The Nineteenth-Century Novel
Critical Essays and Documents

The Nineteenth-Century Novel

Critical Essays and Documents
Revised edition
Edited by Arnold Kettle
at The Open University

HEINEMANN EDUCATIONAL BOOKS
in association with
The Open University Press

Heinemann Educational Books Ltd,
22 Bedford Square, London WC1B 3HH

LONDON   EDINBURGH   MELBOURNE   AUCKLAND
HONG KONG   SINGAPORE   KUALA LUMPUR   NEW DELHI
IBADAN   NAIROBI   JOHANNESBURG
EXETER (NH)   KINGSTON   PORT OF SPAIN

ISBN 0 435 18515 2

Selection and editorial matter copyright © The Open
University 1972, 1981

First published 1972
Reprinted 1976, 1977
Revised edition 1981

Made and printed in Great Britain by
Richard Clay (The Chaucer Press) Ltd,
Bungay, Suffolk

Contents

Introduction to Revised Edition

This anthology of writings on the nineteenth-century novel was designed—and has been revised—with an Open University course in mind. This needs to be said at the outset since the choice of contents would otherwise seem more arbitrary than it is. Having said it, one can, I think, reasonably claim that the interest and value of the collection is by no means dependent on the particular needs of Open University students. Any serious reader of nineteenth-century fiction—student or not—should find here matter of considerable interest, much of it not easily available outside the best, and often all too distant, of libraries.

It might indeed be argued that, all anthologies involving a good deal of arbitrariness, there is something to be said for one in which the selection of items has at least some logic, or even some built-in limitation to it. The Open University course on 'The Nineteenth-Century Novel and its Legacy' has at its centre the study of eleven substantial novels, six of them English (Henry James's *Maisie* being seen in this context as 'English') and five foreign. The choice of novels and novelists—Jane Austen, Emily Bronte, Dickens, George Eliot, James, Hardy, Balzac, Turgenev, Mark Twain, Zola and Tolstoy—was not exactly inevitable (there was special regret in leaving out Melville and Dostoievsky, to mention only the most obvious omissions), but certainly not notably eccentric. Various considerations had to be taken into account. This isn't the place to defend the choice but merely to explain its necessity.

Given the prescribed novels, the principles of choice of contents of this 'Course Reader' also need a few words of explanation. The main point was to make available to Open University students supporting material, of interest in itself, which would also be referred to and discussed in the teaching material provided for the Course. In deciding what these supporting essays should be we* were influenced by a number of considerations of which the need for variety and the limitations of our students' time were perhaps the most important. Just to pick out the critical essay on each novel which the particular teacher considered the best wasn't either enough of a principle or quite the right one: for it might have involved too much repetition of similar critical approaches and too little contrast with that of the teacher concerned. There was also involved (I think it may be confessed) a certain reluctance to submit our Open students to an unrelieved diet of standard 'Eng. Lit.' assumptions and vocabulary.

What in the end we settled for was the sort of arrangement the list of contents indicates. We start with a number of pieces dealing with general problems of novel-reading, not peculiar to the nineteenth century but common to everyone delving at all deeply into the nature of novels. They vary very much in approach and in difficulty. E. M. Forster's famous piece is straightforward and, after years of the lit. crit. industry, must seem a shade old-fashioned. Its merit and purpose is to persuade people not used to thinking much about 'the novel', as opposed to the novel they happen to be reading, that such thought can be both enjoyable and profitable. The intellectual high-jinks of Northrop Frye's brilliant essay on genres and categories are of quite another sort. The less experienced student may find that it involves too formidable a range of reference; though of course you don't have to have read all the books Professor Frye mentions to get what he is driving at. He is deliberately ranging wide because he is trying to bring needed order to a vast and complex subject which most literary historians have funked and few, indeed, have the equipment or courage to tackle at all. The reader who finds Northrop Frye 'difficult' needn't be afraid that he is alone or shamed.

The two short essays by D. H. Lawrence are at once very idiosyncratic and marvellously 'central'. They let you know how one great modern novelist saw the novel and that in itself is

* that is to say, the Course team. All Open University courses are planned and produced by teams. Individual academics are responsible for their own 'units' but a general overall responsibility for the Course rests with the team. So that while responsibility for the *Introduction* is mine, I'm conscious that in an important sense I am writing on behalf of a team, the members of which are listed on page xi.

greatly interesting. But to read them primarily as a display of Lawrence's oddity is to do them, and him, far less than justice. No one else could conceivably have written them, that's true. And of course he is using provocative shock-tactics, rejecting any sort of approach that is remotely academic. Forster, modestly and perhaps a bit coyly unpretentious, was yet speaking to a respectable Cambridge audience. But no university, however open, could have contained Lawrence for long. Yet his essays go bang to the heart of several essential matters. What *is* the novel? What is it *for*? What does it *do* to us? In what ways does or can or should it affect our lives?

The two final contributions to the preliminary, general section are extracts from longer works, and it is to be hoped that they have not been unduly mutilated by being, necessarily, removed from their contexts. Both deal, from contrasting points of view, with some of the most complex yet rewarding facets of novel-criticism. The one, by Wayne C. Booth, is American and for-malist in approach; the other by Georg Lukács, central European and philosophical, specifically Marxist in flavour. Both will seem difficult to readers unfamiliar with the two milieux. Some will find Professor Booth's sophisticated formalism (neither word has normally a pejorative significance in American academic circles) as unpalatable as others find Lukács's handling of philosophical abstractions.

Booth analyses a novel very largely in terms of its technique and literary method. He would doubt, I think, whether one can usefully say much about the 'what' of a novel (what it's saying) except in terms of its 'how' (how it's said). He is so concerned about 'device' and 'artifice' because he sees these factors not as 'extras' added by the cunning novelist to help him express a concept already achieved in his mind, but as integral parts of the very conception itself. Lukács works in a different way. He insistently probes for the social and intellectual content and implications behind and within whatever formal devices the novelist may use; so that the contrast he draws between the novelist who 'relates' and he who 'describes' is at once linked with the whole outlook of the novelist, itself seen in terms of his relationships with his material and with the society within which he lives. Neither Booth nor Lukács in these extracts uses the word 'point-of-view' to describe the novelist's artistic 'position': but if they had done, Booth's 'point-of-view' would refer essentially to the writer's stance as artist while Lukács's would be traced, via his ideology, to his stance in life. Yet, having made this contrast, I don't want to imply that Booth is simply interested in 'form', Lukács in 'content'. Such a simplification would amount to an injustice to both critics, for they would both agree, I feel certain, that between form and content there can in the end be no satisfactory separation. What a man says and how he says it are inextricably intertwined. The difference of their emphases and starting points, however, implies philosophical differences which can't be spirited away and informs not only the critical implications of their two approaches but the whole tone of their discourse.

As I've implied, I don't think most of our students will find either critic easy. But both are eminently worth persevering with as high-level examples of their respective approaches. If Lukács gets more pages than Booth it's because he takes longer to develop his argument and because his incidental references to Tolstoy and Zola have a special relevance for the Course our anthology is serving.

The questions of 'style', 'narrative method' and 'point-of-view' which both Booth and Lukács raise may seem at first to involve giving a disproportionate amount of time to the analysis rather than the appreciation of novels. In fact I don't think it is feasible to separate the two. Directly one asks the question 'What exactly is Jane Austen (or any other novelist) up to?' one is bound to land oneself in some sort of analytical process. To become more conscious of the way a particular writer is operating in a particular novel may not necessarily increase one's pleasure in that novel, though it often can. But that in a more general way a fuller consciousness leads to fuller appreciation seems to me a proposition scarcely open to doubt. An opinion that stands up to argument and experience is better than one that doesn't. It is true that a high-grade analytical apparatus is no guarantee of, much less an alternative to, a sensitive personal response to any novel. But the test of the analysis which a good literary critic provides is that it should sharpen and even sometimes give a whole new dimension to the sensitivity of the reader. It is one of the convictions behind the compilation of this anthology that a reader's pleasure in a novel is more likely to be increased by the intelligent analysis and discussion of the many sorts of issues it raises than by a more rhapsodic attempt to proclaim its beauties.

So perhaps I should, especially bearing in mind that some of our O.U. students will not be experienced in Literature courses, assert very briefly the case for 'criticism' as such, not, of course, as an alternative to reading creative literature, but as an almost essential supplement to it.

To read a novel without attempting to assess it is as unsatisfactory, if not as impossible, as to meet a new group of people without coming to decide, within a reasonable time, which of them you like and trust and which you can't rely on. To some readers the word 'criticism' suggests a spirit at once carping and authoritarian, someone laying down the law as to what you ought to like. But criticism really involves something quite different—assessing the value of things. And it is almost impossible to assess the value of anything without some equipment for defining, explaining, comparing, and arguing about it. I do not think this can ever be, in any precise sense of the term, scientific; which is not to say that one critical statement may not be more valid than another.

There is another—and perhaps equally strong—argument in defence of literary criticism as an activity worth taking seriously. This is that reading is a process involving not only a text but also a reader and that good literary criticism almost always will lead its readers to re-examine and question some quite basic assumptions in their ways of reading. We all tend to imagine that our reading and responses to a text—whether it's a novel, a poem or a newspaper report—are spontaneous and often, indeed, that spontaneity of response is itself a sound basis for praising a piece of literature. But it is not, of course, as simple as that. Our 'spontaneous' responses change with the years. The mind we bring to the reading of a novel may well be 'open' but it isn't blank. One of the helps we get from good criticism is to become more aware of assumptions and habits of mind we have previously taken too much for granted.

Half of the essays that follow in the larger section of the anthology are studies or individual works. The analytical-interpretative essay on the single novel has become an established feature of modern, and especially American, 'English Studies'.

It is a genre that has produced much valuable work and my colleagues and I would claim that every one of the contributions included here has something to say well worth the consideration of any serious reader.

Nevertheless it is perhaps worth spelling out the point (without, I hope, the smallest breath of discourtesy to any of our contributors) that those of us who teach Literature at the Open University don't want our students to accept anything, especially criticism, uncritically. Nor, while convinced of the value—indeed the necessity—of literary criticism, do we regard the methods and emphases developed in the last fifty years or so in British and American universities as necessarily the models which our students should feel themselves under some obligation to applaud and adopt. The turning of 'Eng. Lit.' into a university subject has had negative as well as positive aspects; and if some of our Open University students, ploughing their way through the pages of this anthology, are seized with some sort of impatience or even revulsion, we don't at all ask them to repress these emotions, which may well express a justified reaction against some of the accepted ways of 'treating' literature academically. 'What,' you may suddenly and quite overwhelmingly feel, 'has all this writing to do with a body of literature so various and so delightful, so humane, and as a rule so unselfconscious, as nineteenth-century novels? Is there no better way of thinking about them than this?' The answer is that, if there is, not many people seem to have found it, though also that widespread doubts do certainly sweep the profession, the teachers of English in British universities and colleges, that we may well, over the last half-century, sometimes have taken high roads when the lower road would not only have got us more quickly to where we want to go but might well have taken us somewhere different and more rewarding.

It is not claimed, then, that all or any of our critics are necessarily 'right' about their view of the novel they treat. Some of the essays have been chosen precisely because the approach they contain is considerably at variance with that of the Open University teacher responsible for that novel. For example, Graham Holderness, writing about *Wuthering Heights* in his 'course unit', pays much more attention to local and social considerations than Dorothy van Ghent in her essay on the same novel. Students have to make up their own minds whether the two approaches are irreconcilable, if so which they back, and, in any case, what they have learned from the confrontation.

In the ten years since this Anthology was first published not only has the Open University course it serves been revised (Course A302 becoming A312) but a good deal of critical water has flowed under the bridges. This has, of course, set the (revised) Course team a difficult problem: in particular, how should we respond to the whole area of linguistic-based and French-influenced structuralist and post-structuralist criticism which within the last decade has considerably influenced the way literature is read and taught? The approach of critics like the late Roland Barthes—whether in the end one 'agrees' with it or not—certainly deserves serious consideration. Yet the approaches, concerns, and vocabulary of such critics are so deeply at variance with those which a student opting to take an Open University literature course is likely to anticipate, that the consequent problem cannot well be solved by simply adding to this anthology one or two short but authoritative expositions of the critical theory involved, even if such were available. The most that it has seemed practicable to do is to include an essay—David Lodge's interesting piece on *Middlemarch*—which, in examining one of our set books, draws upon and discusses some of the issues about 'the nineteenth-century realist novel' raised by such an approach.

Alongside these essays in modern critical analysis we have put into this collection a selection of writings which, because they already belong as much to the history of the novel's development as to the history of novel-criticism, are perhaps best called 'documents'.

Balzac's *Preface* (*Avant-propos*) to *The Human Comedy* isn't easily available in English translation. But it is an essay of great importance, not only because it tells us so much about the way one of the greatest of novelists saw his role and his art; but also because it raises explicitly so many critical issues. What is the relation, for instance, between a 'realist' writer's drive for total 'realism' and the moral responsibilities he holds as a social being? Where do the methods of the artist and the sociologist separate and where converge? Is the novelist who sees his characters as 'types' betraying human individuality and uniqueness?

Zola's essay on 'The Experimental Novel', one of the great manifestos of nineteenth-century 'naturalism', continues and develops an examination of many of the issues Balzac had posed half a century earlier. The two throw rewarding light on one another and also on the social developments which separate them. And the two together, in their concern over the 'theory' as well as the practice of their craft, form a most interesting contrast to the attitudes of British novelists who tend not to theorize much about what they are up to. Yet because French theory and practice did come, as the century went on, to influence novelists who wrote in English, it's particularly interesting to compare what Balzac thought of himself with what, with hindsight and ambiguous admiration, the aging Henry James thought of him.

James's piece on Balzac (it is part of the *Preface* to the publication in English of one of Balzac's least typical novels) is written in the full flush of his 'late' and most convoluted style. The reader unfamiliar with the late James is likely, until he grasps its strange speech-rhythms (now so unlike the way anyone talks), to find it very odd. But it is full of generosity as well as eccentricity and is in any case a fine example of an attitude to art almost inconceivable fifty years before.

James on Turgenev (it is really a sort of obituary) has something of the same flavour. It is included partly because it gives a useful short summary of the Russian's achievement but chiefly because, in its emphasis on 'art', on the 'novelists' novelist' aspect of Turgenev, it is in such total contrast to the contemporary review-article (which James had certainly not read) on *On the Eve* by Dobrolyubov. This is one of the classic documents of nineteenth-century novel-criticism and it couldn't conceivably have been written by anyone but a Russian. From it, so polemical in tone, so high-minded yet so down-to-earth, so totally opposed to 'aesthetic' criticism as understood in Western Europe, emerges with great force what literature (including novels) meant to the Russian intelligentsia of the mid-nineteenth century. Dobrolyubov, the young radical (he would be dead within a year), writing under the strict censorship of an autocracy, is using his review to say things he could not have said 'straight' about Russian life and Russian politics. Dobrolyubov and his colleague Chernyshevsky, Lukács has written, 'were genuine, fearless, and uncompromising revolutionaries in the sense in which Marat or St. Just were revolutionaries in the days of the French Revolution'. But he isn't *merely* 'using' Turgenev's novel. To dismiss his discussion of it in such terms would be to miss more than half the point. He is asserting an attitude to literature and to 'realism' as theoretically potent as Balzac's or Zola's, so that 'When Will the Day Come?' is a document as relevant to the study of the novel as an art-form as it is to the student of nineteenth- and twentieth-century Russian history.

Our collection ends, with a certain appropriateness, with F. R. Leavis's essay on *Anna Karenina*. Appropriate because, in our Course, we have reserved a special place for Tolstoy's book as perhaps the supreme achievement among those of the nineteenth-century novelists; but appropriate too because the critic's approach to it is of the kind it is.

Leavis is not interested in 'literary history' or even analysis in the narrower, more academic senses of the terms: his great merit as a literary critic is his insistence on relating literature to life in ways which increase our comprehension and respect for both. His claim that '*Anna Karenina*, in its human centrality, gives us modern man' is precisely the sort of claim which best illustrates our reasons for seeing the nineteenth-century novel as a supremely rewarding field of study.

ARNOLD KETTLE

The Open University
March, 1981

Part One

On General Problems of Novel-Reading

1 E. M. Forster

From *Aspects of the Novel*, Arnold, 1927, Chap, 1, pp. 14–35.

We need a vantage post, for the novel is a formidable mass, and it is so amorphous—no mountain in it to climb, no Parnassus or Helicon, not even a Pisgah. It is most distinctly one of the moister areas of literature—irrigated by a hundred rills and occasionally degenerating into a swamp. I do not wonder that the poets despise it, though they sometimes find themselves in it by accident. And I am not surprised at the annoyance of the historians when by accident it finds itself among them. Perhaps we ought to define what a novel is before starting. This will not take a second. M. Abel Chevalley has, in his brilliant little manual,[1] provided a definition, and if a French critic cannot define the English novel, who can? It is, he says, 'a fiction in prose of a certain extent' (une fiction en prose d'une certaine étendue). That is quite good enough for us, and we may perhaps go so far as to add that the extent should not be less than 50,000 words. Any fictitious prose work over 50,000 words will be a novel for the purposes of these lectures, and if this seems to you unphilosophic will you think of an alternative definition, which will include *The Pilgrim's Progress, Marius the Epicurean, The Adventures of a Younger Son, The Magic Flute, The Journal of the Plague Year, Zuleika Dobson, Rasselas, Ulysses,* and *Green Mansions,* or else will give reasons for their exclusion? Parts of our spongy tract seem more fictitious than other parts, it is true: near the middle, on a tump of grass, stand Miss Austen with the figure of Emma by her side, and Thackeray holding up Esmond. But no intelligent remark known to me will define the tract as a whole. All we can say of it is that it is bounded by two chains of mountains neither of which rises very abruptly—the opposing ranges of Poetry and of History—and bounded on the third side by a sea—a sea that we shall encounter when we come to *Moby Dick.*

In the first place, let us consider the proviso 'English Litera-

[1] Abel Chevalley, *Le Roman Anglais de Notre Temps*, Milford, London.

ture'. 'English' we shall of course interpret as written in English, not as published south of the Tweed or east of the Atlantic, or north of the Equator: we need not attend to geographical accidents, they can be left to the politicians. Yet, even with this interpretation, are we as free as we wish? Can we, while discussing English fiction, quite ignore fiction written in other languages, particularly French and Russian? As far as influence goes, we could ignore it, for our writers have never been much influenced by the continentals. But—for reasons soon to be explained—I want to talk as little as possible about influence during these lectures. My subject is a particular kind of book and the aspects that book has assumed in English. Can we ignore its collateral aspects on the continent? Not entirely. An unpleasant and unpatriotic truth has here to be faced. No English novelist is as great as Tolstoy—that is to say has given so complete a picture of man's life, both on its domestic and heroic side. No English novelist has explored man's soul as deeply as Dostoievsky. And no novelist anywhere has analysed the modern consciousness as successfully as Marcel Proust. Before these triumphs we must pause. English poetry fears no one—excels in quality as well as quantity. But English fiction is less triumphant: it does not contain the best stuff yet written, and if we deny this we become guilty of provincialism.

Now, provincialism does not signify in a writer, and may indeed be the chief source of his strength: only a prig or a fool would complain that Defoe is cockneyfied or Thomas Hardy countrified. But provincialism in a critic is a serious fault. A critic has no right to the narrowness which is the frequent prerogative of the creative artist. He has to have a wide outlook or he has not anything at all. Although the novel exercises the rights of a created object, criticism has not those rights, and too many little mansions in English fiction have been acclaimed to their own detriment as important edifices. Take four at random: *Cranford, The Heart of Midlothian, Jane Eyre, Richard Feverel.* For various personal and local reasons we may be attached to these four books. *Cranford* radiates the humour of the urban midlands, *Midlothian* is a handful out of Edinburgh, *Jane Eyre* is the passionate dream of a fine but still undeveloped woman, *Richard Feverel* exudes farmhouse lyricism and flickers with modish wit. But all four are little mansions, not mighty edifices, and we shall see and respect them for what they are if we stand them for an instant in the colonnades of *War and Peace*, or the vaults of *The Brothers Karamazov*.

I shall not often refer to foreign novels in these lectures, still less would I pose as an expert on them who is debarred from discussing them by his terms of reference. But I do want to emphasize their greatness before we start; to cast, so to speak, this preliminary shadow over our subject, so that when we look back on it at the end we may have the better chance of seeing it in its true lights.

So much for the proviso 'English'. Now for a more important point, the proviso of 'period or periods'. This idea of a period of a development in time, with its consequent emphasis on in-fluences and schools, happens to be exactly what I am hoping to avoid during our brief survey, and I believe that the author of *Gazpacho* will be lenient. Time, all the way through, is to be our enemy. We are to visualize the English novelists not as floating down that stream which bears all its sons away unless they are careful, but as seated together in a room, a circular room, a sort of British Museum reading-room—all writing their novels simultaneously. They do not, as they sit there, think 'I live under Queen Victoria, I under Anne, I carry on the tradi-tion of Trollope, I am reacting against Aldous Huxley'. The fact that their pens are in their hands is far more vivid to them. They are half mesmerized, their sorrows and joys are pouring out through the ink, they are approximated by the act of creation, and when Professor Oliver Elton says, as he does, that 'after 1847 the novel of passion was never to be the same again,' none of them understand what he means. That is to be our vision of them—an imperfect vision, but it is suited to our powers, it will preserve us from a serious danger, the danger of pseudo-scholarship.

Genuine scholarship is one of the highest successes which our race can achieve. No one is more triumphant than the man who chooses a worthy subject and masters all its facts and the leading facts of the subjects neighbouring. He can then do what he likes. He can, if his subject is the novel, lecture on it chrono-logically if he wishes, because he has read all the important novels of the past four centuries, many of the unimportant ones, and has adequate knowledge of any collateral facts that bear upon English fiction. The late Sir Walter Raleigh (who once held this lectureship) was such a scholar. Raleigh knew so many facts that he was able to proceed to influences, and his monograph on the English novel adopts the treatment by period which his unworthy successor must avoid. The scholar, like the philosopher, can contemplate the river of time. He contemplates it not as a whole, but he can see the facts, the personalities, floating past him, and estimate the relations between them, and if his conclusions could be as valuable to us as they are to himself he would long ago have civilized the human race. As you know, he has failed. True scholarship is incommunicable, true scholars rare. There are a few scholars, actual or potential, in the audience to-day, but only a few, and there is certainly none on the platform. Most of us are pseudo-scholars, and I want to consider our characteristics with sympathy and respect, for we are a very large and quite a powerful class, eminent in Church and State, we control the education of the Empire, we lend to the Press such distinction as it consents to receive, and we are a welcome asset at dinner-parties.

Pseudo-scholarship is, on its good side, the homage paid by ignorance to learning. It also has an economic side, on which we need not be hard. Most of us must get a job before thirty, or sponge on our relatives, and many jobs can only be got by passing an exam. The pseudo-scholar often does well in examinations (real scholars are not much good), and even when he fails he appreciates their innate majesty. They are gateways to employment, they have power to ban and bless. A paper on *King Lear* may lead somewhere, unlike the rather far-fetched play of the same name. It may be a stepping-stone to the Local Government Board. He does not often put it to himself openly and say 'That's the use of knowing things, they help you to get on.' The economic pressure he feels is more often subconscious, and he goes to his exam merely feeling that a paper on *King Lear* is a tempestuous and terrible experience but an intensely real one. And whether he be cynical or naïf, he is not to be blamed. As long as learning is connected with earning, as long as certain jobs can only be reached through exams, so long must we take the examination system seriously. If another ladder to employment was contrived, much so-called education would disappear, and no one be a penny the stupider.

It is when he comes to criticism—to a job like the present—that he can be so pernicious, because he follows the method of a true scholar without having his equipment. He classes books before he has understood or read them; that is his first crime. Classification by chronology. Books written before 1847, books written after it, books written after or before 1848. The novel in the reign of Queen Anne, the pre-novel, the ur-novel, the novel of the future. Classification by subject matter—sillier still. The literature of Inns, beginning with *Tom Jones*; the literature of the Women's Movement, beginning with *Shirley*; the literature of Desert Islands, from *Robinson Crusoe* to *The Blue Lagoon*; the literature of Rogues—dreariest of all, though the Open Road runs it pretty close; the literature of Sussex (perhaps the most devoted of the Home Counties); improper books —a serious though dreadful branch of enquiry, only to be pursued by pseudo-scholars of riper years; novels relating to industrialism, aviation, chiropody, the weather. I include the weather on the authority of the most amazing work on the novel that I have met for many years. It came over the Atlantic to me, nor shall I ever forget it. It was a literary manual entitled *Materials and Methods of Fiction*. The writer's name shall be concealed. He was a pseudo-scholar and a good one. He classified novels by their dates, their length, their locality, their sex, their point of view, till no more seemed possible. But he still had the weather up his sleeve, and when he brought it out, it had nine heads. He gave an example under each head, for he was anything but slovenly, and we will run through his list. In the first place the weather can be 'decorative', as in Pierre Loti; then 'utilitarian', as in *The Mill on the Floss* (no Floss, no Mill; no Tullivers); 'illustrative', as in *The Egoist*; 'planned in pre-established harmony', as by Fiona MacLeod; 'in emotional contrast', as in *The Master of Ballantrae*; 'determinative of action', as in a certain Kipling story, where a man proposes to the wrong girl on account of a mud storm; 'a controlling influence', *Richard Feverel*; 'itself a hero', like Vesuvius in *The Last Days of Pompeii*; and ninthly, it can be 'non-existent', as in a nursery tale. I liked him flinging in non-existence. It made everything so scientific and trim. But he himself remained a little dissatisfied, and having finished his classification he said yes, of course there was one more thing, and that was genius; it was useless for a novelist to know that there are nine sorts of weather, unless he has genius also. Cheered by this reflection, he classified novels by their tones. There are only two tones, personal and impersonal, and having given examples of each he grew pensive again and said, 'Yes, but you must have genius too, or neither tone will profit.'

This reference to genius is, again, typical of the pseudo-scholar. He loves mentioning genius, because the sound of the word exempts him from discovering its meaning. Literature is written by geniuses. Novelists are geniuses. There we are; now let us classify them. Which he does. Everything he says may be accurate but all is useless because he is moving round books instead of through them, he either has not read them or cannot read them properly. Books have to be read (worse luck, for it takes a long time); it is the only way of discovering what they contain. A few savage tribes eat them, but reading is the only method of assimilation revealed to the west. The reader must sit down alone and struggle with the writer, and this the pseudo-scholar will not do. He would rather relate a book to the history of its time, to events in the life of its author, to the events it describes, above all to some tendency. As soon as he can use the word 'tendency' his spirits rise, and though those of his audience may sink, they often pull out their pencils at this point and make a note, under the belief that a tendency is portable.

That is why, in the rather ramshackly course that lies ahead of us, we cannot consider fiction by periods, we must not contemplate the stream of time. Another image better suits our powers: that of all the novelists writing their novels at once. They come from different ages and ranks, they have different temperaments and aims, but they all hold pens in their hands, and are in the process of creation. Let us look over their shoulders for a moment and see what they are writing. It may exorcise that demon of chronology which is at present our enemy and which (we shall discover next week) is sometimes their enemy too. 'Oh, what quenchless feud is this, that Time hath with the sons of men,' cries Herman Melville, and the feud goes on not only in life and death but in the by-ways of literary creation and criticism. Let us avoid it by imagining that all the novelists are at work together in a circular room. I shall not mention their names until we have heard their words, because a name brings

associations with it, dates, gossip, all the furniture of the method
we are discarding.

They have been instructed to group themselves in pairs. The
first pair write as follows:

(i) I don't know what to do—not I. God forgive me, but I
am very impatient! I wish—but I don't know what to wish
without a sin. Yet I wish it would please God to take me to
his mercy!—I can meet with none here.—What a world is
this!—What is there in it desirable? The good we hope for
so strangely mixed, that one knows not what to wish for! And
one half of mankind tormenting the other and being tormented themselves in tormenting.

(ii) What I hate is myself—when I think that one has to
take so much, to be happy, out of the lives of others, and
that one isn't happy even then. One does it to cheat one's self
and to stop one's mouth—but that is only, at the best, for a
little. The wretched self is always there, always making us
somehow a fresh anxiety. What it comes to is that it's not,
that it's never, a happiness, any happiness at all, to *take*. The
only safe thing is to give. It's what plays you least false.

It is obvious that here sit two novelists who are looking at
life from much the same angle, yet the first of them is Samuel
Richardson, and the second you will have already identified
as Henry James. Each is an anxious rather than an ardent psychologist. Each is sensitive to suffering and appreciates self-
sacrifice; each falls short of the tragic, though a close approach
is made. A sort of tremulous nobility—that is the spirit that
dominates them—and oh how well they write!—not a word
out of place in their copious flows. A hundred and fifty years of
time divide them, but are not they close together in other ways,
and may not their neighbourliness profit us? Of course as I say
this I hear Henry James beginning to express his regret—no,
not his regret but his surprise—no, not even his surprise but his
awareness that neighbourliness is being postulated of him, and
postulated, must he add, in relation to a shopkeeper. And I hear
Richardson, equally cautious, wondering whether any writer
born outside England can be chaste. But these are surface differences, are indeed additional points of contact. We leave them
sitting in harmony, and proceed to our next pair.

(i) All the preparations for the funeral ran easily and happily under Mrs Johnson's skilful hands. On the eve of the sad occasion she produced a reserve of black sateen, the kitchen steps, and a box of tintacks, and decorated the house with festoons and bows of black in the best possible taste. She tied up the knocker with black crape, and put a large bow over the corner of the steel engraving of Garibaldi, and swathed the bust of Mr Gladstone that had belonged to the deceased with inky swathings. She turned the two vases that had views of Tivoli and the Bay of Naples round, so that these rather brilliant landscapes were hidden and only the plain blue enamel showed, and she anticipated the long contemplated purchase of a tablecloth for the front room, and substituted a violet purple cover for the now very worn and faded raptures and roses in plushette that had hitherto done duty there. Everything that loving consideration could do to impart a dignified solemnity to her little home was done.

(ii) The air of the parlour being faint with the smell of sweet cake, I looked about for the table of refreshments; it was scarcely visible until one had got accustomed to the gloom, but there was a cut-up plum cake upon it, and there were cut-up oranges, and sandwiches, and biscuits, and two decanters that I knew very well as ornaments, but had never seen used in all my life; one full of port, and one of sherry. Standing at this table, I became conscious of the servile Pumblechook in a black cloak and several yards of hat-band, who was alternately stuffing himself, and making obsequious movements to catch my attention. The moment he succeeded, he came over to me (breathing sherry and crumbs) and said in a subdued voice, 'May I, dear sir?' and did.

These two funerals did not happen on the same day. One is that of Mr Polly's father (1920), the other Mrs Gargery's in *Great Expectations* (1860). Yet Wells and Dickens have the same point of view and even use the same tricks of style (cf. the two vases and the two decanters). They are, both, humorists and visualizers who get an effect by cataloguing details and whisking the page over irritably. They are generous-minded; they hate shams and enjoy being indignant about them; they are valuable social reformers; they have no notion of confining books to a library shelf. Sometimes the lively surface of their prose scratches like a cheap gramophone record, a certain poorness of quality appears, and the face of the author draws rather too near to that of the reader. In other words, neither of them has much taste: the world of beauty was largely closed to Dickens, and is entirely closed to Wells. And there are other parallels—for instance their method of drawing character. And perhaps the main difference between them is the difference of opportunity offered to an obscure boy of genius a hundred years ago and forty years ago. The difference is in Wells' favour. He is better educated than his predecessor; in particular the addition of science has strengthened his mind and subdued his hysteria. He registers an improvement in society: Dotheboys Hall has been superseded by the Polytechnic—not any change in the novelist's art.

What about our next pair?

(i) But as for that mark, I'm not sure about it; I don't believe it was made by a nail after all; it's too big, too round, for that. I might get up, but if I got up and looked at it, ten to one I shouldn't be able to say for certain; because once a thing's done, no one ever knows how it happened. O dear me, the mystery of life! The inaccuracy of thought! The ignorance of humanity! To show how very little control of our possessions we have—what an accidental affair this living is after all our civilization—let me just count over a few of the things lost in one lifetime, beginning, for that always seems the most mysterious of losses—what cat would gnaw, what rat would nibble—three pale blue canisters of bookbinding tools? Then there were the birdcages, the iron hoops, the steel skates, the Queen Anne coal-scuttle, the bagatelle-board, the hand-organ —all gone, and jewels too. Opals and emeralds, they lie about the roots of turnips. What a scraping paring affair it is to be sure! The wonder is that I've any clothes on my back, that I sit surrounded by solid furniture at this moment. Why, if one wants to compare life to anything one must liken it to being blown through the Tube at fifty miles an hour....

(ii) Every day for at least ten years together did my father resolve to have it mended; 'tis not mended yet. No family but ours would have borne with it an hour, and what is most astonishing, there was not a subject in the world upon which my father was so eloquent as upon that of door-hinges. And yet, at the same time, he was certainly one of the greatest bubbles to them, I think, that history can produce; his rhetoric and conduct were at perpetual handy-cuffs. Never did the parlour door open but his philosophy or his principles fell a victim to it; three drops of oil with a feather, and a smart stroke of a hammer, had saved his honour for ever.

Inconsistent soul that man is; languishing under wounds which he has the power to heal; his whole life a contradiction to his knowledge; his reason, that precious gift of God to him (instead of pouring in oil), serving but to sharpen his sensibilities, to multiply his pains, and render him more melancholy and uneasy under them! Poor unhappy creature, that he should do so! Are not the necessary causes of misery in this life enough, but he must add voluntary ones to his stock of sorrow? Struggle against evils which cannot be avoided, and submit to others which a tenth part of the trouble they create him would remove from his heart for ever.

By all that is good and virtuous, if there are three drops of oil to be got and a hammer to be found within ten miles of Shandy Hall, the parlour door hinge shall be mended this reign.

The passage last quoted is, of course, out of *Tristram Shandy*. The other passage was from Virginia Woolf. She and Sterne are both fantasists. They start with a little object, take a flutter from it, and settle on it again. They combine a humorous appreciation of the muddle of life with a keen sense of its beauty. There is even the same tone in their voices—a rather deliberate bewilderment, an announcement to all and sundry that they do not know where they are going. No doubt their scales of value are not the same. Sterne is a sentimentalist, Virginia Woolf (except perhaps in her latest work, *To the Lighthouse*) is extremely aloof. Nor are their achievements on the same scale. But their medium is similar, the same odd effects are obtained by it, the parlour door is never mended, the mark on the wall turns out to be a snail, life is such a muddle, oh dear, the will is so weak, the sensations fidgety ... philosophy ... God ... oh dear, look at the mark ... listen to the door—existence ... is really too ... what were we saying?

Does not chronology seem less important now that we have visualized six novelists at their jobs? If the novel develops, is it not likely to develop on different lines from the British Constitution, or even the Women's Movement? I say 'even the Women's Movement' because there happened to be a close association between fiction in England and that movement during the nineteenth century—a connection so close that it has misled some critics into thinking it an organic connection. As women bettered their position the novel, they asserted, became better too. Quite wrong. A mirror does not develop because an historical pageant passes in front of it. It only develops when it gets a fresh coat of quicksilver—in other words, when it acquires new sensitiveness; and the novel's success lies in its own sensitiveness, not in the success of its subject matter. Empires fall, votes are accorded, but to those people writing in the circular room it is the feel of the pen between their fingers that matters most. They may decide to write a novel upon the French or the Russian Revolution, but memories, associations, passions, rise up and cloud their objectivity, so that at the close, when they re-read, some one else seems to have been holding their pen and to have relegated their theme to the background. That 'some one else' is their self no doubt, but not the self that is so active in time and lives under George IV or V. All through history writers while writing have felt more or less the same. They have entered a common state which it is convenient to call inspiration, and, having regard to that state, we may say that History develops, Art stands still.[. . .]

2 Northrop Frye

Specific Continuous Forms

From *The Anatomy of Criticism*, Princeton University Press, pp. 303–14, 1957.

In assigning the term fiction to the genre of the written word, in which prose tends to become the predominating rhythm, we collide with the view that the real meaning of fiction is falsehood or unreality. Thus an autobiography coming into a library would be classified as non-fiction if the librarian believed the author, and as fiction if she thought he was lying. It is difficult to see what use such a distinction can be to a literary critic. Surely the word fiction, which, like poetry, means etymologically something made for its own sake, could be applied in criticism to any work of literary art in a radically continuous form, which almost always means a work of art in prose. Or, if that is too much to ask, at least some protest can be entered against the sloppy habit of identifying fiction with the one genuine form of fiction which we know as the novel.

Let us look at a few of the unclassified books lying on the boundary of 'non-fiction' and 'literature'. Is *Tristram Shandy* a novel? Nearly everyone would say yes, in spite of its easygoing disregard of 'story values'. Is *Gulliver's Travels* a novel? Here most would demur, including the Dewey decimal system, which puts it under 'Satire and Humor'. But surely everyone would call it fiction, and if it is fiction, a distinction appears between fiction as a genus and the novel as a species of that genus. Shifting the ground to fiction, then, is *Sartor Resartus* fiction? If not, why not? If it is, is *The Anatomy of Melancholy* fiction? Is it a literary form or only a work of 'non-fiction' written with 'style'? Is Borrow's *Lavengro* fiction? Everyman's Library says yes; the World's Classics puts it under 'Travel and Topography'.

The literary historian who identifies fiction with the novel is greatly embarrassed by the length of time that the world managed to get along without the novel, and until he reaches his great deliverance in Defoe, his perspective is intolerably cramped. He is compelled to reduce Tudor fiction to a series of tentative essays in the novel form, which works well enough for Deloney but makes nonsense of Sidney. He postulates a great fictional gap in the seventeenth century which exactly covers the golden age of rhetorical prose. He finally discovers that the word novel, which up to about 1900 was still the name of a more or less recognizable form, has since expanded into a catch-all term which can be applied to practically any prose book that is not 'on' something. Clearly, this novel-centred view of prose fiction is a Ptolemaic perspective which is now too complicated to be any longer workable, and some more relative and Copernican view must take its place.

When we start to think seriously about the novel, not as fiction, but as a form of fiction, we feel that its characteristics, whatever they are, are such as make, say, Defoe, Fielding, Austen, and James central in its tradition, and Borrow, Peacock, Melville, and Emily Brontë somehow peripheral. This is not an estimate of merit: we may think *Moby Dick* 'greater' than *The Egoist* and yet feel that Meredith's book is closer to being a typical novel. Fielding's conception of the novel as a comic epic in prose seems fundamental to the tradition he did so much to establish. In novels that we think of as typical, like those of Jane Austen, plot and dialogue are closely linked to the conventions of the comedy of manners. The conventions of *Wuthering Heights* are linked rather with the tale and the ballad. They seem to have more affinity with tragedy, and the tragic emotions of passion and fury, which would shatter the balance of tone in Jane Austen, can be safely accommodated here. So can the supernatural, or the suggestion of it, which is difficult to get into a novel. The shape of the plot is different: instead of manoeuvring around a central situation, as Jane Austen does, Emily Brontë tells her story with linear accents, and she seems to need the help of a narrator, who would be absurdly out of place in Jane Austen. Conventions so different justify us in regarding *Wuthering Heights* as a different form of prose fiction from the novel, a form which we shall here call the romance. Here again we have to use the same word in several different contexts, but romance seems on the whole better than tale, which appears to fit a somewhat shorter form.

The essential difference between novel and romance lies in the conception of characterization. The romancer does not attempt to create 'real people' so much as stylized figures which expand into psychological archetypes. It is in the romance that we find Jung's libido, anima, and shadow reflected in the hero, heroine, and villain respectively. That is why the romance so often radiates a glow of subjective intensity that the novel lacks, and why a suggestion of allegory is constantly creeping in around its fringes. Certain elements of character are released in the romance which makes it naturally a more revolutionary form than the novel. The novelist deals with personality, with characters wearing their *personae* or social masks. He needs the framework of a stable society, and many of our best novelists have been conventional to the verge of fussiness. The romancer deals with individuality, with character *in vacuo* idealized by revery, and, however conservative he may be, something nihilistic and untamable is likely to keep breaking out of his pages.

The prose romance, then, is an independent form of fiction to be distinguished from the novel and extracted from the miscellaneous heap of prose works now covered by that term. Even in the other heap known as short stories one can isolate the tale form used by Poe, which bears the same relation to the full romance that the stories of Chekhov or Katherine Mansfield do to the novel. 'Pure' examples of either form are never found; there is hardly any modern romance that could not be made out to be a novel, and vice versa. The forms of prose fiction are mixed, like racial strains in human beings, not separable like the sexes. In fact the popular demand in fiction is always for a mixed form, a romantic novel just romantic enough for the reader to project his libido on the hero and his anima on the heroine, and just novel enough to keep these projections in a familiar world. It may be asked, therefore, what is the use of making the above distinction, especially when, though undeveloped in criticism, it is by no means unrealized. It is no surprise to hear that Trollope wrote novels and William Morris romances.

The reason is that a great romancer should be examined in terms of the conventions he chose. William Morris should not be left on the side lines of prose fiction merely because the critic has not learned to take the romance form seriously. Nor, in view of what has been said about the revolutionary nature of the romance, should his choice of that form be regarded as an 'escape' from his social attitude. If Scott has any claims to be a romancer, it is not good criticism to deal only with his defects as a novelist. The romantic qualities of *The Pilgrim's Progress*, too, its archetypal characterization and its revolutionary approach to religious experience, make it a well-rounded example of a literary form: it is not merely a book swallowed by English literature to get some religious bulk in its diet. Finally, when Hawthorne, in the preface to *The House of the Seven Gables*, insists that his story should be read as romance and not as novel, it is possible that he meant what he said, even though he indicates that the prestige of the rival form has induced the romancer to apologize for not using it.

Romance is older than the novel, a fact which has developed the historical illusion that it is something to be outgrown, a juvenile and undeveloped form. The social affinities of the romance, with its grave idealizing of heroism and purity, are with the aristocracy (for the apparent inconsistency of this with the revolutionary nature of the form just mentioned, see the introductory comment on the *mythos* of romance in the previous essay). It revived in the period we call Romantic as part of the Romantic tendency to archaic feudalism and a cult of the hero, or idealized libido. In England the romances of Scott and, in less degree, the Brontës, are part of a mysterious Northumbrian renaissance, a Romantic reaction against the new industrialism in the Midlands, which also produced the poetry of Wordsworth and Burns and the philosophy of Carlyle. It is not surprising, therefore, that an important theme in the more bourgeois novel should be the parody of the romance and its ideals. The tradition established by *Don Quixote* continues in a type of novel which looks at a romantic situation from its own point of view, so that the conventions of the two forms make up an ironic compound instead of a sentimental mixture. Examples range from *Northanger Abbey* to *Madame Bovary* and *Lord Jim*.

The tendency to allegory in the romance may be conscious, as in *The Pilgrim's Progress*, or unconscious, as in the very obvious sexual mythopoeia in William Morris. The romance, which deals with heroes, is intermediate between the novel, which deals with men, and the myth, which deals with gods. Prose romance first appears as a late development of Classical mythology, and the prose Sagas of Iceland follow close on the mythical Eddas. The novel tends rather to expand into a fictional approach to history. The soundness of Fielding's instinct in calling *Tom Jones* a history is confirmed by the general rule that the larger the scheme of a novel becomes, the more obviously its historical nature appears. As it is creative history, the novelist usually prefers his material in a plastic, or roughly contemporary state, and feels cramped by a fixed historical pattern. *Waverley* is dated about sixty years back from the time of writing and *Little Dorrit* about forty years, but the historical pattern is fixed in the romance and plastic in the novel, suggesting the general principle that most 'historical novels' are romances. Similarly a novel becomes more romantic in its appeal when the life it reflects has passed away: thus the novels of Trollope were read primarily as romances during the Second World War. It is perhaps the link with history and a sense of temporal context that has confined the novel, in striking contrast to the world-wide romance, to the alliance of time and Western man.

Autobiography is another form which merges with the novel by a series of insensible gradations. Most autobiographies are inspired by a creative, and therefore fictional, impulse to select only those events and experiences in the writer's life that go to build up an integrated pattern. This pattern may be something larger than himself with which he has come to identify himself or simply the coherence of his character and attitudes. We may call this very important form of prose fiction the confession form, following St Augustine, who appears to have invented it, and Rousseau, who established a modern type of it. The earlier tradition gave *Religio Medici*, *Grace Abounding*, and Newman's *Apologia* to English literature, besides the related but subtly different type of confession favored by the mystics.

Here again, as with the romance, there is some value in recognizing a distinct prose form in the confession. It gives several of our best prose works a definable place in fiction instead of keeping them in a vague limbo of books which are not quite literature because they are 'thought', and not quite religion or philosophy because they are Examples of Prose Style. The confession, too, like the novel and the romance, has its own short form, the familiar essay and Montaigne's *livre de bonne foy* is a confession made up of essays in which only the continuous narrative of the longer form is missing. Montaigne's scheme is to the confession what a work of fiction made up of short stories, such as Joyce's *Dubliners* or Boccaccio's *Decameron*, is to the novel or romance.

After Rousseau—in fact in Rousseau—the confession flows into the novel, and the mixture produces the fictional autobiography, the *Künstler-roman*, and kindred types. There is no literary reason why the subject of a confession should always be the author himself, and dramatic confessions have been used in the novel at least since *Moll Flanders*. The 'stream of consciousness' technique permits of a much more concentrated fusion of the two forms, but even here the characteristics peculiar to the confession form show up clearly. Nearly always some theoretical and intellectual interest in religion, politics, or art plays a leading role in the confession. It is his success in integrating his mind on such subjects that makes the author of a confession feel that his life is worth writing about. But this interest in ideas and theoretical statements is alien to the genius of the novel proper, where the technical problem is to dissolve all theory into personal relationships. In Jane Austen, to take a familiar instance, church, state, and culture are never examined except as social data, and Henry James has been described as having a mind so fine that no idea could violate it. The novelist who cannot get along without ideas, or has not the patience to digest them in the way that James did, instinctively resorts to what Mill calls a 'mental history' of a single character. And when we find that a technical discussion of a theory of aesthetics forms the climax of Joyce's *Portrait*, we realize that what makes this possible is the presence in that novel of another tradition of prose fiction.

The novel tends to be extroverted and personal; its chief interest is in human character as it manifests itself in society. The romance tends to be introverted and personal: it also deals with characters, but in a more subjective way. (Subjective here refers to treatment, not subject-matter. The characters of romance are heroic and therefore inscrutable; the novelist is freer to enter his characters' minds because he is more objective.) The confession is also introverted, but intellectualized in content. Our next step is evidently to discover a fourth form of fiction which is extrovert and intellectual.

*   *   *

We remarked earlier that most people would call *Gulliver's Travels* fiction but not a novel. It must then be another form of fiction, as it certainly has a form, and we feel that we are turning from the novel to this form, whatever it is, when we turn from Rousseau's *Emile* to Voltaire's *Candide*, or from Butler's *The Way of All Flesh* to the Erewhon books, or from Huxley's *Point Counterpoint* to *Brave New World*. The form thus has its own traditions, and, as the examples of Butler and Huxley show, has preserved some integrity even under the ascendancy of the novel. Its existence is easy enough to demonstrate, and no one will challenge the statement that the literary ancestry of *Gulliver's Travels* and *Candide* runs through Rabelais and Erasmus to Lucian. But while much has been said about the style and thought of Rabelais, Swift, and Voltaire, very little has been made of them as craftsmen working in a specific medium, a point no one dealing with a novelist would ignore. Another great writer in this tradition, Huxley's master Peacock, has fared even worse, for, his form not being understood, a general impression has grown up that his status in the developfent of prose fiction is that of a slapdash eccentric. Actually, he is as exquisite and precise an artist in his medium as Jane Austen is in hers.

The form used by these authors is the Menippean satire, also more rarely called the Varronian satire, allegedly invented by a Greek cynic named Menippus. His works are lost, but he had two great disciples, the Greek Lucian and the Roman Varro, and the tradition of Varro, who has not survived either except in fragments, was carried on by Petronius and Apuleius. The Menippean satire appears to have developed out of verse satire through the practice of adding prose interludes, but we know it only as a prose form, though one of its recurrent features (seen in Peacock) is the use of identical verse.

The Menippean satire deals less with people as such than with mental attitudes. Pedants, bigots, cranks, parvenus, virtuosi, enthusiasts, rapacious and incompetent professional men of all kinds, are handled in terms of their occupational approach to life as distinct from their social behaviour. The Menippean satire thus resembles the confession in its ability to handle abstract ideas and theories and differs from the novel in its characterization, which is stylized rather than naturalistic, and presents people as mouthpieces of the ideas they represent. Here again no sharp boundary lines can or should be drawn, but if we compare a character in Jane Austen with a similar character in Peacock we can immediately feel the difference between the two forms. Squire Western belongs to the novel, but Thwackum and Square have Menippean blood in them. A constant theme in the tradition is the ridicule of the *philosophus gloriosus*, already discussed. The novelist sees evil and folly as social diseases, but the Menippean satirist sees them as diseases of the intellect, as a kind of maddened pedantry which the *philosophus gloriosus* at once symbolizes and defines.

Petronius, Apuleius, Rabelais, Swift, and Voltaire all use a loose-jointed narrative form often confused with the romance. It differs from the romance, however (though there is a strong admixture of romance in Rabelais), as it is not primarily concerned with the exploits of heroes, but relies on the free play of intellectual fancy and the kind of humorous observation that produces caricature. It differs also from the picaresque form, which has the novel's interest in the actual structure of society. At its most concentrated the Menippean satire presents us with a vision of the world in terms of a single intellectual pattern. The intellectual structure built up from the story makes for violent dislocations in the customary logic of narrative, though the appearance of carelessness that results reflects only the carelessness of the reader or his tendency to judge by a novel-centred conception of fiction.

The word 'satire' in Roman and Renaissance times, meant either of two specific literary forms of that name, one (this one) prose and the other verse. Now it means a structural principle or attitude, what we have called a *mythos*. In the Menippean satires we have been discussing, the name of the form also applies to the attitude. As the name of an attitude, satire is, we have seen, a combination of fantasy and morality. But as the name of a form, the term satire, though confined to literature (for as a *mythos* it may appear in any art, a cartoon, for example), is more flexible, and can be either entirely fantastic or entirely moral. The Menippean adventure story may thus be pure fantasy, as it is in the literary fairy tale. The Alice books are perfect Menippean satires, and so is *The Water-Babies*, which has been influenced by Rabelais. The purely moral type is a serious vision of society as a single intellectual pattern, in other words a Utopia.

The short form of the Menippean satire is usually a dialogue or colloquy, in which the dramatic interest is in a conflict of ideas rather than of character. This is the favorite form of Erasmus, and is common in Voltaire. Here again the form is not invariably satiric in attitude, but shades off into more purely fanciful or moral discussions, like the *Imaginary Conversations* of Landor or the 'dialogue of the dead'. Sometimes this form expands to full length, and more than two speakers are used: the setting then is usually a *cena* or symposium, like the one that looms so large in Petronius. Plato, though much earlier in the field than Menippus, is a strong influence on this type, which stretches in an unbroken tradition down through those urbane and leisurely conversations which define the ideal courtier in Castiglione or the doctrine and discipline of angling in Walton. A modern development produces the country-house weekends in Peacock, Huxley, and their imitators in which the opinions and ideas and cultural interests expressed are as important as the love-making.

The novelist shows his exuberance either by an exhaustive analysis of human relationships, as in Henry James, or of social phenomena, as in Tolstoy. The Menippean satirist, dealing with intellectual themes and attitudes, shows his exuberance in intellectual ways, by piling up an enormous mass of erudition about his theme or in overwhelming his pedantic targets with an avalanche of their own jargon. A species, or rather sub-species, of the form is the kind of encyclopaedic farrago represented by Athenaeus' *Deipnosophists* and Macrobius' *Saturnalia*, where people sit at a banquet and pour out a vast mass of erudition on every subject that might conceivably come up in conversation. The display of erudition had probably been associated with the Menippean tradition by Varro, who was enough of a polymath to make Quintilian, if not stare and gasp, at any rate call him *vir Romanorum eruditissimus*. The tendency to expand into an encyclopaedic farrago is clearly marked in Rabelais notably in the great catalogues of torcheculs and epithets of codpieces and methods of divination. The encyclopaedic compilations produced in the line of duty by Erasmus and Voltaire suggest that a magpie instinct to collect facts is not unrelated to the type of

ability that has made them famous as artists. Flaubert's encyclopaedic approach to the construction of *Bouvard et Pecuchet*
is quite comprehensible if we explain it as marking an affinity
with the Menippean tradition.

This creative treatment of exhaustive erudition is the organizing principle of the greatest Menippean satire in English before
Swift, Burton's *Anatomy of Melancholy*. Here human society
is studied in terms of the intellectual pattern provided by the
conception of melancholy, a symposium of books replaces dialogue, and the result is the most comprehensive survey of human
life in one book that English literature had seen since Chaucer,
one of Burton's favorite authors. We may note in passing the
Utopia in his introduction and his 'digressions', which when
examined turn out to be scholarly distillations of Menippean
forms: the digression of air, of the marvellous journey; the
digression of spirits, of the ironic use of erudition; the digression
of the miseries of scholars, of the satire on the *philosophus
gloriosus*. The word 'anatomy' in Burton's title means a dissection or analysis, and expresses very accurately the intellectualized approach of his form. We may as well adopt it as a convenient name to replace the cumbersome and in modern times
rather misleading 'Menippean satire'.

The anatomy, of course, eventually begins to merge with the
novel, producing various hybrids including the *roman à these*
and novels in which the characters are symbols of social or
other ideas, like the proletarian novels of the thirties in this
century. It was Sterne, however, the disciple of Burton and
Rabelais, who combined them with greatest success. *Tristram
Shandy* may be, as was said at the beginning, a novel, but the
digressing narrative, the catalogues, the stylizing of character
along 'humor' lines, the marvellous journey of the great nose,
the symposium discussions, and the constant ridicule of philosophers and pedantic critics are all features that belong to the
anatomy.

A clearer understanding of the form and traditions of the
anatomy would make a good many elements in the history of
literature come into focus. Boethius' *Consolation of Philosophy*,
with its dialogue form, its verse interludes and its pervading
tone of contemplative irony, is a pure anatomy, a fact of considerable importance for the understanding of its vast influence.

The Compleat Angler is an anatomy because of its mixture of prose and verse, its rural *cena* setting, its dialogue form, its deipnosophistical interest in food, and its gentle Menippean raillery of a society which considers everything more important than fishing and yet has discovered very few better things to do. In nearly every period of literature there are many romances, confessions, and anatomies that are neglected only because the categories to which they belong are unrecognized. In the period between Sterne and Peacock, for example, we have, among romances, *Melmoth the Wanderer*; among confessions, Hogg's *Confessions of a Justified Sinner*; among anatomies, Southey's *Doctor*, Amory's *John Buncle*, and the *Noctes Ambrosianae*.

To sum up then: when we examine fiction from the point of view of form, we can see four chief strands binding it together, novel, confession, anatomy, and romance. The six possible combinations of these forms all exist, and we have shown how the novel has combined with each of the other three. Exclusive concentration on one form is rare: the early novels of George Eliot, for instance, are influenced by the romance, and the later ones by anatomy. The romance-confession hybrid is found, naturally, in the autobiography of a romantic temperament, and is represented in English by the extroverted George Borrow and the introverted De Quincey. The romance-anatomy one we have noticed in Rabelais; a later example is *Moby Dick*, where the romantic theme of the wild hunt expands into an encyclopaedic anatomy of the whale. Confession and anatomy are united in *Sartor Resartus* and in some of Kierkegaard's strikingly original experiments in prose fiction form, including *Either/Or*. More comprehensive fictional schemes usually employ at least three forms: we can see strains of novel, romance, and confession in *Pamela*, of novel, romance, and anatomy in *Don Quixote*, of novel, confession, and anatomy in Proust, and of romance, confession, and anatomy in Apuleius.

I deliberately make this sound schematic in order to suggest the advantage of having a simple and logical explanation for the form of, say *Moby Dick* or *Tristram Shandy*. The usual critical approach to the form of such works resembles that of the doctors in Brobdingnag, who after great wrangling finally pronounced Gulliver a *lusus naturae*. It is the anatomy in particular that has baffled critics, and there is hardly any fiction writer deeply influenced by it who has not been accused of disorderly conduct. The reader may be reminded here of Joyce, for describing Joyce's books as monstrous has become a nervous tic. I find 'demogorgon', 'behemoth', and 'white elephant' in good critics; the bad ones could probably do much better. The care that Joyce took to organize *Ulysses* and *Finnegans Wake* amounted nearly to obsession, but as they are not organized on familiar principles of prose fiction, the impression of shapelessness remains. Let us try our formulas on him.

If a reader were asked to set down a list of things that had most impressed him about *Ulysses*, it might reasonably be somewhat as follows. First, the clarity with which the sights and sounds and smells of Dublin come to life, the rotundity of the character-drawing, and the naturalness of the dialogue. Second, the elaborate way that the story and characters are parodied by being set against archetypal heroic patterns, notably the one provided by the *Odyssey*. Third, the revelation of character and incident through the searching use of the stream-of-consciousness technique. Fourth, the constant tendency to be encyclopaedic and exhaustive both in technique and in subject matter, and to see both in highly intellectualized terms. It should not be too hard for us by now to see that these four points describe elements in the book which relate to the novel, romance, confession, and anatomy respectively. *Ulysses*, then, is a complete prose epic with all four forms employed in it, all of practically equal importance, and all essential to one another, so that the book is a unity and not an aggregate.

This unity is built up from an intricate scheme of parallel contrasts. The romantic archetypes of Hamlet and Ulysses are like remote stars in a literary heaven looking down quizzically on the shabby creatures of Dublin obediently intertwining themselves in the patterns set by their influences. In the 'Cyclops' and 'Circe' episodes particularly there is a continuous parody of realistic patterns by romantic ones which reminds us, though the irony leans in the opposite direction, of *Madame Bovary*. The relation of novel and confession techniques is similar; the author jumps into his characters' minds to follow their stream of consciousness, and out again to describe them externally. In the novel-anatomy combination, too, found in the 'Ithaca' chapter, the sense of lurking antagonism between the personal and intellectual aspects of the scene accounts for much of its pathos. The same principle of parallel contrast holds good for the other three combinations: of romance and confession in 'Nausicaa' and 'Penelope', of confession and anatomy in 'Proteus' and 'The Lotos-Eaters', of romance and anatomy (a rare and fitful combination) in 'Sirens' and parts of 'Circe'.

In *Finnegans Wake* the unity of design goes far beyond this. The dingy story of the sodden HCE and his pinched wife is not contrasted with the archetypes of Tristram and the divine king: HCE is himself Tristram and the divine king. As the setting is a dream, no contrast is possible between confession and novel, between a stream of consciousness inside the mind and the appearances of other people outside it. Nor is the experiential world of the novel to be separated from the intelligible world of the anatomy. The forms we have been isolating in fiction, and which depend for their existence on the commonsense dichotomies of the daylight consciousness, vanish in *Finnegans Wake* into a fifth and quintessential form. This form is the one traditionally associated with scriptures and sacred books, and treats life in terms of the fall and awakening of the human soul and the creation and apocalypse of nature. The Bible is the definitive example of it; the Egyptian Book of the Dead and the Icelandic Prose Edda, both of which have left deep imprints on *Finnegans Wake*, also belong to it.

3 D. H. Lawrence

(i) Why the Novel Matters

First published posthumously in *Phoenix*, Heinemann, 1936. From *Selected Literary Criticism*, ed. A. Beal, Heinemann, 1955, pp. 102-13.

We have curious ideas of ourselves. We think of ourselves as a body with a spirit in it, or a body with a soul in it, or a body with a mind in it. *Mens sana in corpore sano.* The years drink up the wine, and at last throw the bottle away, the body, of course, being the bottle.

It is a funny sort of superstition. Why should I look at my hand, as it so cleverly writes these words, and decide that it is a mere nothing compared to the mind that directs it? Is there really any huge difference between my hand and my brain? Or my mind? My hand is alive, it flickers with a life of its own. It meets all the strange universe in touch, and learns a vast number of things, and knows a vast number of things. My hand, as it writes these words, slips, gaily along, jumps like a grasshopper to dot an *i*, feels the table rather cold, gets a little bored if I write too long, has its own rudiments of thought, and is just as much *me* as is my brain, my mind, or my soul. Why should I imagine that there is a *me* which is more *me* than my hand is? Since my hand is absolutely alive, me alive.

Whereas, of course, as far as I am concerned, my pen isn't alive at all. My pen *isn't me* alive. Me alive ends at my finger-tips.

Whatever is me alive is me. Every tiny bit of my hands is alive, every little freckle and hair and fold of skin. And whatever is me alive is me. Only my finger-nails, those ten little weapons between me and an inanimate universe, they cross the mysterious Rubicon between me alive and things like my pen, which are not alive, in my own sense.

So, seeing my hand is all alive, and me alive, wherein is it just a bottle, or a jug, or a tin can, or a vessel of clay, or any of the rest of that nonsense? True, if I cut it it will bleed, like a can of cherries. But then the skin that is cut, and the veins that bleed, and the bones that should never be seen, they are all just as alive as the blood that flows. So the tin can business, or vessel of clay, is just bunk.

And that's what you learn, when you're a novelist. And that's what you are very liable *not* to know, if you're a parson, or a philosopher, or a scientist or a stupid person. If you're a parson, you talk about souls in heaven. If you're a novelist, you know that paradise is in the palm of your hand, and on the end of your nose, because both are alive; and alive, and man alive, which is more than you can say, for certain, of paradise. Paradise is after life, and I for one am not keen on anything that is *after* life. If you are a philosopher, you talk about infinity, and the pure spirit which knows all things. But if you pick up a novel, you realize immediately that infinity is just a handle to this self-same jug of a body of mine; while as for knowing, if I find my finger in the fire, I know that fire burns, with a knowledge so emphatic and vital, it leaves Nirvana merely a conjecture. Oh, yes, my body, me alive, *knows*, and knows intensely. And as for the sum of all knowledge, it can't be anything more than an accumulation of all the things I know in the body, and you, dear reader, know in the body.

These damned philosophers, they talk as if they suddenly went off in steam, and were then much more important than they are when they're in their shirts. It is nonsense. Every man, philosopher included, ends in his own finger-tips. That's the end of his man alive. As for the words and thoughts and sighs and aspirations that fly from him, they are so many tremulations in the ether, and not alive at all. But if the tremulations reach another man alive, he may receive them into his life, and his life may take on a new colour, like a chameleon creeping from a brown rock on to a green leaf. All very well and good. It still doesn't alter the fact that the so-called spirit, the message or teaching of the philosopher or the saint, isn't alive at all, but just a tremulation upon the ether, like a radio message. All this spirit stuff is just tremulations upon the ether. If you, as man alive, quiver from the tremulation of the ether into new life, that is because you are man alive, and you take sustenance and stimulation into your alive man in a myriad ways. But to say that the message, or the spirit which is communicated to you, is more important than your living body, is nonsense. You might as well say that the potato at dinner was more important.

Nothing is important but life. And for myself, I can absolutely see life nowhere but in the living. Life with a capital L is only man alive. Even a cabbage in the rain is cabbage alive. All things that are alive are amazing. And all things that are dead are subsidiary to the living. Better a live dog than a dead lion. But better a live lion than a live dog. *C'est la vie!*

It seems impossible to get a saint, or a philosopher, or a scientist, to stick to this simple truth. They are all, in a sense, renegades. The saint wishes to offer himself up as spiritual food for the multitude. Even Francis of Assisi turns himself into a sort of angel-cake, of which anyone may take a slice. But an angel-cake is rather less than alive. And poor St Francis might as well apologize to his body, when he is dying: 'Oh, pardon me, my body, the wrong I did you through the years!' It was no wafer, for others to eat.

The philosopher, on the other hand, because he can think, decides that nothing but thoughts matter. It is as if a rabbit, because he can make little pills, should decide that nothing but little pills matter. As for the scientist, he has absolutely no use for me so long as I am man alive. To the scientist, I am dead. He puts under the microscope a bit of dead me, and calls it me. He takes me to pieces, and says first one piece, and then another piece, is me. My heart, my liver, my stomach have all been scientifically me, according to the scientist; and nowadays I am either a brain, or nerves, or glands, or something more up-to-date in the tissue line.

Now I absolutely flatly deny that I am a soul, or a body, or a mind, or an intelligence, or a brain, or a nervous system, or a bunch of glands, or any of the rest of these bits of me. The whole is greater than the part. And therefore, I, who am man alive, am greater than my soul, or spirit, or body, or mind, or consciousness, or anything else that is merely a part of me. I am a man, and alive. I am man alive, and as long as I can, I intend to go on being man alive.

For this reason I am a novelist. And being a novelist, I consider myself superior to the saint, the scientist, the philosopher, and the poet, who are all great masters of different bits of man alive, but never get the whole hog.

The novel is the one bright book of life. Books are not life. They are only tremulations on the ether. But the novel as a tremulation can make the whole man alive tremble. Which is more than poetry, philosophy, science, or any other book-tremulation can do.

The novel is the book of life. In this sense, the Bible is a great confused novel. You may say, it is about God. But it is really about man alive. Adam, Eve, Sarai, Abraham, Isaac, Jacob, Samuel, David, Bath-Sheba, Ruth, Esther, Solomon, Job, Isaiah, Jesus, Mark, Judas, Paul, Peter: what is it but man alive, from start to finish? Man alive, not mere bits. Even the Lord is another man alive, in a burning bush, throwing the tablets of stone at Moses's head.

I do hope you begin to get my idea, why the novel is supremely important as a tremulation on the ether. Plato makes the perfect ideal being tremble in me. But that's only a bit of me. Perfection is only a bit, in the strange make-up of man alive. The Sermon on the Mount makes the selfless spirit of me quiver. But that, too, is only a bit of me. The Ten Commandments set the old Adam shivering in me, warning me that I am a thief and a murderer, unless I watch it. But even the old Adam is only a bit of me.

I very much like all these bits of me to be set trembling with life and the wisdom of life. But I do ask that the whole of me shall tremble in its wholeness, some time or other.

And this, of course, must happen in me, living.

But as far as it can happen from a communication, it can only happen when a whole novel communicates itself to me. The Bible—but *all* the Bible—and Homer, and Shakespeare: these are the supreme old novels. These are all things to all men. Which means that in their wholeness they affect the whole man alive, which is the man himself, beyond any part of him. They set the whole tree trembling with a new access of life, they do not just stimulate growth in one direction.

I don't want to grow in any one direction any more. And, if I can help it, I don't want to stimulate anybody else into some particular direction. A particular direction ends in a *cul-de-sac*. We're in a *cul-de-sac* at present.

I don't believe in any dazzling revelation, or in any supreme Word. 'The grass withereth, the flower fadeth, but the Word of the Lord shall stand for ever'. That's the kind of stuff we've drugged ourselves with. As a matter of fact, the grass withereth, but comes up all the greener for that reason, after the rains. The flower fadeth, and therefore the bud opens. But the Word of the Lord, being man-uttered and a mere vibration on the ether, becomes staler and staler, more and more boring, till at last we turn a deaf ear and it ceases to exist, far more finally than any withered grass. It is grass that renews its youth like the eagle, not any Word.

We should ask for no absolutes, or absolute. Once and for all and for ever, let us have done with the ugly imperialism of any absolute. There is no absolute good, there is nothing absolutely right. All things flow and change, and even change is not absolute. The whole is a strange assembly of apparently incongruous parts, slipping past one another.

Me, man alive, I am a very curious assembly of incongruous parts. My yea! of to-day is oddly different from my yea! of yesterday. My tears of to-morrow will have nothing to do with my tears of a year ago. If the one I love remains unchanged and unchanging, I shall cease to love her. It is only because she changes and startles me into change and defies my inertia, and is herself staggered in her inertia by my changing, that I can continue to love her. If she stayed put, I might as well love the pepper-pot.

In all this change, I maintain a certain integrity. But woe betide me if I try to put my finger on it. If I say of myself, I am this, I am that!—then, if I stick to it, I turn into a stupid fixed thing like a lamp-post. I shall never know wherein lies my integrity, my individuality, my me. I *can* never know it. It is useless to talk about my ego. That only means that I have made up an *idea* of myself, and that I am trying to cut myself out to pattern. Which is no good. You can cut your cloth to fit your coat, but you can't clip bits off your living body, to trim it down to your idea. True, you can put yourself into ideal corsets. But even in ideal corsets, fashions change.

Let us learn from the novel. In the novel, the characters can do nothing but *live*. If they keep on being good, according to pattern, or bad, according to pattern, or even volatile, according to pattern, they cease to live, and the novel falls dead. A character in a novel has got to live, or it is nothing.

We, likewise, in life have got to live, or we are nothing.

What we mean by living is, of course, just as indescribable as what we mean by *being*. Men get ideas into their heads, of what they mean by Life, and they proceed to cut life out to pattern. Sometimes they go into the desert to seek God, sometimes they go into the desert to seek cash, sometimes it is wine, woman, and song, and again it is water, political reform, and votes. You never know what it will be next: from killing your neighbour with hideous bombs and gas that tears the lungs, to supporting a Foundlings' Home and preaching infinite Love, and being co-respondent in a divorce.

In all this wild welter, we need some sort of guide. It's no good inventing Thou Shalt Nots!

What then? Turn truly, honourably to the novel, and see wherein you are man alive, and wherein you are dead man in life. You may love a woman as man alive, and you may be making love to a woman as sheer dead man in life. You may eat your dinner as man alive, or as a mere masticating corpse. As man alive you may have a shot at your enemy. But as a ghastly simulacrum of life you may be firing bombs into men who are neither your enemies nor your friends, but just things you are dead to. Which is criminal, when the things happen to be alive.

To be alive, to be man alive, to be whole man alive: that is the point. And at its best, the novel, and the novel supremely, can help you. It can help you not to be dead man in life. So much of a man walks about dead and a carcass in the street and house, to-day: so much of women is merely dead. Like a pianoforte with half the notes mute.

But in the novel you can see, plainly, when the man goes dead, the woman goes inert. You can develop an instinct for life, if you will, instead of a theory of right and wrong, good and bad.

In life, there is right and wrong, good and bad, all the time. But what is right in one case is wrong in another. And in the novel you see one man becoming a corpse, because of his so-called goodness, another going dead because of his so-called wickedness. Right and wrong is an instinct: but an instinct of the whole consciousness in a man, bodily, mental, spiritual at once. And only in the novel are *all* things given full play, or at least, they may be given full play, when we realize that life itself, and not inert safety, is the reason for living. For out of the full play of all things emerges the only thing that is anything, the wholeness of a man, the wholeness of a woman, man alive, and live woman.

(ii) Morality and the Novel

First published posthumously in *Calendar of Modern Letters*, December 1925. From *Selected Literary Criticism*, ed. A. Beal, Heinemann, 1955, pp. 102–13.

The business of art is to reveal the relation between man and his circumambient universe, at the living moment. As mankind is always struggling in the toils of old relationships, art is always ahead of the 'times', which themselves are always far in the rear of the living moment.

When van Gogh paints sunflowers, he reveals, or achieves, the vivid relation between himself, as man, and the sunflower, as sunflower, at that quick moment of time. His painting does not represent the sunflower itself. We shall never know what the sunflower itself is. And the camera will *visualize* the sunflower far more perfectly than van Gogh can.

The vision on the canvas is a third thing, utterly intangible and inexplicable, the offspring of the sunflower itself and van Gogh himself. The vision on the canvas is for ever incommensurable with the canvas, or the paint, or van Gogh as a human organism, or the sunflower as a botanical organism. You cannot weigh nor measure nor even describe the vision on the canvas. It exists, to tell the truth, only in the much-debated fourth dimension. In dimensional space it has no existence.

It is a revelation of the perfected relation, at a certain moment, between man and a sunflower. It is neither man-in-the-mirror nor flower-in-the-mirror, neither is it above or below or across anything. It is between everything, in the fourth dimension.

And this perfected relation between man and his circumambient universe is life itself, for mankind. It has the fourth-dimensional quality of eternity and perfection. Yet it is momentaneous.

Man and the sunflower both pass away from the moment, in the process of forming a new relationship. The relation between all things changes from day to day, in a subtle stealth of change. Hence art, which reveals or attains to another perfect relationship, will be for ever new.

At the same time, that which exists in the non-dimensional space of pure relationship is deathless, lifeless, and eternal. That is, it gives us the *feeling* of being beyond life or death. We say an Assyrian lion or an Egyptian hawk's head 'lives'. What we really mean is that it is beyond life, and therefore beyond death. It gives us that feeling. And there is something inside us which must also be beyond life and beyond death, since that 'feeling' which we get from an Assyrian lion or an Egyptian hawk's head is so infinitely precious to us. As the evening star, that spark of pure relation between night and day, has been precious to man since time began.

If we think about it, we find that our life *consists in* this achieving of a pure relationship between ourselves and the living universe about us. This is how I 'save my soul' by accomplishing a pure relationship between me and another person, me and other people, me and a nation, me and a race of men, me and the animals, me and the trees or flowers, me and the earth, me and the skies and sun and stars, me and the moon: an infinity of pure relations, big and little, like the stars of the sky: that makes our eternity, for each one of us, me and the timber I am sawing, the lines of force I follow; me and the dough I knead for bread, me and the very motion with which I write, me and the bit of gold I have got. This, if we knew it, is our life and our eternity: the subtle, perfected relation between me and my whole circumambient universe.

And morality is that delicate, for ever trembling and changing *balance* between me and my circumambient universe, which precedes and accompanies a true relatedness.

Now here we see the beauty and the great value of the novel. Philosophy, religion, science, they are all of them busy nailing things down, to get a stable equilibrium. Religion, with its nailed-down One God, who says *Thou shalt, Thou shan't*, and hammers home every time; philosophy, with its fixed ideas; science with its 'laws': they, all of them, all the time, want to nail us on to some tree or other.

But the novel, no. The novel is the highest example of subtle inter-relatedness that man has discovered. Everything is true in its own time, place, circumstance, and untrue outside of its own place, time, circumstance. If you try to nail anything down, in the novel, either it kills the novel, or the novel gets up and walks away with the nail.

Morality in the novel is the trembling instability of the balance. When the novelist puts his thumb in the scale, to pull down the balance to his own predilection, that is immorality.

The modern novel tends to become more and more immoral, as the novelist tends to press his thumb heavier and heavier in the pan: either on the side of love pure love; or on the side of licentious 'freedom'.

The novel is not, as a rule, immoral because the novelist has any dominant *idea*, or *purpose*. The immorality lies in the novelist's helpless, unconscious, predilection. Love is a great emotion. But if you set out to write a novel, and you yourself are in the throes of the great predilection for love, love as the supreme, the only emotion worth living for, then you will write an immoral novel.

Because *no* emotion is supreme, or exclusively worth living for. *All* emotions go to the achieving of a living relationship between a human being and the other human being or creature or thing he becomes purely related to. All emotions, including love and hate, and rage and tenderness, go to the adjusting of the oscillating, unestablished balance between two people who amount to anything. If the novelist puts his thumb in the pan, for love, tenderness, sweetness, peace, then he commits an immoral act: he *prevents* the possibility of a pure relationship, a pure relatedness, the only thing that matters: and he makes inevitable the horrible reaction, when he lets his thumb go, towards hate and brutality, cruelty and destruction.

Life is so made that opposites sway about a trembling centre of balance. The sins of the fathers are visited on the children. If the fathers drag down the balance on the side of love, peace, and production, then in the third or fourth generation the balance will swing back violently to hate, rage, and destruction. We must balance as we go.

And of all the art forms, the novel most of all demands the trembling and oscillating of the balance. The 'sweet' novel is more falsified, and therefore more immoral, than the blood-and-thunder novel.

The same with the smart and smudgily cynical novel, which says it doesn't matter what you do, because one thing is as good as another, anyhow, and prostitution is just as much 'life' as anything else.

This misses the point entirely. A thing isn't life just because somebody does it. This the artist ought to know perfectly well. The ordinary bank clerk buying himself a new straw hat isn't 'life' at all: it is just existence, quite all right, like everyday dinners: but not 'life'.

By life, we mean something that gleams, that has the fourth-dimensional quality. If the bank clerk feels really piquant about his hat, if he establishes a lively relation with it, and goes out of the shop with the new straw on his head, a changed man, be-aureoled, then that is life.

The same with the prostitute. If a man establishes a living relation to her, if only for one moment, then it is life. But if it *doesn't*: if it is just money and function, then it is not life, but sordidness, and a betrayal of living.

If a novel reveals true and vivid relationships, it is a moral work, no matter what the relationships may consist in. If the novelist *honours* the relationship in itself, it will be a great novel.

But there are so many relationships which are not real. When the man in *Crime and Punishment* murders the old woman for sixpence, although it is *actual* enough, it is never quite real. The balance between the murderer and the old woman is gone entirely; it is only a mess. It is actuality, but it is not 'life', in the living sense.

The popular novel, on the other hand, dishes up a *réchauffé* of old relationships: *If Winter Comes*. And old relationships dished up are likewise immoral. Even a magnificent painter like Raphael does nothing more than dress up in gorgeous new dresses relationships, which have already been experienced. And this gives a gluttonous kind of pleasure of the mass: a voluptuousness, a wallowing. For centuries, men say of their voluptuously ideal woman: 'She is a Raphael Madonna.' And women are only just learning to take it as an insult.

A new relation, a new relatedness hurts somewhat in the attaining; and will always hurt. So life will always hurt. Because real voluptuousness lies in re-acting old relationships, and at the best, getting an alcoholic sort of pleasure out of it, slightly depraving.

Each time we strive to a new relation, with anyone or anything, it is bound to hurt somewhat. Because it means the struggle with and the displacing of old connexions, and this is never pleasant. And moreover, between living things at least, an adjustment means also a fight, for each party, inevitably, must 'seek its own' in the other, and be denied. When, in the parties, each of them seeks his own, her own, absolutely, then it is a fight to the death. And this is true of the thing called 'passion'. On the other hand when, of the two parties, one yields utterly to the other, this is called sacrifice, and it also means death. So the Constant Nymph died of her eighteen months of constancy.

It isn't the nature of nymphs to be constant. She should have been constant in her nymph-hood. And it is unmanly to accept sacrifices. He should have abided by his own manhood.

There is, however, the third thing, which is neither sacrifice nor fight to the death: when each seeks only the true relatedness to the other. Each must be true to himself, herself, his own manhood, her own womanhood, and let the relationship work out of itself. This means courage above all things: and then discipline. Courage to accept the life-thrust from within oneself, and from the other person. Discipline, not to exceed oneself any more than one can help. Courage, when one has exceeded oneself, to accept the fact and not whine about it.

Obviously, to read a really new novel will *always* hurt, to some extent. There will always be resistance. The same with new pictures, new music. You may judge of their reality by the fact that they do arouse a certain resistance, and compel, at length, a certain acquiescence.

The great relationship, for humanity, will always be the relation between man and woman. The relation between man and man, woman and woman, parent and child, will always be subsidiary.

And the relation between man and woman will change for ever, and will for ever be the new central clue to human life. It is the *relation itself* which is the quick and the central clue to life, not the man nor the woman, nor the children that result from the relationship, as a contingency.

It is no use thinking you can put a stamp on the relation between man and woman, to keep it in the *status quo*. You can't. You might as well try to put a stamp on the rainbow or the rain.

As for the bond of love, better put it off when it galls. It is an absurdity, to say that men and women *must love*. Men and women will be for ever subtly and changingly related to one another; no need to yoke them with any 'bond' at all. The only morality is to have man true to his manhood, woman to her womanhood, and let the relationship form of itself, in all honour. For it is, to each, *life itself*.

If we are going to be moral, let us refrain from driving pegs through anything, either through each other or through the third thing, the relationship, which is for ever the ghost of both of us. Every sacrificial crucifixion needs five pegs, four short ones and a long one, each one an abomination. But when you try to nail down the relationship itself, and write over it *Love* instead of *This is the King of the Jews*, then you can go on putting in nails for ever. Even Jesus called it the Holy Ghost, to show you that you can't lay salt on its tail.

The novel is a perfect medium for revealing to us the changing rainbow of our living relationships. The novel can help us to live, as nothing else can: no didactic Scripture, anyhow. If the novelist keeps his thumb out of the pan.

But when the novelist *has* his thumb in the pan, the novel becomes an unparalleled perverter of men and women. To be compared only, perhaps, to that great mischief of sentimental hymns, like 'Lead, Kindly Light', which have helped to rot the marrow in the bones of the present generaton.

4 Wayne C. Booth

Telling and Showing

From *The Rhetoric of Fiction*, University of Chicago Press, 1961, Chap. 1, pp. 3–9.

Authoritative 'Telling' in Early Narration.

One of the most obviously artificial devices of the storyteller is the trick of going beneath the surface of the action to obtain a reliable view of a character's mind and heart. Whatever our ideas may be about the natural way to tell a story, artifice is unmistakably present whenever the author tells us what no one in so-called real life could possibly know. In life we never know anyone but ourselves by thoroughly reliable internal signs, and most of us achieve an all too partial view even of ourselves. It is in a way strange, then, that in literature from the very beginning we have been told motives directly and authoritatively without being forced to rely on those shaky inferences about other men which we cannot avoid in our own lives.

'There was a man in the land of Uz, whose name was Job; and that man was perfect and upright, one that feared God, and eschewed evil.' With one stroke the unknown author has given us a kind of information never obtained about real people, even about our most intimate friends. Yet it is information that we must accept without question if we are to grasp the story that is to follow. In life if a friend confided his view that his friend was 'perfect and upright', we would accept the information with qualifications imposed by our knowledge of the speaker's character or of the general fallibility of mankind. We could never trust even the most reliable of witnesses as completely as we trust the author of the opening statement about Job.

We move immediately in Job to two scenes presented with no privileged information whatever: Satan's temptation of God and Job's first losses and lamentations. But we conclude the first section with another judgment which no real event could provide for any observer: 'In all this Job sinned not, nor charged God foolishly.' How do we know that Job sinned not? Who is to pronounce on such a question? Only God himself could know with certainty whether Job charged God foolishly. Yet the author pronounces judgment, and we accept his judgment without question.

It might at first appear that the author does not require us to rely on his unsupported word, since he gives us the testimonial of God himself, conversing with Satan, to confirm his view of Job's moral perfection. And after Job has been pestered by his three friends and has given his own opinion about his experience, God is brought on stage again to confirm the truth of Job's view. But clearly the reliability of God's statements ultimately depends on the author himself; it is he who names God and assures us that this voice is truly His.

This form of artificial authority has been present in most narrative until recent times. Though Aristotle praises Homer for speaking in his own voice less than other poets, even Homer writes scarcely a page without some kind of direct clarification of motives, of expectations, and of the relative importance of events. And though the gods themselves are often unreliable, Homer—the Homer we know—is not. What he tells us usually goes deeper and is more accurate than anything we are likely to learn about real people and events. In the opening lines of the *Iliad*, for example, we are told, under the half-pretense of an invocation, precisely what the tale is to be about: 'the anger of Peleus' son Achilles and its devastation.'[1] We are told directly that we are to care more about the Greeks than the Trojans. We are told that they were 'heroes' with 'strong souls'. We are told that it was the will of Zeus that they should be 'the delicate feasting of dogs'. And we learn that the particular conflict between Agamemnon, 'the lord of men', and 'brilliant' Achilles was set on by Apollo. We could never be sure of any of this information in real life, yet we *are* sure as we move through the *Iliad* with Homer constantly at our elbow, controlling rigorously our beliefs, our interests, and our sympathies. Though his commentary is generally brief and often disguised in simile, we learn from it the precise quality of every heart; we know who dies innocent and who guilty, who foolish and who wise. And we know, whenever there is any reason for us to know, what the characters are thinking: 'the son of Tydeus pondered doubt-

---

[1] Trans. Richmond Lattimore, Routledge and Kegan Paul, 1951. All quotations are from this translation.

fully/ .... Three times in his heart and spirit he pondered turning...' (Book VIII, 167–69).

In the *Odyssey* Homer works in the same explicit and systematic way to keep our judgments straight. Though E. V. Rieu is no doubt correct in calling Homer an 'impersonal' and 'objective' author, in the sense that the life of the real Homer cannot be discovered in his work,[1] Homer 'intrudes' deliberately and obviously to insure that our judgment of the 'heroic', 'resourceful', 'admirable', 'wise' Odysseus will be sufficiently favorable. 'Yet all the gods were sorry for him, except Poseidon, who pursued the heroic Odysseus with relentless malice till the day when he reached his own country.'

Indeed, the major justification of the opening scene in the palace of Zeus is not as mere exposition of the facts of Odysseus' plight. What Homer requires of us is sympathetic involvement in that plight, and Athene's opening reply to Zeus provides authoritative judgment on what is to follow. 'It is for Odysseus that my heart is wrung—the wise but unlucky Odysseus, who has been parted so long from all his friends and is pining on a lonely island far away in the middle of the seas.' To her accusation of neglect, Zeus replies, 'How could I ever forget the admirable Odysseus? He is not only the wisest man alive but has been the most generous in his offerings.... It is Poseidon ... who is so implacable towards him....'

When we come to Odysseus' enemies, the poet again does not hesitate either to speak in his own person or to give divine testimony. Penelope's suitors must look bad to us; Telemachus must be admired. Not only does Homer dwell on Athene's approval of Telemachus, he lays on his own direct judgments with bright colors. The 'insolent', 'swaggering', and 'ruffianly' suitors are contrasted to the 'wise' (though almost helplessly young) Telemachus and the 'good' Mentor. 'Telemachus now showed his good judgment.' Mentor 'showed his good will now by rising to admonish his compatriots.' We seldom encounter the suitors without some explicit attack by the poet: 'This was their boastful way, though it was they who little guessed how matters really

---

[1] The *Odyssey*, trans. E. V. Rieu, Penguin, 1959, p. 10. The quotations that follow are from Rieu's translation, Books I–IV. Different translations give different emphases to Homer's moral judgments, and some use less forceful epithets than does Rieu. But no translator has been able to portray a neutral Homer.

stood.' And whenever there might be some doubt about where a character stands, Homer sets us straight : ' "My Queen," replied Medon, who was by no means a villain....' Hundreds of pages later, when Medon is spared from Odysseus' slaughter, we can hardly be surprised.

The result of all this direct guidance, when it is joined with Athene's divine attestation that the gods 'have no quarrel' with Telemachus and have settled that he 'shall come home safe', is to leave us, as we enter upon Odysseus' first adventure in Book Five, perfectly clear about what we should hope for and what fear; we are unambiguously sympathetic toward the heroes and contemptuous of the suitors. It need hardly be said that another poet, working with the same episodes but treating them from the suitors' point of view, could easily have led us into the same adventures with radically different hopes and fears.[1]

Direct and authoritative rhetoric of the kind we have seen in Job and in Homer's works has never completely disappeared from fiction. But as we all know, it is not what we are likely to find if we turn to a typical modern novel or short story.

> Jim had a great trick that he used to play w'ile he was travelin'. For instance, he'd be ridin' on a train and they'd come to some little town like, well, like, we'll say, like Benton. Jim would look out of the train window and read the signs on the stores.
>
> For instance, they'd be a sign, 'Henry Smith, Dry Goods.' Well, Jim would write down the name and the name of the town and when he got to wherever he was goin' he'd mail back a postal card to Henry Smith at Benton and not sign no name to it, but he'd write on the card, well, somethin' like 'Ask your wife about that book agent that spent the afternoon last week,' or 'Ask your Missus who kept her from gettin' lonesome the last time you was in Carterville.' And he'd sign the card, 'A Friend.'
>
> Of course, he never knew what really come of none of these jokes, but he could picture what probably happened and that was enough.... Jim was a card.

Most readers of Lardner's 'Haircut' (1926) have recognized that Lardner's opinion of Jim is radically different here from the speaker's. But no one in the story has said so. Lardner is not

---

[1] Some readers may fear at this point that I am stumbling blindfold into the 'affective fallacy'. I try to meet their legitimate concern in chaps. iii–v.

present to say so, not, at least, in the sense that Homer is present in his epics. Like many other modern authors, he has effaced himself, renounced the privilege of direct intervention, retreated to the wings and left his characters to work out their own fates upon the stage.

> In sleep she knew she was in her bed, but not the bed she had lain down in a few hours since, and the room was not the same but it was a room she had known somewhere. Her heart was a stone lying upon her breast outside of her; her pulses lagged and paused, and she knew that something strange was going to happen, even as the early morning winds were cool through the lattice....
>
> Now I must get up and go while they are all quiet. Where are my things? Things have a will of their own in this place and hide where they like.... Now what horse shall I borrow for this journey I do not mean to take? ... Come now, Graylie, she said, taking the bridle, we must outrun Death and the Devil....

The relation between author and spokesman is more complex here. Katherine Anne Porter's Miranda ('Pale Horse, Pale Rider' [1936]) cannot be simply classified, like Lardner's barber, as morally and intellectually deficient; the ironies at work among character, author, and reader are considerably more difficult to describe. Yet the problem for the reader is essentially the same as in 'Haircut'. The story is presented without comment, leaving the reader without the guidance of explicit evaluation.

Since Flaubert, many authors and critics have been convinced that 'objective' or 'impersonal' or 'dramatic' modes of narration are naturally superior to any mode that allows for direct appearances by the author or his reliable spokesman. Sometimes the complex issues involved in this shift have been reduced to a convenient distinction between 'showing', which is artistic, and 'telling', which is inartistic. 'I shall not *tell* you anything,' says a fine young novelist in defense of his art. 'I shall allow you to eavesdrop on my people, and sometimes they will tell the truth and sometimes they will lie, and you must determine for yourself when they are doing which. You do this every day. Your butcher says, "This is the best," and you reply, "That's *you* saying it." ' Shall my people be less the captive of their desires than your butcher? I can *show* much, but show only.... You will no more expect the novelist to tell you precisely *how* something is said than you will expect him to stand by your chair and hold your book.'[1]

But the changed attitudes toward the author's voice in fiction raise problems that go far deeper than this simplified version of point of view would suggest. Percy Lubbock taught us forty years ago to believe that 'the art of fiction does not begin until the novelist thinks of his story as a matter to be *shown*, to be so exhibited that it will tell itself'.[2] He may have been in some sense right—but to say so raises more questions than it answers.

Why is it that an episode 'told' by Fielding can strike us as more fully realized than many of the scenes scrupulously 'shown' by imitators of James or Hemingway? Why does some authorial commentary ruin the work in which it occurs, while the prolonged commentary of *Tristram Shandy* can still enthral us? What, after all, does an author do when he 'intrudes' to 'tell' us something about his story? Such questions force us to consider closely what happens when an author engages a reader fully with a work of fiction; they lead us to a view of fictional technique which necessarily goes far beyond the reductions that we have sometimes accepted under the concept of 'point of view'.

Two stories from the 'Decameron'

Our task will be simpler if we begin with some stories written long before anyone worried very much about cleaning out the rhetorical impurities from the house of fiction. The stories in Boccaccio's *Decameron*, for example, seem extremely simple— perhaps even simple-minded and inept—if we ask of them the questions which many modern stories invite us to ask. It is bad enough that the characters are what we call two-dimensional, with no revealed depths of any kind; what is much worse, the 'point of view' of the narrator shifts among them with a total disregard for the kind of technical focus or consistency generally admired today. But if we read these stories in their own terms, we soon discover a splendid and complex skill underlying the simplicity of the effect.

[1] Mark Harris, 'Easy Does It Not', in *The Living Novel*, ed. Granville Hicks, Macmillan Co., New York, 1957, p. 117.
[2] *The Craft of Fiction*, Cape, 1921, p. 62.

The material of the ninth story of the fifth day is in itself conventional and shallow indeed. There was once a young lover, Federigo, who impoverished himself courting a chaste married woman, Monna Giovanna. Rejected, he withdrew to a life of poverty, with only a beloved falcon remaining of all his former possessions. The woman's husband died. Her son, who had grown fond of Federigo's falcon, became seriously ill and asked Monna to obtain the falcon for his comfort. She reluctantly went to Federigo to request the falcon. Federigo was overwhelmed with excitement by her visit, and he was determined, in spite of his poverty, to entertain her properly. But his cupboard was bare, so he killed the falcon and served it to her. They discovered their misunderstanding, and the mother returned empty-handed to her boy, who soon died. But the childless widow, impressed by Federigo's generous gesture in offering his falcon, chose him for her second husband.

Such a story, reduced in this way to a bare outline, could have been made into any number of fully realized plots with radically different effects. It could have been a farce, stressing Federigo's foolish extravagance, his ridiculous antics in trying to think of something to serve his beloved for breakfast, and the absurdity of the surprise ending. It could have been a meditative or a comic piece on the ironical twists of fate, emphasizing the transformation in Monna from proud resistance to quick surrender—something of the order of Christopher Fry's *A Phoenix Too Frequent* as derived from Petronius. It could have been a sardonic tale written from the point of view of the husband and son who, like the falcon, must be killed off, as it were, to make the survivors happy. And so on.

As it is, every stroke is in a direction different from these. The finished tale is designed to give the reader the greatest possible pleasure in the sympathetic comedy of Monna's and Federigo's deserved good fortune, to make the reader delight in this instance of the announced theme for all the tales told on the fifth day: 'good fortune befalling lovers after divers direful or disastrous adventures'.[1] Though one never views these characters or their disastrous adventures in anything like a tragic light, and though, in fact, one laughs at the excesses of Federigo's passion and at

---

[1] Trans. J. M. Rigg, Everyman, 1930. All quotations are from this edition.

his willingness to pursue it even to poverty, our laughter must always be sympathetic. Much as Federigo deserves his disasters, in the finished tale he also deserves the supreme good fortune of winning Monna.

To insure our pleasure in such an outcome—a pleasure which might have been mild indeed considering that there are nine other tales attempting something like the same effect—the two main characters must be established with great precision. First the heroine, Monna Giovanna, must be felt to be thoroughly worthy of Federigo's 'extravagant' love. In a longer, different kind of story, this might have been done by showing her in virtuous action; one could take whatever space were required for episodes dramatizing her as worthy of Federigo's fantastic devotion. But here economy is at least as important as precision. And the economical method of imposing her virtues on the reader is for the narrator to *tell* us about them, supporting his telling with some judiciously chosen, and by modern standards very brief and unrealistic, episodes. These can be of two kinds, either in the form of what James was later to call 'going behind' to reveal the true workings of the heroine's mind and heart or in the form of overt action. Thus, the narrator begins by describing her as the 'fairest' and 'most elegant', and as 'no less virtuous than fair'. In a simple story of this kind, her beauty and elegance require for validation no more than Federigo's dramatized passion. Our belief in her virtue, however—certainly in Boccaccio a more unlikely gift than beauty and elegance—is supported both by her sustained chastity in the face of his courtship and, far more important, by the quality of what is revealed whenever we enter her thoughts.

Whereupon the lady was silent a while, bethinking her what she should do. She knew that Federigo had long loved her, and had never had so much as a single kind look from her: wherefore she said to herself:—How can I send or go to beg of him his falcon, which by what I hear is the best that ever flew, and moreover is his sole comfort? And how could I be so unfeeling as to seek to deprive a gentleman of the one solace that is now left him? And so, albeit she very well knew that she might have the falcon for the asking, she was perplexed, and knew not what to say, and gave her son no answer. At length, however, the love she bore the boy carried the day, and she made up her mind, for his contentment ... to go herself and fetch him the falcon.

The interest in this passage lies of course in the moral choice that it presents and in the effect upon our sentiments that is implicit in that choice. Though the choice is in one respect a relatively trivial one, it is far more important than most choices faced by the characters who people Boccaccio's world. Dramatized at greater length, it could in fact have been made into the central episode for the story—though the story that resulted would be a far different one from what we now have. As it is treated here, the choice is given precisely the degree of importance it should have in the whole. Because we experience Monna's thoughts and feelings at first hand, we are forced to agree with the narrator's assessment of her great worth. She is not simply virtuous in conventional matters like chastity, but she is also capable of moral delicacy in more fundamental matters: unlike the majority of Boccaccio's women, she is above any casual manipulation of her lover for her own purposes. Even this delicacy, admirable in itself, can be overridden by a more important value, 'the love she bore the boy'. Yet all this is kept strictly serviceable to our greater interest in Federigo and the falcon; there is never any question of our becoming sidetracked into deep psychological or sentimental involvement with her as a person.

Because the narrator has *told* us what to think of her, and then *shown* her briefly in support of his claims, all the while keeping our sympathy and admiration carefully subordinated to the comic effect of the whole, we can move to the most important episode with our expectations clear and—in their own kind— intense. We can move to Monna's relatively long and wonderfully delicate speech to Federigo requesting the falcon, with our hopes centered clearly on the 'good fortune' of their ultimate union.

If all this skilful presentation of the admirable Monna is to succeed, we must see Federigo himself as an equally admirable, though not really heroic, figure. Too much moral stature will spoil the comedy; too little will destroy our desire for his success. It is not enough to show his virtues through his actions; his only admirable act is the gift of the falcon and that might be easily interpreted in itself as a further bit of foolish extravagance. Unless the story is to be lengthened unduly with episodes showing that he is worthy, in spite of his extravagance, the narrator must give us briefly and directly the necessary information about his true character. He is therefore described, unobtrusively but in terms that only an omniscient narrator could use with success, as 'gallant', 'full of courtesy', 'patient', and most important of all, as 'more in love than ever before'; the world of *his* desires is thus set off distinctly from the world of many of the other tales, where love is reduced for comic purposes to lust.

These completely straightforward statements of the narrator's opinions are supported by what we see of Federigo's own mind. His comic distress over not having anything to feed his beloved visitor, and his unflinching sacrifice of the bird, are rendered in intimate detail, with frequent—though by modern standards certainly shallow—inside views; his poverty 'was brought home to him', he was 'distressed beyond measure', he 'inwardly' cursed 'his evil fortune'. 'Sorely he longed that the lady might not leave his house altogether unhonoured, and yet to crave help of his own husbandman was more than his pride could brook.' All this insures that the wonderful comedy of the breakfast will be the comedy of sympathetic laughter: we are throughout completely in favor of Federigo's suit. And our favor is heightened by the method of presenting the scene of discovery. 'No sooner had Federigo apprehended what the lady wanted, than, *for grief that 'twas not in his power to serve her* ... he fell a-weeping....' At first Monna supposed that ' 'twas only because he was loath to part with the brave falcon that he wept.' We might have made the same mistake but for the author's help provided in the clause I have italicized.

Once we have become assured of his character in this way, Federigo's speeches, like Monna Giovanna's, become the equivalent of inside views, because we know that everything he says is a trustworthy reflection of his true state of mind. His long speech of explanation about the falcon serves, as a result, to confirm all we have learned of him; when he concludes, 'I doubt I shall never know peace of mind more', we believe in his sincerity, though of course we know with complete certainty, and have known from the beginning, that the story is to end with 'good fortune'.

Having seen this much, we need little more. To make Monna
the heiress as provided in the will, her son must die in a passage
only one or two lines longer than the one or two lines earlier
given to the death of the husband. Her 'inward commendation'
of Federigo's 'magnanimity' leads her to the decision to marry
him rather than a wealthy suitor: 'I had rather have a man without wealth than wealth without a man.' Federigo *is* a man, as we
know by now. Though his portrait is conventional, 'flat', 'two-
dimensional', it includes everything we need. We can thus accept
without irony the narrator's concluding judgment that married
to such a wife he lived happily to the end of his days. Fiammetta's auditors all 'praised God that He had worthily rewarded
Federigo'.

If we share in the pleasure of seeing the comic but worthy hero
worthily rewarded, the reason is thus not to be found in any
inherent quality of the materials but rather in the skilful construction of a living plot out of materials that might have been
used in many different ways. The deaths of the husband and
son, which in the finished version are merely conveniences for
Federigo's exaltation, would in any truly impartial account
occupy considerably more space than Federigo's anxiety over
not having to serve his mistress. Treated impartially, the boy's
death would certainly be dramatized as fully as the mother's
hesitation about troubling Federigo for his falcon. But the
demands of this plot are for a technique that wins us to Federigo's
side.

Quite obviously this technique cannot be judged by modern
standards of consistency; the story could not have been written
from a consistent point of view without stretching it to three
times its present length and thereby losing its taut comic force.
To tell it entirely through Federigo's eyes would require a much
longer introductory section, and the comedy of the visit to fetch
the falcon would be partially lost if we did not see more of the
preparation for it than Federigo can possibly be aware of. Yet
since it is primarily Federigo's story, to see it through Monna's
eyes would require a great deal of manipulation and extension.
Such conjectural emendations are in a way absurd, since they
almost certainly would never have occurred to Boccaccio. But
they help to make emphatic the great gap that separates Boccaccio's technique from the more obviously rigorous methods

we have come to look for. In this story there is no important revelation of truth, no intensity of illusion, no ironic complexity, no prophetic vision, no rich portrayal of moral ambiguities. There is some incidental irony, it is true, but the greatness of the whole resides in unequivocal intensity not of illusion but of comic delight produced in extraordinarily brief compass.

Any temptation we might have to attribute its success to unconscious or accidental primitivism can be dispelled by looking at the radically different experience offered by other tales. Since his different effects are based on different moral codes, Boccaccio can never assume that his readers will hold precisely the correct attitudes as they approach any one story. He certainly does not assume that his readers will approve of the license of his most licentious tales. Even Dioneo, the most lewd of all the ten narrators, must spend a good deal of energy manipulating us into the camp of those who can laugh with a clear conscience at his bawdy and often cruel stories. In the potentially distressing tale of how the holy man, Rustico, debauches the young and innocent Alibech by teaching her how to put the devil in hell (third day, tenth tale), great care is taken with the character and ultimate fate of the simple-minded girl in order to lead us to laugh at conduct that in most worlds, including the world in which Boccaccio lived, would be considered cruel and sacrilegious rather than comic.

If Dioneo, the lusty young courtier, must use care with his rhetoric in a bawdy tale, Fiammetta, the lovely lady, must use even more when she comes to praise infidelity. On the seventh day the subject is 'the tricks which, either for love or for their deliverance from peril, ladies have heretofore played their husbands, and whether they were by the said husbands detected, or no'. In 'The Falcon' Fiammetta worked to build admiration for the virtue of Federigo and Monna Giovanna; she now (fifth tale) employs a different rhetoric. Since her task is to insure our delight in the punishment of a justifiably jealous husband, her commentary tells us directly what is borne out by our views of the husband's mind: he is 'a poor creature, and of little sense' who deserves what he gets. More important, she prefaces the story with a little oration, about one-seventh of the length of the whole story, setting our values straight: 'For which reason, to sum up, I say that a wife is rather to be commended than censured, if she take her revenge upon a husband that is jealous without cause.'

In support of this general argument, the whole tale is manipulated in such a way as to make the reader desire the comic punishment of the husband. Most of it is seen through the eyes of the woman, with great stress on her comic suffering at the hands of the great bullying fool. The climax is his full punishment, in the form of a clever, lashing speech from his wife. Few readers can feel that he has received anything but what he deserves when Fiammetta concludes that the cuckold's wife has now earned her 'charter of indulgence'.

These extremes by no means exhaust the variety of norms that we are led to accept by the shift rhetoric as we move through the *Decameron*. The standards of judgment change so radically, in fact, that it is difficult to discern any figure in Boccaccio's carpet.[1] I shall try later on to deal with some of the issues raised when an author heightens specific effects at the expense of his general notions of moral truth or reality. What is important here is to recognize the radical inadequacy of the telling-showing distinction in dealing with the practice of this one author. Boccaccio's artistry lies not in adherence to any one supreme manner of narration but rather in his ability to order various forms of telling in the service of various forms of showing.

---

[1] Erich Auerbach, for example, complains that he can find no basic moral attitude and no clear approach to reality lying back of all the tales. So long as he considers what Boccaccio does 'for the sake of the comic effect', he has nothing but praise for his 'critical sense' of the world, 'firm yet elastic in perspective, which, without abstract moralizing, allots phenomena their specific, carefully nuanced moral value' (*Mimesis: The Representation of Reality in Western Literature*, Berne, 1946, trans. Willard Trask, Anchor Books, 1957, p. 193). It is only on the level of the most general qualities, common to all the stories despite the differing needs of the moment, that Auerbach encounters difficulties and complains of the 'vagueness and uncertainty' of Boccaccio's 'early humanism' (p. 102). Auerbach's account is valuable in showing how Boccaccio's style, in so far as it is common to all of the tales, serves as a kind of rhetoric convincing the reader of the reality of his world.

5 Georg Lukács

Narrate or Describe?

A preliminary discussion of
Naturalism and Formalism

To be radical is to grasp things by the roots. The root
of humanity, however, is man himself.

Marx

Written in 1936. First published in Britain in *Writer and Critic*, trans.
A. Khan, Merlin Press, London, 1970, pp. 110–35.

I

Let's start *in medias res*! In two famous modern novels Zola's
Nana and Tolstoy's *Anna Karenina*, horse races are depicted.
How do the two writers approach their task?

The description of the race is a brilliant example of Zola's
virtuosity. Every possible detail at a race is described precisely,
colourfully and with sensuous vitality. Zola provides a small
monograph on the modern turf; every phase from the saddling
of the horses to the finish is investigated meticulously. The
Parisian public is depicted in all the brilliance of a Second-
Empire fashion show. The manœuvring behind the scenes, too,
is presented in detail. The race ends in an upset, and Zola
describes not only the surprise outcome but also the betting
fraud responsible for it. However, for all its virtuosity the description is mere filler in the novel. The events are loosely
related to the plot and could easily be eliminated; the sole connection arises from the fact that one of Nana's many fleeting
lovers is ruined in the swindle.

Another link to the main plot is even more tenuous, hardly
an integral element in the action of the novel at all—and is thus
even more representative of Zola's creative method: the victorious horse is named Nana. Surprisingly, Zola actually under-
lines this tenuous chance association. The victory of the
coquette's namesake is symbolic of her own triumph in Parisian
high society and demi-monde.

In *Anna Karenina* the race represents the crisis in a great drama. Vronsky's fall means an overturning in Anna's life. Just before the race she had realized that she was pregnant and, after painful hesitation, had informed Vronsky of her condition. Her shock at Vronsky's fall impels the decisive conversation with her husband. The relationships of the protagonists enter a new critical phase because of the race. The race is thus no mere tableau but rather a series of intensely dramatic scenes which provide a turning point in the plot.

The absolute divergence of intentions in the scenes in the two novels is further reflected in the creative approaches. In Zola the race is *described* from the standpoint of an observer; in Tolstoy it is *narrated* from the standpoint of a participant.

Vronsky's ride is thoroughly integrated into the total action of the novel. Indeed, Tolstoy emphasizes that it is no mere incidental episode but an event of essential significance in Vronsky's life. The ambitious officer has been frustrated in advancing his military career by a set of circumstances, not the least of which is his relationship with Anna. For him a victory in the race in the presence of the court and of the aristocracy offers one of the few remaining opportunities for furthering his career. All the preparations for the race and all the events of the race itself are therefore integral to an important action, and they are recounted in all their dramatic significance. Vronsky's fall is the culmination of a phase in his personal drama. With it Tolstoy breaks off the description of the race. The fact that Vronsky's rival subsequently overtook him can be noted in passing later.

But the analysis of the epic concentration in this scene is not yet exhausted by any means. Tolstoy is not describing a 'thing', a horse-race. He is recounting the vicissitudes of human beings. That is why the action is narrated twice, in true epic fashion, and not simply picturesquely described. In the first account, in which Vronsky was the central figure as a participant in the race, the author had to relate with precision and sophistication everything of significance in the preparations and in the race itself. But in the second account Anna and Karenin are the protagonists. Displaying his consummate epic artistry, Tolstoy does not introduce this account of the race immediately after the first. Instead he first recounts earlier events in Karenin's day and explores Karenin's attitude towards Anna. Thus he is able to present the race as the climax of the entire day. The race itself develops into an inner drama. Anna watches Vronsky alone, oblivious to all other events in the race and to the success and failure of all other participants. Karenin watches no one but Anna, following her reactions to what happens to Vronsky. This scene, almost devoid of dialogue, prepares for Anna's outburst on the way home, when she confesses her relations with Vronsky to Karenin.

Here the reader or writer educated in the 'modern' school may protest: 'Granted that these do represent two different fictional approaches, does not the very linking of the race with the destinies of the protagonists make the race itself a chance event, simply an opportunity for the dramatic catastrophe? And does not Zola's comprehensive, monographic, effective description provide an accurate picture of a social phenomenon?'

The key question is: what is meant by 'chance' in fiction? Without chance all narration is dead and abstract. No writer can portray life if he eliminates the fortuitous. On the other hand, in his representation of life he must go beyond crass accident and elevate chance to the inevitable.

Is it thoroughness of description that renders something artistically 'inevitable'? Or does inevitability arise out of the relationship of characters to objects and events, a dynamic interaction in which the characters act and suffer? Linking Vronsky's ambition to his participation in the race provides quite another mode of artistic necessity than that which is possible with Zola's exhaustive description. Objectively, attendance at or participation in a race is only an incident in life. Tolstoy integrated such an incident into a critical dramatic context as tightly as it was possible to do. The race is, on the one hand, merely an occasion for the explosion of a conflict, but, on the other hand, through its relationship to Vronsky's social ambitions—an important factor in the subsequent tragedy—it is far more than a mere incident.

There are examples in literature of more obvious contrasts of the two approaches to inevitability and accident in the representation of fictional subject matter.

Compare the description of the theatre in the same Zola novel with that in Balzac's *Lost Illusions*. Superficially there is much similarity. The opening night, with which Zola's novel begins, decides Nana's career. The première in Balzac signifies a turning point in Lucien de Rubempré's life, his transition from unrecognized poet to successful but unscrupulous journalist.

In this chapter Zola, with characteristic and deliberate thoroughness, describes the theatre only from the point of view of the audience. Whatever happens in the auditorium, in the foyer or in the loges, as well as the appearance of the stage as seen from the hall, is described with impressive artistry. But Zola's obsession with monographic detail is not satisfied. He devotes another chapter to the description of the theatre as seen from the stage. With no less descriptive power he depicts the scene changes, the dressing-rooms, etc., both during the performance and the intermissions. And to complete this picture, he describes in yet a third chapter a rehearsal, again with equal conscientiousness and virtuosity.

This meticulous detail is lacking in Balzac. For him the theatre and the performance serve as the setting for an inner drama of his characters: Lucien's success, Coralie's theatrical career, the passionate love between Lucien and Coralie, Lucien's subsequent conflict with his former friends in the D'Arthèz circle and his current protector Lousteau, and the beginning of his campaign of revenge against Mme de Bargeton, etc.

But what is represented in these battles and conflicts—all directly or indirectly related to the theatre? The state of the theatre under capitalism: the absolute dependence of the theatre upon capital and upon the press (itself dependent upon capital); the relationship of the theatre to literature and of journalism to literature; the capitalistic basis for the connection between the life of an actress and open and covert prostitution.

These social problems are posed by Zola, too. But they are simply described as social facts, as results, as *caput mortuum* of a social process. Zola's theatre director continually repeats: 'Don't say theatre, say bordello.' Balzac, however, depicts *how* the theatre *becomes* prostituted under capitalism. The drama of his protagonists is simultaneously the drama of the institution in which they work, of the things with which they live, of the setting in which they fight their battles, of the objects through which they express themselves and through which their interrelationships are determined.

This is admittedly an extreme case. The objective factors in a man's environment are not always and inevitably so intimately linked to his fate. They can provide instruments for his activity and for his career and even, as in Balzac, turning points in his fortunes. But they may also simply provide the setting for his activity and for his career.

Does the contrast in approach we have just noted arise where there is a simple literary representation of a setting?

In the introductory chapter to his novel *Old Mortality*, Walter Scott depicts a marksmanship contest during some national holiday in Scotland after the Restoration, organized as part of a campaign to revive feudal institutions, as a review of the military power of the Stuart supporters and as a provocation for unmasking disaffection. The parade takes place on the eve of the revolt of the oppressed Puritans. With extraordinary epic artistry Walter Scott assembles on the parade ground all the opposing elements about to explode in bloody conflict. In a series of grotesque scenes during the military review, he exposes the hopeless anachronism of the feudal institutions and the stubborn resistance of the population to their revival. In the subsequent contest he exposes the contradictions within each of the two hostile parties; only the moderates on both sides take part in the sport. In the inn we see the brutal outrages of the royal mercenaries and encounter Burley, later to become the leader of the Puritan uprising, in all his gloomy magnificence. In effect, in narrating the events of this military review and describing the entire setting, Walter Scott introduces the factions and protagonists of a great historical drama. In a single stroke he sets us in the midst of a decisive action.

The description of the agricultural fair and of the awarding of prizes to the farmers in Flaubert's *Madame Bovary* is among the most celebrated achievements of description in modern realism. But Flaubert presents only a 'setting'. For him the fair is merely background for the decisive love scene between Rudolf and Emma Bovary. The setting is incidental, merely 'setting'. Flaubert underscores its incidental character; by interweaving and counterposing official speeches with fragments of love dialogue, he offers an ironic juxtaposition of the public and private banality of the petty bourgeoisie, accomplishing this parallel with consistency and artistry.

But there remains an unresolved contradiction: this incidental setting, this accidental occasion for a love scene, is simultaneously an important event in the world of the novel; the minute description of this setting is absolutely essential to Flaubert's purpose, that is, to the comprehensive exposition of the social milieu. The ironic juxtaposition does not exhaust the significance of the description. The 'setting' has an independent existence as an element in the representation of the environment. The characters, however, are nothing but observers of this setting. To the reader they seem undifferentiated, additional elements of the environment Flaubert is describing. They become dabs of colour in a painting which rises above a lifeless level only insofar as it is elevated to an ironic symbol of philistinism. The painting assumes an importance which does not arise out of the subjective importance of the events, to which it is scarcely related, but from the artifice in the formal stylization.

Flaubert achieves his symbolic content through irony and consequently on a considerable level of artistry and to some extent with genuine artistic means. But when, as in the case of Zola, the symbol is supposed to embody social monumentality and is supposed to imbue episodes otherwise meaningless, with great social significance, true art is abandoned. The metaphor is over-inflated in the attempt to encompass reality. An arbitrary detail, a chance similarity, a fortuitous attitude, an accidental meeting—all are supposed to provide direct expression of important social relationships. There are innumerable possible examples in Zola's work, like the comparison of Nana with the golden fleece, which is supposed to symbolize her disastrous effect on the Paris of before 1870. Zola himself confessed to such intentions, declaring: 'In my work there is a hypertrophy of real detail. From the springboard of exact observation it leaps to the stars. With a single beat of the wings, the truth is exalted to the symbol.'

In Scott, Balzac or Tolstoy we experience events which are inherently significant because of the direct development of the characters in the events and because of the general social significance emerging in the unfolding of the characters' lives. We are the audience to events in which the characters take active part. We ourselves experience these events.

In Flaubert and Zola the characters are merely spectators,

more or less interested in the events. As a result, the events themselves become only a tableau for the reader, or, at best, a series of tableaux. We are merely observers.

II

The opposition between experiencing and observing is not accidental. It arises out of divergent basic positions about life and about the major problems of society and not just out of divergent artistic methods of handling content or one specific aspect of content.

Only after making this assertion can we attempt a concrete investigation of our problem. As in other areas of life, in literature there are no 'pure' phenomena. Engels once noted ironically that 'pure' feudalism had existed only in the constitution of the ephemeral Kingdom of Jerusalem. Yet feudalism obviously was an historical reality and as such is a valid subject for scientific investigation. There are no writers who renounce description absolutely. Nor, on the other hand, can one claim that the outstanding representatives of realism after 1848, Flaubert and Zola, renounced narration absolutely. What is important here are philosophies of composition, not any illusory 'pure' phenomenon of narration or description. What is important is knowing how and why description, originally one of the many modes of epic art (undoubtedly a subordinate mode), became the principal mode. In this development the character and function of description underwent a fundamental transformation from what it had been in the epic.

In his critique of Stendhal's *Charterhouse of Parma*, Balzac had emphasized the importance of description as a mode of modern fiction. In the novel of the eighteenth century (Le Sage, Voltaire, etc.) there had scarcely been any description, or at most it had played a minimal, scarcely even a subordinate, role. Only with romanticism did the situation change. Balzac pointed out that the literary direction he followed, of which he considered Walter Scott the founder, assigned great importance to description.

But after emphasizing the contrast with the 'aridity' of the seventeenth and eighteenth centuries and associating himself with the modern method, he adduced a whole series of stylistic criteria for defining the new literary direction. According to Balzac, description was only one stylistic mode among several. He particularly emphasized the new significance of the dramatic element in fiction.

The new style developed out of the need to adapt fiction to provide an adequate representation of new social phenomena. The relationship of the individual to his class had become more complicated than it had been in the seventeenth and eighteenth centuries. Formerly a summary indication of the background, external appearance and personal habits of an individual (as in Le Sage) had sufficed for a clear and comprehensive social characterization. Individualization was accomplished almost exclusively through action, through the reactions of characters to events.

Balzac recognized that this method could no longer suffice. Rastignac is an adventurer of quite another sort to Gil Blas. The precise description of the filth, smells, meals and service in the Vauquier pension is essential to render Rastignac's particular kind of adventurism comprehensible and real. Similarly, Grandet's house and Gobseck's apartment must be described accurately and in precise detail in order to represent two contrasting usurers, differing as individuals and as social types.

But apart from the fact that the description of the environment is never 'pure' description but is almost always transformed into action (as when old Grandet repairs his decayed staircase himself), description for Balzac provides nothing more than a base for the new, decisive element in the composition of the novel: the dramatic element. Balzac's extraordinarily multifaceted, complicated characterizations could not possibly emerge with such impressive dramatic effectiveness if the environmental conditions in their lives were not depicted in such breadth. In Flaubert and Zola description has an entirely different function.

Balzac, Stendhal, Dickens and Tolstoy depict a bourgeois society consolidating itself after severe crises, the complicated laws of development operating in its formation, and the tortuous transitions from the old society in decay to the new society in birth. They themselves actively experienced the crises in this development, though in different ways. Goethe, Stendhal and Tolstoy took part in the wars which were the midwives of the revolutions; Balzac was a participant in and victim of the feverish speculations of emerging French capitalism; Goethe and Stendhal served as government officials; and Tolstoy, as landowner and as participant in various social organizations (the census and famine commissions, for example) directly experienced important events of the transitional upheaval.

In their public activity as well as in their private lives, they followed the tradition of the writers, artists and scientists of the Renaissance and of the Enlightenment, men who participated variously and actively in the great social struggles of their times, men whose writing was the fruit of such rich, diverse activity. They were not 'specialists' in the sense of the capitalist division of labour.

With Flaubert and Zola it was otherwise. They started their creative work after the June uprising in a firmly established bourgeois society. They did not participate actively in the life of this society; indeed they refused to do so. In this refusal lay the tragedy of the important generation of artists of the transitional period. This renunciation of social activity was above all a manifestation of their disposition, an expression of their hate, revulsion and contempt for the political and social order of their time. People who made peace with the order turned into soulless, lying apologists for capitalism. But Flaubert and Zola had too much integrity. For them the only solution to the tragic contradiction in their situation was to stand aloof as observers and critics of capitalist society. At the same time they became specialists in the craft of writing, writers in the sense of the capitalist division of labour. The book had become merchandise, the writer, a salesman of this merchandise—unless he had been born a coupon clipper. In Balzac we still see the gloomy magnificence of primary accumulation in the realm of culture. Goethe and Tolstoy can still exhibit the aristocratic disdain of those who do not live exclusively from writing. But Flaubert becomes a voluntary ascetic, and Zola is constrained by material pressures to be a writer in the sense of the capitalist division of labour.

New styles, new ways of representing reality, though always linked to old forms and styles, never arise from any immanent dialectic within artistic forms. Every new style is socially and historically determined and is the product of a social development. But to recognize the determining factors in the formation of artistic styles is not to assign equal artistic value or rank to these styles. Necessity can also be necessity for the artistically false, distorted and corrupt. The alternatives, experiencing and observing, correspond to what was socially determined for writers of two different periods of capitalism. Narration and description represent the principal modes of fiction appropriate to these periods.

To distinguish the two modes effectively, we can counterpose statements by Goethe and Zola regarding the relationship of observation to creation. 'I have never,' said Goethe, 'contemplated nature with poetic purpose in mind. But my early landscape sketching and later investigations in natural science trained me to a constant, precise observation of nature. Little by little I became so well acquainted with nature in its smallest details that when I need something as a poet, I find it at hand and do not easily err against truth.' Zola also expressed himself clearly about his method of approaching a subject: 'A naturalistic novelist wants to write a novel about the world of the theatre. He starts out with this general idea *without possessing a single fact or character*. His first task will be to take notes on what he can learn about the world he wants to describe. He has known this actor, attended that performance.... Then he will speak with the people who are best informed about this material, he will collect opinions, anecdotes, character portraits. That is not all. He will then read documents. *Finally* he will visit the locale itself and spend *some days* in a theatre to become familiar with the minutest details; he will spend his evenings in the dressing room of an actress and will absorb the atmosphere as much as possible. And once this documentation is complete, the novel will write itself. The novelist must only arrange the facts logically.... *Interest is no longer concentrated on originality of plot; on the contrary, the more* banal and general it is, the more typical it becomes.' [Emphasis by G.L.]

These are two basically divergent styles. Two basically divergent approaches to reality. [...]

IV

[...] Narration establishes proportions, description merely levels.

Goethe demands that epic poetry treat all events as past in contrast to the drama, which contemporizes all action. Thus Goethe perceptively defines the stylistic distinction between epic and drama. Drama in principle stands on a much higher level of abstraction than the epic. A drama is concentrated about a single conflict; whatever does not pertain directly or indirectly to the conflict must be excluded as a disturbing, superfluous element. The opulence of a dramatist like Shakespeare results from a varied and rich conception of the conflict itself. In the exclusion of all details not pertaining to the conflict, there is no fundamental difference between Shakespeare and the Greeks.

Goethe insisted that the action of the epic be set in the past because he understood that only thus could there be an effective poetic selection of the essential elements within the varied richness of life and only thus could there be a representation of the essential elements that would promote the illusion of life in its full breadth. The criteria for determining whether a detail is pertinent, whether it is essential, must be more generous in the epic than in the drama and must encompass more complex and indirect relationships. Within this broader and fuller conception of the essential, however, selection is still as rigorous as for the drama. What does not pertain to the subject here too is ballast, no less an impediment than in the drama.

The involved complexity of patterns of life is clarified only at the conclusion. Only in activity are particular personal qualities in the totality of a character revealed as important and decisive. Only in practical activity, only in the complicated intercatenation of varied acts and passions is it possible to determine what objects, what institutions, etc., significantly influence men's lives and how and when this influence is effected. Only at the conclusion can these questions be resolved and reviewed. Life itself sorts out the essential elements in the subjective as well as in the objective world. The epic poet who narrates a single life or an assemblage of lives retrospectively makes the essential aspects selected by life clear and understandable. But the observer, necessarily a contemporary to what he observes, loses himself in a whirlwind of details of apparently equal significance, for life has not done its selecting through the test of practice. The use of the past tense in the epic is thus a basic technique prescribed by reality for achieving artistic order and organization.

Of course, the reader does not know the conclusion in advance. He possesses an abundance of details of which he cannot always and immediately determine the importance. Certain expectations are awakened which the later course of the narrative will confirm or refute. But the reader is involved in a rich web of variegated motivations; the author in his omniscience knows the special significance of each petty detail for the final solution and for the final revelation of character since he introduces only details that contribute to his goals. The reader takes confidence from the author's omniscience and feels at home in the fictional world. If he cannot foretell the events, he feels confident about the direction which the events will take because of their inner logic and because of the inner necessity in the characters. Perhaps he does not know everything about the future progress of the action and the future evolution of the characters, but in general he knows more than the characters themselves.

Indeed, with the gradual exposition of their significance, the details are seen in a new light. When, for example, in his short story 'After the Ball', Tolstoy describes with subtle touches the self-sacrifice of the father of the hero's fiancée for his daughter, the reader accepts the information without grasping its significance. Only after the account of the running of the gauntlet, where the same tender father acts as the brutal commander at an execution, is the suspense resolved. Tolstoy demonstrates his epic artistry in maintaining the unity within this suspense by avoiding depicting the old officer as a dehumanized 'product' of czarism and by showing instead how the czarist régime transforms people decent and self-sacrificing in their private lives into passive and even eager instruments of its brutality. It is clear that all the nuances of the events at the ball could be revealed only in retrospect from the gauntlet scene. The 'contemporary' observer, who could not view the ball from this perspective or retrospectively at all, would have had to see and describe other, insignificant and superficial details.

The necessary distance in narration, which permits the selection of the essential after the action, is not lost when true epic poets use the first-person point of view, where a character is himself the narrator, as in this Tolstoy short story. Even in a novel in diary form like Goethe's *Werther*, individual passages are set back in time, if only a short period of time, to provide the perspective necessary for the selection of details essential for revealing the effect of events and people upon Werther.

Only in this perspective can characters assume definite outline without at the same time losing their capacity to change. As a matter of fact, with this approach their transformation can proceed as an enrichment, as a fulfilment of the outline with ever more intense vitality. Tension in the novel results from this evolution; it is a suspense regarding the success or failure of characters with whom we have become acquainted.

That is why in masterworks of epic art the conclusion can be anticipated from the very beginning. In the opening lines of the Homeric epics the content and conclusion are even summarized.

How then does suspense arise? Indubitably it does not arise out of an aesthetic interest in how the *poet* goes about arriving at his goal. It arises rather from the natural human curiosity regarding the capacities *Odysseus* will yet disclose and the obstacles he has still to overcome to achieve his goal. In the Tolstoy story we know from the outset that the love of the hero-narrator will not result in marriage. The suspense therefore is not in what will happen to his love but in how the hero developed his present maturity and sense of irony. The tension in genuine epic always develops out of concern for the destinies of the characters.

Description contemporizes everything. Narration recounts the past. One describes what one sees, and the spatial 'present' confers a temporal 'present' on men and objects. But it is an illusory present, not the present of immediate action of the drama. The best modern narrative has been able to infuse the dramatic element into the novel by transferring events into the past. But the contemporaneity of the observer making a description is the antithesis of the contemporaneity of the drama.

Static situations are described, states or attitudes of mind of human beings or conditions of things—still lives.

Representation declines into genre, and the natural principle of epic selection is lost. One state of mind at any moment and of itself without relation to men's activity is as important or as irrelevant as another. And this equivalence is even more blatant when it comes to objects. In a narrative it is reasonable to mention only those aspects of a thing which are important to its function in a specific action. In and of itself everything has innumerable qualities. When a writer attempts as an observer and describer to achieve a comprehensive description, he must either reject any principle of selection, undertake an inexhaustible labour of Sisyphus or simply emphasize the picturesque and superficial aspects best adapted to description.

In any case, the loss of the narrative interrelationship between objects and their function in concrete human experiences means a loss of artistic significance. Objects can then acquire significance only through direct association with some abstract concept which the author considers essential to his view of the world. But an object does not thereby achieve poetic significance; significance is assigned to it. The object is made a symbol. As this process demonstrates, the aesthetic approach of naturalism inevitably engenders formalist methods of fiction.

But the loss of inner significance and hence of any epic order and hierarchy among objects and events does not stop at mere levelling and transformation of an imitation of life into a still life. Bringing characters to life and representing objects on the basis of immediate, empirical observation is a process with its own logic and its own mode of accentuation. Something much worse than mere levelling results—a reversed order of significance, a consequence implicit in the descriptive method since both the important and the unimportant are described with equal attention. For many writers this process leads to genre description deprived of all human significance.

With devastating irony Friedrich Hebbel dissected a typical exponent of this genre-like description, Adalbert Stifter, who, thanks to Nietzsche, has been elevated to a classic of German reaction. Hebbel demonstrates how the pressing problems of mankind vanish in Stifter; all basic aspects of life are smothered under a blanket of delicately delineated minutiae. 'Because moss shows up more impressively if the painter ignores the tree, and the tree stands out better if the forest disappears, there is a general cry of exultation, and artists whose powers scarcely suffice to render the pettiest aspects of nature and who instinctively do not attempt loftier tasks are exalted above others who do not depict the dance of the gnats because it is scarcely visible next to the dance of the planets. The "peripheral" begins to bloom everywhere; the mud on Napoleon's boot at the moment of the hero's abdication is as painstakingly portrayed as the spiritual conflict in his face.... In short, the comma puts on coat-tails and in its lofty complacency smiles haughtily at the sentence to which it owes its existence.'

Hebbel astutely defines the other basic danger latent in description: the danger of details becoming important in themselves. With the loss of the art of narration, details cease to be transmitters of concrete aspects of the action and attain significance independent of the action and of the lives of the characters. Any artistic relationship to the composition as a whole is lost. The false contemporaneity in description brings a disintegration of the composition into disconnected and autonomous details. Nietzsche, observing with an acute eye symptoms of decadence in art and life, defined the stylistic impact of this process on the individual sentence. 'The individual word,' he declared, 'becomes sovereign and leaps out of the sentence, the sentence bursts its bounds to obscure the sense of the page; the page acquires life at the expense of the whole—the whole is no longer a whole. But this is the picture of every decadent style... the vitality, vibrance and exuberance of life withdraws into the minute image; whatever is left over lacks life.... The whole is no longer alive; it is a synthetic, contrived artifact.'

The autonomy of the details has varied effects, all deleterious, on the representation of men's lives. On the one hand, writers strive to describe details as completely, plasticly and picturesquely as possible; in this attempt they achieve an extraordinary artistic competence. But the description of things no longer has anything to do with the lives of characters. Not only are things described out of any context with the lives of the characters, attaining an independent significance that is not their due within the totality of the novel, but the very manner in which they are described sets them in an entirely different sphere from that in which the characters move. The more naturalistic writers become, the more they seek to portray only common characters of the everyday world and to provide them only with thoughts, emotions and speech of the everyday world—the harsher the disharmony. The dialogue sinks into the arid, flat prose of everyday bourgeois life: the description declines into the strained artificiality of a synthetic art. The characters have no connection at all with the objects described.

But if the relationship is established on the basis of description, the situation becomes even worse. Then the author describes everything from the point of view of the psychology of his characters. Not only is a consequent representation of reality impossible in such an approach (except in an extremely subjective first-person novel), but, in addition, there is no possibility of artistic composition. The author's point of view jumps from here to there, and the novel reels from one perspective to another. The author loses the comprehensive vision and omniscience of the old epic narrators. He sinks consciously to the level of his characters and sometimes knows only as much about situations as they do. The false contemporaneity of description transforms the novel into a kaleidoscopic chaos.

Thus every epic relationship disappears in the descriptive style. Lifeless, fetishized objects are whisked about in an amorphous atmosphere. Epic relationships are not simply successive; and when in description individual pictures or sketches are arranged chronologically, epic relationship is not thereby established. In genuine narration an author can render a chronological series of events lifelike and meaningful only by utilizing approaches of considerable complexity. In narration the writer must move with the greatest deftness between past and present so that the reader may grasp the real causality of the epic events. And only the experience of this causality can communicate the sense of a real chronological, concrete, historical sequence, as in the double narration of the race in Tolstoy's *Anna Karenina*. Similarly, with what art does Tolstoy in *Resurrection* expose bit by bit the background to the relationship between Nechlyudov and Maslova, introducing an additional detail whenever the illumination of a moment in the past is needed to advance the action another step!

Description debases characters to the level of inanimate

objects; as a result a basic principle of epic composition is abandoned. The writer using the descriptive method starts out with *things*. (We have seen how Zola conceives the writer's confrontation of a subject. The actual core of his novels is a complex of facts: money, the mine, etc.) The consequence of this approach is that the varied manifestations of a complex of objects determine the organization of the novel, as in *Nana*, where the theatre is described in one chapter from the viewpoint of the audience and in another from backstage. The characters' lives, the careers of the protagonists, merely constitute a loose thread for attaching and grouping a series of pictures of objects, pictures which are ends in themselves.

Matching this spurious objectivity is an equally spurious subjectivity. For from the standpoint of epic interrelationships not much is gained when a simple succession of events provides the motive principle of the composition or when a novel is based on the lyrical, self-orientated subjectivity of an isolated individual; a succession of subjective impressions no more suffices to establish an epic interrelationship than a succession of fetishized objects, even when these are inflated into symbols. From an artistic point of view, the individual pictures in both cases are as isolated and unrelated to each other as pictures in a museum.

Without the interaction of struggle among people, without testing in action, everything in composition becomes arbitrary and incidental. No psychology, no matter how refined, and no sociology, no matter how pseudo-scientific, can establish epic relationships within this chaos.

The levelling inherent in the descriptive method makes everything episodic. Many modern writers look contemptuously at the old-fashioned, complicated methods by which the old novelists set their plots into motion and elaborated an epic composition with all its involved interaction and conflict. Thus Sinclair Lewis contrasts Dickens's method of composition with Dos Passos' to the latter's advantage: 'And the classical method— oh yes, was painstakingly spun out. Through an ill-fated coincidence Mr Jones and Mr Smith are sent out in the same coach so that something pathetic and entertaining may occur. In *Manhattan Transfer* people do not run into each other on the road but meet in the most natural fashion.' 'The most natural fashion' implies that the characters either fall into no relationships at all or at best into transient and superficial relationships, that they appear suddenly and just as suddenly disappear, and that their personal lives—since we scarcely know them—do not interest us in the least, and that they take no active part in a plot but merely promenade with varying attitudes through the externalized objective world described in the novel. That is certainly 'natural' enough. The question is: what is the result for the art of narration?

Dos Passos is no common talent and Sinclair Lewis is an outstanding writer. Thus what Sinclair Lewis says in the same essay about Dickens's and Dos Passos' characterization is significant: 'Of course Dos Passos created no such enduring characters as Pickwick, Micawber, Oliver, Nancy, David and his aunt, Nicholas, Smike, and at least forty others, and he will never succeed in doing so.' An invaluable admission and quite honest. But if Sinclair Lewis is right, and undoubtedly he is, what then is the artistic value of the 'most natural fashion' of relating characters to the action?

Part Two

On Nineteenth-Century Novels

6 Hubert Teyssandier

On *Mansfield Park*

From *Les formes de la création romanesque à l'époque de Walter Scott et de Jane Austen*, Paris, Didier–Erudition, 1977, pp. 127–56.

Translated by Kate Patterson and Hubert Teyssandier.

Mansfield Park[1] has the basic ingredients of a classic love story which sets the hero and heroine face to face and leads to a happy ending after all obstacles have been removed. However, Jane Austen's story does not have a linear progression, and the obstacles in it are due not to external contingencies but to the sheer complexity of the relationships within a group which consists of eight characters at the start of the novel: four young men and four young women, all of marriageable age. This obvious symmetry cuts across another symmetry of equal importance: four of the characters belong to the Bertram family and the other four wish to marry into it. The four children of Sir Thomas Bertram, Baronet, of Mansfield Park (Northamptonshire), are Tom, the eldest son, who leads a dissipated life and runs heavily into debt, Edmund, who is about to be ordained and embodies all the moral qualities that his brother lacks, and two daughters, Maria and Julia, who are both in different degrees arrogant, ambitious, and passionate. There is also a cousin, Fanny Price, who has been attached to the group of Bertram children since early childhood, Sir Thomas having taken responsibility for her upbringing, in order to assist her impoverished parents. Similar to Edmund in her moral qualities, Fanny completes the initial pattern by providing the antithesis to Maria and Julia. The narrative then introduces a sixth character belonging to the same age group, Mr Rushworth, who has just inherited a fortune and a vast estate (Sotherton Court), which redeems his personal insignificance. Finally, Mary Crawford and her brother Henry arrive from London, bringing with them all the false values that are traditionally associated with the city, and set up house with their brother-in-

[1] All quotations are from the Penguin edition of *Mansfield Park*, with introduction and notes by Tony Tanner (Penguin English Library, 1966); the figures indicate the page numbers.

law, the rector of Mansfield, a few hundred yards away from the Bertrams' house.

So by the end of the first fifty pages the group is complete, and it becomes easy to recognize the customary oppositions between arrogance and modesty, dissipation and prudence, worldliness and moral seriousness. But one also finds, superimposed on these traditional elements, the complex system of symmetrical relationships that develops between the characters, and which bears the mark of all the tensions arising from their rivalries and inner conflicts. The following diagrams bring out the successive transformations of these relationships, through the progressive elimination (two by two) of all the characters, until the hero and the heroine (Edmund and Fanny) are left face to face:

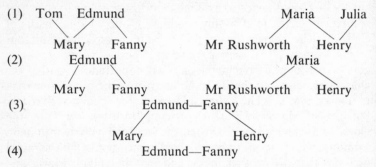

The first diagram shows the initial relationships between the four Bertram children and the four characters who are more or less closely associated with their group: ever since her childhood, Fanny has been linked to her cousin Edmund by a sisterly affection that will later grow into perfect love; the rich and foolish Mr Rushworth is engaged to Maria who has accepted him out of ambition; as for the two Londoners, one is interested in the two brothers and the other in the two sisters, and while Mary hesitates between Tom and Edmund, Henry undertakes to make both Maria and Julia fall in love with him. After enjoying her hour of glory when she shares Henry Crawford's seat on the 'barouche box' as they drive to Sotherton ('Happy Julia! Unhappy Maria!', 109), Julia loses the match in the rivalry that opposes her to her sister, while Tom, who takes no interest in Mary, retires of his own accord and becomes lost in the fashionable life of seaside resorts. This new situation brings us to the second diagram and the double rivalry which opposes, on the one hand, the seductress and the cousin, in their pursuit of Edmund, and on the other hand, the seducer and the rich fiancé, in their pursuit of Maria: these new relationships are made perceptible through the formation of groups at the beginning of the walk on the Sotherton estate (118). The symmetry of this double figure then falls apart when Maria, who has been deserted by Henry Crawford, decides to marry Mr Rushworth, and disappears with him from the world of Mansfield. A new symmetry is immediately established (diagram 3), and this time it is made perceptible through the distribution of couples at the beginning of the ball at Mansfield: the first two dances unite Fanny and Henry, as well as Mary and Edmund, while Fanny observes Edmund across the space that separates them (283). Finally, as a result of the collapse of the Rushworths' marriage and Maria's elopement with Henry, Mansfield is rid of the Crawfords' presence, and the affection that has linked Edmund and Fanny since childhood, finds its predictable conclusion. Thus, the complexity of the initial situation is eventually reduced through successive simplifications to the unity of perfect love.

Within this pattern of relationships, the central moral opposition is between the two protagonists, Edmund and Fanny, and their antagonists, Henry and Mary, the 'villains' of the story, who conspire together to undermine from within the integrity of the world of Mansfield. This confrontation between immoralism and morality is almost always implicit; and it is expressed not so much by elementary contrasts between vice and virtue, as by recurrent metaphors. These include medical metaphors like the one in the following passage where Mrs Grant is addressing Henry and Mary:

'You are as bad as your brother, Mary; but we will cure you both. Mansfield shall cure you both—and without any taking in. Stay with us and we will cure you.'
    The Crawfords, without wanting to be cured, were very willing to stay. (79)

The reverse side of this hope of a moral cure, is the risk of contamination to which Mansfield Park is exposed through the Crawfords' presence. And in fact, fostered by the amateur theatricals, another 'infection' for which Mr Yates is responsible ('My friend Yates brought the infection from Ecclesford', 200), the moral sickness causes two victims (Maria and Julia), and threatens to cause two more (Edmund and Fanny). Similarly, the play-acting metaphors have a moral significance beyond their literal meaning, and talent in this sphere is presented as a sign of insincerity. For Henry acts better than Tom or Edmund: 'Mr Crawford was considerably the best actor of all' (185); and Maria, who joins Henry in the same dangerous game, 'acted well—too well' (185); whereas Fanny cannot and will not act:

> 'Indeed you must excuse me. I could not act anything if you were to give me the world. No, indeed, I cannot act.' (168)

This indirect mode of presentation, working through moral metaphors, is far from the technique of rigid contrasts that prevailed in the moralistic tales of the period. Moreover, the four main characters, that is the two heroes and the two villains, lose the schematic outlines of the types from which they are derived; and instead of simply representing the confrontation between good and evil, all four of them are governed by unconscious motives or torn by inner contradictions. Edmund, who has been compared to Edgar Mandlebert in Fanny Burney's *Camilla* (1796), may exhibit the moral preoccupations of the traditional hero, but he is far from perfect. For he sometimes acts against his conscience, while resorting to dubious self-justifications; and so the moral hero comes down from his pedestal: 'Edmund had descended from that moral elevation which he had maintained before' (179). Lost in self-deception, he finds good reasons for going back on his refusal to play in *Lover's Vows*, and prepares to take a part as Mary Crawford's partner. Later, he manages to persuade himself that the undeniable 'dissimilarity' between Mary and himself shows how well they complement each other (345); and he finally replaces the real object of his desire by an imaginary creation that satisfies his moral standards. The victim of his own passion and his powers of self-delusion, he is also torn between the affection that attaches him to Fanny and the attraction that draws him towards Mary; and he tries to reconcile these irreconcilable forces in the dream of a double love embracing both women—the sisterly confidante and the seductress:

'I would not have the shadow of a coolness arise,' he repeated, his voice sinking a little, 'between the two dearest objects I have on earth.' (270)

Edmund's false arguments and impossible dreams bring to the surface his unconscious or semiconscious motives, with the result that the type of the moral hero loses its flat and abstract simplicity in the windings of a tormented conscience.

Similarly, the creation of Fanny owes a good deal to the stereotyped heroines of moralistic tales; but some of the traditional character traits appear in contexts that give them a special significance. For example, Fanny's tears are not an attribute of virtue but her response to moments of physical exhaustion combined with mental anguish; in particular, they reflect her momentary disorientation after a sudden change of place: the young Fanny (aged ten) cries when she first arrives at Mansfield (50), and when she returns to her own family eight years later, the sobs that convey 'her various emotions of pain and pleasure' (377), are again the effect of noise and fatigue. Lacking the unreal and serene perfection of the traditional heroine, she also experiences the 'agitation' of 'jealousy' (180), and sometimes reveals latent feelings of aggression through her vehement condemnation of both her rival and her hero:

> She looked over the letter again. ' "So very fond of me!" 'tis nonsense all. She loves nobody but herself and her brother. Her friends leading her astray for years! She is quite as likely to have led *them* astray. They have all, perhaps, been corrupting one another; but if they are so much fonder of her than she is of them, she is the less likely to have been hurt, except by their flattery. "The only woman in the world, whom he ever could think of as a wife." I firmly believe it. It is an attachment to govern his whole life. Accepted or refused, his heart is wedded to her for ever. . . .' (414)

Another constant trait of Fanny's character, which is indicated with remarkable insistance, is the sense of guilt that she often experiences in the absence of any objective error:

> Mrs Norris had been talking to her the whole way from Northampton of her wonderful good fortune, and the extraordinary degree of gratitude and good behaviour which it

ought to produce, and her consciousness of misery was therefore increased by the idea of its being a wicked thing for her
not to be happy. (50)

Reproaching herself for not feeling sufficiently sad when Sir
Thomas leaves or sufficiently happy when he returns, she also
feels 'dreadfully guilty' (332) for not loving the man her uncle and
cousin would like to see her marry (316), and occasionally doubts
the purity of her own motives, as when she accuses herself of
egoism for her refusal to play in *Lovers' Vows* (174). The roots of
this vague and persistent guilt lie below the threshold of consciousness, and reflect the sufferings and insoluble conflicts that
result from Fanny's personal situation. For her feeling that she
enjoys a privileged position is accompanied by her fear that she
may not be worthy of it; and the moral imperatives that forbid
her to accept Henry Crawford go against the more accommodat-
ing code of her adopted milieu, which she nevertheless wishes to
obey. Finally, the innocent Fanny takes on herself the fault of
others, and feels them more intensely than the real culprits:

> Fanny seemed to herself never to have been shocked before.
> There was no possibility of rest. The evening passed, without a
> pause of misery, the night was totally sleepless. She passed only
> from feelings of sickness to shudderings of horror; and from
> hot fits of fever to cold . . .—it was too horrible a confusion
> of guilt, too gross a complication of evil, for human nature, not
> in a state of utter barbarism, to be capable of! (429–30)

Here the language of traditional moral reprobation gathers
strength from personally experienced guilt, as if Fanny were
anticipating Mrs Norris's reproaches and making herself assume
responsibility for the sins of Maria and Henry (435). In this way,
the stock figure of the angelic heroine acquires verisimilitude
and is seen to go through the real sufferings of existence.

A profound and original transformation of traditional character traits is also apparent in the creation of the two Crawfords,
the 'villain' and 'villainess' of the story. Henry Crawford, who
aroused the admiration of Henry Austen ('He admires H. Crawford: I mean properly, as a clever, pleasant man'),[1] is characterized not by black and boundless malice, but more subtly, by

[1] *Letters*, ed. R. W. Chapman, 2nd edn., Oxford University Press, 1952
(1964), pp. 377–8 (March 1814).

perverted standards of judgement, which lead him to substitute aesthetic evaluations for moral ones. For example, in church, the delivery of the texts interests him more than their content ('nineteen times out of twenty I am thinking how such a prayer ought to be read, and longing to have it to read myself', 338); and imagining himself as the preacher, he emphasizes the formal qualities of the sermon: 'I could not preach, but to the educated; to those who were capable of estimating my composition' (338). In short, with Henry Crawford, the diabolic figure of the villain is transformed into an immoral aesthete. Henry also assumes the traditional role of the seducer, although he lacks the appropriate physical features. His first appearance reveals him to be 'absolutely plain, black and plain' (77); and after looking him up and down with contempt, the tall Mr Rushworth criticizes him for his smallness: 'Handsome! Nobody can call such an undersized man handsome' (129). Then the development of Henry's character leads him to depart even more from his initial role, and to discover through the game of seduction the torments of a sincerity that he has never known before. At first, he considers love to be no more than a worldly pastime, his aim being to make others love him without falling in love himself:

'. . . my plan is to make Fanny Price in love with me.' (239)

However, in this last endeavour the rules of the game are reversed, and Henry becomes the rejected lover. Trapped into experiencing the passion that he has hitherto acted, he also comes to discover another, hidden part of himself, as if the game had been a permanent denial of his inmost reality. At this point in the story, the game-player becomes serious, and the aesthete begins to look for moral certainties. But then, losing control of the situation, Henry succumbs to Maria's advances, just as he was hoping to find salvation with Fanny. Thus, the villain ceases to be an unreal, monolithic figure, and in this last episode, Henry is shown to be torn between contradictory desires, like Edmund; but unlike Edmund, he lacks the necessary strength of character to assert his own will.

Mary Crawford, Henry's sister and accomplice, 'a young woman who had been mostly used to London' (74), has the 'lively dark eye' and the provocative airs of the age-old seductress:

A young woman, pretty, lively, with a harp as elegant as herself; and both placed near a window, cut down to the ground, and opening on a little lawn, surrounded by shrubs in the rich foliage of summer, was enough to catch any man's heart. (95)

Mary's language, which is also provocative, is distinguished from that of the other characters by a number of vulgarities which seem, in the context, to be signs of a moral flaw: 'worse than anything—quite disgusting' (83); 'Of *Rears*, and *Vices* [Rear- and Vice-Admirals], I saw enough' (91); 'What a difference a vowel makes!—if his rents were but equal to his rants!' (387). Mary's cynicism, which here takes the form of a pun, is also expressed on several occasions by incisive epigrams. These set up immoralism as a code of conduct, and ring out with the crisp finality of the speeches in a Restoration comedy:

'. . . Selfishness must always be forgiven you know, because there is no hope of a cure.' (98)

'. . . A large income is the best recipe for happiness I ever heard of . . .' (226)

Loving to dazzle and to draw attention to herself, Mary makes a display of her egoism and mercenary ambitions. But in fact, far from revealing her true character, her provocative ways make her more enigmatic; and it becomes tempting to infer mysterious depths behind the mask of the seductress. Mary's cynical humour may be merely an assumed role, disguising, though not entirely hiding, more disinterested motives. On the other hand, flippancy may also be the way in which a woman determined to realize her desires, gives a socially acceptable form to her powerful, aggressive instincts.

'If I lose the game, it shall not be from not striving for it' (251): taken literally, Mary's remark expresses her determination to win the round in the game of cards called 'speculation': but on a metaphorical reading, the ambitions in question are of a different nature. The aim of her first efforts when she arrives at Mansfield, is to marry Tom, heir to the Bertram estate and fortune:

Matrimony was her object, provided she could marry well, and having seen Mr Bertram in town, she knew that objection could no more be made to his person than to his situation in life. While she treated it as a joke, therefore, she did not forget to think of it seriously. (75)

However, as in the case of Henry, the situation is reversed; and against her own interests and reiterated convictions, Mary transfers her affection to the younger brother who has chosen the career of a clergyman with seven hundred pounds a year. The growth of this love, which is undoubtedly sincere, seems to indicate a transformation of Mary's character. But then her taste for flippancy and cynical humour makes a spectacular reappearance in the scene where she talks about Tom's illness and the fears for his life, while joking about the profit that she may derive from his death:

> '. . . Poor young man!—If he is to die, there will be *two* poor young men less in the world; and with a fearless face and bold voice would I say to any one, that wealth and consequence could fall into no hands more deserving of them . . .' (423)

Still, the vitality and spontaneity that Mary displays at other moments, suggest a different woman from the one who is absorbed in matrimonial calculations. This contradiction between exuberance and calculating cynicism hints at the presence of inner conflicts between incompatible impulses. But behind Mary's scintillating exterior, the core of her character remains to the last an impenetrable mystery. So although in contrast to the two protagonists, the two antagonists retain to some extent the role of villains, the contrasts dissolve into the complexity and ambiguity of human behaviour and motives.

Turning from the characters to the places in the novel, one finds that here too traditional stereotypes have been used and also refined. As was customary in the moralistic tales of the period, the spatial organization of *Mansfield Park* serves to formulate the central moral themes. However, whether real or imaginary, the places are not exhausted by their moral significance; rather they acquire a solid presence and become firmly anchored in a three-dimensional world. Limited at first to Mansfield and the surrounding countryside, this world then expands to include London and Portsmouth, and finally contracts again as the narrative returns to its point of departure, with the characters distributed between Mansfield parsonage and the Bertrams' house. Between all these different places, the exact distances are always given so that every scene and event is precisely located. For example, the parsonage is half a mile away from the house:

The houses, though scarcely half a mile apart, were not within sight of each other; but by walking fifty yards from the hall door, she could look down the park, and command a view of the parsonage and all its demesnes, gently rising beyond the village road; and in Dr Grant's meadow she immediately saw the group—Edmund and Miss Crawford both on horseback, riding side by side, Dr and Mrs Grant, and Mr Crawford, with two or three grooms, standing about and looking on. (97)

Here the scene is set in a perspective view of the landscape and Fanny's loneliness is measured in terms of the distance separating her from the group that is suddenly revealed to her, at the point where the view opens out onto the surrounding countryside. Mrs Norris's house is situated on the other side of the park (61), and the distance separating it from the Bertrams' house becomes a torment for Fanny, on account of all the useless errands that Mrs Norris inflicts upon her, on the pretext that she needs to take more exercise:

'. . . And as for Fanny's just stepping down to my house for me, it is not much above a quarter of a mile, I cannot think I was unreasonable to ask it. How often do I pace it three times a-day, early and late, ay and in all weathers too, and say nothing about it.' (103)

Then going from Mansfield to Sotherton, along 'ten miles of indifferent road' (72), some of the characters (Henry, Maria, Julia) find that their feelings are altered, and that the change of place brings about a change of attitude:

When they came within the influence of Sotherton associations, it was better for Miss Bertram, who might be said to have two strings to her bow. She had Rushworth-feelings, and Crawford-feelings, and in the vicinity of Sotherton, the former had considerable effect. (110)

Similarly, Fanny's journey from Mansfield to Portsmouth, and her return, take place in a recognizable setting of winter roads ('the dirty month of February' (370)), and then a spring-time landscape (434); while on the way, Fanny experiences the successive effects of travel on her spirits and feelings:

The novelty of travelling, and the happiness of being with William, soon produced their natural effect on Fanny's spirits, when Mansfield Park was fairly left behind, and by the time their first stage was ended, and they were to quit Sir Thomas's carriage, she was able to take leave of the old coachman, and send back proper messages, with cheerful looks. (369)

When Fanny arrives her outlook changes in such a way that the ideal gives way to the real place, and vice versa. For Portsmouth, which has been transfigured by 'the remembrance of all her earliest pleasures' (364), now loses its aura in the ugliness of everyday life; whereas Mansfield, now remote in time and space, becomes the setting for a perfect existence.

The places in the story also assert their presence through the specificity of their components; and these too provide objective correlatives for the central moral themes. For example, the topography of Sotherton estate is imagined with a precision that is not merely descriptive. Similarly, each of the rooms in the Bertrams' house has its appointed purpose: Fanny's lowly status is expressed by the two rooms that are assigned to her—'the little white attic' and 'the east room'—where the Bertrams relegate all the decorative objects that they consider unworthy of the reception rooms; the billiard room, for a while the theatre, is at first the scene of permitted distractions and later that of dangerous games; Sir Thomas's study is the seat of his authority, and the alterations that are made in it during his absence, in order to make room for the actors' entrances, constitute a violation of the order that he embodies. The countryside around the house can be glimpsed in the course of walks and journeys; and Thornton Lacey, Edmund's future living, is the complete picture of a Northamptonshire village: a farmer can be seen mending a hedge in sight of a stream, a church and a parsonage which are framed in the foreground by a farm-yard and a blacksmith's shop (249–50). Then around the Prices' small house the town of Portsmouth is outlined with its dock-yard (395), its draw-bridge (370), and its ramparts from which the sea is visible in a shimmer of 'ever-varying hues' (401).

In the case of London, the reality of the place is solely due to the minor characters who are associated with it. For the function of these characters who are neither seen nor heard, and who only exist through the memories and conversations of others, is to create the moral atmosphere of the capital, while also completing the definition of the main characters to whose set they belong. So although the city is never described in the detail of its streets and houses, the Crawfords' milieu is vividly evoked by references to their acquaintances: Admiral Crawford keeps dubious company, Mrs Fraser and Lady Stornaway regret having married for money (356–7), the Twickenhams are agreeable but hardly reputable people (436), and on the fringe of all this veiled and open corruption, Mr Harding, 'an old and most particular friend' of Sir Thomas (437), represents a moral code that has become obsolete in London. Then other places, which might have been no more than names, come to life through the characters who are mentioned in connection with them. For example, Ramsgate appears in Tom Bertram's anecdote about the Sneyd sisters (83); and Henry Crawford's remarks about his agent Maddison (403) hint at the injustices that are committed and the personal tragedies that take place on his estate at Everingham. The minor characters and marginal places therefore fulfil a vital function, by relating certain characters to different environments from those in which they are seen to develop, and by adding an extra dimension of width and depth to the limited world of the action.

Now the main differences between the various places in the story (Mansfield Park, the parsonage, Sotherton, then London and Portsmouth) depend on money, accompanied by specific intellectual and moral characteristics. Mansfield Park is the country estate of a distinguished family whose fortune consists of its plantations in Antigua and the seven thousand pounds that Lady Bertram brought as her dowry. Sotherton estate represents a greater and more secure fortune, but owing to the stupidity of its owner, this wealth lacks moral radiance:

'If this man had not twelve thousand a year, he would be a very stupid fellow.' (73)

Mansfield parsonage superimposes two degrees of wealth. Mr and Mrs Grant represent the genteel life style that comes from a comfortable income (a thousand pounds a year in the time of Mr Norris (41)); and with all his material needs well satisfied, the rector of the village does not look beyond his next meal. The Crawfords' fortune is more considerable (Mary has twenty thousand pounds, Henry four thousand pounds a year, (73, 144)); and once they have arrived the Grants' house acquires the glamour of affluence, embodied in these two brilliant but morally unsound personalities. For accustomed to what contemporary novelists described as 'the vortex of the fashionable life', the Crawfords bring to Mansfield all the vices and perils of London.

Then in the later chapters of the novel, the action leaves the limits of the initial setting, circumscribed by Mansfield and Sotherton, and moves towards London and Portsmouth. From the point of view of the narrative technique, Portsmouth is the new centre, receiving all the echoes from a crisis that is enacted elsewhere. But for the characters involved in the crisis, the point of convergence is London: the Rushworths leave Sotherton for their house in Wimpole Street, the Crawfords leave the parsonage and return to their starting point, and Edmund too sets out for London in the hope of meeting Mary again. Indeed, the capital becomes 'the vortex of dissipation' that threatens to engulf all the characters; and between Wimpole Street and Twickenham, Henry and Maria seal their doom. Combining the greatest affluence with the greatest immorality, London is therefore of all the places in the story, the one that remains most faithful to its traditional definition; though it is nevertheless distinguished from the stereotypes of the city by the complex, fully developed characters that are its products.

After the different ways of being rich represented by Mansfield, Sotherton, and London, the Portsmouth episode adds the image of poverty, and the moral shortcomings that in this case accompany it. Utter destitution has always had its place in moralistic tales, since it gives the rich an opportunity to exhibit their generosity. On the other hand, poverty without misery, the drabness of existence in joyless surroundings, is a less common theme, and one less conducive to tearful sentiment. Crushed by their relative poverty, the Prices are listless and incapable; and in their cramped and badly kept house, they live in chaos and lack consideration for each other:

> It was the abode of noise, disorder, and impropriety. Nobody was in their right place, nothing was done as it ought to be.
>
> (381)

No longer accustomed to this way of life after all the years that she has spent away from Portsmouth, Fanny is here confronted with the repellent sight of badly washed dishes and badly served food:

. . . her eyes could only wander from the walls marked by her father's head, to the table cut and knotched by her brothers, where stood the tea-board never thoroughly cleaned, the cups and saucers wiped in streaks, the milk a mixture of motes floating in thin blue, and the bread and butter growing every minute more greasy than even Rebecca's hands had first produced it. (428)

The butter, milk, cups, and other objects that Fanny now finds offensive, have the virtue of passing unnoticed at the Bertrams' house; and this contrast provided by the Price household leads to a re-evaluation of Mansfield which now appears in Fanny's memory enhanced by all the refinements of hushed and graceful living:

> At Mansfield, no sounds of contention, no raised voice, no abrupt bursts, no tread of violence was ever heard; all proceeded in a regular course of cheerful orderliness; everybody had their due importance; everybody's feelings were consulted. (384)

Thus, the two life styles that are represented by Portsmouth and Mansfield, the two places that are furthest apart in the world of the novel, are fundamentally opposed to each other, both at the level of material conditions and at that of human relationships: in Portsmouth, domestic chaos is accompanied by a state of anarchy where everyone tries to assert themselves at the expense of the others; whereas Mansfield, viewed from Portsmouth, becomes a place of order where life is harmoniously governed by a code of good manners and mutual respect.

Yet the real Mansfield remains distinct from this distant, idealized vision; and the obvious superiority of the Bertrams' life style is not accompanied by the moral perfection that novelists generally associated with the houses of the gentry. Unlike Percy-hall in Maria Edgeworth's *Patronage* (1814), which retains its integrity in the face of external dangers, Mansfield Park is far from being exemplary. Rather it is marked by such deep internal flaws that the whole moral edifice begins to totter, badly supported by its natural defenders. For despite all the differences that separate Mansfield from Portsmouth, the two places are linked by the common inadequacies of the two sisters:

Of her two sisters, Mrs Price very much more resembled Lady

Bertram than Mrs Norris. She was a manager by necessity, without any of Mrs Norris's inclination for it, or any of her activity. Her disposition was naturally easy and indolent, like Lady Bertram's; and a situation of similar affluence and do-nothing-ness would have been much more suited to her capacity, than the exertions and self-denials of the one, which her imprudent marriage had placed her in. (382)

Wealth mitigates the effects of indolence but does not remove its evils; and while Lady Bertram's domestic duties are taken over by others, her dumb and complacent idleness creates a moral vacuum that leads in the long run to disastrous consequences for the whole family:

To the education of her daughters, Lady Bertram paid not the smallest attention. She had not time for such cares. She was a woman who spent her days in sitting nicely dressed on a sofa, doing some long piece of needlework, of little use and no beauty, thinking more of her pug than her children, but very indulgent to the latter, when it did not put herself to incon-venience, guided in every thing important by Sir Thomas, and in smaller concerns by her sister. (55)

While not malicious, Lady Bertram takes little interest in those around her, withdrawing into a state of lethargy between her niece and her poodle, and approving of every thing that does not ruffle her habitual composure. Meanwhile, the void left by the inadequate mother is filled by the overwhelming activity of Mrs Norris, the possessive aunt, who runs the whole household, and brings on disaster, by the arbitrary way in which she flatters the vanity of the two Bertram girls and humiliates the poor relation: 'Remember, wherever you are, you must be the lowest and last' (232). At the same time, her continual insincerity, which is partly unconscious, effectively helps to poison the moral atmosphere of Mansfield: although thrifty to the point of avarice, she pretends, and at times believes herself, to be generous; although intrusive, she would like to be thought discreet ('I hate to be worrying and officious' (205)); although indifferent, she is lavish with her terms of endearment: 'dear Sir Thomas', 'good old Mrs Whitaker', 'good old Wilcox', 'dearest Mrs Rushworth', 'poor dear sister Price' (107, 132, 258, 260, 367). In the absence of Sir Thomas, who misguidedly places his trust in her, Mrs Norris takes over all his responsibilities; and Maria's ill-fated marriage is concluded under her authority. Indeed, she becomes the main destructive principle within the family order, while also caricaturing all the traditional values that Mansfield stands for, substituting tyranny for authority, and officiousness for genuine concern.

Sir Thomas represents a more subtle deviation from the same system of values; and his affected and highly idiosyncratic language betrays the disturbing weakness of the order that he embodies. Fully conscious of his role as head of the family, he acts throughout with excessive solemnity. He also lives up to his position by adopting all the artifices of an elevated language, while avoiding current expressions ('There is something in this which my comprehension does not reach' (316)), and sometimes piling up so many negatives that he becomes quite unintelligible ('though I cannot but presume on having been no unacceptable companion myself' (315)). Sir Thomas is therefore a formal speaker rather than a conversationalist; and the reprimand that he gives his eldest son, on finding himself obliged to settle Tom's debts, sums up well all the main characteristics of his style, as well as his moral outlook:

> 'I blush for you, Tom,' said he, in his most dignified manner; 'I blush for the expedient which I am driven on, and I trust I may pity your feelings as a brother on the occasion. You have robbed Edmund for ten, twenty, thirty years, perhaps for life, of more than half the income which ought to be his. It may hereafter be in my power, or in your's (I hope it will), to procure him better preferment; but it must not be forgotten, that no benefit of that sort would have been beyond his natural claims on us, and that nothing can, in fact, be an equivalent for the certain advantage which he is now obliged to forego through the urgency of your debts.' (58)

The content of this speech is fully in line with the conventional morality of the period; but its studied grandiloquence, bordering on parody, deflects attention from what is being said to the form of expression: here Sir Thomas is simply holding forth, while taking up an appropriately dignified stance. So in his case, moral sense deteriorates into pompous rhetoric and stern words become a substitute for upright behaviour: 'principle, active principle, had been wanting' (448). Behind a façade of unflinching rigour, the education of his daughters has taught them no more than a verbal knowledge of right and wrong; with the result that they have discarded moral and religious values in favour of wordly ambitions:

> They had been instructed theoretically in their religion, but never required to bring it into daily practice. To be distinguished for elegance and accomplishments—the authorized object of their youth—could have had no useful influence that way, no moral effect on the mind. (448)

The elder daughter's marriage is a fatal repetition of Sir Thomas's fundamental error; and in the same way, the whole traditional order, for which the family house is a symbol, begins to disintegrate when it comes into contact with the world, not through villainous scheming, but simply through the cumulative effect of its own internal flaws and weaknesses. Thus, sapped by its insincerity and hollow rhetoric, the world of Mansfield Park represents the breakdown of a system of values that has degenerated into an empty respect of conventions.

After the final crisis, the scattered family reassemble at the house; and their world is regenerated by their recognition of the harm that they have done, and by the banishment of the worst offenders. Tom, whose theatricals have helped to spread the infection, acknowledges his responsibility and becomes a reformed character (447); Julia, who is less to blame than Maria, finds the way back to Mansfield having learnt humility: 'She was humble and wishing to be forgiven' (447); Sir Thomas reproaches himself and rediscovers the true meaning of the moral and religious principles that he has really been neglecting, although he thought that he was putting them into practice. Meanwhile, Maria, the most guilty of all, finds herself punished by perpetual banishment; and Mrs Norris, whose flattery and pernicious influence amount to complicity in her niece's misconduct, chooses to accompany her into exile, thus ridding Mansfield of a presence that has become unbearable to Sir Thomas:

> To be relieved from her, therefore, was so great a felicity, that had she not left bitter remembrances behind her, there might have been danger of his learning almost to approve the evil which produced such a good. (450)

The Grants, close relatives of the other great offender, are also to disappear from Mansfield. Then, after some time has passed, Edmund and Fanny, now reunited for good, move into the parsonage; and the house that has sheltered the Crawfords' tempting immorality becomes a place of virtue. The couple's final happiness is described with subdued irony, and presented as the inevitable conclusion of the novel in which they have been the hero and heroine:

> My Fanny indeed at this very time, I have the satisfaction of knowing, *must*[1] have been happy in spite of every thing. She *must* have been a happy creature in spite of all that she felt or thought she felt, for the distress of those around her. (446)

> His happiness in knowing himself to have been so long the beloved of such a heart, *must* have been great enough to warrant any strength of language in which he could cloathe it to her or to himself; it *must* have been a delightful happiness! (455)

Edmund and Fanny must be happy, because their merits deserve to be rewarded, and because romantic conventions, which are observed here with apparent fidelity, positively require a happy ending.

However, the irony is all on the surface in the last chapter; and the conventions that are displayed but not derided remain peripheral to the deeper moral purpose that here becomes explicit. For the guilt of the characters does not dissolve into the unreal light of a redeemed world, but emerges as one of the most insistent themes, accompanied by a solemn emphasis on the irreversible nature of past error. In such a context, the opening sentence of the chapter ('Let other pens dwell on guilt and misery' (446)) can only be meant to underline the importance of the two subjects that are supposedly omitted. Time may be able to do 'almost every thing' (446), but it cannot erase what is irreparable; and Maria is never to know a 'second spring of hope or character' (449). As for Sir Thomas, he gathers together 'all that remained to him of domestic felicity' (455), and overcomes to some extent the painful awareness of his own faults; but he remains unable to free himself completely from a permanent sense of guilt:

> These were the circumstances and the hopes which gradually brought their alleviation to Sir Thomas, deadening his sense of

---

[1] My italics in this quotation and the following ones.

what was lost, and in part reconciling him to himself; though the anguish arising from the conviction of his own errors in the education of his daughters, was never to be entirely done away. (447)

So the inner demons that are responsible for the fall of Mansfield Park leave deeper scars than the villains of traditional novels; and the moral world is regenerated but not transfigured, being too marked by the past crisis ever to return to a state of innocence.

Lastly, even the happy aspects of this ending are subtly differentiated from the conventional image of happiness, which is briefly recalled by the negative formula in the following passage:

> With so much true merit and true love, and *no want of fortune or friends*, the happiness of the married cousins must appear as secure as earthly happiness can be. (456)

Here wealth and earthly blessings, which were presented by many novelists of the period as essential attributes of happiness, become secondary to the inner light of spiritual fulfilment. The hero and heroine do not lack 'fortune or friends'; but the final emphasis is not so much on their human successes, as on the peace of mind that they attain after their trials and sufferings. Moreover, this ending seems to be prefigured by Fanny's earlier meditation on the stars, which also combines earthly and spiritual contentment:

> 'Here's harmony!' said she. 'Here's repose! Here's what may leave all painting and all music behind, and what poetry only can attempt to describe. Here's what may tranquillize every care, and lift the heart to rapture! When I look out on such a night as this, I feel as if there could be neither wickedness nor sorrow in the world; and there certainly would be less of both if the sublimity of Nature were more attended to, and people were carried more out of themselves by contemplating such a scene.' (139)

The tranquillity that is symbolized here by the natural world is presented in the closing pages as the ultimate goal of all human efforts; and while Sir Thomas tries to become reconciled to himself, Edmund conquers his first love, and Fanny loses her habitual sadness in the certainty of a happy future. Thus, Mansfield Park has to live with its history; but the calm after the final crisis echoes the harmony that is revealed in the summer sky.

7 Dorothy van Ghent

'On *Wuthering Heights*,

From *The English Novel: Form and Function*, Harper and Row, 1961, pp. 153–70.

Emily Brontë's single novel is, of all English novels, the most treacherous for the analytical understanding to approach. It is treacherous not because of failure in its own formal controls on its meaning—for the book is highly wrought in form—but because it works at a level of experience that is unsympathetic to, or rather, simply irrelevant to the social and moral reason. One critic has spoken of the quality of feeling in this book as 'a quality of suffering':

> It has anonymity. It is not complete. Perhaps some ballads represent it in English, but it seldom appears in the main stream, and few writers are in touch with it. It is a quality of experience the expression of which is at once an act of despair and an act of recognition or of worship. It is the recognition of an absolute hierarchy. This is also the feeling in Aeschylus. It is found amongst genuine peasants and is a great strength. Developing in places which yield only the permanent essentials of existence, it is undistracted and universal.[1]

We feel the lack of 'completeness', which this critic refers to, in the nature of the dramatic figures that Emily Brontë uses: they are figures that arise on and enact their drama on some ground of the psychic life where ethical ideas are not at home, at least such ethical ideas as those that inform our ordinary experience of the manners of men. They have the 'anonymity' of figures in dreams or in religious ritual. The attitude toward life that they suggest is rather one of awed contemplation of an unregenerate universe than a feeling for values or disvalues in types of human intercourse. It is an attitude that is expressed in some of the great Chinese paintings of the middle Ages, where the fall of a torrent from an enormous height, or a single huge wave breaking under the moon, or a barely indicated chain of distant mountains lost among mists, seems to be animated by some mysterious,

[1] G. D. Klingopulos, 'The Novel as Dramatic Poem (II): "Wuthering Heights," ' in *Scrutiny* XIV, 1946–1947.

universal, half-divine life which can only be 'recognized', not understood.

The strangeness that sets *Wuthering Heights* apart from other English novels does not lie alone in the attitude that it expresses and the level of experience that it defines, for something of the same quality of feeling exists, for instance, in Conrad's work. Its strangeness is the perfect simplicity with which it presents its elemental figures almost naked of the web of civilized habits, ways of thinking, forms of intercourse, that provides the familiar background of other fiction. Even Conrad's adventurers, no matter how far they may go into the 'heart of darkness', carry with them enough threads of this web to orient them socially and morally. We can illustrate what we mean by this simplicity, this almost nakedness, if we compare Emily Brontë's handling of her materials with Richardson's handling of materials that, in some respects, are similar in kind. For example, the daemonic character of Heathcliff, associated as it is with the wildness of heath and moors, has a recognizable kinship with that of Love-lace, daemonic also, though associated with town life and sophisticated manners. Both are, essentially, an anthropomor-phized primitive energy, concentrated in activity, terrible in effect. But Emily Brontë insists on Heathcliff's gypsy lack of origins, his lack of orientation and determination in the social world, his equivocal status on the edge of the human. When Mr Earnshaw first brings the child home, the child is an 'it', not a 'he', and 'dark almost as if it came from the devil'; and one of Nelly Dean's last reflections is, 'Is he a ghoul or a vampire?' But Richardson's Lovelace has all sorts of social relationships and determinations, an ample family, economic orientation, col-lege acquaintances, a position in a clique of young rakes; and Richardson is careful, through Lovelace's own pen, to offer various rationalizations of his behavior, each in some degree cogent. So with the whole multifold *Clarrisa*-myth: on all sides it is supported for the understanding by historically familiar morality and manners. But *Wuthering Heights* is almost bare of such supports in social rationalization. Heathcliff might *really* be a demon. The passion of Catherine and Heathcliff is too simple and undeviating in its intensity, too uncomplex, for us to find in it any echo of practical social reality. To say that the motivation of this passion is 'simple' is not to say that it is easy to define: much easier to define are the motivations that are somewhat complex and devious, for this is the familiar nature of human motivations. We might associate perfectly 'simple' motivations with animal nature or extra-human nature, but by the same token the quality of feeling involved would resist analysis.

But this nakedness from the web of familiar morality and manners is not quite complete. There is the framework formed by the convention of narration (the 'point of view'): we see the drama through the eyes of Lockwood and Nelly Dean, who belong firmly to the world of practical reality. Sifted through the idiom of their commonplace vision, the drama taking place among the major characters finds contact with the temporal and the secular. Because Lockwood and Nelly Dean have witnessed the incredible violence of the life at the Heights, or rather, because Nelly Dean has witnessed the full span and capacity of that violence and because Lockwood credits her witness, the drama is oriented in the context of the psychologically familiar. There is also another technical bulwark that supports this uneasy tale in the social and moral imagination, and that is its extension over the lives of two generations and into a time of ameliorated and respectable manners. At the end, we see young Cathy teaching Hareton his letters and correcting his boorishness (which, after all, is only the natural boorishness consequent on neglect, and has none of the cannibal unregeneracy of Heathcliff in it); the prospect is one of decent, socially responsible domesticity. For this part of the tale, Lockwood alone is sufficient witness; and the fact that now Nelly Dean's experienced old eyes and memory can be dispensed with assures us of the present reasonableness and objectivity of events, and even infects retrospection on what has happened earlier—making it possible for the dream-rejecting reason to settle complacently for the 'naturalness' of the entire story. If ghosts have been mentioned, if the country people swear that Heathcliff 'walks', we can, with Lockwood at the end, affirm our skepticism as to 'how anyone could ever imagine unquiet slumbers for the sleepers in that quiet earth'.

Let us try to diagram these technical aspects of the work, for the compositional soundness of *Wuthering Heights* is owing to them. We may divide the action of the book into two parts, following each other chronologically, the one associated with the earlier generation (Hindley and Catherine and Heathcliff, Edgar, and Isabella Linton), the other with the later generation (young Cathy and Linton and Hareton). The first of these actions is centered in what we shall call a 'mythological romance'—for the astonishingly ravenous and possessive, perfectly amoral love of Catherine and Heathcliff belongs to that realm of the imagination where myths are created. The second action, centered in the protracted effects of Heathcliff's revenge, involves two sets of young lives and two small 'romances': the childish romance of Cathy and Linton, which Heathcliff manages to pervert utterly; and the successful assertion of a healthy, culturally viable kind of love between Cathy and Hareton, asserted as Heathcliff's cruel energies flag and decay. Binding the two 'actions' is the perduring figure of Heathcliff himself, demon-lover in the first, paternal ogre in the second. Binding them also is the framing narrational convention or 'point of view': the voices of Nelly Dean and Lockwood are always in our ears; one or the other of them is always present at a scene, or is the confidant of someone who was present; through Lockwood we encounter Heathcliff at the beginning of the book, and through his eyes we look on Heathcliff's grave at the end. Still another pattern that binds the two actions is the repetition of what we shall call the 'two children' figure—two children raised virtually as brother and sister, in a vibrant relationship of charity and passion and real or possible metamorphosis. The figure is repeated, with variations, three times, in the relationships of the main characters. Of this we shall speak again later. The technical continuities or patterning of the book could, then be simplified in this way:

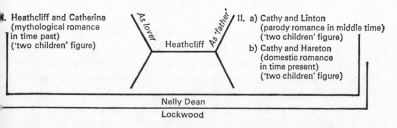

What, concretely, is the effect of this strict patterning and binding? What does it 'mean'? The design of the book is drawn in the spirit of intense compositional rigor, of *limitation*; the characters act in the spirit of passionate immoderacy, of *excess*. Let us consider this contrast a little more closely. Essentially, *Wuthering Heights* exists for the mind as a tension between two kinds of reality: the raw, inhuman reality of anonymous natural energies, and the restrictive reality of civilized habits, manners, and codes. The first kind of reality is given to the imagination in the violent figures of Catherine and Heathcliff, portions of the flux of nature, children of rock and heath and tempest, striving to identify themselves as human, but disrupting all around them with their monstrous appetite for an inhuman kind of intercourse, and finally disintegrated from within by the very energies out of which they are made. It is this vision of a reality radically alien from the human that the ancient Chinese landscape paintings offer also. But in those ancient paintings there is often a tiny human figure, a figure that is obviously that of a philosopher, for instance, or that of a peasant—in other words, a human figure decisively belonging to and representing a culture —who is placed in diminutive perspective beside the enormously cascading torrent, or who is seen driving his water buffalo through the overwhelming mists or faceless snows; and this figure is outlined sharply, so that, though it is extremely tiny, it is very definite in the giant surrounding indefiniteness. The effect is one of contrast between finite and infinite, between the limitation of the known and human, and the unlimitedness of the unknown and the nonhuman. So also in *Wuthering Heights*: set over against the wilderness of inhuman reality is the quietly secular, voluntarily limited, safely human reality that we find in the gossipy concourse of Nelly Dean and Lockwood, the one an old family servant with a strong grip on the necessary emotional economies that make life endurable, the other a city visitor in the country, a man whose very disinterestedness and facility of feeling and attention indicate the manifold emotional economies by which city people particularly protect themselves from any disturbing note of the ionic discord between civilized life and the insentient wild flux of nature in which it is islanded. This second kind of reality is given also in the romance of Cathy and Hareton, where book learning and gentler manners and domestic charities form a little island of complacence. The tension between these two kinds of reality, their inveterate opposition and at the same time their *continuity* one with another, provides at once the content and the form of *Wuthering Heights*. We see the tension graphically in the diagram given above. The inhuman excess of Heathcliff's and Catherine's passion, an excess that is carried over into the second half of the book by Heathcliff's revenge, an excess everywhere present in language[1] —in verbs and modifiers and metaphors that seethe with a brute fury—this excess is held within a most rigorous pattern of repeated motifs and of what someone has called the 'Chinese box' of Nelly Dean's and Lockwood's interlocution. The form of the book, then—a form that may be expressed as a tension between the impulse to excess and the impulse to limitation or economy —*is* the content. The form, in short, is the book itself. Only in the fully wrought, fully realized, work of art does form so exhaust the possibilities of the material that it identifies itself with these possibilities.

If there has been any cogency in what we have said above, we should ask now how it is that the book is able to represent dramatically, in terms of human 'character', its vision of the inhuman. After all, Catherine and Heathcliff *are* 'characters', and not merely molecular vibrations in the primordial surge of things; indeed, they are so credibly characterized that Hollywood has been able to costume and cosmeticize them. As 'characters', what are they? As lovers, what kind of love is theirs? They gnash and foam at each other. One could borrow for them a line from a poem by John Crowe Ransom describing lovers in hell: 'Stuprate, they rend each other when they kiss.' This is not 'romantic love', as that term has popular meaning; and it is not even sexual love, naturalistically considered—the impulse to destruction is too pure in it, too simple and direct. Catherine says she *is* Heathcliff, and the implication is not of the possibility of a 'mating', for one does not 'mate' with oneself. Similarly, after her death, when Heathcliff howls that he cannot live without his *life*, he cannot live without his *soul* (and Nellie says that he 'howled, not like a man, but like a savage beast'), the relationship and the destiny suggested are not those of adult

[1] Mark Schorer examines this aspect of *Wuthering Heights* in his essay 'Fiction and the "Analogical Matrix",' in *Critiques and Essays on Modern Fiction*, The Ronald Press Company, New York, 1952.

human lovers, because the complex attendant motivations of adult life are lacking. But the emotional implications of Catherine's and Heathcliff's passion are never 'adult', in the sense of there being in that passion any recognition of the domestic and social responsibilities, and the spiritual complexities, of adult life. Whatever could happen to these two, if they could be happily together, would be something altogether asocial, amoral, savagely irresponsible, wildly impulsive : it would be the enthusiastic, experimental, quite random activity of childhood, occult to the socialized adult. But since no conceivable *human* male and female, not brutish, not anthropologically rudimentary, could be together in this way as adults, all that we can really imagine for the grown-up Catherine and Heathcliff, as 'characters' on the human plane, is what the book gives of them— their mutual destruction by tooth and nail in an effort, through death, to get back to the lost state of gypsy freedom in childhood.

Caught in the economical forms of adult life—concepts of social and intellectual 'betterment' (such as lead Catherine to marry Edgar Linton), the frames of wealth and property ownership (which Heathcliff at first exploits in order to 'raise' himself to Catherine's standard, and then as an engine of revenge against both the Earnshaws and the Lintons), marital relationships, and parenthood—they are, for the imagination, 'humanized', endowed with 'character', at least to the extent that we see their explosive confusions, resistances, and misery convulsing the forms usual to human adulthood. Their obsession, their prime passion, is also 'human' although it is utterly destructive of the values signified by that word : the passion to lose the self in some 'otherness', whether in complete identification with another person (an identification for which 'mating' is a surrogate only of a temporary and lapsing kind), or by absorption into 'nature'—but it is a passion that is tabooed for the socialized adult, disguised, held in check by the complex cultural economies, safely stabled in the unconscious, at best put to work in that darkness to turn the mill of other objectives. This regressive passion is seen in uncompromised purity in Catherine and Heathcliff, and it opens the prospect of disintegration— disintegration into the unconsciousness of childhood and the molecular fluidity of death—in a word, into anonymous natural energy.

If the story of Catherine and Heathcliff had not been a story told by an old woman as something that had had its inception many years ago, if the old woman who tells the story had not been limited in imagination and provincial in her sympathies, if the story had been dramatized immediately in the here-and-now and not at a temporal remove and through a dispassioned intermediator, it is doubtful that it would resonate emotionally for us or carry any conviction—even any 'meaning'. Because of the very fact that the impulses it represents are taboo, they can conveniently be observed only at a remove, as someone else's, as of the past, and from the judicial point of view of conventional manners. The 'someone else's' and the 'long ago' are the mind's saving convention for making a distance with itself such as will allow it perspective. Thus the technical *displacement* of Heathcliff's and Catherine's story into past time and into the memory of an old woman functions in the same way as dream displacements: it both censors and indulges, protects and liberates.

Significantly, our first real contact with the Catherine-Heathcliff drama is established through a dream—Lockwood's dream of the ghost-child at the window. Lockwood is motivated to dream the dream by the most easily convincing circumstances; he has fallen asleep while reading Catherine's diary, and during his sleep a tempest-blown branch is scratching on the windowpane. But why should Lockwood, the well-mannered urbanite, dream *this*?

> I pulled its wrist on to the broken pane, and rubbed it to and fro till the blood ran down and soaked the bedclothes...

The image is probably the most cruel one in the book. Hareton's hanging puppies, Heathcliff's hanging the springer spaniel, Hindley's forcing a knife between Nelly's teeth or throwing his baby over the staircase, Catherine's leaving the blue print of her nails on Isabella's arm, Heathcliff stamping on Hindley's face—these images and others like them imply savagery or revengefulness or drunkenness or hysteria, but always a motivating set of emotional circumstances. But this is the punctilious Lockwood—whose antecedents and psychology are so insipid that we care little about them—who scrapes the dream-waif's wrist back and forth on broken glass till the blood runs down and soaks the bedclothes. The cruelty of the dream is the gratuitousness of the violence wrought on a child by an emotionally unmotivated vacationer from the city, dreaming in a strange bed. The bed is an old-fashioned closet bed ('a large oak case ... it formed a little closet' with a window set in it): its paneled sides Lockwood has 'pulled together' before going to sleep. The bed is like a coffin (at the end of the book, Heathcliff dies in it, behind its closed panels); it had been Catherine's bed, and the movable panels themselves suggest the coffin in which she is laid, whose 'panels' Heathcliff bribes the sexton to remove at one side. Psychologically, Lockwood's dream has only the most perfunctory determinations, and nothing at all of result for the dreamer himself, except to put him uncomfortably out of bed. But poetically the dream has its reasons, compacted into the image of the daemonic child scratching at the pane, trying to get from the 'outside' 'in', and of the dreamer in a bed like a coffin, released by that deathly privacy to indiscriminate violence. The coffin-like bed shuts off any interference with the wild deterioration of the psyche. Had the dream used any other agent than the effete, almost epicene Lockwood, it would have lost this symbolic force; for Lockwood, more successfully than anyone else in the book, has shut out the powers of darkness (the pun in his name is obvious in this context); and his lack of any dramatically thorough motivation for dreaming the cruel dream suggests those powers as existing autonomously, not only in the 'outsideness' of external nature, beyond the physical windowpane, but also within, even in the soul least prone to passionate excursion.

The windowpane is the medium, treacherously transparent, separating the 'inside' from the 'outside', the 'human' from the alien and terrible 'other'. Immediately after the incident of the dream, the time of the narrative is displaced into the childhood of Heathcliff and Catherine, and we see the two children looking through the window of the Lintons' drawing room.

'Both of us were able to look in by standing on the basement, and clinging to the ledge, and we saw—ah! it was beautiful—a splendid place carpeted with crimson, and crimson-covered chairs and tables, and a pure white ceiling bordered by gold, a shower of glass-drops hanging in silver chains from the centre, and shimmering with little soft tapers. Old Mr and

Mrs Linton were not there; Edgar and his sister had it entirely to themselves. Shouldn't they have been happy? We should have thought ourselves in heaven!'

Here the two unregenerate waifs look *in* from the night on the heavenly vision of the refinements and securities of the most privileged human estate. But Heathcliff rejects the vision: seeing the Linton children blubbering and bored there (*they* cannot get *out*!), he senses the menace of its limitations; while Catherine is fatally tempted. She is taken in by the Lintons, and now it is Heathcliff alone outside looking through the window.

'The curtains were still looped up at one corner, and I resumed my station as a spy; because, if Catherine had wished to return, I intended shattering their great glass panes to a million of fragments, unless they let her out. She sat on the sofa quietly ... the woman-servant brought a basin of warm water, and washed her feet; and Mr Linton mixed a tumbler of negus, and Isabella emptied a plateful of cakes into her lap ... Afterwards, they dried and combed her beautiful hair ...'

Thus the first snare is laid by which Catherine will be held for a human destiny—her feet washed, cakes and wine for her delectation, her beautiful hair combed (the motifs here are limpid as those of fairy tale, where the changeling in the 'otherworld' is held there mysteriously by bathing and by the strange new food he has been given to eat). By her marriage to Edgar Linton, Catherine yields to that destiny; later she resists it tormentedly and finds her way out of it by death. Literally she 'catches her death' by throwing open the window.

'Open the window again wide: fasten it open! Quick, why don't you move?' [she says to Nelly].
'Because I won't give you your death of cold,' I answered.
'You won't give me a chance of life, you mean,' she said ...

In her delirium, she opens the window, leans out into the winter wind, and calls across the moors to Heathcliff,

'Heathcliff, if I dare you now, will you venture? ... Find a way, then! ... You are slow! ... you always followed me!'

On the night after her burial, unable to follow her (though he digs up her grave in order to lie beside her in the coffin from which the side panels have been removed), he returns to the Heights *through the window*—for Hindley has barred the door —to wreak on the living the fury of his frustration. It is years later that Lockwood arrives at the Heights and spends his uncomfortable night there. Lockwood's outcry in his dream brings Heathcliff *to the window*, Heathcliff who has been caught ineluctably in the human to grapple with its interdictions long after Catherine has broken through them. The treachery of the windows is that Catherine lost now in the 'other', can look through the transparent membrane that separates her from humanity, can scratch on the pane, but cannot get 'in', while Heathcliff, though he forces the window open and howls into the night, cannot get 'out'. When he dies, Nelly Dean discovers the window swinging open, the window of that old-fashioned coffin-like bed where Lockwood had had the dream. Rain has been pouring in during the night, drenching the dead man. Nelly says,

> I hasped the window; I combed his black long hair from his forehead; I tried to close his eyes: to extinguish, if possible, that frightful, life-like gaze of exultation before any one else beheld it. They would not shut: they seemed to sneer at my attempts...

Earlier, Heathcliff's eyes have been spoken of as 'the clouded windows of hell' from which a 'fiend' looks out. All the other uses of the 'window' that he has spoken of here are not figurative but perfectly naturalistic uses, though their symbolic value is inescapable. But the fact that Heathcliff's eyes refuse to close in death suggests the symbol in a metaphorical form (the 'fiend' has now got 'out', leaving the window open), elucidating with simplicity the meaning of the 'window' as a separation between the daemonic depths of the soul and the limited and limiting lucidities of consciousness, a separation between the soul's 'otherness' and its humanness.

There is still the difficulty of defining, with any precision, the quality of the daemonic that is realized most vividly in the conception of Heathcliff, a difficulty that is mainly due to our tendency always to give the 'daemonic' some ethical status—that is, to relate it to an ethical hierarchy. Heathcliff's is an archetypal figure, untraceably ancient in mythological thought—an imaged recognition of that part of nature which is 'other' than the human soul (the world of the elements and the animals) and of that part of the soul itself which is 'other' than the conscious part. But since Martin Luther's revival of this archetype for modern mythology, it has tended to forget its relationship with the elemental 'otherness' of the outer world and to identify itself solely with the dark functions of the soul. As an image of soul work, it is ethically relevant, since everything that the soul does —even unconsciously, even 'ignorantly' (as in the case of Oedipus)—offers itself for ethical judgment, whereas the elements and the animals do not. Puritanism perpetuated the figure for imagination; Milton gave it its greatest aesthetic splendor, in the fallen angel through whom the divine beauty still shone; Richardson introduced it, in the person of Lovelace, to an infatuated middle class; and always the figure was ethically relevant through the conception of 'sin' and 'guilt'. (Let us note here, however, the ambivalence of the figure, an ambivalence that the medieval devil does not have. The medieval devil is a really ugly customer, so ugly that he can even become a comedy figure—as in the medieval moralities. The daemonic archetype of which we are speaking here is deeply serious in quality because of his ambivalence: he is a fertilizing energy and profoundly attractive, and at the same time horribly destructive to civilized institutionalism. It is because of his ambivalence that, though he is the 'enemy', ethically speaking, he so easily takes on the stature and beauty of a hero, as he does in the Satan of *Paradise Lost*.) In Byron's *Manfred*, the archetype underwent a rather confusing sea-change, for Manfred's crime is, presumably, so frightful that it cannot be mentioned, and the indefinable nature of the crime blurs the edges of the figure and cuts down its resonance in the imagination (when we guess that the crime might be incest, we are disposed to find this a rather paltry equation for the Byronic incantation of guilt); nevertheless, the ethical relevancy of the figure remains. Let us follow it a little further, before returning to Emily Brontë's Heathcliff. In the later nineteenth century, in the novels of Dostoievsky, it reappears with an enormous development of psychological subtlety, and also with a great strengthening and clarification of its ethical significance. In the work of André Gide, it undergoes another sea-change: the archetypal daemonic figure now becomes the principle of progress, the spirit of free investigation and creative experience; with this reorientation, it becomes positively ethical rather than negatively so. In Thomas Mann's *Doctor Faustus*, it reverts to its earlier and more constant significance, as the type of the instinctive part of the soul, a great and fertilizing power, but ethically unregenerative and therefore a great danger to ethical man.

Our interest in sketching some phases of the history of this archetype has been to show that it has had, in modern mythology, constantly a status in relation to ethical thought. The exception is Heathcliff. Heathcliff is no more ethically relevant than is flood or earthquake or whirlwind. It is as impossible to speak of him in terms of 'sin' and 'guilt' as it is to speak in this way of the natural elements or the creatures of the animal world. In him, the type reverts to a more ancient mythology and to an earlier symbolism. *Wuthering Heights* so baffles and confounds the ethical sense because it is not informed with that sense at all: it is profoundly informed with the attitudes of 'animism', by which the natural world—that world which is 'other' than and 'outside of' the consciously individualized human—*appears* to act with an energy similar to the energies of the soul; to be permeated with soul energy but of a mysterious and alien kind that the conscious human soul, bent on securing itself through civilization, cannot identify itself with as to purpose; an energy that can be propitiated, that can at times be canalized into humanly purposeful channels, that *must* be given religious recognition both for its enormous fertility and its enormous potential destructiveness. But Heathcliff does have human shape and human relationships; he is, so to speak, 'caught in' the human; two kinds of reality intersect in him— as they do, with a somewhat different balance, in Catherine; as they do, indeed, in the other characters. Each entertains, in some degree, the powers of darkness—from Hindley, with his passion for self-destruction (he, too, wants to get 'out'), to Nelly Dean, who in a sense 'propitiates' those powers with the casuistry of her actions, and even to Lockwood, with his sadistic dream. Even in the weakest of these souls there is an intimation of the dark Otherness, by which the soul is related psychologically to the inhuman world of pure energy, for it carries within itself an 'otherness' of its own, that inhabits below consciousness.

The imagery of the windowpane is metamorphic, suggesting a total change of mode of being by the breaking-through of a separating medium that exists between consciousness and the 'other'. The strangest and boldest and most radiant figuration that Emily Brontë has given to her subject is the 'two children' figure, also a metamorphic figure of break-through and transformation. The *type* or classic form of this figure is a girl with golden hair and a boy with dark hair and shadowed brow, bound in kinship and in a relationship of charity and passion, and with a metamorphosis of some kind potential in the relationship. The beautiful dark boy will be brightened, made angelic and happy, by the beautiful golden girl: this, apparently, is what *should* happen. But the dynamics of the change are not perfectly trustworthy. In one of Emily Brontë's poems, describing a child who might be the child Heathcliff, the ambivalent dark boy will evidently sink further into his darkness.

> I love thee, boy; for all divine,
> All full of God thy features shine.
> Darling enthusiast, holy child,
> Too good for this world's warring wild,
> Too heavenly now but doomed to be
> Hell-like in heart and misery.[1]

In the 1850 printing of the Brontë poems (the printing supervised by the Brontë sisters) two companion pieces appear under the title 'The Two Children', in the first of which the dark boy is still unchanged.

> Frowning on the infant,
> Shadowing childhood's joy,
> Guardian angel know not
> That melancholy boy...[2]

In the second of these companion pieces, the golden child is evoked, and now the change in the dark one is promised.

> Child of Delight! with sunbright hair,
> And seablue, seadeep eyes;
> Spirit of Bliss, what brings thee here,
> Beneath these sullen skies?

[1] *The Complete Poems of Emily Jane Brontë*, edited by C. W. Hatfield, Columbia University Press, New York, 1941, p. 121.
[2] Ibid., p. 229.

> Thou shouldest live in eternal spring,
> Where endless day is never dim;
> Why, Seraph, has thy erring wing
> Borne thee down to weep with him?

She answers that she is 'not from heaven descended', but that she has seen and pitied 'that mournful boy'.

> And I swore to take his gloomy sadness,
> And give to him my beamy joy...'[1]

Here, with the change of the dark child, the golden child will be changed also, for she will take his 'gloomy sadness'. In another set of verses, the light-dark contrast is turned around bewilderingly.

> And only *he* had locks of light,
> And *she* had raven hair;
> While now, his curls are dark as night,
> And hers as morning fair.[2]

What really seems to be implied by all these shifts is not a mere exchange of characteristics but a radical identification of the two children, so that each can appear in the mode of the other, the bright one in the mode of darkness and the dark one in the mode of light.

In still another of those poems that dramatize affairs in the kingdom of Gondal that occupied Emily Brontë's youthful fantasy, a brooding phantom figure haunts the moonlit grounds of a castle. Its face is 'divinely fair', but on its 'angel brow'

> Rests such a shade of deep despair
> As nought divine could ever know.

Apparently the cause of his death was adoration of another man's wife ('Lord Alfred's idol queen'), and it is for this reason that his spirit is 'shut from heaven—an outcast for eternity'. The woman for whom he died is represented as an 'infant fair', looking from a golden frame in a portrait gallery.

> And just like his its ringlets bright,
> Its large dark eye of shadowy light,

---

[1] Ibid., p. 230.
[2] Ibid., p. 174.

Its cheeks' pure hue, its forehead white,
And like its noble name.

A deliberate confusion of the planes of reality—a shifting into
the life inside the picture frame (like the shifts 'through the
window' in *Wuthering Heights*), and with it a shifting from despairing adulthood into childhood—is suggested with the following questions:

> And did he never smile to see
> Himself restored to infancy?

> Never part back that golden flow
> Of curls, and kiss that pearly brow,
> And feel no other earthly bliss
> Was equal to that parent's kiss?[1]

The suggestions are those of metamorphic changes, but all under
the aspect of frustration: the despairing lover cannot get
through the picture frame where the child is. Other motifs here
are reminiscent of those of *Wuthering Heights*. The spectral
lover is an ambivalent figure, of divine beauty, but an outcast
from heaven. Kinship is suggested between him and the child in
the picture ('And just like his its ringlets bright ... And like its
noble name'), and one is left to imagine that 'Lord Alfred's idol
queen' was his sister, wherefore the frustration of their love. The
last stanza quoted above remarks ambiguously on the parental
feeling involved in the relationship: is it not the infant who is
the 'parent' here? Parental charity is the feeling of the golden
'guardian angel' for her dark charge in 'The Two Children'
poems, as it is, in a degree, of Catherine for Heathcliff during
their childhood, and of young Cathy first for Linton and then
for Hareton. The fact that, in the poem, both the infant and the
spectral lover have golden hair seems, in this elusive fantasy,
to be a mark of perversion of the metamorphic sequence, at
least of its having gone awry (as in the case, too, of young Cathy
and Linton, who is not dark but fair).

In the relationship of Catherine and Heathcliff, the fantasy
has its typical form. She is golden, he is dark. His daemonic
origin is always kept open, by reiterations of the likelihood that
he is really a ghoul, a fiend, an offspring of hell, and not merely

[1] Ibid., pp. 177–178.

so in behavior. And Catherine also, like the guardian child in
'The Two Children' poems, is 'not from heaven descended':
she has furious tantrums, she lies, she bites, her chosen toy is a
whip. They are raised as brother and sister; there are three references to their sleeping in the same bed as infants. She scolds and
orders and mothers and cherishes him ('much too fond of him'
as a child, Nelly says). The notions of somatic change and discovery of noble birth, as in fairy tale, are deliberately played
with; as, when Catherine returns from her first sojourn at the
Lintons' and Heathcliff asks Nelly to 'make him decent' he
says, comparing himself with Edgar,

> 'I wish I had light hair and a fair skin, and was dressed and
> behaved as well, and had a chance of being as rich as he will
> be!'

and Nelly answers,

> 'You're fit for a prince in disguise ... Were I in your place, I
> would frame high notions of my birth...'

(If Heathcliff is really of daemonic origin, he is, in a sense, indeed of 'high birth', a 'prince in disguise', and might be expected,
like the princes of fairy tale, to drop his 'disguise' at the crisis
of the tale and be revealed in original splendor: the dynamics
of the 'two children' figure also points to that potential transformation.) Some alluring and astonishing destiny seems possible
for the two. *What* that phenomenon might be or mean, we cannot know, for it is frustrated by Catherine's marriage to Edgar,
which dooms Heathcliff to be 'hell-like in heart and misery'.
Catherine's decision dooms her also, for she is of the same
daemonic substance as Heathcliff, and a civilized marriage and
domesticity are not sympathetic to the daemonic quality.

With the second generation, the 'two children' figure is distorted and parodied in the relationship of Catherine's daughter
and Heathcliff's son. Young Cathy, another 'child of delight,
with sunbright hair', has still some of the original daemonic
energy, but her 'erring wing' has brought her down to 'weep
with' a *pale-haired* and pallid little boy whose only talents are
for sucking sugar candy and torturing cats. She does her best,
as infant mother, to metamorphose him, but he is an ungrateful
and impossible subject. Her passionate charity finally finds her

'married' to his corpse in a locked bedroom. With Cathy and Hareton Earnshaw, her cousin on her mother's side, the 'two children' are again in their right relationship of golden and dark, and now the pathos of the dark child cures the daemon out of the golden one, and the maternal care of the golden child raises the dark one to civilized humanity and makes of him a proper husband.

In these several pairs, the relationship of kinship has various resonances. Between Catherine and Heathcliff, identity of 'kind' is greatest, although they are foster brother and sister only. The foster kinship provides an imaginative implicit reason for the unnaturalness and impossibility of their mating. Impassioned by their brother-and-sisterlike identity of kind, they can only destroy each other, for it is impossible for two persons to *be* each other (as Catherine says she 'is' Heathcliff) without destruction of the physical limitations that individualize and separate. In Emily Brontë's use of the symbolism of the incest motive, the incestual impulse appears as an attempt to make what is 'outside' oneself identical with what is 'inside' oneself—a performance that can be construed in physical and human terms only by violent destruction of personality bounds, by rending of flesh and at last by death.

With Catherine's daughter and young Linton, who are cousins, the implicit incestuousness of the 'two children' figure is suggested morbidly by Linton's disease and by his finally becoming a husband only as a corpse. With Cathy and Hareton Earnshaw, also cousins, Victorian 'ameliorism' finds a way to sanction the relationship by symbolic emasculation; Cathy literally teaches the devil out of Hareton, and 'esteem' between the two takes the place of the old passion for identification. With this successful metamorphosis and mating, the daemonic quality has been completely suppressed, and, though humanity and civilization have been secured for the 'two children', one feels that some magnificent bounty is now irrecoverable. The great magic, the wild power, of the original two has been lost.

We are led to speculate on what the bounty might have been,[1] had the windowpane not stood between the original pair, had

[1] A stimulating and enlightening interpretation of the book is to be found in Richard Chase's 'The Brontës, or Myth Domesticated,' in *Forms of Modern Fiction*, edited by William Van O'Connor, University of Minnesota Press, 1948.

the golden child and the dark child not been secularized by a spelling book. Perhaps, had the ideal and impossible eventuality taken place, had the 'inside' and the 'outside', the bright child and the dark one, become identified in such a way that they could freely assume each other's modes, then perhaps the world of the animals and the elements—the world of wild moor and barren rock, of fierce wind and attacking beast, that is the strongest palpability in *Wuthering Heights*—would have offered itself completely to human understanding and creative intercourse. Perhaps the dark powers that exist within the soul, as well as in the outer elemental world, would have assumed the language of consciousness, or consciousness would have bravely entered into companionship with those dark powers and transliterated their language into its own. Emily Brontë's book has been said to be nonphilosophical—as it is certainly nonethical; but all philosophy is not ethics, and the book seizes, at the point where the soul feels itself cleft within and in cleavage from the universe, the first germs of philosophic thought, the thought of the duality of human and nonhuman existence, and the thought of the cognate duality of the psyche.

8 G. Robert Stange

Expectations Well Lost: Dickens's Fable for his time

From *College English* XVI, 1954–55, 9–17.

Great Expectations is a peculiarly satisfying and impressive novel. It is unusual to find in Dickens's work so rigorous a control of detail, so simple and organic a pattern. In this very late novel the usual features of his art—proliferating sub-plots, legions of minor grotesques—are almost entirely absent. The simplicity is that of an art form that belongs to an ancient type and concentrates on permanently significant issues. *Great Expectations* is conceived as a moral fable; it is the story of a young man's development from the moment of his first self-awareness, to that of his mature acceptance of the human condition.

So natural a theme imposes an elemental form on the novel: the over-all pattern is defined by the process of growth, and Dickens employs many of the motifs of folklore. The story of Pip falls into three phases which clearly display a dialectic progression. We see the boy first in his natural condition in the country, responding and acting instinctively and therefore virtuously. The second stage of his career involves a negation of child-like simplicity; Pip acquires his 'expectations', renounces his origins, and moves to the city. He rises in society, but since he acts through calculation rather than through instinctive charity, his moral values deteriorate as his social graces improve. This middle phase of his career culminates in a sudden fall, the beginning of a redemptive suffering which is dramatically concluded by an attack of brain fever leading to a long coma. It is not too fanciful to regard this illness as a symbolic death; Pip rises from it regenerate and percipient. In the final stage of growth he returns to his birthplace, abandons his false expectations, accepts the limitations of his condition, and achieves a partial synthesis of the virtue of his innocent youth and the melancholy insight of his later experience.

Variants of such a narrative are found in the myths of many heroes. In Dickens's novel the legend has the advantage of providing an action which appeals to the great primary affections and serves as unifying center for the richly conceived minor themes and images which form the body of the novel. It is a signal virtue of this simple structure that it saves *Great Expectations* from some of the startling weaknesses of such excellent but inconsistently developed novels as *Martin Chuzzlewit* or *Our Mutual Friend*.

The particular fable that Dickens elaborates is as interesting for its historical as for its timeless aspects. In its particulars the story of Pip is the classic legend of the nineteenth century: *Great Expectations* belongs to that class of education or development-novels which describe the young man of talents who progresses from the country to the city, ascends in the social hierarchy, and moves from innocence to experience. Stendhal in *Le Rouge et le Noir*, Balzac in *Le Père Goriot* and *Les Illusions perdues*, use the plot as a means of dissecting the post-Napoleonic world and exposing its moral poverty. This novelistic form reflects the lives of the successful children of the century, and usually expresses the mixed attitudes of its artists. Dickens, Stendhal, Balzac communicate their horror of a materialist society, but they are not without admiration for the possibilities of the new social mobility: *la carrière ouverte aux talents* had a personal meaning for all three of these energetic men.

Pip, then, must be considered in the highly competitive company of Julien Sorel, Rubempré, and Eugène de Rastignac. Dickens's tale of lost illusions, however, is very different from the French novelists'; *Great Expectations* is not more profound than other development-novels, but it is more mysterious. The recurrent themes of the genre are all there: city is posed against country, experience against innocence; there is a search for the true father; there is the exposure to crime and the acceptance of guilt and expiation. What Dickens's novel lacks is the clarity and, one is tempted to say, the essential tolerance of the French. He could not command either the saving ironic vision of Stendhal or the disenchanted practicality and secure Catholicism of Balzac. For Dickens, always the Victorian protestant, the issues of a young man's rise or fall are conceived as a drama of the individual conscience; enlightenment (partial at best) is to be found only in the agony of personal guilt.

With these considerations and possible comparisons in mind I should like to comment on some of the conspicuous features of *Great Expectations*. The novel is interesting for many reasons: it demonstrates the subtlety of Dickens's art; it displays a consistent control of narrative, imagery, and theme which gives meaning to the stark outline of the fable, and symbolic weight to every character and detail. It proves Dickens's ability (which has frequently been denied) to combine his genius for comedy with his fictional presentation of some of the most serious and permanently interesting of human concerns.

The principal themes are announced and the mood of the whole novel established in the opening pages of *Great Expectations*. The first scene with the boy Pip in the graveyard is one of the best of the superbly energetic beginnings found in almost all Dickens's mature novels. In less than a page we are given a character, his background, and his setting; within a few paragraphs more we are immersed in a decisive action. Young Pip is first seen against the background of his parents' gravestones—monuments which communicate to him no clear knowledge either of his parentage or of his position in the world. He is an orphan who must search for a father and define his own condition. The moment of this opening scene, we learn, is that at which the hero has first realized his individuality and gained his 'first most vivid and broad impression of the identity of things'. This information given the reader, the violent meeting between Pip and the escaped convict abruptly takes place.

The impression of the identity of things that Pip is supposed to have received is highly equivocal. The convict rises up like a ghost from among the graves, seizes the boy suddenly, threatens to kill him, holds him upside down through most of their conversation, and ends by forcing the boy to steal food for him. The children of Dickens's novels always receive rather strange impressions of things, but Pip's epiphany is the oddest of all, and in some ways the most ingenious. This encounter in the graveyard is the germinal scene of the novel. While he is held by the convict Pip sees his world upside down; in the course of Dickens's fable the reader is invited to try the same view. This particular change of viewpoint is an ancient device of irony, but an excellent one: Dickens's satire asks us to try reversing the accepted senses of innocence and guilt, success and failure, to think of the world's goods as the world's evils.

A number of ironic reversals and ambiguous situations develop out of the first scene. The convict, Magwitch, is permanently grateful to Pip for having brought him food and a file with which to take off his leg-iron. Years later he expresses his gratitude by assuming in secrecy an economic parenthood; with the money he has made in Australia he will, unbeknownst to Pip, make 'his boy' a gentleman. But the money the convict furnishes him makes Pip not a true gentleman, but a cad. He lives as a flâneur in London, and when he later discovers the disreputable source of his income is snobbishly horrified.

Pip's career is a parable which illustrates several religious paradoxes: he can gain only by losing all he has; only by being defiled can he be cleansed. Magwitch returns to claim his gentleman, and finally the convict's devotion and suffering arouse Pip's charity; by the time Magwitch has been captured and is dying Pip has accepted him and come to love him as a true father. The relationship is the most important one in the novel: in sympathizing with Magwitch Pip assumes the criminal's guilt; in suffering with and finally loving the despised and rejected man he finds his own real self.

Magwitch did not have to learn to love Pip. He was naturally devoted to 'the small bundle of shivers', the outcast boy who brought him the stolen food and the file in the misty graveyard. There is a natural bond, Dickens suggests, between the child and the criminal; they are alike in their helplessness; both are repressed and tortured by established society, and both rebel against its incomprehensible authority. In the first scene Magwitch forces Pip to commit his first 'criminal' act, to steal the file and food from his sister's house. Though this theft produces agonies of guilt in Pip, we are led to see it not as a sin but as an instinctive act of mercy. Magwitch, much later, tells Pip: 'I first become aware of myself, down in Essex, a thieving turnips for my living.' Dickens would have us, in some obscure way, conceive the illicit act as the means of self-realization.

In the opening section of the novel the view moves back and forth between the escaped criminal on the marshes and the harsh life in the house of Pip's sister, Mrs Joe Gargery. The 'criminality' of Pip and the convict is contrasted with the socially approved cruelty and injustice of Mrs Joe and her respectable friends. The elders who come to the Christmas feast at the Gargerys' are pleased to describe Pip as a criminal: the young are, according to Mr Hubble, 'naterally wicious'. During this most bleak of Christmas dinners the child is treated not only as outlaw, but as animal. In Mrs Joe's first speech Pip is called a 'young monkey'; then, as the spirits of the revellers rise, more and more comparisons are made between boys and animals. Uncle Pumblechook, devouring his pork, toys with the notion of Pip's having been born a 'Squeaker':

'If you had been born such, would you have been here now? Not you. . . .'

'Unless in that form,' said Mr Wopsle, nodding towards the dish.

'But I don't mean in that form, sir,' returned Mr Pumblechook, who had an objection to being interrupted; 'I mean, enjoying himself with his elders and betters, and improving himself with their conversation, and rolling in the lap of luxury. Would he have been doing that? No, he wouldn't. And what would have been your destination?' turning on me again. 'You would have been disposed of for so many shillings according to the market price of the article, and Dunstable the butcher would have come up to you as you lay in your straw, and he would have whipped you under his left arm, and with his right he would have tucked up his frock to get a penknife from out of his waistcoat-pocket, and he would have shed your blood and had your life. No bringing up by hand then. Not a bit of it!'

This identification of animal and human is continually repeated in the opening chapters of the novel, and we catch its resonance throughout the book. When the two convicts—Pip's 'friend' and the other fugitive, Magwitch's ancient enemy—are captured, we experience the horror of official justice, which treats the prisoners as if they were less than human: 'No one seemed surprised to see him, or interested in seeing him, or glad to see him, or sorry to see him, or spoke a word, except that somebody in the boat growled as if to dogs, "Give way, you!"' And the prison ship, lying beyond the mud of the shore, looked to Pip 'like a wicked Noah's ark'.

The theme of this first section of the novel—which concludes with the capture of Magwitch and his return to the prison ship—might be called 'the several meanings of humanity'. Only the three characters who are in some way social outcasts—Pip, Magwitch, and Joe Gargery the child-like blacksmith—act in charity and respect the humanity of others. To Magwitch Pip is distinctly not an animal, and not capable of adult wickedness: 'You'd be but a fierce young hound indeed, if at your time of life you could help to hunt a wretched warmint.' And when, after he is taken, the convict shields Pip by confessing to have stolen the Gargerys' pork pie, Joe's absolution affirms the dignity of the man:

> 'God knows you're welcome to it—so far as it was ever mine,' returned Joe, with a saving remembrance of Mrs Joe. 'We don't know what you have done, but we wouldn't have you starved to death for it, poor miserable fellow-creatur.— Would us, Pip?'

The next section of the narrative is less tightly conceived than the introductory action. Time is handled loosely; Pip goes to school, and becomes acquainted with Miss Havisham of Satis House and the beautiful Estella. The section concludes when Pip has reached early manhood, been told of his expectations, and has prepared to leave for London. These episodes develop, with variations, the theme of childhood betrayed. Pip himself renounces his childhood by coming to accept the false social values of middle-class society. His perverse development is expressed by persistent images of the opposition between the human and the non-human, the living and the dead.

On his way to visit Miss Havisham for the first time, Pip spends the night with Mr Pumblechook, the corn-chandler, in his lodgings behind his shop. The contrast between the aridity of this old hypocrite's spirit and the viability of his wares is a type of the conflict between natural growth and social form. Pip looks at all the shopkeeper's little drawers filled with bulbs and seed packets and wonders 'whether the flower-seeds and bulbs ever wanted of a fine day to break out of those jails and bloom'. The imagery of life repressed is developed further in the descriptions of Miss Havisham and Satis House. The first detail Pip notices is the abandoned brewery where the once active ferment has ceased; no germ of life is to be found in Satis House or in its occupants.

> ...there were no pigeons in the dove-cot, no horses in the

stable, no pigs in the sty, no malt in the storehouse, no smells of grains and beer in the copper or the vat. All the uses and scents of the brewery might have evaporated with its last reek of smoke. In a by-yard, there was a wilderness of empty casks....

On top of these casks Estella dances with solitary concentration, and behind her, in a dark corner of the building, Pip fancies that he sees a figure hanging by the neck from a wooden beam, 'a figure all in yellow white, with but one shoe to the feet; and it hung so, that I could see that the faded trimmings of the dress were like earthy paper, and that the face was Miss Havisham's'.

Miss Havisham *is* death. From his visits to Satis House Pip acquires his false admiration for the genteel; he falls in love with Estella and fails to see that she is the cold instrument of Miss Havisham's revenge on human passion and on life itself. When Pip learns he may expect a large inheritance from an unknown source he immediately assumes (incorrectly) that Miss Havisham is his benefactor; she does not undeceive him. Money, which is also death, is appropriately connected with the old lady rotting away in her darkened room.

Conflicting values in Pip's life are also expressed by the opposed imagery of stars and fire. Estella is by name a star, and throughout the novel stars are conceived as pitiless: 'And then I looked at the stars, and considered how awful it would be for a man to turn his face up to them as he froze to death, and see no help or pity in all the glittering multitude.' Estella and her light are described as coming down the dark passage of Satis House 'like a star', and when she has become a woman she is constantly surrounded by the bright glitter of jewelry.

Joe Gargery, on the other hand, is associated with the warm fire of the hearth or forge. It was his habit to sit and rake the fire between the lower bars of the kitchen grate, and his workday was spent at the forge. The extent to which Dickens intended the contrast between the warm and the cold lights—the vitality of Joe and the frigid glitter of Estella—is indicated in a passage that describes the beginnings of Pip's disillusionment with his expectations:

When I woke up in the night ... I used to think, with a weariness on my spirits, that I should have been happier and better if I had never seen Miss Havisham's face, and had risen to manhood content to be partners with Joe in the honest old forge. Many a time of an evening, when I sat alone looking at the fire, I thought, after all, there was no fire like the forge fire and the kitchen fire at home.

Yet Estella was so inseparable from all my restlessness and disquiet of mind, that I really fell into confusion as to the limits of my own part in its production.

At the end of the novel Pip finds the true light on the homely hearth, and in a last twist of the father-son theme, Joe emerges as a true parent—the only kind of parent that Dickens could ever fully approve, one that remains a child. The moral of this return to Joe sharply contradicts the accepted picture of Dickens as a radical critic of society: Joe is a humble country-man who is content with the place in the social order he has been appointed to fulfill. He fills it 'well and with respect'; Pip learns that he can do no better than to emulate him.

The second stage of Pip's three-phased story is set in London, and the moral issues of the fiction are modulated accordingly. Instead of the opposition between custom and the instinctive life, the novelist treats the conflict between man and his social institutions. The topics and themes are specific, and the satire, some of it wonderfully deft, is more social than moral. Not all Dickens's social message is presented by means that seem adequate. By satirizing Pip and his leisure class friends (The Finches of the Grove, they call themselves) the novelist would have us realize that idle young men will come to a bad end. Dickens is here expressing the Victorian Doctrine of Work—a pervasive notion that both inspired and reassured his industrious contemporaries.

The difficulty for the modern reader, who is unmoved by the objects of Victorian piety, is that the doctrine appears to be the result, not of moral insight, but of didactic intent; it is presented as statement, rather than as experience or dramatized perception, and consequently it never modifies the course of fictional action or the formation of character. The distinction is crucial: it is between the Dickens who *sees* and the Dickens who *professes*; often between the good and the bad sides of his art.

The novelist is on surer ground when he comes to define the nature of wealth in a mercantile society. Instead of moralistic condemnation we have a technique that resembles parable. Pip eventually learns that his ornamental life is supported, not by Miss Havisham, but by the labor and suffering of the convict Magwitch:

'I swore arterwards, sure as ever I spec'lated and got rich, you should get rich. I lived rough, that you should live smooth; I worked hard that you should be above work. What odds, dear boy? Do I tell it fur you to feel a obligation? Not a bit. I tell it, fur you to know as that there dunghill dog wot you kept life in, got his head so high that he could make a gentleman—and, Pip, you're him!'

The convict would not only make a gentleman but own him. The blood horses of the colonists might fling up the dust over him as he was walking but, 'I says to myself, "If I ain't a gentleman, nor yet ain't got no learning, I'm the owner of such. All on you owns stock and land; which on you owns a brought-up London gentleman?"'

In this action Dickens has subtly led us to speculate on the connections between a gentleman and his money, on the dark origins of even the most respectable fortunes. We find Magwitch guilty of trying to own another human being, but we ask whether his actions are any more sinful than those of the wealthy *bourgeois*. There is a deeper moral in the fact that Magwitch's fortune at first destroyed the natural gentleman in Pip, but that after it was lost (it had to be forfeited to the state when Magwitch was finally captured) the 'dung-hill dog' did actually make Pip a gentleman by evoking his finer feelings. This ironic distinction between 'gentility' and what the father of English poetry meant by 'gentilesse' is traditional in our literature and our mythology. In *Great Expectations* it arises out of the action and language of the fiction; consequently it moves and persuades us as literal statement never can.

The middle sections of the novel are dominated by the solid yet mysterious figure of Mr Jaggers, Pip's legal guardian. Though Jaggers is not one of Dickens's greatest characters he is heavy with implication; he is so much at the center of this fable that we are challenged to interpret him—only to find that his meaning is ambiguous. On his first appearance Jaggers strikes a characteristic note of sinister authority:

He was a burly man of an exceedingly dark complexion,

with an exceedingly large head and a correspondingly large hand. He took my chin in his large hand and turned up my face to have a look at me by the light of the candle.... His eyes were set very deep in his head, and were disagreeably sharp and suspicious....

'How do you come here?'

'Miss Havisham sent for me, sir,' I explained.

'Well! Behave yourself. I have a pretty large experience of boys, and you're a bad set of fellows. Now mind!' said he, biting the side of his great forefinger, as he frowned at me, 'you behave yourself.'

Pip wonders at first if Jaggers is a doctor. It is soon explained that he is a lawyer—what we now ambiguously call a *criminal* lawyer—but he is like a physician who treats moral malignancy with the doctor's necessary detachment from individual suffering. Jaggers is interested not in the social operations of the law, but in the varieties of criminality. He exudes an antiseptic smell of soap and is described as washing his clients off as if he were a surgeon or a dentist.

Pip finds that Jaggers has 'an air of authority not to be disputed ... with a manner expressive of knowing something secret about every one of us that would effectually do for each individual if he chose to disclose it'. When Pip and his friends go to dinner at Jaggers's house Pip observes that he 'wrenched the weakest parts of our dispositions out of us'. After the party his guardian tells Pip that he particularly liked the sullen young man they called Spider: ' "Keep as clear of him as you can. But I like the fellow, Pip; he is one of the true sort. Why if I was a fortune-teller.... But I am not a fortune-teller," he said.... "You know what I am don't you?" ' This question is repeated when Pip is being shown through Newgate Prison by Jaggers's assistant, Wemmick. The turnkey says of Pip: 'Why then ... he knows what Mr Jaggers is.'

But neither Pip nor the reader ever fully knows what Mr Jaggers is. We learn, along with Pip, that Jaggers has manipulated the events which have shaped the lives of most of the characters in the novel; he has, in the case of Estella and her mother, dispensed a merciful but entirely personal justice; he is the only character who knows the web of secret relationships that are finally revealed to Pip. He dominates by the strength of his knowledge the world of guilt and sin—called *Little Britain*—of which his office is the center. He has, in brief, the powers that an artist exerts over the creatures of his fictional world, and that a god exerts over his creation.

As surrogate of the artist, Jaggers displays qualities of mind —complete impassibility, all-seeing unfeelingness—which are the opposite of Dickens's, but of a sort that Dickens may at times have desired. Jaggers can be considered a fantasy figure created by a novelist who is forced by his intense sensibility to re-live the sufferings of his fellow men and who feels their agonies too deeply.

In both the poetry and fiction of the nineteenth century there are examples of a persistent desire of the artist *not to care*. The mood, which is perhaps an inevitable concomitant of Romanticism, is expressed in Balzac's ambivalence toward his great character Vautrin. As arch-criminal and Rousseauistic man, Vautrin represents all the attitudes that Balzac the churchman and monarchist ostensibly rejects, yet is presented as a kind of artist-hero, above the law, who sees through the social system with an almost noble cynicism.

Related attitudes are expressed in the theories of art developed by such different writers as Flaubert and Yeats. While—perhaps because—Flaubert himself suffered from hyperaesthesia, he conceived the ideal novelist as coldly detached, performing his examination with the deft impassivity of the surgeon. Yeats, the 'last Romantic', found the construction of a mask or anti-self necessary to poetic creation, and insisted that the anti-self be cold and hard—all that he as poet and feeling man was not.

Dickens's evocation of this complex of attitudes is less political than Balzac's, less philosophical than Flaubert's or Yeats's. Jaggers has a complete understanding of human evil but, unlike the living artist, can wash his hands of it. He is above ordinary institutions; like a god he dispenses justice, and like a god displays infinite mercy through unrelenting severity:

'Mind you, Mr Pip,' said Wemmick, gravely in my ear, as he took my arm to be more confidential; 'I don't know that Mr Jaggers does a better thing than the way in which he keeps himself so high. He's always so high. His constant height is of a piece with his immense abilities. That Colonel durst no more take leave of *him*, than that turnkey durst ask him his intentions respecting a case. Then between his height and them, he slips in his subordinate—don't you see?—and so he has 'em soul and body.'

Pip merely wishes that he had 'some other guardian of minor abilities'.

The final moral vision of *Great Expectations* has to do with the nature of sin and guilt. After visiting Newgate Pip, still complacent and self-deceived, thinks how strange it was that he should be encompassed by the taint of prison and crime. He tries to beat the prison dust off his feet and to exhale its air from his lungs; he is going to meet Estella, who must not be contaminated by the smell of crime. Later it is revealed that Estella, the pure, is the bastard child of Magwitch and a murderess. Newgate is figuratively described as a greenhouse, and the prisoners as plants carefully tended by Wemmick, assistant to Mr Jaggers. These disturbing metaphors suggest that criminality is the condition of life. Dickens would distinguish between the native, inherent sinfulness from which men can be redeemed, and that evil which destroys life: the sin of the hypocrite or oppressor, the smothering wickedness of corrupt institutions. The last stage of Pip's progression is reached when he learns to love the criminal and to accept his own implication in the common guilt.

Though Dickens's interpretation is theologically heterodox, he deals conventionally with the ancient question of free will and pre-destination. In one dramatic paragraph Pip's 'fall' is compared with the descent of the rock slab on the sleeping victim in the Arabian Nights tale: Slowly, slowly, 'all the work, near and afar, that tended to the end, had been accomplished; and in an instant the blow was struck, and the roof of my stronghold dropped upon me'. Pip's fall was the result of a chain of pre-determined events but he was, nevertheless, responsible for his own actions; toward the end of the novel Miss Havisham gravely informs him: 'You have made your own snares. *I* never made them.'

The patterns of culpability in *Great Expectations* are so intricate that the whole world of the novel is eventually caught in a single web of awful responsibility. The leg-iron, for example, which the convict removed with the file Pip stole for him is found by Orlick and used as a weapon to brain Mrs Joe. By this fearsome chain of circumstance Pip shares the guilt for his sister's death.

Profound and suggestive as is Dickens's treatment of guilt and expiation in this novel, to trace its remoter implications is to find something excessive and idiosyncratic. A few years after he wrote *Great Expectations* Dickens remarked to a friend that he felt always as if he were wanted by the police—'irretrievably tainted'. Compared to most of the writers of his time the Dickens of the later novels seems to be obsessed with guilt. The way in which his development-novel differs from those of his French compeers emphasizes an important qualty of Dickens's art. The young heroes of *Le Rouge et le Noir* and *Le Père Goriot* proceed from innocence, through suffering to learning. They are surrounded by evil, and they can be destroyed by it. But Stendhal, writing in a rationalist tradition, and Balzac displaying the worldliness that only a Catholic novelist can command, seem astonishingly cool, even callous, besides Dickens. *Great Expectations* is outside either Cartesian or Catholic rationalism; profound as only an elementally simple book can be, it finds its analogues not in the novels of Dickens's English or French contemporaries, but in the writings of that other irretrievably tainted artist, Fyodor Dostoievsky.

9 Honoré de Balzac

Preface (Avant-propos) to *The Human Comedy*

Translated by Petra Morrison for the Open University, 1972.

To explain why I have given the title of *The Human Comedy* to a labour which I undertook nearly thirteen years ago, I will need to describe the thinking behind it, narrate its origin and outline its structure as if I were a completely disinterested person. This is not as difficult as the public might think. A small output produces great self-satisfaction; but a large one engenders infinite modesty. In saying this I am bearing in mind the examinations of their own works which Corneille, Molière and other great authors made; it may be impossible to match them in their fine conceptions, but one can still try to resemble them in their approach.

The first idea of *The Human Comedy* came to me like a dream, like one of those impossible projects which one toys with and then allows to flit away; a chimera which smiles, showing its woman's face, and then straightway spreads its wings and soars into the sky of fantasy. But this chimera, like many chimeras, changed into reality; she gave orders and imposed a tyranny which I was compelled to obey.

The idea sprang from a comparison between Humanity and Animality.

It would be a mistake to think that the great argument which recently erupted between Cuvier and Geoffroi Saint-Hilaire centred on a scientific innovation. *Unity of substance*, the idea that all animal life shares a common essence, had already under different names preoccupied the greatest minds of the last two centuries. Re-read the extraordinary works of the mystic writers, such as Swedenborg and Saint-Martin, who have been concerned with the sciences in their relations with the infinite, and the writings of the inspired naturalists like Leibniz, Buffon, Charles Bonnet, etc.; consider Leibniz's monads, Buffon's organic molecules, Needham's vegetative force, and the *interlocking* of similar elements of Charles Bonnet, who was bold enough to write in 1760 that 'animals grow just as plants do'. In all of these you will find the rudiments of the great law concerning *the self as it perceives itself*, which is at the base of *unity of substance*. There is only one animal. The Creator used the same, single template for all the beings he organized. The animal is a principle which derives its external form, or more exactly the differences in its form, from the environments in which it develops. Zoological species result from these differences. Geoffroi Saint-Hilaire's propounding and defending of this way of thinking, which happens also to agree with our ideas about the divine power, will be to his eternal honour; he defeated Cuvier on this important scientific issue, and his triumph was hailed in the last article ever written by the great Goethe.

I had adopted this way of thinking long before the discussions which arose from it, and I saw that in this sense Society resembled Nature. For does not Society make man, according to the milieux in which he acts, into as many different men as there are varieties in zoology? The differences between a soldier, a worker, an administrator, a lawyer, an idler, a learned man, a statesman, a merchant, a sailor, a poet, a pauper or a priest, are harder to grasp, but they are just as considerable as those differences which separate the wolf, the lion, the ass, the crow, the shark, the seal, the ewe and so on. Consequently just as there are Zoological Species, there always have been and always will be Social Species. Buffon did magnificent work in trying to represent the whole of the zoological world in one book; so is there not a similar task to be done for Society? But Nature has set limits for animal species, by which Society cannot be contained.

When Buffon had portrayed the lion, he could describe the lioness in several sentences; whereas in Society the woman is not always merely the female of the male. There can be two completely dissimilar beings in one household. A merchant's wife sometimes deserves to be the wife of a prince, and often a prince's wife hardly compares with the wife of an artist. The Social State, being Nature plus Society, contains elements of chance which Nature would not permit. The describing of Social Species, consequently, is at least double the task of describing Animal Species, even if we consider only the two sexes. Finally, there are few dramas and little confusion among animals; they fight each other, that is all. Men, too, fight each other, but their degree of intelligence complicates the combat in another way. Some learned gentlemen still will not admit that Animality spills over into Humanity in an immense flood of life; but the grocer nevertheless becomes a peer of France, and the noble sometimes descends to the lowest social rank. Furthermore, Buffon found the life of animals excessively simple. Animals have little furniture, they have neither arts nor sciences; whereas through some law which has yet to be worked out, man tends to make concrete his life, morality and thought in everything that he appropriates to his needs. Leeuwenhoek, Swammerdam, Spallanzani, Réaumur, Charles Bonnet, Müller, Haller and other patient zoologists have shown us how interesting animal behaviour is, but to my eyes, at least, animals' habits are always alike, for evermore; whereas the habits, clothing, words and dwellings of a prince, banker, artist, bourgeois, priest or poor man are entirely unlike, and change with different civilizations.

Thus the task at hand has a threefold shape: men, women and things, i.e. people and the material form they give to their thinking: in short, man and life, for life clothes us.

Can anyone have read the dry and tiresome recitals of facts known as *histories* and not noticed that the writers of every period, in Egypt, Persia, Greece and Rome, have forgotten to give us the history of manners and morals? Petronius's piece* on the private life of the Romans stimulates rather than satisfies our curiosity. It was after noticing this immense lacuna in the field of history that the Abbé Barthélémy devoted his life to recreating Greek ways, in his story of the young Anacharsis.

But how can one make the drama interesting to the three or four thousand types of character which make up a Society? How can one please at once the poet, the philosopher and the masses who want poetry and philosophy served up as exciting images? I could grasp the importance and poetry of such a history of the human heart, but I could see no way of writing it; for until our day even the most famous story-tellers concentrated their talent on creating one or two typical characters, on depicting a single facet of life. It was with this thought in mind that I read the works of Walter Scott. Walter Scott, that

* [*The Satyricon.*]

modern innovator and minstrel, was at that period conferring a
gigantic stature on a literary form unjustly labelled secondary.
For indeed, is not the second of these two propositions truly
the harder one: firstly, to put into order facts which are much
the same for every nation, to research the spirit of obsolete
laws, to formulate theories which lead whole peoples astray, or,
like certain metaphysicians, to explain existence; or secondly,
to relate civil life to Daphnis and Chloe, Roland, Amadis, Pan-
urge, Don Quixote, Manon Lescaut, Clarissa and Lovelace,
Robinson Crusoe, Gil Blas, Ossian, Julie d'Etanges, Uncle
Toby, Werther, René, Corinne, Adolphe, Paul and Virginie,
Jeanie Deans, Claverhouse, Ivanhoe, Manfred and Mignon? For
to begin with, these literary characters, who last longer and
remain more real than the generations which saw their birth,
usually stay alive only on the condition of forming a powerful
image of the present. They are drawn up from the depths of
their century; the whole human heart beats within their shell,
and there is often a whole philosophy hidden in them. And it
is in this way that Walter Scott gave the philosophical value of
history to the novel, that literary form which through the
centuries has encrusted with immortal diamonds the poetic
crown of those countries where literature is cultivated. He gave
the novel the spirit of former times; he united in it drama,
dialogue, portraiture, landscape and description; he included
both the marvellous and the factual, those elements of epic; he
made the most humble, familiar forms of speech jostle with
poetry. But, since he did not so much formulate a system as
find his voice in the heat of creation or through the logic of that
creation, he did not think of linking his works together so as
to set up a complete history, of which each chapter would have
been a novel, and each novel a period of time. It was through
noticing this failure to connect (which I must observe by no
means diminishes the Scotsman's greatness) that I perceived the
system I could use to perform my task. Although I was, so to
speak, dazzled by Walter Scott's astonishing, always consistent,
fertility, I did not despair, for I realized that this talent of his
was rooted in the infinite variety of human nature. Chance is
the greatest novelist in the world: one has only to study it in
order to be fertile. French Society was to be the historian, I had
only to be the secretary. I would draw up the inventory of the

vices and virtues, collect the main effects of the passions, portray characters, select the principal events of Society, and compose types by combining the traits of several homogeneous characters; and I might thus succeed in writing that history forgotten by so many historians, the history of manners and morals. With much patience and courage I would write the book for nineteenth-century France which, to our regret, Rome, Athens, Tyre, Memphis, Persia and India have failed to bequeath to us; the kind of book which the brave and patient Monteil following the Abbé Barthélémy's example, tried to write for the Middle Ages, though he chose an unfortunate form for it.

But my work was nothing as yet. A writer could, if he adopted this method of rigorously literal reproduction, become a more or less faithful, happy, patient or courageous painter of human types, narrator of the dramas of private life, archaeologist of social furniture, classifier of professions, and recorder of good and evil; but if I was to deserve the praises which any artist must aspire to, I must needs study the *causes or central cause* of these social facts, and discover the meaning hidden in that immense assembly of faces, passions and events. Finally, after I had sought—I do not say found—this cause or social motivator, would it not be necessary to meditate on the principles of nature, and see in what respects Societies move away from or closer to the eternal rule of truth and beauty? In spite of such wide premises, which in themselves could constitute a work, the work needed a conclusion in order to be whole. Depicted thus, Society was to carry within itself the seeds of its own development.

The law of the writer is what makes him a writer and, I am not afraid to say it, the equal and perhaps the superior of the statesman; this law binds him to make some kind of decision on human affairs, to be absolutely devoted to principles. Macchiavelli, Hobbes, Bossuet, Leibniz, Kant and Montesquieu create the science applied by statesmen. St Peter and St Paul created the systems followed by popes. 'A writer,' as Bonald said, 'must have firm opinions on morals and politics, he must consider himself a teacher of men; for if men are merely to doubt they have no need of teachers.' These great words, which are the law equally of the royalist writer and the democratic one, were adopted by me as a creed early on. Therefore, when anyone wants to use my own work to contradict me, he will find that he has misinterpreted some irony; or he will mistakenly turn against me what is in fact the speech of one of my characters— a pet manoeuvre of calumniators. Now for the inner meaning, the spirit of the work; here are its basic principles.

Man is neither good nor evil, he is born with instincts and aptitudes; Society, far from depraving him as Rousseau claimed, perfects him and makes him better; but his personal interest, at the same time, strengthens his bad tendencies enormously. Since Christianity, and especially Catholicism, is a comprehensive system for the repressing of man's depraved tendencies (as I said in *The Country Doctor**), it is the major element of Social Order.

An attentive study of the panorama of society, which is moulded from life, as it were, with all its good and its evil, produces this lesson; if thought, or passion which contains both thought and feeling, is the main social element, it is also the main socially destructive element. In this sense social life resembles human nature. Nations only acquire longevity by moderating their way of living. Teaching, or even better educating, by Religious Bodies is therefore the great principle of existence for nations, since it is the sole means of diminishing the sum of evil and of increasing the sum of good in every Society. Thought, the principle of all evils and virtues, can only be trained, tamed and directed by religion. The sole possible religion is Christianity (see in *Louis Lambert,** the letter written from Paris where the young mystic philosopher, with reference to Swedenborg's doctrine, explains how there has only been one religion since the beginning of the world). Christianity has created modern nations and it will preserve them. Hence, indubitably, the necessity of the monarchical principle. Catholicism and Royalty are two twin principles. As for the limits which Institutions must impose on these two principles so that they are not allowed to develop to their absolute extremes, for everything absolute is bad, everyone will agree that a preface as succinct as this one must be cannot become a political treatise. And consequently I cannot enter into, either, the religious or the political debates of the moment. I write in the light of two eternal Truths: Religion and Monarchy, two necessities which contemporary events confirm, and which every sensible writer

* [Novels included in *The Human Comedy*.]

should try to lead our country back to. I am not the enemy of Election, for it is an excellent principle for establishing law, but I reject Election *taken as sole social force*, especially if it is as badly organized as it is today, for it does not represent the impressive minorities with the ideas and interests which a monarchist government would share. Election when it covers every area of life gives us government by the masses, the only kind which is not responsible and where tyranny has no limits, for it claims the authority of *law*. Consequently I regard the Family and not the Individual as the true social unit. On this subject, at the risk of being thought retrograde, I place myself with Bossuet and Bonald, rather than following modern innovators. Since Election has become the sole social force, however, there is no need to infer the slightest contradiction between my acts and my thinking if I take part in an election myself. An engineer may announce that such and such a bridge is about to collapse and is dangerous for everybody to use; and he will use it himself if it is the only way to reach the town. Napoleon adapted Election to the spirit of our country admirably. As a result even the least of the delegates of his *Corps Législatif* (legislative body) were the most famous orators of the parliamentary Chambers under the Restoration. No Chamber has ever matched the *Corps Législatif* when they were compared man for man. The electoral system of the Empire, therefore, given modifications determined by the difference in time, is indisputably a better system than the present one.

Some people may think this statement smacks of pride and smugness. They will want to quarrel with my trying to be a historian when I am a novelist, and will require me to justify my politics. But here I am simply answering a need, that is all. The work I have undertaken will have the length of a history; I still need to provide it with its yet hidden central cause, with principles and a morality.

In this edition I am obliged to suppress prefaces which were published in order to answer essentially transitory criticisms; but I wish to retain one remark concerning such criticism.

Writers who have an aim—and it may be a return to the principles found in the past for precisely the reason that they are eternal—must always clear the ground. Now anyone who brings his own contribution to the domain of ideas, or publicizes a wrong, or identifies evil in order to destroy it, is always considered immoral. The reproach of immorality has invariably been levelled at every courageous writer; it is, furthermore, the last accusation made against a poet when there are no others left to make. If you are true in your portrayals, and manage, by dint of daily and nightly labour, to write the most difficult language in the world, the word immoral is thrown in your face. Socrates was immoral, Jesus Christ was immoral: both were persecuted in the name of the Societies which they overthrew or reformed. When one wants to kill someone, one accuses him of immorality. This manoeuvre, so familiar among political parties, is a disgrace to all those who use it. Luther and Calvin knew exactly what they were doing when they used the damage done to their material interests to shield them! And so they lived out their natural life.

As I was depicting the whole of Society and grasping it in all the immensity of its upheavals, it happened—it was bound to happen—that one particular story contained more evil than good, that one section of the fresco represented a group of wrong-doers; and criticism cried immorality, without noting the morality of another section which was designed to form a perfect contrast. As criticism was blind to the general structure, I pardoned it; which was all the easier since one can no more prevent criticism than one can prevent the use of sight, language and judgement. The time when I will be judged impartially has not yet come. And besides, the writer who cannot make himself face critical fire should no more set up to write than a traveller who counts on a perpetually clear sky should set out on a journey. On this point, it only remains for me to note that even the most conscientious moralists seriously doubt that Society can offer as many good actions as evil ones; yet in the panorama which I have created of Society there are more virtuous than reprehensible characters. In my work all wrongdoings, transgressions and crimes, from the smallest to the gravest, receive their punishment whether it be human or divine, sensational or secret. I have done better than the historian, I am freer. Cromwell lived here on earth with no punishment other than what thought could inflict on him. Nonetheless there has been disagreement between different schools of thought; even Bossuet was gentle on the great regicide. The usurper William of Orange, and that other usurper Hugues Capet, both died at a ripe old age, having lived under no more threats or fears than did Henri IV and Charles I. Take the lives of Catherine II and Louis XVI; they would seem to rule out the existence of any form of morality, if we judged them in terms of the morality which governs details, for as Napoleon said, for Kings as for Statesmen there is a lesser and a greater morality. My SCENES OF POLITICAL LIFE are based on this fine reflection. The law of history is not, as it is for the novel, to aim towards ideal beauty. History is, or should be, what it was in reality; whereas *the novel must be the world improved*, to quote Madame Necker, one of the most distinguished minds of the last century. But the novel would be worthless if in the midst of this august deceit, it were not true in its details. Walter Scott was obliged to conform to the ideas of an essentially hypocritical country, and consequently, in terms of humanity, he was false in his portrayal of woman, because his models were Protestant ones. The Protestant woman has no ideal. She can be chaste, pure, virtuous; but her love cannot grow, it will always be calm and well-behaved like a duty performed. It would seem that the Virgin Mary hardened the hearts of the sophists who banished her and her treasures of mercy from heaven. In Protestantism, there is nothing left for woman after she has transgressed; whereas in the Catholic Church, the hope of pardon makes her sublime. Hence there is only one woman for the Protestant writer, whereas the Catholic writer finds a new woman in each new situation. If Walter Scott had been Catholic, and had set himself the task of accurately describing the different Societies which have succeeded each other in Scotland, then, perhaps, the portrayer of Effie and of Alice (the two characters which in his old age he regretted having created) would have accepted the passions, with their transgressions and punishments, and the virtues which repentance teaches them. Passion is humanity, entire. Without it, religion, history, the novel and art would be useless.

In seeing me amass so many facts and paint them as they are, with passion as the central element, some people have wrongly imagined that I belonged to the sensualist or materialist schools, which are two facets of the same thing, pantheism. But perhaps it was easy, perhaps they were bound to make that mistake. I do not in the least share the belief in the indefinite progress of

Societies; I believe in man's progress over himself. Consequently those who wish to believe that I consider man to be a finite creature, are making an absurd mistake. My book *Séraphita*,* which portrays the doctrine of the Christian Buddha in action, strikes me as being an adequate rebuttal to this accusation, which I must admit, however, has never been put forward with much force.

In certain sections of my long work, I have tried to popularize astonishing facts; I could refer to them, perhaps, as marvels of electricity, which changes in man into an incalculable power; but in what way do the phenomena of brain and nerves, demonstrating as they do the existence of a new moral world, disturb the sure and necessary relationships between God and every world? How could they topple Catholic dogmas? Suppose that indisputable facts one day caused us to rank thought among those fluids which reveal their presence only by their effects, their substance escaping our senses however many mechanical aids are used to extend them; this would produce the same result as Christopher Columbus's observation of the roundness of the earth, or Galileo's demonstration of its rotation. Our future would remain the same. Animal magnetism, with whose miracles I have been familiar since 1820; the distinguished researches of Gall, Lavater's successor; the work of all those who for the last fifty years have explored thought much as opticians have explored that almost identical substance, light; all these, in the final run, make one lean towards both the mystics, those disciples of the apostle John, and towards the great thinkers who have established the spiritual world, the sphere where man's relations with God are revealed.

If the meaning of my structure is properly grasped, it will be recognized that I attach the same weight to the acts of individual life, their causes and principles, and to common everyday facts however secret or obvious, as other historians have hitherto attached to events in the public life of nations. The unknown battle which is fought in a valley of the Indre between passion and Madame de Mortsauf (*The Lily of the Valley**) is possibly every bit as important as the most famous of known battles. For in one, the glory of a conqueror is at stake; in the other, it is a matter of heaven. The misfortunes of the two Birotteaus, priest

* [Novels included in *The Human Comedy*.]

144 Honoré de Balzac

and perfumer, are for me the misfortunes of humanity. The Ditch-Digger (*The Country Doctor**) and Madame Graslin (*The Country Priest**) constitute a comprehensive picture of womanhood. We suffer like these people every day. A hundred times I have had to do what Richardson only did once. Lovelace has a thousand forms, for social corruption takes on the colours of all the milieux in which it develops. Clarissa, on the other hand, that beautiful image of passionate virtue, is drawn in lines of a disheartening purity. To create many virgins one has to be Raphael. In this sense, literature may be a lower form than painting. So may I be permitted to point out how many irreproachably virtuous figures there are in the published portions of my work; Pierrette Lorrain, Ursule Mirouët, Constance Birotteau, the Ditch-Digger, Eugénie Grandet, Marguerite Claës, Pauline de Villenoix, Madame Jules, Madame de La Chanterie, Eve Chardon, Mademoiselle d'Esgrignon, Madame Firmiani, Agathe Rouget, Renée de Maucombe. And furthermore, many background characters may be less in evidence but still provide equally good examples of the domestic virtues. Consider, too, Joseph Lebas, Genestas, Benassis, the priest Bonnet, Doctor Minoret, Pillerault, David Séchard, the two Birotteaus, the priest Chaperon, the judge Popinot, Bourgeat, the Sauviats, Tascherons and many others; do they not solve the difficult literary problem of how to make a virtuous character interesting?

This was no mean task, portraying the two or three thousand outstanding types of character of a period, for briefly, that is the sum of types which each generation produces, and which *The Human Comedy* will contain. This number of faces and characters, this multitude of existences, demanded frames, and even whole picture-galleries, if I can be pardoned the expression. Hence the natural and already familiar divisions of my work into SCENES OF PRIVATE LIFE, PROVINCIAL LIFE, PARISIAN LIFE, POLITICAL LIFE, MILITARY LIFE and COUNTRY LIFE. These six divisions constitute the whole of the STUDIES OF MORALS which form the general history of Society, what our ancestors would have called its chronicle. And moreover, these six divisions correspond to more general ideas. Each of them has its own

* [Novels included in *The Human Comedy*.]

meaning and direction, and formulates a period of human life. I will repeat here, more succinctly, what Félix Davin, that young talent lost to literature through a premature death, wrote of my work when he had investigated its structure. The SCENES OF PRIVATE LIFE represent childhood and adolescence, and the transgressions of both, just as the SCENES OF PROVINCIAL LIFE represent the age of passions, calculations, interests and ambition. Then the SCENES OF PARISIAN LIFE present a panorama of the tastes, vices and all the excesses stimulated by the particular morality of capital cities, where extremes of both evil and good are encountered. Each of these three parts has its own local colour: the social antithesis of Paris and the provinces provided me with immense resources. Not only men, but also the principal events of life, can be formulated by types. There are situations—typical phases—which are represented in all kinds of existence, and I have tried above all else to pinpoint such situations accurately. I have tried to give an idea of the different regions of our beautiful country. My work has its geography, as it has its genealogy and its families, its places and its things, its people and its facts; as it has its heraldry, its nobles and its bourgeois, its craftsmen and its peasants, its politicians and its dandies, its army: in fact, its whole world!

Having portrayed social life in these three divisions, I then needed to show exceptional lives, which affect the interests of several people or of everyone, and which are in a sense beyond the general law: hence the SCENES OF POLITICAL LIFE. Then, having completed that vast picture of society, was it not necessary to show it in its most violent state, leaving its home ground for defence or conquest? Hence the SCENES OF MILITARY LIFE, which is still the least finished division of the work, but which I will leave room for in this edition so that it can form part of it when completed. And finally, the SCENES OF COUNTRY LIFE are in a way the evening of this long day, if I can so term the drama of society. This division contains the purest characters, and the application of the great principles of politics, order and morality.

Such is the whole foundation of comedies and tragedies, crowded with people, on which the Second Part of my work, the *PHILOSOPHICAL STUDIES*, is erected. Here the social mechanics of every event are demonstrated, and the ravages of thought portrayed, each emotion in its turn. In a sense, its first book,

The Wild Ass' Skin links the STUDIES OF MORALS to the PHILO-
SOPHICAL STUDIES, the link being an almost oriental fantasy
where Life itself is portrayed at grips with Desire, the principle
of all Passion.

Then comes the Third Part, the ANALYTICAL STUDIES, of which
I will say nothing for only one of them has been published, *The
Physiology of Marriage*.

Later on I will provide two other works in this Third Part.
Firstly, *A Pathology of Social Life* and then *An Anatomy of
Education* and *A Monograph on Virtue*.

As you see what still remains for me to do, you may well
say what my publishers said to me: God grant you a long life!
My only wish is not to be so tormented by people and things as
I have been since I undertook this awesome task. I have had one
consolation, however, for which I thank God; the greatest
talents and finest natures of this time, and the sincerest friends,
as great in private life as the others are in public life, have
shaken my hand and wished me courage. And why should I
not admit that these friendships, and these gestures made here
and there by strangers, have sustained me in my career? They
have strengthened me both against unjust attacks, and the
calumny which has so often pursued me, and against myself,
against discouragement and that too lively hopefulness whose
words are mistaken for excessive self-satisfaction. I had resolved to face attacks and insults with a stoic impassiveness; but
on two occasions, cowardly slurs have made it necessary for
me to defend myself. Those who think insults should be pardoned may regret that I showed my expertise in literary spar-
ring; but there are others, Christians, who hold that we live in
a time where it is good to show how silence has its own
generosity.

While we are on the subject, I must point out that I only
acknowledge as mine those works that bear my name. Besides
The Human Comedy, my only output is the *Hundred Droll
Stories*, two plays and individual articles which are, moreover
signed. This is my indisputable right. But this disclaimer, even
though it affects works on which I have collaborated, is dictated less by self-love than by honesty. If people are to persist
in attributing to me works of which I hold the copyright, but
which in literary terms I do not in the least regard as mine, I

will simply let them have their say, for the same reason as I will refuse to respond to attacks and slurs.

The immensity of my scheme which embraces both the history and criticism of Society, an analysis of its evils and a discussion of its principles, authorizes me, I think, to give this work the title under which it appears today: *The Human Comedy*. Is this ambitious? Or is it only just? This is what the public will decide, when the work is finished.

Paris, July 1842

10 Henry James

(i) Honoré de Balzac

From *Notes on Novelists with Some Other Notes*, Charles Scribner's Sons, 1942, pp. 24–43.

I

Stronger than ever, even than under the spell of first acquaintance and of the early time, is the sense—thanks to a renewal of intimacy and, I am tempted to say, of loyalty—that Balzac stands signally apart, that he is the first and foremost member of his craft, and that above all the Balzac-lover is in no position till he has cleared the ground by saying so. The Balzac-lover alone, for that matter, is worthy to have his word on so happy an occasion as this[1] about the author of *La Comédie humaine*, and it is indeed not easy to see how the amount of attention so inevitably induced could at the worst have failed to find itself turning to an act of homage. I have been deeply affected, to be frank, by the mere refreshment of memory, which has brought in its train moreover consequences critical and sentimental too numerous to figure here in their completeness. The authors and the books that have, as we say, done something for us, become part of the answer to our curiosity when our curiosity had the freshness of youth, these particular agents exist for us, with the lapse of time, as the substance itself of knowledge: they have been intellectually so swallowed, digested and assimilated that we take their general use and suggestion for granted, cease to be aware of them because they have passed out of sight. But they have passed out of sight simply by having passed into our lives. They have become a part of our personal history, a part of ourselves, very often, so far as we may have succeeded in best expressing ourselves. Endless, however, are the uses of great persons and great things, and it may easily happen in these cases that the connection, even as an 'excitement'—the form mainly of the connections of youth—is never really broken. We have largely been living on our benefactor—which is the high-

[1] The appearance of a translation of the *Deux Jeunes Mariées* in *A Century of French Romance*.

est acknowledgment one can make; only, thanks to a blest law that operates in the long run to rekindle excitement, we are accessible to the sense of having neglected him. Even when we may not constantly have read him over the neglect is quite an illusion, but the illusion perhaps prepares us for the finest emotion we are to have owed to the acquaintance. Without having abandoned or denied our author we yet come expressly back to him, and if not quite in tatters and in penitence like the Prodigal Son, with something at all events of the tenderness with which we revert to the parental threshold and hearthstone, if not, more fortunately, to the parental presence. The beauty of this adventure, that of seeing the dust blown off a relation that had been put away as on a shelf, almost out of reach, at the back of one's mind, consists in finding the precious object not only fresh and intact, but with its firm lacquer still further figured, gilded and enriched. It is all overscored with traces and impressions—vivid, definite, almost as valuable as itself—of the recognitions and agitations it originally produced in us. Our old—that is our young—feelings are very nearly what page after page most gives us. The case has become a case of authority *plus* association. If Balzac in himself is indubitably wanting in the sufficiently common felicity we know as charm, it is this association that may on occasion contribute the grace.

The impression then, confirmed and brightened, is of the mass and weight of the figure and of the extent of ground it occupies; a tract on which we might all of us together quite pitch our little tents, open our little booths, deal in our little wares, and not materially either diminish the area or impede the circulation of the occupant. I seem to see him in such an image moving about as Gulliver among the pigmies, and not less good-natured than Gulliver for the exercise of any function, without exception, that can illustrate his larger life. The first and the last word about the author of *Les Contes drolatiques* is that of all novelists he is the most serious—by which I am far from meaning that in the human comedy as he shows it the comic is an absent quantity. His sense of the comic was on the scale of his extraordinary senses in general, though his expression of it suffers perhaps exceptionally from that odd want of elbow-room—the penalty somehow of his close-packed, pressed-down contents—which reminds us of some designedly beautiful thing but half-disengaged from the clay or the marble. It is the scheme and the scope that are supreme in him, applying this moreover not to mere great intention, but to the concrete form, the proved case, in which we possess them. We most of us aspire to achieve at the best but a patch here and there, to pluck a sprig or a single branch, to break ground in a corner of the great garden of life. Balzac's plan was simply to do everything that could be done. He proposed to himself to 'turn over' the great garden from north to south and from east to west; a task —immense, heroic, to this day immeasurable—that he bequeathed us the partial performance of, a prodigious ragged clod, in the twenty monstrous years representing his productive career, years of concentration and sacrifice the vision of which still makes us ache. He had indeed a striking good fortune, the only one he was to enjoy as an harassed and exasperated worker: the great garden of life presented itself to him absolutely and exactly in the guise of the great garden of France, a subject vast and comprehensive enough, yet with definite edges and corners. This identity of his universal with his local and national vision is the particular thing we should doubtless call his greatest strength were we preparing agreeably to speak of it also as his visible weakness. Of Balzac's weaknesses, however, it takes some assurance to talk; there is always plenty of time for them; they are the last signs we know him by—such things truly as in other painters of manners often come under the head of mere exuberance of energy. So little in short do they earn the invidious name even when we feel them as defects.

What he did above all was to read the universe, as hard and as loud as he could, *into* the France of his time; his own eyes regarding his work as at once the drama of man and a mirror of the mass of social phenomena the most rounded and registered, most organized and administered, and thereby most exposed to systematic observation and portrayal, that the world had seen. There are happily other interesting societies, but these are for schemes of such an order comparatively loose and incoherent, with more extent and perhaps more variety, but with less of the great enclosed and exhibited quality, less neatness and sharpness of arrangement, fewer categories, subdivisions, juxtapositions. Balzac's France was both inspiring enough for an immense prose epic and reducible enough for a report or a chart. To allow his achievement all its dignity we should doubt-less say also treatable enough for a history, since it was as a patient historian, a Benedictine of the actual, the living painter of his living time, that he regarded himself and handled his material. All painters of manners and fashions, if we will, are historians, even when they least don the uniform: Fielding, Dickens, Thackeray, George Eliot, Hawthorne among ourselves. But the great difference between the great Frenchman and the eminent others is that, with an imagination of the highest power, an unequalled intensity of vision, he saw his subject in the light of science as well, in the light of the bearing of all its parts on each other, and under pressure of a passion for exactitude, an appetite, the appetite of an ogre, for *all* the kinds of facts. We find I think in the union here suggested something like the truth about his genius, the nearest approach to a final account of him. Of imagination on one side all compact, he was on the other an insatiable reporter of the immediate, the material, the current combination, and perpetually moved by the historian's impulse to fix, preserve and explain them. One asks one's self as one reads him what concern the poet has with so much arithmetic and so much criticism, so many statistics and documents, what concern the critic and the economist have with so many passions, characters and adventures. The contradiction is always before us; it springs from the inordinate scale of the author's two faces; it explains more than anything else his eccentricities and difficulties. It accounts for his want of grace, his want of the light-ness associated with an amusing literary form, his bristling surface, his closeness of texture, so rough with richness, yet so productive of the effect we have in mind when we speak of not being able to see the wood for the trees.

A thorough-paced votary, for that matter, can easily afford to declare at once that this confounding duality of character does more things still, or does at least the most important of all—introduces us without mercy (mercy for ourselves I mean) to the oddest truth we could have dreamed of meeting in such a connection. It was certainly *a priori* not to be expected we should feel it of him, but our hero is after all not in his magnifi-cence totally an artist: which would be the strangest thing possible, one must hasten to add, were not the smallness of the practical difference so made even stranger. His endowment and his effect are each so great that the anomaly makes at the most a difference only by adding to his interest for the critic. The critic worth his salt is indiscreetly curious and wants ever to know how and why—whereby Balzac is thus a still rarer case for him, suggesting that exceptional curiosity may have exceptional rewards. The question of what makes the artist on a great scale is interesting enough; but we feel it in Balzac's company to be nothing to the question of what on an equal scale frustrates him. The scattered pieces, the *disjecta membra* of the character are here so numerous and so splendid that they prove misleading; we pile them together, and the heap assuredly is monumental; it forms an overtopping figure. The genius this figure stands for, none the less, is really such a lesson to the artist as perfection itself would be powerless to give; it carries him so much further into the special mystery. Where it carries him, at the same time, I must not in this scant space attempt to say—which would be a loss of the fine thread of my argument. I stick to our point in putting it, more concisely, that the artist of the *Comédie humaine* is half smothered by the historian. Yet it belongs as well to the matter also to meet the question of whether the historian himself may not be an artist—in which case Balzac's catastrophe would seem to lose its excuse. The answer of course is that the reporter, however philosophic, has one law, and the originator, however substantially fed, has another; so that the two laws can with no sort of harmony or congruity make, for the finer sense, a common household. Balzac's catastrophe—so to name it once again—was in this perpetual conflict and final impossibility, an impossibility that explains his defeat on the classic side and extends so far at times as to make us think of his work as, from the point of view of beauty, a tragic waste of effort.

What it would come to, we judge, is that the irreconcilability of the two kinds of law is, more simply expressed, but the irreconcilability of two different ways of composing one's effect. The principle of composition that his free imagination would have, or certainly might have, handsomely imposed on him is perpetually dislocated by the quite opposite principle of the earnest seeker, the inquirer to a useful end, in whom nothing is free but a born antipathy to his yokefellow. Such a production as *Le Curé de village*, the wonderful story of Madame Graslin, so nearly a masterpiece yet so ultimately not one, would be, in this connection, could I take due space for it, a perfect illustration. If, as I say, Madame Graslin's creator was confined by his doom to patches and pieces, no piece is finer than the first half of the book in question, the half in which the picture is determined by his unequalled power of putting people on their feet, planting them before us in their habit as they lived—a faculty nourished by observation as much as one will, but with the inner vision all the while wide awake, the vision for which ideas are as living as facts and assume an equal intensity. This intensity, greatest indeed in the facts, has in Balzac a force all its own, to which none other in any novelist I know can be likened. His touch communicates on the spot to the object, the creature evoked, the hardness and permanence that certain substances, some sorts of stone, acquire by exposure to the air. The hardening medium, for the image soaked in it, is the air of his mind. It would take but little more to make the peopled world of fiction as we know it elsewhere affect us by contrast as a world of rather gray pulp. This mixture of the solid and the vivid is Balzac at his best, and it prevails without a break, without a note not admirably true, in *Le Curé de village*—since I have named that instance—up to the point at which Madame Graslin moves out from Limoges to Montégnac in her ardent passion of penitence, her determination to expiate her strange and undiscovered association with a dark misdeed by living and working for others. Her drama is a particularly inward one, interesting, and in the highest degree, so long as she herself, her nature, her behaviour, her personal history and the relations in which they place her, control the picture and feed our illusion. The firmness with which the author makes them play this part, the whole constitution of the scene and of its developments from the moment we cross the threshold of her dusky stuffy old-time birth-house, is a rare delight, producing in the reader that sense of local and material immersion which is one of Balzac's supreme secrets. What characteristically befalls, however, is that the spell accompanies us but part of the way—only until, at a given moment, his attention ruthlessly transfers itself from inside to outside, from the centre of his subject to its circumference.

This is Balzac caught in the very fact of his monstrous duality, caught in his most complete self-expression. He is clearly quite unwitting that in handing over his *data* to his twin-brother the impassioned economist and surveyor, the insatiate general inquirer and reporter, he is in any sort betraying our confidence, for his good conscience at such times, the spirit of edification in him, is a lesson even to the best of us, his rich robust temperament nowhere more striking, no more marked anywhere the great push of the shoulder with which he makes his theme move, overcharged though it may be like a carrier's van. It is not therefore assuredly that he loses either sincerity or power in putting before us to the last detail such a matter as, in this case, his heroine's management of her property, her tenantry, her economic opportunities and visions, for these are cases in which he never shrinks nor relents, in which positively he stiffens and terribly towers—to remind us again of M. Taine's simplifying word about his being an artist doubled with a man of business. Balzac was indeed doubled if ever a writer was, and to that extent that we almost as often, while we read, feel ourselves thinking of him as a man of business doubled with an artist. Whichever way we turn it the oddity never fails, nor the wonder of the ease with which either character bears the burden of the other. I use the word burden because, as the fusion is never complete—witness in the book before us the fatal break of 'tone', the one unpardonable sin for the novelist—we are beset by the conviction that but for this strangest of dooms one or other of the two partners might, to our relief and to his own, have been disembarrassed. The disembarrassment, for each, by a more insidious fusion, would probably have conduced to the mastership of interest proceeding from form, or at all events to the search for it, that Balzac fails to embody. Perhaps the possibility of an artist constructed on such strong lines is one of those fine things that are not of this world, a mere dream of the fond critical spirit. Let these speculations and condonations at least pass as the amusement, as a result of the high spirits—if high spirits be the word—of the reader feeling himself again in touch. It was not of our author's difficulties—that is of his difficulty, the great one—that I proposed to speak, but of his immense clear action. Even that is not truly an impression of ease, and it is strange and striking that we are in fact so attached by his want of the unity that keeps surfaces smooth and dangers down as scarce to feel sure at any moment that we shall not come back to it with most curiosity. We are never so curious about successes as about interesting failures. The more reason therefore to speak promptly, and once for all, of the scale on which, in its own quarter of his genius, success worked itself out for him.

It is to that I *should* come back—to the infinite reach in him of the painter and the poet. We can never know what might have become of him with less importunity in his consciousness of the machinery of life, of its furniture and fittings, of all that, right and left, he causes to assail us, sometimes almost to suffocation, under the general rubric of *things*. Things, in this sense with him, are at once our delight and our despair; we pass from being inordinately beguiled and convinced by them to feeling that his universe fairly smells too much of them, that the larger ether, the diviner air, is in peril of finding among them scarce room to circulate. His landscapes, his 'local colour'—thick in his pages at a time when it was to be found in his pages almost alone—his towns, his streets, his houses, his Saumurs, Angoulêmes, Guérandes, his great prose Turner-views of the land of the Loire, his rooms, shops, interiors, details of domesticity and traffic, are a short list of the terms into which he saw the real as clamouring to be rendered and into which he rendered it with unequalled authority. It would be doubtless more to the point to make our profit of this consummation than to try to reconstruct a Balzac planted more in the open. We hardly, as the case stands, know most whether to admire in such an example as the short tale of 'La Grenadière' the exquisite feeling for 'natural objects' with which it overflows like a brimming wine-cup, the energy of perception and description which so multiplies them for beauty's sake and for the love of their beauty, or the general wealth of genius that can calculate, or at least count, so little and spend so joyously. The tale practically exists for the sake of the enchanting aspects involved—those of the embowered white house that nestles on its terraced hill above the great French river, and we can think, frankly, of no one else with an equal amount of business on his hands who would either have so put himself out for aspects or made them almost by themselves a living subject. A born son of Touraine, it must be said, he pictures his province, on every pretext and occasion, with filial passion and extraordinary breadth. The prime aspect in his scene all the while, it must be added, is the money aspect. The general money question so loads him up and weighs him down that he moves through the human comedy, from beginning to end, very much in the fashion of a camel, the ship of the desert, surmounted with a cargo. 'Things' for him are francs and centimes more than any others, and I give up as inscrutable, unfathomable, the nature, the peculiar avidity of his interest in them. It makes us wonder again and again what then is the use on Balzac's scale of the divine faculty. The imagination, as we all know, may be employed up to a certain point in inventing uses for money; but its office beyond that point is surely to make us forget that anything so odious exists. This is what Balzac never forgot; his universe goes on expressing itself for him, to its furthest reaches, on its finest sides, in the terms of the market. To say these things, however, is after all to come out where we want, to suggest his extraordinary scale and his terrible completeness. I am not sure that he does not see character too, see passion, motive, personality, as quite in the order of the 'things' we have spoken of. He makes them no less concrete and palpable, handles them no less directly and freely. It is the whole business in fine—that grand total to which he proposed to himself to do high justice—that gives him his place apart, makes him, among the novelists, the largest weightiest presence. There are some of his obsessions—that of the material, that of the financial, that of the 'social', that of the technical, political, civil —for which I feel myself unable to judge him, judgment losing itself unexpectedly in a particular shade of pity. The way to judge him is to try to walk all round him—on which we see how remarkably far we have to go. He is the only member of his order really monumental, the sturdiest-seated mass that rises in our path.

II

We recognize none the less that the finest consequence of these re-established relations is linked with just that appearance in him, that obsession of the actual under so many heads, that makes us look at him, as we would at some rare animal in captivity, between the bars of a cage. It amounts to a sort of suffered doom, since to be solicited by the world from all quarters at once, what is that for the spirit but a denial of escape? We feel his doom to be his want of a private door, and that he felt it, though more obscurely, himself. When we speak of his want of charm therefore we perhaps so surrender the question as but to show our own poverty. If charm, to cut it short, is what he lacks, how comes it that he so touches and holds us that—above all if we be actual or possible fellow-workers—we are uncomfortably conscious of the disloyalty of almost any shade of surrender? We are lodged perhaps by our excited sensibility in a dilemma of which one of the horns is a compassion that savours of patronage; but we must resign ourselves to that by reflecting that our partiality at least takes nothing away from him. It leaves him solidly where he is and only brings us near, brings us to a view of *all* his formidable parts and properties. The conception of the *Comédie humaine* represents them all, and represents them mostly in their felicity and their triumph —or at least the execution does: in spite of which we irresistibly find ourselves thinking of him, in reperusals, as most essentially the victim of a cruel joke. The joke is one of the jokes of fate, the fate that rode him for twenty years at so terrible a pace and with the whip so constantly applied. To have wanted to do so much, to have thought it possible, to have faced and in a manner resisted the effort, to have felt life poisoned and consumed by such a bravery of self-committal—these things form for us in him a face of trouble that, oddly enough, is not appreciably lighted by the fact of his success. It was the having to do so much that was the trap, whatever possibilities of glory might accompany the good faith with which he fell into it. What accompanies *us* as we frequent him is a sense of the deepening ache of that good faith with the increase of his working consciousness, the merciless development of his huge subject and of the rigour of all the conditions. We see the whole thing quite as if Destiny had said to him: 'You want to "do" France, presumptuous, magnificent, miserable man—the France of revolutions, revivals, restorations, of Bonapartes, Bourbons, republics, of war and peace, of blood and romanticism, of violent change and intimate continuity, the France of the first half of your century? Very well; you most distinctly *shall*, and you shall particularly let me hear, even if the great groan of your labour do fill at moments the temple of letters, how you like the job.' We must of course not appear to deny the existence of a robust joy in him, the joy of power and creation, the joy of the observer and the dreamer who finds a use for his observations and his dreams as fast as they come. The *Contes drolatiques* would by themselves sufficiently contradict us, and the savour of the *Contes drolatiques* is not confined to these productions. His work at large tastes of the same kind of humour, and we feel him again and again, like any other great healthy producer of these matters, beguiled and carried along. He would have been, I dare say, the last not to insist that the artist has pleasures forever indescribable; he lived in short in his human comedy with the largest life we can attribute to the largest capacity. There are particular parts of his subject from which, with our sense of his enjoyment of them, we have to check the impulse to call him away—frequently as I confess in this relation that impulse arises.

The relation is with the special element of his spectacle from which he never fully detaches himself, the element, to express it succinctly, of the 'old families' and the great ladies. Balzac frankly revelled in his conception of an aristocracy—a conception that never succeeded in becoming his happiest; whether, objectively, thanks to the facts supplied him by the society he studied, or through one of the strangest deviations of taste that the literary critic is in an important connection likely to encounter. Nothing would in fact be more interesting than to attempt a general measure of the part played in the total comedy, to his imagination, by the old families; and one or two contributions to such an attempt I must not fail presently to make. I glance at them here, however, the delectable class, but as most representing on the author's part free and amused creation; by which too I am far from hinting that the amusement is at all at their expense. It is in their great ladies that the old families most shine out for him, images of strange colour and form, but 'felt', as we say, to their finger-tips, and extraordinarily interesting as a mark of the high predominance—predominance of character, of cleverness, of will, of general 'personality'—that almost every scene of the Comedy attributes to women. It attributes to them in fact a recognized, an uncontested supremacy; it is through them that the hierarchy of old families most expresses itself; and it is as surrounded by them even as some magnificent indulgent pasha by his overflowing seraglio that Balzac sits most at his ease. All of which reaffirms—if it be needed—that his inspiration, and the sense of it, were even greater than his task. And yet such betrayals of spontaneity in him make for an old friend at the end of the chapter no great difference in respect to the pathos—since it amounts to that—of his genius-ridden aspect. It comes to us as we go back to him that his spirit had fairly made of itself a cage in which he was to turn round and round, always unwinding his reel, much in the manner of a criminal condemned to hard labour for life. The cage is simply the complicated but dreadfully definite French world that built itself so solidly in and roofed itself so impenetrably over him.

It is not that, caught there with him though we be, we ourselves prematurely seek an issue: we throw ourselves back, on the contrary, for the particular sense of it, into his ancient superseded comparatively *rococo* and quite patriarchal France—patriarchal in spite of social and political convulsions; into his old-time antediluvian Paris, all picturesque and all workable, full, to the fancy, of an amenity that has passed away; into his intensely differentiated sphere of *la province,* evoked in each sharpest or faintest note of its difference, described systematically as narrow and flat, and yet attaching us if only by the contagion of the author's overflowing sensibility. He feels in his vast exhibition many things, but there is nothing he feels with the communicable shocks and vibrations, the sustained fury of perception—not always a fierceness of judgment, which is another matter—that *la province* excites in him. Half our interest in him springs still from our own sense that, for all the convulsions, the revolutions and experiments that have come and gone, the order he describes is the old order that our sense of the past perversely recurs to as to something happy we have irretrievably missed. His pages bristle with the revelation of the lingering earlier world, the world in which places and people still had their queerness, their strong marks, their sharp type, and in which, as before the platitude that was to come, the observer with an appetite for the salient could by way of precaution fill his lungs. Balzac's appetite for the salient was voracious, yet he came, as it were, in time, in spite of his so often speaking as if what he sees about him is but the last desolation of the modern. His conservatism, the most entire, consistent and convinced that ever was—yet even at that much inclined to whistling in the dark as if to the tune of 'Oh how mediæval I *am*!'—was doubtless the best point of view from which he could rake his field. But if what he sniffed from afar in that position was the extremity of change, we in turn feel both subject and painter drenched with the smell of the past. It is preserved in his work as nowhere else—not vague nor faint nor delicate, but as strong to-day as when first distilled.

It may seem odd to find a conscious melancholy in the fact that a great worker succeeded in clasping his opportunity in such an embrace, this being exactly our usual measure of the felicity of great workers. I speak, I hasten to reassert, all in the name of sympathy—without which it would have been detestable to speak at all; and the sentiment puts its hand instinctively on the thing that makes it least futile. This particular thing then is not in the least Balzac's own hold of his terrible mass of matter; it is absolutely the convolutions of the serpent he had with a magnificent courage invited to wind itself round him. We must use the common image—he had created his Frankenstein monster. It is the fellow-craftsman who can most feel for him—it being apparently possible to read him from another point of view without getting really into his presence. We undergo with him from book to book, from picture to picture, the convolutions of the serpent, we especially whose refined performances are given, as we know, but with the small common or garden snake. I stick to this to justify my image just above of his having been 'caged' by the intensity with which he saw his general matter as a whole. To see it always as a whole is our wise, our virtuous effort, the very condition, as we keep in mind, of superior art. Balzac was in this connection then wise and virtuous to the most exemplary degree; so that he doubtless ought logically but to prompt to complacent reflections. No painter ever saw his general matter nearly so much as a whole. Why is it then that we hover about him, if we are real Balzacians, not with cheerful chatter, but with a consideration deeper in its reach than any mere moralizing? The reason is largely that if you wish with absolute immaculate virtue to look at your matter as a whole and yet remain a theme for cheerful chatter, you must be careful to take some quantity that will not hug you to death. Balzac's active intention was, to vary our simile, a beast with a hundred claws, and the spectacle is in the hugging process of

which, as energy against energy, the beast was capable. Its victim
died of the process at fifty, and if what we see in the long gallery
in which it is mirrored is not the defeat, but the admirable resistance, we none the less never lose the sense that the fighter is shut
up with his fate. He has locked himself in—it is doubtless his
own fault—and thrown the key away. Most of all perhaps the
impression comes—the impression of the adventurer committed
and anxious, but with no retreat—from the so formidably concrete nature of his plastic stuff. When we work in the open, as it
were, our material is not classed and catalogued, so that we have
at hand a hundred ways of being loose, superficial, disingenuous,
and yet passing, to our no small profit, for remarkable. Balzac
had no 'open'; he held that the great central normal fruitful
country of his birth and race, overarched with its infinite social
complexity, yielded a sufficiency of earth and sea and sky. We
seem to see as his catastrophe that the sky, all the same, came
down on him. He couldn't keep it up—in more senses than one.
These are perhaps fine fancies for a critic to weave about a
literary figure of whom he has undertaken to give a plain account;
but I leave them so on the plea that there are relations in which,
for the Balzacian, criticism simply drops out. That is not a
liberty, I admit, ever to be much encouraged; critics in fact are
the only people who have a right occasionally to take it. There
is no such plain account of the *Comédie humaine* as that it
makes us fold up our yard-measure and put away our note-book
quite as we do with some extraordinary character, some mysterious and various stranger, who brings with him his own
standards and his own air. There is a kind of eminent presence
that abashes even the interviewer, moves him to respect and
wonder, makes him, for consideration itself, not insist. This
takes of course a personage sole of his kind. But such a personage precisely is Balzac.

III

By all of which have I none the less felt it but too clear that I
must not pretend in this place to take apart the pieces of his
immense complicated work, to number them or group them or
dispose them about. The most we can do is to pick one up here

and there and wonder, as we weigh it in our hand, at its close compact substance. That is all even M. Taine could do in the longest and most penetrating study of which our author has been the subject. Every piece we handle is so full of stuff, condensed like the edibles provided for campaigns and explorations, positively so charged with distilled life, that we find ourselves dropping it, in certain states of sensibility, as we drop an object unguardedly touched that startles us by being animate. We seem really scarce to want anything to *be* so animate. It would verily take Balzac to detail Balzac, and he has had in fact Balzacians nearly enough affiliated to affront the task with courage. The *Répertoire de la Comédie humaine* of MM. Anatole Cerfberr and Jules Christophe is a closely-printed octavo of 550 pages which constitutes in relation to his characters great and small an impeccable biographical dictionary. His votaries and expositors are so numerous that the Balzac library of comment and research must be, of its type, one of the most copious. M. de Lovenjoul has laboured all round the subject; his *Histoire des œuvres* alone is another crowded octavo of 400 pages; in connection with which I must mention Miss Wormeley, the devoted American translator, interpreter, worshipper, who in the course of her own studies has so often found occasion to differ from M. de Lovenjoul on matters of fact and questions of date and of appreciation. Miss Wormeley, M. Paul Bourget and many others are examples of the passionate piety that our author can inspire. As I turn over the encyclopedia of his characters I note that whereas such works usually commemorate but the ostensibly eminent of a race and time, every creature so much as named in the fictive swarm is in this case preserved to fame : so close is the implication that to have *been* named by such a dispenser of life and privilege is to be, as we say it of baronets and peers, created. He infinitely divided moreover, as we know, he subdivided, altered and multiplied his heads and categories—his 'Vie Parisienne', his 'Vie de province', his 'Vie politique', his 'Parents pauvres', his 'Etudes philosophiques', his 'Splendeurs et misères des courtisanes', his 'Envers de l'histoire contemporaine' and all the rest; so that nominal reference to them becomes the more difficult. Yet without prejudice either to the energy of conception with which he mapped out his theme as with chalk on a huge blackboard, or to the prodigious patience with which he executed his plan, practically filling in with a wealth of illustration, from sources that to this day we fail to make out, every compartment of his table, M. de Lovenjoul draws up the list, year by year, from 1822 to 1848, of his mass of work, giving us thus the measure of the tension represented for him by almost any twelvemonth. It is wholly unequalled, considering the quality of Balzac's show, by any other eminent abundance.

I must be pardoned for coming back to it, for seeming unable to leave it; it enshrouds so interesting a mystery. How was so solidly systematic a literary attack on life to be conjoined with whatever workable minimum of needful intermission, of free observation, of personal experience? Some small possibility of personal experience and disinterested life must, at the worst, from deep within or far without, feed and fortify the strained productive machine. These things were luxuries that Balzac appears really never to have tasted on any appreciable scale. His published letters—the driest and most starved of those of any man of equal distinction—are with the exception of those to Madame de Hanska, whom he married shortly before his death, almost exclusively the audible wail of a galley-slave chained to the oar. M. Zola, in our time, among the novelists, has sacrificed to the huge plan in something of the same manner, yet with goodly modern differences that leave him a comparatively simple instance. His work assuredly has been more nearly dried up by the sacrifice than ever Balzac's was—so miraculously, given the conditions, was Balzac's to escape the anticlimax. Method and system, in the chronicle of the tribe of *Rougon-Macquart*, an economy in itself certainly of the rarest and most interesting, have spread so from centre to circumference that they have ended by being almost the only thing we feel. And then M. Zola has survived and triumphed in his lifetime, has continued and lasted, has piled up and, if the remark be not frivolous, enjoyed in all its *agréments* the reward for which Balzac toiled and sweated in vain. On top of which he will have had also his literary great-grandfather's heroic example to start from and profit by, the positive heritage of a *fils de famille* to enjoy, spend, save, waste. Balzac had frankly no heritage at all but his stiff subject, and by way of model not even in any direct or immediate manner that of the inner light and kindly admonition of his genius. Nothing adds more to the strangeness of his general performance than his having failed so long to find his inner light, groped for it almost ten years, missed it again and again, moved straight away from it, turned his back on it, lived in fine round about it, in a darkness still scarce penetrable, a darkness into which we peep only half to make out the dreary little waste of his numerous *œuvres de jeunesse*. To M. Zola was vouchsafed the good fortune of settling down to the *Rougon-Macquart* with the happiest promptitude; it was as if time for one look about him—and I say it without disparagement to the reach of his look—had sufficiently served his purpose. Balzac moreover might have written five hundred novels without our feeling in him the faintest hint of the breath of doom, if he had only been comfortably capable of conceiving the short cut of the fashion practised by others under his eyes. As Alexandre Dumas and George Sand, illustrious contemporaries, cultivated a personal life and a disinterested consciousness by the bushel, having, for their easier duration, not too consistently known, as the true painter knows it, the obsession of the thing to be done, so Balzac was condemned by his constitution itself, by his inveterately seeing this 'thing to be done' as part and parcel, as of the very essence, of his enterprise. The latter existed for him, as the process worked and hallucination settled, in the form, and the form only, of the thing done, and not in any hocus-pocus about doing. There was no kindly convenient escape for him by the little swinging back-door of the thing *not* done. He desired—no man more—to get out of his obsession, but only at the other end, that is by boring through it. 'How then, thus deprived of the outer air almost as much as if he were gouging a passage for a railway through an Alp, *did* he live?' is the question that haunts us—with the consequence for the most part of promptly meeting its fairly tragic answer. He did *not* live—save in his imagination, or by other aid than he could find there; his imagination was all his experience; he had provably no time for the real thing. This brings us to the rich if simple truth that his imagination alone did the business, carried through both the conception and the execution—as large an effort and as proportionate a success, in all but the vulgar sense, as the faculty when equally handicapped was ever concerned in. Handicapped I say because this interesting fact about him, with the claim it makes, rests on the ground, the high distinction, that more than all the rest of us put together he went in, as we say, for detail, circumstance and specification, proposed to himself *all* the connections of every part of his matter and the full total of the parts. The whole thing, it is impossible not to keep repeating, was what he deemed treatable. One really knows in all imaginative literature no undertaking to compare with it for courage, good faith and sublimity. There, once more, was the necessity that rode him and that places him apart in our homage. It is no light thing to have been condemned to become provably sublime. And looking through, or trying to, at what is beneath and behind, we are left benevolently uncertain if the predominant quantity be audacity or innocence.

It is of course inevitable at this point to seem to hear the colder critic promptly take us up. He undertook the whole thing—oh exactly, the ponderous person! But *did* he 'do' the whole thing, if you please, any more than sundry others of fewer pretensions? The retort to this it can only be a positive joy to make, so high a note instantly sounds as an effect of the inquiry. Nothing is more interesting and amusing than to find one's self recognizing both that Balzac's pretensions were immense, portentous, and that yet, taking him—and taking *them*—altogether, they but minister in the long run to our fondness. They affect us not only as the endearing eccentricities of a person we greatly admire, but fairly as the very condition of his having become such a person. We take them thus in the first place for the very terms of his plan, and in the second for a part of that high robustness and that general richness of nature which made him in face of such a project believe in himself. One would really scarce have liked to see such a job as *La Comédie humaine* tackled without swagger. To think of the thing really as practicable *was* swagger, and of the very rarest order. So to think assuredly implied pretensions, pretensions that risked showing as monstrous should the enterprise fail to succeed. It is for the colder critic to take the trouble to make out that of the two parties to it the body of pretension remains greater than the success. One may put it moreover at the worst for him, may recognize that it is in the matter of opinion still more than in the matter of knowledge that Balzac offers himself as universally competent. He has flights of judgment—on subjects the most special as well as the most general—that are vertiginous and on his alighting from which we greet him with a special indulgence. We can easily imagine him to respond, confessing humorously—if he had only time—to such a benevolent understanding smile as would fain hold our own eyes a moment. Then it is that he would most show us his scheme and his necessities and how in operation they all hang together. *Naturally* everything about everything, though how he had time to learn it is the last thing he has time to tell us; which matters the less, moreover, as it is not over the question of his knowledge that we sociably invite him, as it were (and remembering the two augurs behind the altar) to wink at us for a sign. His convictions it is that are his great pardonable 'swagger'; to them in particular I refer as his general operative condition, the constituted terms of his experiment, and not less as his consolation, his support, his amusement by the way. They embrace everything in the world— that is in his world of the so parti-coloured France of his age: religion, morals, politics, economics, physics, esthetics, letters, art, science, sociology, every question of faith, every branch of research. They represent thus his equipment of ideas, those ideas of which it will never do for a man who aspires to constitute a State to be deprived. He must take them with him as an ambassador extraordinary takes with him secretaries, uniforms, stars and garters, a gilded coach and a high assurance. Balzac's opinions are his gilded coach, in which he is more amused than anything else to feel himself riding, but which is indispensably concerned in getting him over the ground. What more inevitable than that they should be intensely Catholic, intensely monarchical, intensely saturated with the real genius—as between 1830 and 1848 he believed it to be—of the French character and French institutions?

Nothing is happier for us than that he should have enjoyed his outlook before the first half of the century closed. He could then still treat his subject as comparatively homogeneous. Any country could have a Revolution—every country *had* had one. A Restoration was merely what a revolution involved, and the Empire had been for the French but a revolutionary incident, in addition to being by good luck for the novelist an immensely pictorial one. He was free therefore to arrange the background of the comedy in the manner that seemed to him best to suit anything so great; in the manner at the same time prescribed according to his contention by the noblest traditions. The church, the throne, the noblesse, the bourgeoisie, the people, the peasantry, all in their order and each solidly kept in it, these were precious things, things his superabundant insistence on the price of which is what I refer to as his exuberance of opinion. It was a luxury for more reasons than one, though one, presently to be mentioned, handsomely predominates. The meaning of that exchange of intelligences in the rear of the oracle which I have figured for him with the perceptive friend bears simply on his pleading guilty to the purport of the friend's discrimination. The point the latter makes with him—a beautiful cordial critical point—is that he truly cares for nothing in the world, thank goodness, so much as for the passions and embroilments of men and women, the free play of character and the sharp revelation of type, all the real stuff of drama and the natural food of novelists. Religion, morals, politics, economics, esthetics would be thus, as systematic matter, very well in their place, but quite secondary and subservient. Balzac's attitude is again and again that he cares for the adventures and emotions because, as his last word, he cares for the good and the greatness of the State—which is where his swagger, with a whole society on his hands, comes in. What we on our side in a thousand places gratefully feel is that he cares for his monarchical and hierarchical and ecclesiastical society because it rounds itself for his mind into the most congruous and capacious theatre for the repertory of his innumerable comedians. It has above all, for a painter abhorrent of the superficial, the inestimable benefit of the accumulated, of strong marks and fine shades, contrasts and complications. There had certainly been since 1789 dispersals and confusions enough, but the thick tradition, no more at the most than half smothered, lay under them all. So the whole of his faith and no small part of his working omniscience were neither more nor less than that historic sense which I have spoken of as the spur of his invention and which he possessed as no other novelist has done. We immediately feel that to name it in connection with him is to answer every question he suggests and to account for each of his idiosyncrasies in turn. The novel, the tale, however brief, the passage, the sentence by itself, the situation, the person, the place, the motive exposed, the speech reported—these things were in his view history, with the absoluteness and the dignity of history. This is the source both of his weight and of his wealth. What is the historic sense after all but animated, but impassioned knowledge seeking to enlarge itself? I have said that his imagination did the whole thing, no other explanation—no reckoning of the possibilities of personal saturation—meeting the mysteries of the case. Therefore his imagination achieved the miracle of absolutely resolving itself into multifarious knowledge. Since history proceeds by documents he constructed, as he needed them, the documents too—fictive sources that imitated the actual to the life. It was of course a terrible business, but at least in the light of it his claims to creatorship are justified—which is what was to be shown.

(ii) Ivan Turgenev

From *Library of World's Best Literature*, ed. Charles Dudley Warner, International Society, New York, 1897, pp. 117–23.

There is perhaps no novelist of alien race who more naturally than Ivan Turgenev inherits a niche in a Library for English readers; and this is not because of any advance or concession that in his peculiar artistic independence he ever made, or could dream of making, such readers, but because it was one of the effects of his peculiar genius to give him, even in his lifetime, a special place in the regard of foreign publics. His position is in this respect singular; for it is his Russian savor that as much as anything has helped generally to domesticate him.

Born in 1818, at Orel in the heart of Russia, and dying in 1883, at Bougival near Paris, he had spent in Germany and France the latter half of his life; and had incurred in his own country in some degree the reprobation that is apt to attach to the absent—the penalty they pay for such extension or such beguilement as they may have happened to find over the border. He belonged to the class of large rural proprietors of land and serfs; and with his ample patrimony, offered one of the few examples of literary labor achieved in high independence of the question of gain—a character that he shares with his illustrious contemporary Tolstoy, who is of a type in other respects so different. It may give us an idea of his primary situation to imagine some large Virginian or Carolinian slaveholder, during the first half of the century, inclining to 'Northern' views; and becoming (though not predominantly under pressure of these, but rather by the operation of an exquisite genius) the great American novelist—one of the great novelists of the world. Born under a social and political order sternly repressive, all Turgenev's deep instincts, all his moral passion, placed him on the liberal side; with the consequence that early in life, after a period spent at a German university, he found himself, through the accident of a trifling public utterance, under such suspicion in high places as to be sentenced to a term of tempered exile—confinement to his own estate. It was partly under these circumstances perhaps that he gathered material for the work from the appearance of which his reputation dates—*A Sportsman's Sketches*, published in two volumes in 1852. This admirable collection of impressions of homely country life, as the old state of servitude had made it, is often spoken of as having borne to the great decree of Alexander II the relation borne by Mrs Beecher Stowe's famous novel to the emancipation of the Southern slaves. Incontestably, at any rate, Turgenev's rustic studies sounded, like *Uncle Tom's Cabin*, a particular hour: with the difference, however, of not having at the time produced an agitation—of having rather presented the case with an art too insidious for instant recognition, an art that stirred the depths more than the surface.

The author was designated promptly enough, at any rate, for such influence as might best be exercised at a distance: he travelled, he lived abroad; early in the sixties he was settled in Germany; he acquired property at Baden-Baden, and spent there the last years of the prosperous period—in the history of the place—of which the Franco-Prussian War was to mark the violent term. He cast in his lot after that event mainly with the victims of the lost cause; setting up a fresh home in Paris—near which city he had, on the Seine, a charming alternate residence —and passing in it, and in the country, save for brief revisitations, the remainder of his days. His friendships, his attachments, in the world of art and of letters, were numerous and distinguished; he never married; he produced, as the years went on, without precipitation or frequency; and these were the years during which his reputation gradually established itself as, according to the phrase, European—a phrase denoting in this case, perhaps, a public more alert in the United States even than elsewhere.

Tolstoy, his junior by ten years, had meanwhile come to fruition; though, as in fact happened, it was not till after Turgenev's death that the greater fame of *War and Peace* and of *Anna Karenina* began to be blown about the world. One of the last acts of the elder writer, performed on his death-bed, was to address to the other (from whom for a considerable term he had been estranged by circumstances needless to reproduce) an appeal to return to the exercise of the genius that Tolstoy had already so lamentably, so monstrously forsworn. 'I am on my death-bed; there is no possibility of my recovery. I write you expressly to tell you how happy I have been to be your contemporary, and to utter my last, my urgent prayer. Come back, my friend, to your literary labors. That gift came to you from the source from which all comes to us. Ah, how happy I should be could I think you would listen to my entreaty! My friend, great writer of our Russian land, respond to it, obey it!' These words, among the most touching surely ever addressed by one great spirit to another, throw an indirect light—perhaps I may even say a direct one—upon the nature and quality of Turgenev's artistic temperament; so much so that I regret being without opportunity, in this place, to gather such aid for a portrait of him as might be supplied by following out the unlikeness between the pair. It would be too easy to say that Tolstoy was, from the Russian point of view, for home consumption, and Turgenev for foreign : *War and Peace* has probably had more readers in Europe and America than *A Nest of Gentlefolk* or *On the Eve* or *Smoke*—a circumstance less detrimental than it may appear to my claim of our having, in the Western world, supremely adopted the author of the latter works. Turgenev is in a peculiar degree what I may call the novelists' novelist—an artistic influence extraordinarily valuable and ineradicably established. The perusal of Tolstoy—a wonderful mass of life—is an immense event, a kind of splendid accident, for each of us : his name represents nevertheless no such eternal spell of method, no such quiet irresistibility of presentation, as shines, close to us and lighting our possible steps, in that of his precursor. Tolstoy is a reflector as vast as a natural lake; a monster harnessed to his great subject—all human life!—as an elephant might be harnessed, for purposes of traction, not to a carriage, but to a coach-house. His own case is prodigious, but his example for others dire: disciples not elephantine he can only mislead and betray.

One by one, for thirty years, with a firm, deliberate hand, with intervals and patiences and waits, Turgenev pricked in his sharp outlines. His great external mark is probably his concision: an ideal he never threw over—it shines most perhaps even when he is least brief—and that he often applied with a rare felicity. He has masterpieces of a few pages; his perfect things are sometimes his least prolonged. He abounds in short tales, episodes clipped as by the scissors of Atropos; but for a direct translation of the whole we have still to wait—depending meanwhile upon the French and German versions, which have been, instead of the original text (thanks to the paucity among us of readers of Russian), the source of several published in English. For the novels and *A Sportsman's Sketches* we depend upon the nine volumes (1897) of Mrs Garnett. We touch here upon the remarkable side, to our vision, of the writer's fortune—the anomaly of his having constrained to intimacy even those who are shut out from the enjoyment of his medium, for whom that question is positively prevented from existing. Putting aside extrinsic intimations, it is impossible to read him without the conviction of his being, in the vividness of his own tongue, of the strong type of those made to bring home to us the happy truth of the unity, in a generous talent, of material and form—of their being inevitable faces of the same medal; the type of those, in a word, whose example deals death to the perpetual clumsy assumption that subject and style are—æsthetically speaking, or in the living work—different and separate things. We are conscious, reading him in a language not his own, of not being reached by his personal tone, his individual accent.

It is a testimony therefore to the intensity of his presence, that so much of his particular charm does reach us; that the mask turned to us has, even without his expression, still so much beauty. It is the beauty (since we must try to formulate) of the finest presentation of the familiar. His vision is of the world of character and feeling, the world of the relations life throws up at every hour and on every spot; he deals little, on the whole, in the miracles of chance—the hours and spots over the edge of time and space; his air is that of the great central region of passion and motive, of the usual, the inevitable, the intimate— the intimate for weal or woe. No theme that he ever chooses but strikes us as full; yet with all have we the sense that their animation comes from within, and is not pinned to their backs like the pricking objects used of old in the horse-races of the Roman carnival, to make the animals run. Without a patch of 'plot' to draw blood, the story he mainly tells us, the situation he mainly gives, runs as if for dear life. His first book was practically full evidence of what, if we have to specify, is finest in him—the effect, for the commonest truth, of an exquisite envelope of poetry. In this medium of feeling—full, as it were, of all the echoes and shocks of the universal danger and need— everything in him goes on; the sense of fate and folly and pity and wonder and beauty. The tenderness, the humor, the variety of *A Sportsman's Sketches* revealed on the spot an observer with a rare imagination. These faculties had attached themselves, together, to small things and to great: to the misery, the simplicity, the piety, the patience, of the unemancipated peasant; to all the natural wonderful life of earth and air and winter and summer and field and forest; to queer apparitions of country neighbors, of strange local eccentrics; to old-world practices and superstitions; to secrets gathered and types disinterested and impressions absorbed in the long, close contacts with man and nature involved in the passionate pursuit of game. Magnificent in stature and original vigor, Turgenev, with his love of the chase, or rather perhaps of the inspiration he found in it, would have been the model of the mighty hunter, had not such an image been a little at variance with his natural mildness, the softness that often accompanies the sense of an extraordinary reach of limb and play of muscle. He was in person the model rather of the strong man at rest: massive and towering, with the voice of innocence and the smile almost of childhood. What seemed still more of a contradiction to so much of him, however, was that his work was all delicacy and fancy, penetration and compression.

If I add, in their order of succession, *Rudin, Fathers and Sons, Spring Floods*, and *Virgin Soil*, to the three novels I have (also in their relation of time) named above, I shall have indicated the larger blocks of the compact monument, with a base resting deep and interstices well filled, into which that work disposes itself. The list of his minor productions is too long to draw out: I can only mention, as a few of the most striking—*A Correspondence*, *The Wayside Inn*, *The Brigadier*, *The Dog*, *The Jew*, *Visions*, *Mumu*, *Three Meetings*, *A First Love*, *The Forsaken*, *Assia*, *The Journal of a Superfluous Man*, *The Story of Lieutenant Yergunov*, *A King Lear of the Steppe*. The first place among his novels would be difficult to assign: general opinion probably hesitates between *A Nest of Gentlefolk* and *Fathers and Sons*. My own predilection is great for the exquisite *On the Eve*; though I admit that in such company it draws no supremacy from being exquisite. What is less contestable is that *Virgin Soil* —published shortly before his death, and the longest of his fiction—has, although full of beauty, a minor perfection.

Character, character expressed and exposed, is in all these things what we inveterately find. Turgenev's sense of it was the great light that artistically guided him; the simplest account of him is to say that the mere play of it constitutes in every case his sufficient drama. No one has had a closer vision, or a hand at once more ironic and more tender, for the individual figure. He sees it with its minutest signs and tricks—all its heredity of idiosyncracies, all its particulars of weakness and strength, of ugliness and beauty, of oddity and charm; and yet it is of his essence that he sees it in the general flood of life, steeped in its relations and contacts, struggling or submerged, a hurried particle in the stream. This gives him, with his quiet method, his extraordinary breadth; dissociates his rare power to particularize from dryness or hardness, from any peril of caricature. He understands so much that we almost wonder he can express anything; and his expression is indeed wholly in absolute projection, in illustration, in giving of everything the unexplained and irresponsible specimen. He is of a spirit so human that we almost wonder at his control of his matter; of a pity so deep and so general that we almost wonder at his curiosity. The element of poetry in him is constant, and yet reality stares through it without the loss of a wrinkle. No one has more of that sign of the born novelist which resides in a respect unconditioned for the freedom and vitality, the absoluteness when summoned, of the creatures he invokes; or is more superior to the strange and

second-rate policy of explaining or presenting them by reprobation or apology—of taking the short cuts and anticipating the
emotions and judgments about them that should be left, at the
best, to the perhaps not most intelligent reader. And yet his
system, as it may summarily be called, of the mere particularized report, has a lucidity beyond the virtue of the cruder
moralist.

If character, as I say, is what he gives us at every turn, I
should speedily add that he offers it not in the least as a synonym,
in our Western sense, of resolution and prosperity. It wears the
form of the almost helpless detachment of the short-sighted
individual soul; and the perfection of his exhibition of it is in
truth too often but the intensity of what, for success, it just does
not produce. What works in him most is the question of the will;
and the most constant induction he suggests, bears upon the sad
figure that principle seems mainly to make among his country-
men. He had seen—he suggests to us—its collapse in a thousand
quarters; and the most general tragedy, to his view, is that of
its desperate adventures and disasters, its inevitable abdication
and defeat. But if the men, for the most part, let it go, it takes
refuge in the other sex; many of the representatives of which, in
his pages, are supremely strong—in wonderful addition, in
various cases, to being otherwise admirable. This is true of such
a number—the younger women, the girls, the 'heroines' in
especial—that they form in themselves, on the ground of moral
beauty, of the finest distinction of soul, one of the most striking
groups the modern novel has given us. They are heroines to the
letter, and of a heroism obscure and undecorated: it is almost
they alone who have the energy to determine and to act. Elena,
Lisa, Tatyana, Gemma, Marianna—we can write their names
and call up their images, but I lack space to take them in turn.
It is by a succession of the finest and tenderest touches that they
live; and this, in all Turgenev's work, is the process by which
he persuades and succeeds.

It was his own view of his main danger that he sacrificed too
much to detail; was wanting in composition, in the gift that con-
duces to unity of impression. But no novelist is closer and more
cumulative; in none does distinction spring from a quality of
truth more independent of everything but the subject, but the
idea itself. This idea, this subject, moreover—a spark kindled

by the innermost friction of things—is always as interesting as an unopened telegram. The genial freedom—with its exquisite delicacy—of his approach to this 'innermost' world, the world of our finer consciousness, has in short a side that I can only describe and commemorate as nobly disinterested; a side that makes too many of his rivals appear to hold us in comparison by violent means, and introduce us in comparison to vulgar things.

11 N. A. Dobrolyubov

When Will the Day Come? *
On the Eve,
a novel by I. S. Turgenev, Russky Vestnik,
Nos. 1-2, 1860

First published in *Sovremennik*, No. 3, 1860. From *Selected Philosophical Essays*, trans. Fineberg, Foreign Languages Publishing House, Moscow, 1948, pp. 388-438.

> Schlage die Trommel und fürchte dich nicht.
> *Heine.*

Aesthetic criticism has now become the hobby of sentimental young ladies. In conversation with them the devotees of pure art may hear many subtle and true observations, and then they can sit down and write a review in the following style. 'Here is the content of Mr Turgenev's new novel' (follows a summary of the story). 'This faint sketch is enough to show how much life and poetry, of the freshest and most fragrant kind, is to be found in this novel. But only by reading the novel itself can one obtain a true idea of that feeling for the most subtle poetical shades of life, of that keen psychological analysis, of that profound understanding of the hidden streams and currents of public thought, and of that friendly and yet bold attitude towards reality which constitute the distinguishing features of Mr Turgenev's talent. See, for example, how subtly he has noted these psychological features' (then comes a repetition of a part of the summary, followed by an excerpt from the novel); 'read this wonderful scene which is depicted with such grace and charm' (excerpt); 'recall this poetical living picture' (excerpt), 'or this lofty and bold delineation' (excerpt). 'Does not this penetrate to the depths of one's soul, compel the heart to beat faster, animate and ornament our lives, exalt before us human dignity and the great, eternal significance of the sacred ideas of truth, goodness and beauty! *Comme c'est joli, comme c'est delicieux!'*

* [This article has had, for reasons of space, to be cut by more than a third; but its essential points and proportions have been maintained.]

We are unable to write pleasant and harmless reviews of this sort because we are little acquainted with sentimental young ladies. Openly confessing this, and disclaiming the role of 'cultivator of the aesthetic tastes of the public', we have chosen for ourselves a different task, one more modest and more commensurate with our abilities. We simply wish to sum up the data that are scattered throughout the author's work, and which we accept as accomplished facts, as phenomena of life that confront us. This is not a complicated task, but it is one that must be undertaken because, what with the multiplicity of their occupations and the need for relaxation, people are rarely willing to go into all the details of a literary production, to analyse, verify and put in their proper places all the figures that combine to make this intricate report on one of the sides of our social life and then to ponder over the result, over what it promises, and what obligations it imposes upon us. But such verification and reflection will be very useful in the case of Mr Turgenev's new novel.

We know that the devotees of pure aesthetics will at once accuse us of wanting to thrust our own views upon the author and to set tasks for his talent. We shall therefore make the following reservation, tedious though it may be to do so. No, we have no wish to thrust anything upon the author; we say at the very outset that we do not know what object the author had in view, or what views prompted him to write the story that constitutes the contents of the novel *On the Eve*. The important thing for us is not so much what the author *wanted* to say, as what he *said*, even unintentionally, simply in the process of truthfully reproducing the facts of life. We prize every talented production precisely because it enables us to study the facts of our own lives which, without these facts are so little exposed to the gaze of the ordinary observer. To this day there is no publicity in our lives except official publicity; everywhere we encounter not living but official persons, persons who are serving in one sphere or another; in government offices we meet clerks, at balls we meet dancers, in clubs—cardplayers, in theatres—hairdressers' clients, and so forth. Everybody hides his spiritual life as far away from the public gaze as possible; everybody looks at us as much as to say: 'I have come here to dance, or to show my coiffure. That being the case, be satisfied with the fact that I am going about my business, and please don't take it into your head to question me about my feelings and my ideas.' And indeed, nobody makes any attempt to make anybody confess, nobody is interested in anyone; everybody in society goes his own way, regretting that he must come together with others on official occasions as, for example, a first night at the opera, an official banquet, or at a meeting of some committee or other. Under these circumstances, how is a man who does not devote himself exclusively to the observation of social habits to study and learn what life is? On top of all this there is the variety, even opposites, in the different circles and classes of our society! Ideas which have become banal and out of date in one circle are still hotly debated in another; what some regard as inadequate and weak, others regard as excessively sharp and bold, and so forth. We have no other way of knowing what is defeated, what is victorious, or what is beginning to permeate and predominate in the moral life of society than through literature, and mainly through its artistic productions. The author-artist, although not troubling to draw any general conclusions about the state of public thought and morality, is always able to grasp their most essential features, throw a vivid light upon them and place them before the eyes of thinking people. That is why we think that as soon as it is recognized that an author-artist possesses talent, *i.e.*, the ability to feel and depict the phenomena with lifelike truth, this very recognition creates legitimate ground for taking his productions as a basis for the discussion of the milieu, the epoch, which prompted the author to write this or that production. And here the criterion of the author's talent will be the breadth of his conception of life, the degree to which the images he has created are permanent and comprehensive.

We have deemed it necessary to say this in order to justify our method, namely, to interpret the phenomena of life itself on the basis of a literary production, without attributing to the author any preconceived ideas or aims. The reader perceives that we regard as important precisely those productions in which life is expressed as it is and not according to a program previously drawn up by the author. We did not discuss *A Thousand Souls*,* for example, because, in our opinion, the whole social side of this novel was forcibly adjusted to a preconceived idea. Hence,

* [A novel by A. F. Pisemsky.]

there is nothing to discuss here except the degree of skill the author displayed in composing his work. It is impossible to rely on the truth and living reality of the facts delineated by the author because his inner attitude towards these facts is not simple and truthful. We see an entirely different attitude of an author towards his subject in Mr Turgenev's new novel, as indeed we see in most of his novels. In *On the Eve* we see the inescapable influence of the natural course of social life and thought, to which the author's own thoughts and imagination were involuntarily adjusted.

In expressing the view that the main task of the literary critic is to explain the phenomena of reality which called a given artistic production into being, we must add that in the case of Mr Turgenev's novels this task acquires a special meaning. Mr Turgenev may be rightly described as the painter and bard of the morality and philosophy which have reigned among the educated section of our society during the past twenty years. He very soon divined the new requirements, the new ideas that were permeating the public mind, and in his works he, as a rule, devoted (as much as circumstances would permit) attention to the question that was about to come up next, and which was already beginning vaguely to stir society. We hope to trace the whole of Mr Turgenev's literary activity on a future occasion, and so we shall not deal with it at length now; we shall only say that it is to this sensitiveness that the author displays towards the living strings of society, to this ability of his to respond forthwith to every noble thought and honest sentiment which is only just beginning to penetrate the minds of the best people, that we largely ascribe the success which Mr Turgenev has always enjoyed among the Russian public. It goes without saying that his literary talent too has contributed a great deal to this success, but our readers know that Mr Turgenev's talent is not of the Titanic kind, which by sheer poetic expression alone captivates you, thrills you and compels you to sympathize with a phenomenon, or an idea, with which you were not in the least inclined to sympathize. Not a turbulent and impulsive power but, on the contrary, gentleness and a kind of poetic moderation are the characteristic features of his talent. That is why we believe that he could not have roused the general sympathy of the public had he dealt with questions and requirements that were totally alien to his readers, or which had not yet arisen in society. Some readers would have noted the charm of the poetical descriptions in his novels, the subtlety and profundity with which he portrayed different individuals and situations; but there can be no doubt that this alone would not have been enough to make the author's success and fame permanent. Even the most attractive and talented narrator must, if he fails to display this responsive attitude towards modern times, share the fate of Mr Fet, whom people praised at one time, but of whose work only about half of his best poems are remembered by only about a half a score of admirers. It is his responsive attitude towards modern times that has saved Mr Turgenev and has guaranteed him permanent success among the reading public. A certain profound critic once rebuked Mr Turgenev for having in his works so strongly reflected 'all the vacillations of public thought'. We, on the contrary, regard this as the most vital feature of Mr Turgenev's talent; and we believe that it is this feature of his talent that explains the sympathy, almost enthusiasm, with which all his productions have been received up till now.

Thus, we may boldly assert that if Mr Turgenev touches upon any question in a story of his, if he has depicted any new aspect of social relationships, it can be taken as a guarantee that this question is rising, or soon will rise, in the mind of the educated section of society; that this new aspect is beginning to make itself felt and will soon stand out sharply and clearly before the eyes of all. That is why, every time a story by Mr Turgenev appears, our curiosity is roused and we ask: what sides of life are depicted in it, what question does it touch upon? [...]

[...] In Mr Turgenev's new novel we meet with situations and types that differ from those we have been accustomed to find in his previous works. The social demand for action, for real action, incipient contempt for dead, abstract principles and passive virtue are expressed in the whole structure of the new novel. Everybody who reads this essay has undoubtedly read *On the Eve*, hence, instead of summarizing the story we shall only make a brief sketch of its principal characters.

The heroine of the story is a girl with a serious turn of mind, possessing an energetic will and a heart filled with humane strivings. Her development has been very peculiar owing to special domestic circumstances.

Her father and mother were very narrow-minded but not vicious; her mother was even favorably distinguished for her kindness and soft heart. From her childhood Helena* was free from the yoke of that domestic despotism which crushes so many beautiful characters in the bud. She grew up alone, without friends, absolutely free: no formalism restricted her. Nikolai Artyomich Stakhov, her father, was a rather dull-witted person, but he regarded himself as a philosopher of the sceptical school and kept himself aloof from domestic life, at first only admiring his little Helena, who revealed unusual abilities at an early age. While she was little, Helena worshipped her father. But Stakhov's relations with his wife were not altogether satisfactory. He married Anna Vassilyevna for her dowry, he had no feeling towards her whatever, he treated her almost with contempt and left her for the society of Augustina Christianovna, who fooled and fleeced him. Anna Vassilyevna, a sick and sensitive woman, after the type of Maria Dmitriyevna in *A Nest of Gentlefolk*, meekly bore her lot but could not refrain from complaining about it to everybody at home and, incidentally, even to her daughter. Thus, Helena soon became her mother's confidante, one to whom to pour out her woes, and involuntarily she became the judge between her and her father. Owing to Helena's impressionable nature this greatly influenced the development of her inner strength. The less she could do practically in this matter the more work she found for her mind and imagination. Compelled from her earliest years to watch the relationships between those she loved, participating with both heart and mind in the explanation of these relationships and in passing judgment upon them, Helena early trained herself to think independently and to form a conscious opinion about everything around her. The domestic relationships of the Stakhov's are very briefly sketched in Mr Turgenev's novel, but this sketch gives us profoundly true indications which explain a great deal in the early development of Helena's character. She was an impressionable and clever child; her position between her mother and father early prompted her to serious reflection and early raised her to an independent, authoritative role. She placed herself on the level of her elders and put them before the bar of her judgment.

* [Helena, Elena or Yelena are alternative transliterations of the Russian name.]

Her reflections were not cold, however; her whole soul merged with them, because the matter affected people who were extremely close and extremely dear to her, whose relationships were bound up with her most sacred sentiments and her most vital interests. That is why her reflections directly affected the disposition of her heart. She ceased to worship her father and acquired a passionate attachment to her mother, whom she regarded as an oppressed and suffering being. Her love for her mother, however, did not rouse the contrary feeling of hostility towards her father, who was neither a villain, a positive fool nor a domestic tyrant. He was just an ordinary mediocrity, and Helena cooled towards him instinctively and later, perhaps, consciously decided that there was nothing lovable about him. But soon she observed that her mother too was a mediocrity, and passionate love and respect for her gave way in her heart to a mere sense of pity and condescension. Mr Turgenev very aptly describes her attitude towards her mother when he says that she 'treated her mother as if she were an ailing grandmother'. The mother admitted to herself that she was beneath her daughter; the father, however, as soon as his daughter began to surpass him in intellect, which was not a very difficult matter, cooled towards her, decided that she was queer, and dropped her.

Meanwhile Helena's feelings of sympathy and humanity grew and expanded. Of course, the pain she felt at the sight of the suffering of others was originally caused in her childish heart by the downtrodden appearance of her mother long before she began to understand what the trouble was about. This pain was always with her, it accompanied her at every step she took in her development, it gave an exceptionally pensive bent to her thoughts, and it gradually called forth and defined in her active strivings, all of which she directed towards a passionate and irresistible yearning for the good and happiness of all. [...]

[...] But the active strivings of the soul mature and grow strong only if there is scope and freedom for them. One must test one's strength several times, suffer reverses and collisions, learn to know what various efforts cost and how various obstacles have to be overcome in order to acquire the courage and determination which are necessary for an active struggle, in order to learn one's strength and be able to find commensurate work for it. Notwithstanding the freedom of her development,

Helena could not find sufficient outlets for her strength and was unable to satisfy her strivings. Nobody prevented her from doing what she wanted to do, but there was nothing to do. She was not restricted by the pedantry of systematic education and was therefore able to educate herself without acquiring the multitude of prejudices that are inseparable from systems, courses and routine education in general. She read a great deal and with interest, but reading alone could not satisfy her; the only effect it had upon her was that her power of reasoning developed more than her other powers, and her intellectual requirements even began to exceed the living strivings of her heart. Nor could the giving of alms, tending pups and kittens, and protecting flies from spiders satisfy her. When she grew older and wiser she could not fail to see how shallow this activity was, and moreover, these occupations called for very little effort and could not fill her life. She wanted something bigger, something higher, but what it was she did not know; even if she did know she could not set to work at it. This explains why she was always in such a state of agitation, why she was always expecting and looking for something, and that is why her very appearance became so peculiar.

'Her whole being, the expression on her face, her *attentive and somewhat timid, clear, but unsteady gaze, her smile which seemed to be strained, and her low uneven voice* expressed something nervous, electrical, something *impulsive and hasty. . . .*'

Clearly, she is still beset by vague doubts about herself, she has not yet determined her role. She has realized what she does not need and remains proud and independent amidst the habitual circumstances of her life; but she does not yet know what she needs, and above all she does not understand what she must do to achieve what she needs, and that is why her whole being is strained, uneven and impulsive. She is waiting, living on the eve of something. . . . She is ready for vigorous, energetic activity, but she is unable to set to work by herself, alone.

This timidity, this virtual passivity of the heroine combined with her abundance of inner strength and her tormenting thirst for activity astonishes us and makes us think that there is something unfinished about Helena's personality. But this very unfinished state of Helena's personality, her lack of a practical role, reveals precisely the living connection between Mr Turgenev's heroine and the whole of the educated section of our society. In the way Helena's character is conceived, at bottom, it is an exceptional one, and if she were indeed presented everywhere as expressing her views and strivings she would have been alien to Russian society and would not have had that intimate meaning for us that she has now. She would have been a fictitious character, a plant unskilfully transplanted to our soil from some foreign land. But Mr Turgenev's true sense of reality did not permit him to make the practical activities of his heroine fully coincide with her theoretical concepts and the inner promptings of her soul. Our public life does not yet provide an author with the materials for this. At present we observe throughout our society only an awakening desire to get down to real work, a realization of the banality of the various beautiful toys, of the lofty phrases and inert forms with which we have amused and fooled ourselves for so long. But we have not yet emerged from the sphere in which we were able to sleep so peacefully, and we do not yet know very well where the exit is; if anybody does know, he is still afraid to open the door. This difficult and painful transitional state of society inevitably leaves its impress on works of art that are produced under these conditions. There may be individual strong characters in society, individuals may achieve a high level of moral development, and so such personalities appear in literary productions. But all this remains only in the portrayal of the characters of these persons, it is not carried over into life; the possibility of its existence is assumed, but it is not seen in real life. [...]

[...] In Mr Turgenev's Helena we now see an attempt to create an energetic and active character, and it cannot be said that the author's portrayal of this character is unsuccessful. If we have rarely met women like Helena, many of us, of course, have observed even in the most ordinary women the embryo of one or other of the essential features of Helena's character, the potential development of many of her strivings. As an ideal personage, constituted of the finest elements that are developing in our society, Helena is intelligible and close to us. Her strivings are defined for us very clearly; she seems to serve as an answer to the question and doubts of Olga, who, while living with Stolz, is yearning and longing for something which she herself cannot define. The portrait of Helena explains this longing, which inevitably overcomes every decent Russian, no matter how good his own circumstances may be. Helena is thirsting to perform good deeds, she is looking for the means to create happiness around herself, because she cannot conceive of herself enjoying peace of mind, let alone happiness, if she is surrounded by suffering, unhappiness, poverty and the humiliation of her dear ones.

But what activities commensurate with these inner demands could Mr Turgenev provide for his heroine? It is difficult to answer this question even in the abstract, and it is probably still less possible for a Russian author of the present day to create such activities in his art. There is no scope for such activities, and the author is, willy-nilly, obliged to compel his heroine to display her lofty strivings in a shallow way, by giving alms and saving abandoned kittens. She is unable, and afraid, to undertake activities which call for great strain and struggle. All around her she sees one thing oppressing another, and precisely because of her humane and sympathetic disposition she tries to keep aloof from everything in order to avoid oppressing others herself. At home her influence is not felt at all; her father and mother are like strangers to her; they stand in awe of her authority, but she never offers them advice or instruction, or makes demands of them. She has a companion living in the house, a young, good-natured German girl named Zoya, but Helena keeps aloof from her, scarcely ever speaks to her, and their relations are very cold. There is also the young artist Shubin, about whom we shall speak in a moment; Helena annihilates him with her withering criticism, but she never dreams of exercising any influence over him, although this would have been extremely beneficial for him. There is not a single instance throughout the story where the yearning to do good induces Helena to intervene in the affairs of those around her and to exercise her influence in any way. We do not think that this is due to a casual oversight on the author's part. No, up to very recently we saw, not among women but among men, a special type who towered and shone above society and took pride in standing aloof from the surrounding milieu. 'It is impossible to keep pure in this environment,' they said, 'and besides, this environment is so shallow and banal that it is far better to keep out of it.' And they did indeed keep out of it; they did not make a single energetic attempt to improve this banal environment. Their self-exclusion from it was regarded as the only honest way out of their situation, and was glorified as an act of heroism. Naturally, having such examples and concepts before him, the author had no better means of depicting Helena's domestic life than by describing her as standing entirely aloof from that life. As we have said, however, in the story Helena's impotence is attributed to a special cause, which springs from her feminine, humane sentiments: she dreads all collisions not because she lacks courage, but because she is afraid that she may offend or harm somebody. Having never experienced a full and active life, she still imagines that her ideals can be achieved without a struggle, without causing anybody any harm. After one incident (when Insarov heroically threw a drunken German into a pond), she made the following entry in her diary:

'No, he will stand no nonsense, and he has the courage to take up the cudgels on another's behalf. But why that anger, those quivering lips and that venom in his eyes? But perhaps it cannot be otherwise? Perhaps a man, a fighter, cannot remain meek and mild?'

This simple idea had only just entered her mind, and then only in the form of a question which she is unable to answer.

In this state of indefiniteness, of inaction, in spite of a continuous yearning for something, Helena lives until she reaches the age of twenty. Sometimes she feels exceedingly depressed; she realizes that she is wasting her strength, that her life is empty. She says to herself: 'If I got a place as a serving maid I would feel much better, I am sure.' This feeling of depression is intensified by the fact that she meets with no sympathy from anybody, she can find no one to support her. Sometimes it seems to her that she wants something that nobody else wants, that nobody in all Russia is thinking about.... She becomes frightened and the need for sympathy grows stronger, and she longs intensely and agitatedly for another soul that would understand her, that would respond to her innermost sentiments, that would help her and teach her what to do. A desire arises within her to surrender herself to somebody, to merge her being with somebody, and the lone independence in which she stands among those immediately around her becomes repugnant to her.

'From the age of sixteen she lived her own life, but it was a lonely life. Her soul flared up and died down alone, she beat her wings against the bars like a bird in a cage; but there was no cage, nobody restricted her, nobody restrained her, nevertheless, she struggled and pined. Sometimes she did not understand herself; she even feared herself. Everything around her seemed to her to be either senseless or unintelligible. "How is it possible to live without love? But there is no one to love," she mused, and these thoughts, these sensations frightened her.'

It is in this state of mind and heart that she comes upon the scene in the story, in the summer, at a country house in Kuntsovo. In a short space of time three men appear before her, one of whom attracts her whole soul. Incidentally, there is a fourth man, introduced casually, but not one of the unwanted type, whom we shall also count. Three of these gentlemen are Russians, the fourth is a Bulgarian, and him Helena regards as her ideal. Let us look at all these gentlemen. [...]

[Dobrolyubov here discusses in some detail the characters and roles of the three young men, Shubin, Bersenev and Insarov and then poses the question:]

[...] What then is the significance of the *Bulgarian's* appearance in this story? Why a Bulgarian and not a Russian? Are there no such characters among Russians, are Russians incapable of loving passionately and persistently, incapable of recklessly marrying for love? Or is this only a whim of the author's imagination, and it is useless seeking any particular meaning in it? As much as to say: 'Well, he went and took a Bulgarian, and there's an end to it. He might just as well have taken a Gypsy, or a Chinese, perhaps....'

The answers to these questions depend upon one's views concerning the entire meaning of the story. We think that the Bulgarian's place here could indeed have been taken by a man of some other nationality, by a Serb, a Czech, an Italian or a Hungarian, but not by a Pole or a Russian. Not a Pole, because a Pole is entirely out of the question. But why not a Russian? That is the question at issue, and we shall try to answer it to the best of our ability.

The point is that the principal personage in *On the Eve* is Helena, and it is in relation to her that we must examine the other personages in the story. She expresses that vague longing for something, that almost unconscious but irresistible desire for a new way of life, for a new type of people, which the whole of Russian society, and not only its so-called educated section, now feels. Helena so vividly expresses the finest strivings of our present society and she brings out the utter hollowness of the common everyday life of this society in such prominent relief, that one involuntarily feels like drawing a detailed parallel. Here all would be in their place: Stakhov, who is by no means malicious, but is featherbrained and stupidly puts on airs; Anna Vassilyevna, whom Shubin calls a hen; the German companion towards whom Helena is so cold; dreamy but sometimes profound Uvar Ivanovich, who is disturbed only by the news of the counter-bombardment; and even the mean footman, who reports Helena to her father when everything is all over.... But parallels of this kind, while undoubtedly revealing a playful imagination, become overstrained and ludicrous when they go into great detail. We shall therefore refrain from going into details and confine ourselves to a few observations of a most general nature.

Helena's development is not based on deep learning, or on wide experience of life; the finest, the ideal side of her character blossomed, grew and matured at the sight of the meek sufferings. of the person who was dear to her, at the sight of the poor, the sick and the oppressed, whom she found and saw everywhere, even in her dreams. Is it not with impressions like these that all the best characters in Russian society grew and were moulded? Is it not in the character of every truly decent person in this country to hate all violence, tyranny and oppression, and to wish to help the weak and the oppressed? We do not say: '*activity* in protecting the weak from the strong' because this is not the case; we say *wish*, which is exactly the case with Helena. We too are glad to perform a good deed when it concerns only the positive side, *i.e.*, when it does not call for a struggle, when no outside opposition is anticipated. We give alms, arrange theatrical performances for charitable purposes, and even sacrifice part of our fortunes if need be; all on the condition, however, that the matter ends here, that we will not have to encounter and combat all sorts of unpleasantness for the sake of some poor or wronged person. We have the 'desire actively to do good', and we have the strength to do it; but fear, lack of confidence in our strength and, lastly, our ignorance of what is to be done, constantly check us and, without knowing why, we suddenly find ourselves outside of social life, cold and alien to its interests, exactly like Helena and all those around her. And yet the *desire* still seethes in every-body's breast (we mean in the breasts of those who do not strive artificially to supress it) and we are all seeking, thirsting, wait-ing ... waiting for someone to tell us what is to be done. It is with the anguish of perplexity, almost of despair, that Helena writes in her diary:

> 'Oh, if only somebody said to me: this is what you must do! Be good—that is not enough. Do good ... yes, that is the main thing in life. *But how is one to do good?*'

Who in our society, conscious of possessing a loving heart, has not, in his torment, put this question to himself? Who has not confessed to himself that all the forms of activity in which his desire to do good has manifested itself, as far as it was pos-sible, have been significant and pitiful? Who has not felt that there is something different, something more lofty, that we could have done, but did not do because we did not know how to pro-ceed about it? ... Who can solve our doubts? We long for this solution, we seek it eagerly in the bright moments of our exist-ence, but we cannot find it anywhere. It seems to us that every-body around us is either tormented by the same perplexity that torments us, or has crushed his own feelings in his heart and confines himself to pursuing only his petty, selfish, animal interests. And so life passes, day after day, until it dies in a man's heart, and day after day a man waits and hopes that the next day will be better, that his doubts will be solved tomorrow, that somebody will tell us how to do good....

Russian society has been longing and waiting like this for quite a long time; and how many times have we, like Helena, erred in thinking that the one we had been waiting for had arrived and then cooled off? Helena became passionately attached to Anna Vassilyevna, but Anna Vassilyevna turned out to be a spineless nonentity.... At one time Helena felt well-disposed towards Shubin in the same way as our society at one time became enthusiastic about art, but it turned out that Shubin lacked real content, there were only sparkle and whims about him; and absorbed in her searching, Helena could not stop to admire trinkets. For a moment she was interested in serious learning, in the person of Bersenev, but serious learning turned out to be modest, beset by doubt, learning that was waiting for a number one to lead him. What Helena needed was a man without a number, a man who was not waiting for a lead, an independent man, who irresistibly strove towards his goal and carried others with him. At last such a man appeared in the person of Insarov and in him Helena found her ideal, in him she found the man who could tell her how to do good.

But why could not Insarov have been a Russian? After all, he does nothing in the story, he only intends to do something; this much a Russian could have done. Insarov's character could have been encased in a Russian skin, particularly in the way it expresses itself in the story. In the story his character expresses itself in that he loves strongly and resolutely; but is it impossible for a Russian to love in this way?

All this is true, nevertheless the sympathies of Helena, of the girl as we understand her, could not turn towards a Russian with the same justification and with the same naturalness as they turned towards this Bulgarian. All Insarov's charm lies in the grandeur and sacredness of the idea which permeates his whole being. Thirsting to do good, but not knowing how, Helena is instantly and profoundly captivated by the mere relation of his aims, even before she has seen him. 'Liberate one's country,' she says, 'these are words that one even fears to utter—they are so grand!' And she feels that she has found the word her heart has been longing for, that she is satisfied, that no higher goal than this can be striven for, and that her whole life, her whole future will be filled with activities if only she follows this man. And so she tries to study him, she wants to peer into his soul, to share his dreams, to learn the details of his plans. He has only one idea: his country and its freedom, an idea which is constantly with him and has merged with his being; Helena is satisfied, she is pleased with the clarity and definiteness of his aim, the serenity and firmness of his heart, with the grandeur of the very idea, and soon she herself becomes the echo of this idea which inspires him.

'When he talks about his country,' she writes in her diary, 'he seems to grow and grow, his face becomes handsomer, his voice becomes like steel, and it seems as though there is not a man in the world before whom his eyes would droop. And he not only talks, he has done things, and will do things. I will ask him about it. . . .'

Several days later she writes again:

'But it is strange, though, that up till now, until I was twenty, I have never loved anybody! It seems to me that D (I will call him D, I like that name: Dmitri) has such a serene soul because he has devoted himself entirely to his cause, to his dream. Why should he worry? Whoever devotes himself to a cause entirely . . . entirely . . . entirely, knows little worry, he has nothing to answer for. It is not what *I want*, it is what *it* wants.'

Realizing this she wants to merge herself with him in such a way that *not she* should want, but that *he*, and *that* which inspires him, should want. We can fully understand her position; and we are sure that the whole of Russian society, even if it is not yet carried away by the personality of Insarov as she is, will understand that Helena's feelings are real and natural.

We say that society will not be carried away, and we base this statement on the assumption that *this* man Insarov is, after all, an alien to us. Mr Turgenev himself, who has so thoroughly studied the finest part of our society, did not find it possible to make him *our man*. Not only did he bring him from Bulgaria, but he refrained from making his hero sufficiently endearing to us merely as a man. This, if you look at it even from the literary standpoint, is the main artistic defect in the novel. We know one of the principal reasons for this, one over which the author had no control, and therefore we are not blaming Mr Turgenev for this. Nevertheless, the pale sketch of Insarov affects the impression we obtain from the story. The grandeur and beauty of Insarov's idea are not brought out with full force so that we are not imbued with it sufficiently to compel us to exclaim with proud inspiration: we shall follow you! And yet this idea is so sacred, so exalted. . . . Far less humane, even utterly false ideas, vividly brought out in artistic images, have exercised a feverish effect upon society; the Charles Moores, the Werthers and the Pechorins had a crowd of imitators. Insarov will have no such imitators. True, it was difficult for him to express his ideas fully, living as he did in Moscow and doing nothing; he could not indulge in rhetorical outpourings! But from the story we learn little about him even as a man; his inner world is inaccessible to us; what he does, what he thinks, what he hopes for, what changes his relationships undergo, his views on the course of events, on life that is sweeping past our eyes, are concealed from us. Even his love for Helena is not fully revealed to us. We know that he loves her passionately, but how he becomes imbued with this passion, what it is about Helena that attracts him, how deep this passion is, when he becomes aware of it and decides to go away—all these inner details about Insarov's personality, and many others which Mr Turgenev is able to depict with such subtle poetic skill, are kept from us. As a living image, as a real personality, Insarov is extremely remote from us, and this explains why *On the Eve* produces upon the public such a faint and partly even unfavourable impression compared with Mr Turgenev's previous stories, which portray characters whom the author had studied down to the minutest detail, and for whom he had felt such a lively sympathy. We realize that Insarov must be a good man and that Helena must love him with all the ardour of her soul because she sees him in real life and not in a story. But he is near and dear to us only as a representative of an idea, which attracts us, as it did Helena, like a flash of light and lights up the gloom of our existence. That is why we understand how natural are Helena's feelings towards Insarov, that is why we ourselves, pleased with his indomitable loyalty to an idea, fail to realize at first that he is depicted for us only in pale and general outline.

And yet some want him to be a Russian! 'No, he could not be a Russian!' exclaims Helena herself in answer to a regret that had arisen in her own heart that he was not a Russian. Indeed, there are no such Russians, there should not and cannot be such, at all events at the present time. We do not know how the new generations are developing and will develop, but those that we see in action today have not by any means developed in such a way as to resemble Insarov. Every individual's development is influenced not only by his private relationships, but by the entire social atmosphere in which it is his lot to live. One social atmosphere will develop heroic trends, another will develop peaceful inclinations, a third irritates, a fourth soothes. Russian life is so well arranged that everything in it induces calm and peaceful slumber, and every sleepless person seems, and not without good reason, to be a troublesome character and absolutely unwanted by society. Indeed, compare the conditions under which Insarov's life begins and passes with those met with in the life of every Russian.

Bulgaria is enslaved, she is groaning under the Turkish yoke. We, thank God, are not enslaved by anybody, we are free, we are a great people who more than once have decided with our arms the destinies of kingdoms and nations; we are the masters of others, but we have no masters. . . .

In Bulgaria there are no social rights and guarantees, Insarov says to Helena: 'If only you knew what a bounteous land my country is, and yet she is being torn and trampled upon. We have been robbed of everything: our church, our rights, our land; the vile Turks drive us like cattle, we are slaughtered. . . .' Russia, on the contrary, is a well-ordered state, she has wise laws which protect the rights of citizens and define their duties; here justice reigns and beneficent publicity flourishes. Nobody is robbed of his church, and religion is not restricted in any way, on the contrary, the zeal of preachers in admonishing the errant is encouraged; far from anybody being robbed of rights and land, these are even granted to those who hitherto have not possessed them; nobody is driven like cattle.

'In Bulgaria,' says Insarov, 'every peasant, every beggar, and I—we all want the same thing, we all have the same goal.' There is no such monotony in Russian life in which every class, even every circle, lives its own separate life, has its own separate goal and strivings, has its own appointed place. With the good social order prevailing here each one need be concerned only with the pursuit of his own welfare, and for this purpose there is no need whatever to merge with the whole nation in one common idea, as they do in Bulgaria.

Insarov was still an infant when a Turkish Aga kidnapped his mother and afterwards murdered her, and then his father was shot because he wanted to avenge his mother by stabbing the Aga. Which Russian could ever gain such impressions in his life? Can anything like this be conceived of in Russia? Of course, criminals may be found anywhere, but if, in this country, an Aga kidnapped and afterwards killed another man's wife, the husband would not be allowed to avenge her, because we have laws, before which all are equal, and which punish crimes irrespective of persons.

In short, Insarov imbibed hatred for enslavers and discontent with the present state of things with his mother's milk. There was no need for him to exert himself, to resort to a long series of syllogisms to be able to determine the direction of his activities. Since he is not lazy, and no coward, he knows what to do and how to behave. There is no need for him to take up many tasks at once. And besides his task is so *easily understood*, as Shubin says: 'All you have to do is to kick the Turks out—that's not much!' Moreover, Insarov knows that he is doing right not only in his own conscience, but also before the court of humanity: his idea will meet with the sympathy of every decent man. Try and picture something like this in Russian society. It is inconceivable.... Translated into Russian, Insarov would turn out to be nothing more than a robber, a representative of the 'antisocial element', with whom the Russian public are so familiar from the learned investigations of Mr Solovyov, which have been published in *Russky Vestnik*. Who, we ask, could love such a man? What well-bred and clever girl would not flee from him in horror?

Is it clear now why a Russian could not have taken the place of Insarov? Characters like his are, of course, born in Russia in no small number, but they cannot develop as freely and express themselves as frankly as Insarov does. A contemporary Russian Insarov will always remain timid and dual-natured, he will lie low, express himself with various reservations and equivocations ... and it is this that reduces confidence in him. Sometimes he may even prevaricate and contradict himself, and it is well known that people usually prevaricate for their own gain, or out of cowardice. What sympathy can one feel towards a covetous man and a coward, especially when one's soul longs for action and seeks for a great mind and a strong hand to lead it?

True, minor heroes appear among us who somewhat resemble Insarov in courage and in sympathy for the oppressed. But in our society they are ludicrous Don Quixotes. The distinguishing feature of a Don Quixote is that he does not know what he is fighting for, or what will come of his efforts, and these minor heroes display this feature to a remarkable degree. For example, they may suddenly take it into their heads that it is necessary to save the peasants from the tyranny of the squires and simply refuse to believe that there is no tyranny here at all, that the rights of the squires are strictly defined by the law, and must remain inviolable as long as these laws exist; that to rouse the peasants against this tyranny means not liberating them from the squires, but making them, in addition, liable to a penalty under the law. Or, for example, they may set themselves the task of protecting the innocent from miscarriages of justice, as if the judges in this country administer the law according to their own arbitrary will. Everybody knows that in this country everything is done according to the law, and that to interpret the law one way or another it is not heroism that is needed, but skill in legal quibbling. And so our Don Quixotes simply beat the air. ... Or they may suddenly take it into their heads to eradicate bribery, and what a torment they will make of the lives of poor officials who take ten kopeks or so for some little service rendered! Our heroes who will set out to protect sufferers will make the lives of these poor officials unbearable. It is, of course, a noble and lofty task, but do these unwise people deserve our sympathy? We are not referring to those cold slaves to duty who act in this way simply in their official capacity; we have in mind Russians who really and sincerely sympathize with the oppressed, and are even ready to fight in their defence. But it is these who turn out to be useless and ludicrous, because they fail to understand the general character of the environment in which they are operating. How can they understand it when they themselves are in it, when their tops, so to speak, are pushing upwards, while their roots are, after all, embedded in this very soil? They want to alleviate their neighbours' sufferings, but these sufferings spring from the very milieu in which both the sufferers and the would-be alleviators of suffering live. What can be done here? Turn this whole milieu upside down? If so, they will have to turn themselves upside down. Get into an empty packing case and turn it upside down with yourself inside it! What efforts you will be compelled to exert! If you stand outside of the packing case, however, you can easily turn it over with just one push. Insarov's advantageous position is that he is

not inside the packing case; the oppressors of his country are the
Turks, with whom he has nothing in common. All he has to do
is go up and push them as hard as his strength will allow. The
Russian heroes, however, belonging, as a rule, to the educated
section of society, are themselves vitally connected with what
must be overthrown. They are in the position of what a son of
a Turkish Aga, for example, would be if he took it into his head
to liberate Bulgaria from the Turks. It is difficult even to conceive of such a situation; but even if it occurred, if this son of
an Aga wanted to avoid appearing like a stupid and ludicrous
fellow, he would have to renounce everything that connects him
with the Turks—his faith, his nationality, his relatives and
friends, and the material advantages of his social position. It
must be admitted that this is frightfully difficult, and determination of this kind requires a somewhat different development
from that which the son of a Turkish Aga usually receives. It
is not much easier for a Russian to be a hero. This explains why
sympathetic and energetic characters in this country content
themselves with petty and unnecessary bravado and fail to rise
to real and serious heroism, *i.e.*, renouncing the entire complex
of concepts and practical relationships which bind them to the
social milieu. Their timidity in face of the host of enemy forces is
reflected even in their theoretical development; they are afraid,
or are unable, to delve down to the roots, and setting out, for
example, to punish evil, they only attack some minor manifestation of it and wear themselves out frightfully before they have
time even to look for the source of this evil. They are reluctant to
put the axe to the tree on which they themselves grew, and so
they try to assure themselves, and others, that all the rot is only
on the surface, that it is only necessary to scrub it off and all will
be well. Dismiss a few corrupt officials from the service, appoint
trustees over a few squires' estates, and expose the tapster at
one tavern who is selling diluted vodka and justice will reign
supreme, the peasants all over Russia will live in bliss, and the
tavern licensing system will become a splendid thing for the
people. Many sincerely believe this and do indeed waste all their
strength on efforts of this kind, and for this they quite seriously
regard themselves as heroes.

We were told about a hero of this type who, it was said, was a
man of extraordinary energy and talent. While still a student at

the high school he started a row with one of the tutors because the latter was appropriating the paper intended for the use of the students. The affair took a bad turn; our hero managed to get into trouble also with the school inspector and the headmaster and was expelled. He began to prepare to enter the university and meanwhile gave private lessons. At the very first house at which he gave these lessons, he saw the mother of his pupils slap the face of her housemaid. He flared up, raised a scandal in the house, called the police and formally charged the mistress with cruelly ill-treating her servant. A lengthy investigation ensued, but, of course, he could not prove anything and barely escaped severe punishment for laying false information and for slander. After that he could get no more private lessons. With great difficulty, thanks to somebody's special intercession, he obtained a situation in the government service. One day he was asked to copy a decision of an extremely absurd nature. Unable to restrain himself, he challenged this decision. He was told to hold his tongue, but he persisted in his protest. After that he was told to clear out. Having nothing to do, he accepted the invitation of an old school chum of his to stay in the country with him during the summer. When he arrived in the village and saw what went on there he began to tell his friend, his friend's father, and even the steward of the estate and the peasants that it was illegal to compel the peasants to perform *barshchina* for more than three days, that it was outrageous to flog them without trial and sentence, that it was dishonourable to drag peasant women into the house at night, and so forth. The upshot was that the peasants who had agreed with what he said were flogged, and the old squire ordered the carriage to be brought round for him and asked him to leave and never show his face in those parts again if he wanted to keep a whole skin. Pulling through the summer somehow, our hero entered the university in the autumn, and he succeeded in doing so only because, at the examinations, he was given innocuous questions to answer which gave him no scope for argument. He took up medicine and really studied hard; but during his practical course, when a professor expounded the intricacies of the science at the bedside of a patient, he could never restrain himself from interrupting when the professor revealed the obsolescence of his views, or quackery; as soon as the latter said anything of that nature he at once butted in and tried to prove that he was talking nonsense. As a result of all this, our hero was not allowed to remain on as a post-graduate student, was not sent abroad for further study, but was appointed to a hospital in some remote district. No sooner did he arrive there than he exposed the superintendent and threatened to lodge a complaint against him. One day he caught the superintendent red-handed and lodged a complaint, but for this he received a reprimand from the head doctor. When he received this reprimand he, of course, protested very loudly and was soon dismissed from the hospital. . . . After that he received an appointment to go with some expedition or other, and here he took up the cudgels on behalf of the soldiers and quarrelled with the chief of the expedition and with the official in charge of the food supplies. As his protests were unavailing, he sent a report to headquarters complaining that the men were being starved owing to the malpractices of the officials and that the chief of the expedition was conniving at this. When the party reached its destination an investigator arrived and interrogated the soldiers. The latter stated that they had no complaints. Our hero became indignant, was disrespectful to the General Staff doctor, and a month later was reduced to the rank of assistant feldscher. He remained in this post for two weeks, but unable to stand the deliberately brutal treatment to which he was subjected, he shot himself.

An extraordinary case, a strong and impulsive character, is that not so? And yet, look what he perished for. There was nothing in his actions that would not represent the direct duty of any honest man in his place; but he must possess considerable heroism to act in this way, he must have self-sacrificing determination to die for the sake of doing good. The question arises: since he possessed this determination, would it not have been better to have exercised it for some bigger cause, so that something really useful might have been achieved? The whole trouble is, however, that he did not realize the necessity and the possibility of such a cause, and he did not understand what was going on around him, he refused to see the conspiracy that went on around him, he refused to see what went on before his very eyes, and imagined that every manifestation of evil that he noticed was nothing more than an abuse, which could only be a rare exception, of the system which in itself was splendid. Holding views such as these, the Russian hero can, of course, do nothing more than confine himself to petty details without thinking of the general, whereas Insarov always subordinated the particular to the general, convinced that the particular too, 'will not get away'. Thus, in answer to Helena's question as to whether he avenged his father's murder, he said:

> 'I did not search for the murderer. I did not search for him, not because I could not kill him—I would have done that with a clear conscience—but because there is no time for private vengeance when the liberation of a nation is at stake. One would have hindered the other. But the murderer will not get away. His time will come too.'

It is this love for the general cause, this premonition which gives him the strength coolly to bear private wrong, that makes the Bulgarian Insarov far and away superior to all the Russian heroes, who have no conception whatever of a general cause.

Incidentally, even of such heroes there are very few in this country, and most of these do not hold out to the end. Far more numerous among the educated section of our society is another category of men—those who indulge in reflection. Among these there are also many who, although able to reflect, understand nothing, but of these we shall not speak. We wish to point only to those men who really have bright minds, men who after a long period of doubt and searching, attained the integrity and clarity of ideas which Insarov attained without exceptional effort. These people know where the root of evil lies and they know what must be done to put a stop to evil; they are deeply and sincerely imbued with the idea they attained at last. But they no longer possess the strength for practical activity; they have strained themselves to such an extent that their characters seem to have sagged and become enfeebled. They welcome the approach of the new way of life, but they cannot go out to meet it, and they cannot satisfy the fresh sentiments of a man who is thirsting to do good and is looking for a leader. [...]

Helena found no resource in Russia after she met Insarov and conceived of a different life. That is why she could neither remain in Russia nor return home after her husband's death. The author understood this perfectly well, and preferred to leave her fate unknown rather than bring her back to her father's

house and compel her to live for the rest of her life in sad loneliness and idleness in her native Moscow. Her mother's appeal,
which reached her almost at the moment she lost her husband,
failed to soften her repugnance for this banal, colourless and
inactive life. 'Return to Russia? What for? What shall I do in
Russia?' she wrote to her mother, and went off to Zara to be
swallowed up by the waves of insurrection.

What a good thing it was that she took this decision! Indeed,
what awaited her in Russia? Could she have an object in life, or
even life itself? Return to the unfortunate cats and flies?
Give to beggars money that she herself did not earn, but obtained
God knows how? Rejoice at Shubin's successes in his art? Discuss Schelling with Bersenev, read *Moskovskiye Vedomosti* to
her mother, and see *rules* parading in the public arena in the
shape of various Kurnatovskys and nowhere see real deeds performed, or even feel the breath of a new life.... And gradually,
slowly and painfully wilt, wither and die?... No, once having
tasted a different life, having breathed a different air, it was
easier for her to rush into danger, however grave, than to condemn herself to this painful torture, to this slow execution....
And we are glad that she escaped from our life and did not confirm by her own example that hopelessly mournful and heart-
rending prophecy of the poet which is so invariably and
ruthlessly confirmed by the fate of the finest, the chosen characters in Russia:

> Remote from nature and the sun,
> Remote from light and art,
> Remote from life and love
> Your youth flashes by,
> Your living feelings die,
> Your dreams fade away.
> And your life will pass unseen
> In a deserted, nameless land,
> In an unchartered land—
> And vanish like a cloud of smoke
> In the dull and foggy sky
> In autumn's boundless gloom....*

It remains for us now to sum up the various features scat-

* [From Tyuchev's poem, 'To My Countrywoman' (1850).]

tered through this essay (for the incompleteness and incoherence of which we ask our readers to excuse us) and draw a general conclusion.

Insarov, being consciously and completely engrossed by a great idea of liberating his country and being ready to play an active part in this, could not develop and reveal his talents in present-day Russian society. Even Helena, who was able to love him so fully and merge herself completely with his ideas, could not remain in Russian society, even among her near and dear ones. And so, there is no room among us for great ideas and great sentiments? ... All heroic and active people must fly from us if they do not wish to die of idleness, or perish in vain? Is that not so? Is this not the idea that runs through the novel that we have reviewed?

We think not. True, we lack an open field for wide activity; true, our life is spent in petty affairs, in scheming, intriguing, scandalmongering and meanness; true, our civic leaders are hardhearted and often thickheaded; our wiseacres will not do a thing to achieve the triumph of their convictions, our liberals and reformers base their schemes on legal subtleties and not on the groans and cries of their unhappy fellow men. All this is true, and all this is seen to some extent in *On the Eve*, as well as in dozens of other novels that have appeared recently. Nevertheless we think that *today* there is already room for great ideas and sentiments in our society, and that the time is not far distant when it will be possible to put these ideas into practice.

The point is that, bad as our present way of life is, the appearance of types like Helena has proved to be possible. And not only have such characters become possible in life, they have already been grasped by the artists' mind, they have been introduced into literature, they have been elevated to a type. Helena is an ideal personage, but her features are familiar to us, we understand and sympathize with her. What does this show? It shows that the basis of her character—love for the suffering and the oppressed and a desire to do good and weary search for the one who could show how good can be done—all this is at last being felt in the best section of our society. And this feeling is so strong and so near to realization that it is no longer, as before, dazzled either by brilliant but sterile minds and talents, by conscientious but abstract learning, by official virtues, nor even by kind, generous but passive hearts. To satisfy our feeling our thirst, something more is needed; we need a man like Insarov— but a Russian Insarov.

What do we need him for? We ourselves said above that we do not need hero liberators, that we were a nation of rulers, not of slaves....

Yes, we are safeguarded against outside dangers; even if we were obliged to wage an external struggle we can be calm about it. We have always had sufficient heroes to perform deeds of valour on the battlefield, and the raptures which even at the present day our young ladies go into at the sight of an officer's uniform and moustaches is irrefutable proof that our society knows how to appreciate these heroes. But have we not many internal enemies? Is it not necessary to wage a struggle against them? And is not heroism needed for such a struggle? But where are the men among us who are capable of action? Where are the men of integrity who have been from childhood imbued with a single idea, who have merged themselves with that idea so thoroughly that they must either achieve this triumph or perish in the attempt? There are no such men among us, be- cause up to now our social environment has been unfavourable for their development. It is from this environment, from its banality and pettiness, that we must be liberated by the new men whose appearance is so impatiently and eagerly awaited by all that is best, all that is fresh in our society.

It is as yet difficult for such a hero to appear; the conditions for his development, and particularly for the first manifestations of his activity, are extremely unfavourable, and his task is far more complicated and difficult than Insarov's. An external enemy, a privileged oppressor can be attacked and vanquished far more easily than an internal enemy, whose forces are spread everywhere in a thousand different shapes, elusive and invulner- able, harassing us on all sides, poisoning our lives, giving us no rest, and preventing us from surveying the battlefield. This inter- nal enemy cannot be combated with ordinary weapons; we can liberate ourselves from him only by dispelling the raw, foggy atmosphere of our lives in which he was born, grew up and gained strength, and by surrounding ourselves with an atmos- phere in which he will be unable to breathe.

Is this possible? When will it be possible? Of these two

questions a categorical answer can be given only to the first. Yes, it is possible, and for the following reasons. We said above that our social environment suppresses the development of personalities like Insarov. But now, we may add the following: this environment has now reached the stage when it itself can facilitate the appearance of such a man. Eternal banality, pettiness and apathy cannot be the lawful lot of man, and the people who constitute our social environment and who are fettered by its conditions have long ago realized the harshness and absurdity of these conditions. Some are dying of ennui, others are striving with all their might to go away, to escape from this oppression. Various ways of escape have been invented, various means have been employed to infuse some animation into the deadliness and rottenness of our lives, but they have all proved to be feeble and ineffective. Now, at last, concepts and demands are appearing, such as those that we saw in the case of Helena; these demands meet with sympathy in society; nay, more, efforts are being made to put them into effect. This shows that the old social routine is passing away a little more vacillation, a few more powerful words and favourable factors, and active men will appear!

Above we hinted that in our society the determination and energy of a strong character are killed at their birth also by that idyllic admiration of everything in the world, by that proneness for indolent self-satisfaction and somnolent repose with which every one of us, when still a child, meets everything around us, and to inculcate us with which every effort is made by means of various counsels and admonitions. Lately, however, things have changed very much in this respect too. Everywhere, and in all things, we observe the growth of self-realization, everywhere the unsoundness of the old order of things is understood, everybody is waiting for reform and rectification, and nobody now lulls his children to sleep with songs about the inconceivable perfection of the present state of things in every corner of Russia. On the contrary, today everybody is waiting, everybody is hoping, and children are now growing up imbued with hopes and dreams of a brighter future, and are not forcibly tied to the corpse of the obsolete past. When their turn comes to set to work they will put into it the energy, consistency and harmony of heart and mind of which we could scarcely obtain even a theoretical conception.

Then a full, sharp and vividly depicted image of a Russian Insarov will appear in literature. We shall not have to wait long for him; the feverishly painful impatience with which we are expecting his appearance in real life is the guarantee of this. We need him, without him our lives seem to be wasted, and every days means nothing in itself, but is only the eve of another day. That day will come at last! At all events, the eve is never far from the next day; only a matter of one night separates them.

12 U. C. Knoelpflmacher

(i) George Eliot and Science

From *Religious Humanism and the Victorian Novel*, Princeton University Press, 1965, pp. 27–32, 41–44.

In a famous letter to Charles Kingsley, T. H. Huxley bluntly demands a conversion to the 'spirit of science' by those who, like Kingsley or F. D. Maurice, were trying to preserve the religion of 'that great and powerful instrument for good or evil, the Church of England'.[1] To Huxley, the budding neo-Darwinism of Kingsley is a desirable token of things to come, for, if religion 'is to be saved from being shivered into fragments by the advancing tide of science ... it must be by the efforts of men who, like yourself, see your way to the combination of the Church with the spirit of science.'[2] It is highly doubtful whether at the time of his letter, 1860, Huxley would have pointed to the recent work of a new novelist, his former colleague on the *Westminster Review*, as an example of this combination. It is certain that Kingsley would hardly have cherished the work of 'Miss Evans, the infidel esprit fort', for his model.[3] Yet in the years to come, a majority of Victorians were to regard George Eliot as one who combined at least the 'essence' of the Church with the predominant 'spirit of science'. George Eliot's qualifications were unquestionable. At the end of the novelist's career, an anonymous reviewer surveyed her work and ascribed to it the empirical attitude of positivism, an attitude compressed in the simple statement that 'we have no knowledge of anything but phenomena and our knowledge of phenomena is relative, not absolute'.[4] Decades later, Frederic Harrison tacitly concurred with this estimate when he remembered George Eliot as 'one who, possessed of an immense and *scientific* culture, had long meditated on burning social and moral questions'.[5]

[1] Leonard Huxley, *Life and Letters of Thomas Henry Huxley*, Macmillan and Co., 1900, I, 238.

[2] Ibid.

[3] Quoted by Margaret Thorp, *Charles Kingsley*, Princeton University Press, 1933, p. 93. Kingsley's scorn of 'Miss Evans' was partly prompted by her adverse reviews of Maurice's *Sermons* and of his own *Westward Ho!*

[4] *London Quarterly Review*, XLVII, January 1877, 447.

[5] *Autobiographic Memoirs*, Macmillan and Co., 1911, II, 108 (italics added).

George Eliot's 'scientific culture' was solidified in the early fifties when, as a contributor to the *Westminster Review*, she was surrounded by men such as Huxley, Owen, and Spencer, at a time when Spencer himself was publishing his historic essay on 'The Development Hypothesis' and when George Henry Lewes began his popularization of Comte's philosophy of the sciences.[1] After her union with Lewes, a man esteemed by Darwin and Lyell for 'the thoroughness of his knowledge in their departments',[2] George Eliot remained abreast of all the major scientific and pseudoscientific developments of the time. Evolutionism confirmed her in the empiricist position she was to maintain for the remainder of her life, but it also sharpened her urgent need of imposing a new moral order on the amoral, perennially changing, and hence totally relative cosmos it had established. Her desire for clarity led her to accept the phenomenalism of the new 'spirit'; yet its reduction of a purposive universe to a sequence of fortuitous evolutionary processes was distasteful to the residual religiosity of the former Evangelical enthusiast, who had already been forced to part with the mysticism of her 'other-worldly' religion.

George Eliot's remarks about *The Origin of Species*, a work she read, assimilated, and correctly evaluated within days after its publication, reveal this same duality: her sure grasp of the book's relevance for the 'spirit of science' clashes with her suddenly aroused religious sensibility—a collision quite similar to that which she was to exploit artistically, more than a decade later, through the opposed points of view of Tertius Lydgate and Dorothea Brooke. Writing to her lifelong friend, Barbara Bodichon, she prophesies that Darwin's study will make 'an epoch'. She welcomes the 'long-celebrated naturalist' (who was to become her and Lewes's friend) as an important latecomer to the ranks of the evolutionists and applauds *The Origin of Species* as 'the expression of his thorough adhesion, after long years of

---

[1] Herbert Spencer's work appeared in the *Leader* in 1852; it anticipated some of Darwin's conclusions and earned him the support of Huxley. At the time, Marian Evans' close friendship with Spencer was expected to lead to their marriage.

[2] Quoted in a letter from Charles Eliot Norton to George William Curtis, January 29, 1869, *The George Eliot Letters*, ed. Gordon S. Haight, Oxford University Press, 1954–1955, v, 8. Hereafter this edition shall be referred to as *GEL*.

study, to the Doctrine of Development'. By its fearless contribution to the expansion of human knowledge, the book exemplifies the very truth of the evolutionary 'doctrine' tested in its pages: 'So the world gets on step by step towards brave clearness and honesty!' But deep spiritual misgivings follow this shrill exclamation. The 'clearness' and 'honesty' of a devotion to unvarnished truth, even this truth itself, are apparently insufficient to assuage these reservations: 'But to me the Development theory and all other explanations of processes by which things came to be, produce a feeble impression compared with the mystery that lies under the processes.'[1]

Such pronouncements, significant as they are, must not be overestimated. Since her early childhood Marian Evans had displayed an unusual interest in the natural sciences; it was her desire for precision, however much at odds with her hankering for 'mystery', which had, after all, produced her initial break with Christianity in 1842. Thus, despite her ever latent reservations about the 'Development theory', she never doubted that its basic explanations of the 'processes by which things came to be' had to be accepted unflinchingly. To a large extent, these explanations even acted as a partial substitute for the moral order she had lost. The Calvinism of her schooldays had instilled in her a belief in rigid laws extracted by a strict and implacable deity; it had stressed the irrevocable 'consequences' of human behavior: every single act, or gesture, or thought could lead to the salvation or damnation of the believer. Although science forever removed this Calvinist deity, it allowed George Eliot— and fellow Puritan renegades such as T. H. Huxley—to convert it into an equally implacable but this-worldly power as capable of punishing 'the great evils of disobedience to natural laws' as of rewarding a submission to 'the great and fundamental truths of Nature and [to] the laws of her operation'.[2] Science reduced the salvation of the soul to the survival of the species, but its grim emphasis on 'consequences' was almost identical to that of the old religion. Huxley's assumption that all conduct was to be guided by a strict observation of 'the natural consequences of actions',[3] was a belief that George Eliot (who had already

[1] All quotations in this paragraph are from *GEL*, III, 227.
[2] 'A Liberal Education; and Where to Find It', *Science and Education: Essays*, London, 1894, p. 86.
[3] Ibid., p. 84.

absorbed Bray's crude 'philosophy of necessity' and the historical determinism of Mill and Hegel) not only echoed but also
translated into the complex causal sequences of her novels.

There were further links. The close introspection of her early
Puritanism, with its meticulous dissection of the hidden motives
which prompted men to selfish actions, its deep sense of human
depravity and concomitant belief in self-denial, found outlets
in the new emphasis on a man-centred order. Metaphysics had
been dissolved into psychology and Victorian psychologists such
as Lewes believed that their main task consisted in a careful
differentiation of man's faculties from those of the animals with
which he shared a basic instinct of self-preservation and self-
gratification. Man's animality, however, his innate egoism, could
be tempered by a stoic acceptance of the natural order and his
willingness to annul the self in the general advancement of his
fellow men. The affective emotions of the 'heart'—altruism and
self-denial—and the thinking capacity of the 'head', could allow
him, as a member of the social organism, to rely on the accumulation of human experience and to rise above his instinctual
nature: 'Human Knowledge is pre-eminently distinguished
from Animal Knowledge by this collective experience.'[1]

On the whole, then, George Eliot accepted the 'spirit of
science' which had reduced 'mystery' to a series of verifiable
processes. Though far more reluctantly than T. H. Huxley or
John Tyndall, the optimist Mr Stockton of Mallock's *New
Republic*, she believed that the future advancement of society
would have to be founded on the 'natural knowledge' provided
by empiricism. In his epoch-making Belfast *Address*, Tyndall
proclaimed that this knowledge was sufficient to cope with man's
major problems, all of which, he admitted, may well be 'the
manifestation of a Power absolutely inscrutable to the intellect
of man'.[2] This strict adherence to empirical truth has a two-
fold value: it concentrates on tangible realities and it also
eliminates that inscrutable 'Power' from its domain. This separation, Tyndall argued, is absolutely necessary. Though science
is 'able to comprehend the machinery' of all organic matter,
including that of man, the prime mover 'which sets it in motion'

[1] George Henry Lewes, *The Study of Psychology*, London, 1879, p. 166.
[2] *Address Delivered before the British Association Assembled at Belfast*,
London, 1874, pp. 57–58.

eludes its scrutiny. 'Man the *object* is separated by an impassable gulf from man the *subject*. There is no motor energy in intellect to carry it without logical rupture from the one to the other.'

With the exception of *Daniel Deronda*, where an inscrutable 'Power' seems to operate, George Eliot's novels respect Tyndall's gulf of separation. The chain of events that governs *Adam Bede* or *The Mill on the Floss*, whether labeled as Bray's moral 'law of consequences' or as Tyndall's intelligible 'machinery', is reducible to component links of cause and effect, although its prime mover remains unexamined. In *Middlemarch* this causality assumes even larger proportions, but, although it extends to the extramundane reach of Casaubon's 'Dead Hand', it is again worked out within the limits of verifiable evidence. By a characteristic Victorian manipulation, free will coexists with determinism and an immortality of sorts with spiritual extinction.[1] For George Eliot, like Tyndall, is eager to leave the 'immovable basis of the religious sentiment' untouched. To her, even more than to the jubilant scientist proclaiming the future absorption of religion by science, a 'reasonable satisfaction' of this sentiment is 'the problem of problems at the present hour'.

To Tyndall this problem is easily solved. The scientist, he feels, may, after all, cross the 'boundary of the experimental evidence' and worship in 'that Matter' which the religions of the past 'have hitherto covered with opprobrium', 'the promise and potency of all terrestrial Life'. And here science can simply appropriate the sensibility of those dying 'religious theories, schemes and systems' whose cosmogonies it has already replaced: 'And grotesque in relation to scientific culture as many of the religions of the world have been and are—dangerous, nay destructive, to the dearest privileges of freemen as some of them undoubtedly have been, and would, if they could, be again—it will be wise to recognize them as the forms of a force, mischievous, if permitted to intrude on the region of *knowledge*, over which it holds no command, but capable of being guided to noble issues in the region of *emotion*, which is its proper and elevated sphere.'

How this 'region of emotion' is to be reached, Tyndall does not say. But his statements provide a gloss to George Eliot's

---

[1] See 'The Metaphysics of *Middlemarch*', below.

novels. Her ideal religious characters are those ministers—the Tryans, Irwines, Kenns, or Lyons, who are willing to exclude their dogmatic convictions from the realm of emotional fellowship, or those who, like the astronomer Sephardo in *The Spanish Gipsy* or the Reverend Mr Farebrother in *Middlemarch*, balance their scientific understanding of 'man the object' with a compassionate feeling for 'man the subject'. On the other hand, the characters whose zealotry intrudes upon the 'regions of knowledge', such as Savonarola in *Romola* or Bulstrode in *Middlemarch*, are inevitably punished by the consequences engendered by their actions. Even those idealists, like the ethereal Dinah Morris or Dorothea Brooke, who deny the realities of physical knowledge in their religious enthusiasm, must become re-educated in the ways of Nature.

And yet, in the over-all weighting of *Middlemarch*, though still respecting Tyndall's basic separation, George Eliot very deliberately tips the scales towards the 'religious sentiment'. In *Daniel Deronda*, which was published two years after the Belfast *Address*, she crosses the 'boundary of experimental evidence', enters 'the region of emotion', and tries to satisfy the 'problem of problems at the present hour' by rejecting many of the standards she had shared with Huxley or Tyndall. For science alone was unable to conduct her into this region: Darwin persisted in a wholly 'unscientific' personal religion; Huxley adopted an aloof and dispassionate stoicism. Even Comte's utilitarian disregard for the Bible was distasteful to a writer brought up on its poetry. It was George Eliot's need to recover this poetry that gave her the power to go beyond Tyndall and made her traditionalism so similar to that of Matthew Arnold. It was her schooling in the biblical criticism of her time and the work of Ludwig Feuerbach in particular which allowed her to retain an 'essence' of Christianity and provided her with a new symbology for her novels.

(ii) The 'Metaphysics' of Middlemarch

From *Religious Humanism and the Victorian Novel*, Princeton University Press, 1965, pp. 106–115.

The Victorian clash of science and religion rekindled the age-old dispute over man's free will. Natural science pointed to a uniformity of cause and effect and questioned the spontaneity of human will in a world seemingly dominated by the mechanistic processes of evolution. Plagued by theories which regarded man as a new Adam limited by the 'natural' laws of development, Victorian thinkers could no longer echo Dr Johnson's forceful assertion, 'Sir, we *know* our will is free, and *there's* an end on't.'[1] Instead, they were forced into painstaking reassessments. One of the first acts of the newly founded Metaphysical Society was to poll its members on their individual definitions of 'Will'. The lines thus drawn, theologians and intuitionists could battle scientists and empiricists over a redefinition of the Libertarian doctrine.[2] To the one camp, Will remained synonymous with conscious choice; to the extremists in the other, it became a function of matter and thus wholly resolvable into physiological phenomena.

Summing up this conflict from his own empiricist standpoint, George Henry Lewes argued in his *Study of Psychology* that Dr Johnson's statement no longer had the same validity for an age imbued with evolutionary thought. To Lewes, the exercise of choice is not equivalent to free will, for an 'inexorable subjection to conditions' rules all our choice: 'actions, sensations, emotions, and thoughts are subject to causal determination no less rigorously than the movements of the planets or the fluctuations of the waves.'[3] And yet, though the individual organism is 'swept along in the great current of natural forces' that operate within and without it, man is nonetheless conscious of a Will based on his power of choice. To resolve this apparent paradox,

---

[1] *Boswell's Life of Johnson*, ed R. W. Chapman, Oxford University Press, 1953, p. 411.
[2] Cf. Alan Willard Brown, *The Metaphysical Society: Victorian Minds in Crisis, 1869–1880*, Columbia University Press pp. 47–54, 68, *et passim*.
[3] George Henry Lewes, *The Study of Psychology*, London, 1879, p. 102.

Lewes cites the 'individual movement' of sailors on the deck of a ship 'swept onwards by the waves': 'Each sailor knows that he moves with the vessel, but knows also that he is free to move to and fro on deck.' A consciousness of freedom can prevent man from yielding completely to the external and internal forces which propel him; in the realm of ethics, man's volition may overcome his desires, themselves the result of the 'conditions' to which he is subjected. Human volition can thus become 'the abstract expression of the product of Experience, it is educable, and become amenable to the Moral Law'.

Lewes's rather wishful compromise allows him to escape the implications of a purely mechanistic view of life, such as T. H. Huxley's belief that all human activities, including man's will, are rooted in the protoplasm which makes up the 'physical basis of life'. To Lewes, the mind is not a 'function of the Organism' but an 'entity operating on and through the Organism'; this 'Organism' is, in turn, 'to a great extent self-regulatively variable'. But Lewes is unwilling to venture beyond this qualified statement; his empirical standards do not permit him to go much further. Man is free only in 'the sense that we have a range of motives surveyed by a Personality which is the incorporation of our past experience, and carries the prevision of alternative futures'. Lewes is silent as to the nature of this 'Personality'; he does not say whether he regards it, like Samuel Butler after him, as a vital power extending beyond the span of an individual life. Instead, he insists that, as a psychologist, he is bent only on a scientific interpretation of the 'conditions' which make up human conduct. Like Freud, decades later, he reduces theology into 'science' by quitting, as he says, 'the metaphysical for the biological point of view'. 'The only question therefore is, What are the conditions? It is the task of the psychologist to specify them.'

The *Study of Psychology* was the last part of Lewes's incomplete *chef-d'oeuvre*, the ambitious *Problems of Life and Mind* (1873–1879). It was published by George Eliot in the year after his death. George Eliot's own *Middlemarch*—and in a different way, her *Daniel Deronda*—must be placed against Lewes's inquiries, as well as against those of other contemporaries concerned with the Libertarian controversy. As a novelist, George Eliot assumes a 'task' analogous to that which Lewes prescribed for his 'psychologist'. She surveys the 'range of motives' of her characters with an eye to 'past experience' and, in doing so, cautiously assesses 'the prevision of alternative futures'. The choices offered to the novel's individual characters are examined not only from the 'biological point of view' demanded by Lewes but also from that of a moralist and fabulist employing a very similar scientific idiom in order to determine and verify the existence of higher ethical truths. As we shall see in the next chapter, George Eliot eventually abandoned the analytical manner of *Middlemarch* in order to turn to a more elevated form of presenting these truths in *Daniel Deronda*, her final novel, where she deliberately flaunts the causal and 'inexorable subjection of conditions' which, according to Lewes governs all our action. In *Middlemarch*, however, she sets up a complex deterministic system governed by what she alternately calls 'the train of causes' (ch. 61), 'the force of circumstances' (ch. 36), the 'rush of unintended consequences' (ch. 57), or, perhaps most appropriately, 'the irony of events' (ch. 46).

In the scheme of *Middlemarch* this 'irony of events' affects the individual wills of all the characters who are, like Lewes's sailors, swept along by the inexorable stream of human progress. As we have seen already, Dorothea—the story of whose 'errant will' provides the main line of action—and her fellow-seekers for perfection, Lydgate and Ladislaw, are all desirous of higher 'effects'. Fred and Rosamond Vincy likewise want to make an 'impression' on the world. That revengeful pair, Featherstone and Casaubon, hope to affect the lives of their survivors through the provisions made in their last 'wills'. The banker Bulstrode's own desire to control human destiny is masked by his sanctimonious deference to the mandate of a 'Divine Will'. And yet, without exception, the wills of all these characters are blunted.

Bulstrode succumbs to the pressures of past actions he has tried to ignore (and which, according to Lewes's psychological determinism, are an integral part of his 'personality'). Lydgate, Bulstrode's unwilling associate, is similarly caught in a causal web, paralyzed by his yoke to a feebler being capable of seeing 'causes and effects which lay within the track of her own tastes and interests' (ch. 58). Featherstone's dying wish to alter his last will is countered by Mary Garth, who by her choice and 'without a will of her own' thereby alters the lot of Fred Vincy, her fiancé. Similarly, Casaubon's posthumous demands are defied by a matured Dorothea, who chooses to marry young 'Will' the Radical (who is in turn tamed by her influence, just as Lewes's 'Will' becomes 'educable' and 'amenable to Moral Law'). Thus, on the whole, the volition of all characters is checked by 'the irony of events' and must be tempered by experience or, what amounts to the same thing, by a conformity to prosaic 'conditions' of existence. Caleb Garth, the very voice for this conformity, concludes sadly at one point: 'For my part, I wish there was no such thing as a will.' Although, in context, Caleb's words merely refer to the stipulations in Featherstone's testament, they are misinterpreted by an indignant listener: 'That's a strange sentiment to come from a Christian man, by God! ... I should like to know how you will back that up, Garth!' (ch. 35). Caleb remains silent, but the answer is obvious. Backed up by experience, Caleb, his daughter Mary, and his son-in-law and disciple, Fred Vincy, as well as the matured Dorothea and her second husband, abandon all 'great expectations'. The effects of their being can become 'diffusive' only upon their recognition and acceptance of the 'conditions' established by a power greater than themselves.

In *Middlemarch* this power is not supernatural. It is merely the summation of human actions, the cumulative wills of past and present which make George Eliot's 'irony of events' quite similar to the World-Will of Schopenhauer or to the evolutionary 'current of natural forces' postulated by Lewes.[1] The novel's intricate network of causal connections approaches the mechanism of these 'natural forces'. Characters and events are linked within the realm of probability. Their interaction and the effects of this interaction are examined by an ironic, but sympathetic novelist-observer and by her reader, both of whom can momentarily detach themselves from their own submission to similar laws or 'conditions'. George Eliot likens her fictional chains of

[1] According to Antonio Aliotta, *The Idealistic Reaction Against Science*, Macmillan and Co., 1914, the voluntarism of Schopenhauer seemed to supply 'the metaphysical view best suited to explain the process of evolution' and to provide 'that which was lacking in a mechanical theory' (p. 29). Lewes rejected Schopenhauer's all-encompassing definition of Will, although there are several correspondences between their thought. George Eliot recommended an 1853 article by John Oxenford as 'one of the best' on Schopenhauer (*GEL*, II, 95); it is said to have secured the philosopher's reputation in England and to have stimulated his belated recognition in Germany.

reaction to those of the experimental scientist: 'In watching effects, if only of an electric battery, it is often necessary to change our place and examine a particular mixture ...' (ch. 40). Yet, unlike Thomas Hardy, she is unwilling to aggrandize the deterministic sequences she portrays into a pattern conforming to an invariable cosmic order or into a monumental vision of the 'World as Evil'.[1] Nor does her determinism lead her to worship at the foot of an abstraction such as Auguste Comte's 'Grand Être', which, like her own concept of tradition and culture, combines a cumulative past with the needs of the present.[2] Instead, George Eliot answers as an artist and moralist the question that Lewes poses as a psychologist: 'What are the conditions?'

In *Middlemarch* the conditions created by the 'irony of events' stress man's dependence on the actions of his fellow man. To George Eliot, as to Matthew Arnold, a 'consciousness of the not ourselves', of powers beyond the scope of the individual will, makes for 'righteousness'. God, immortality, providence may not exist: yet man must therefore act as if they do. The believing skeptics of Middlemarch, the Garths and the Farebrothers, are didactically rewarded by the same deterministic sequences they recognize and obey. On the other hand, the 'irony of events' is enlisted to shatter the scientific *hybris* of Lydgate or the fanaticism of Bulstrode. *Middlemarch* tests the efficacy of ethical conduct. But it separates conduct from faith in a God and reduces mystery to a verifiable experience. Although George Eliot was to reintroduce 'mystery' in *Daniel Deronda*, in *Middlemarch* she can be accused of the same inconsistencies evident in the work of those Victorian thinkers who likewise confused the unknowable with the unknown. As if aware of the possibility of such an imputation, she defends herself in chapter 61 of the

---

[1] Lewes, like George Eliot, rejects any mechanical view based on a 'rigorous invariableness of sequence, irrespective of any variations in the conditions', an invariableness which well applies to the fatalistic world of Hardy's novels (*The Study of Psychology*, p. 110).

[2] Comte classified human progress according to three 'states' or stages: the theological or imaginative, the metaphysical or abstract, and the scientific or positive. It is noteworthy that George Eliot inverts the order in *Middlemarch* by giving supremacy to the nonscientific, but imaginative, Dorothea. The young widow's escape from the grasp of Casaubon's 'Dead Hand' is also in defiance of Comte's favorite aphorism that 'the living are governed by the dead'.

216   U. C. Knoelpflmacher

novel by taking her epigraph from Johnson's *Rasselas*: ' "Inconsistencies," answered Imlac, "cannot both be right, but im-
puted to man they may both be true." ' Though hailed as the
most 'philosophic' of novelists by her contemporaries, George
Eliot reminds the reader that she is concerned with an artistic
interpretation of 'truth' and not with the resolution of metaphysical inconsistencies. Transplanted to the medium of fiction,
her world-picture can create a greater semblance of truth than
its numerous counterparts in the philosophical and critical essays
of her contemporaries. Lewes's speculations have been superseded by the advent of Freudianism; the anti-mechanist doctrines
of Spencer and Butler have been dismissed by stricter thinkers.
Even the heated debates of the Metaphysical Society ended in a
lame stalemate by an acceptance of the conclusion that 'if free
will does not exist, we must and do act as if it did'.[1] Though
unsatisfactory from a philosophical standpoint, this same conclusion carries an air of authenticity when borne out by the
intricate 'irony of events' which governs in *Middlemarch*.

Like the work of so many a Victorian 'truth-seeker', *Middlemarch* thrives on paradox. It is a mystic's rejection of religion
and a rationalist's plea for irrationality. It contains a scrupulous
'scientific' dissection of character by a writer hostile to the aims
of science. Part of the novel's success in its emulation of 'truth'
lies in George Eliot's ability to recreate in its poetic *architec-
tonicè* the very same tension that Matthew Arnold had regarded
as being inimical to poetry. No other novel by George Eliot
approaches the detachment of *Middlemarch*; no other novel
before *The Ambassadors* uses complementary points of view to
a greater effect. The endless oppositions of *Middlemarch* define,
modify, and redefine characters and actions alike. Even the titles
of the various parts of the book are carefully counterpointed.
As Mr Brooke so helpfully volunteers, 'Everything is symbolical,
you know' (ch. 34).

Balance is all in *Middlemarch*. George Eliot the rationalist
corrects George Eliot the enthusiast; Dorothea the enthusiast
corrects Lydgate the rationalist. Although this balance is occasionally broken, the author qualifies her 'gushiness' through a
steady sense of humor; she softens her satiric denunciations by
an all-inclusive sympathy. She becomes a 'Bat of erudition' in

[1] Brown, *The Metaphysical Society*, p. 103.

the creation of Mr Casaubon; she spouts lusty provincialisms in portraying her 'Philistine' louts. At times George Eliot speaks through the witty Mrs Cadwallader, at times through Dorothea and through Tertius Lydgate. But she is closest perhaps to Mary Garth, the homely observer without illusions. Of all the characters, Mary alone is able to laugh at the human scene: '... people were so ridiculous with their illusions, carrying their fool's caps unawares, thinking their own lies opaque while everybody else's were transparent ...' (ch. 33).

Middlemarch carries the imprint of Mary Garth's observation. Despite the novel's 'high seriousness' and despite the starkness of its description of Lydgate's fall and Dorothea's Pyrrhic victory, the world it reproduces is only potentially tragic. *Middlemarch* does portray a relentless and gloomy evolutionary process; it laments for a lost age of faith and exhibits its makeshift 'modes of religion' with wistfulness and reluctance. But in its over-all compromise, its 'middle' march between religious despair and religious affirmation, George Eliot's masterpiece implies a confidence in man's ability to surmount his enslavement to time and change. It finds in time present and time past a possibility of future redemption. *Middlemarch* is neither tragedy nor comedy. It is the tragicomedy of human progress.

13 David Lodge

Middlemarch and the Idea of the Classic Realist Text

Paper presented at the George Eliot Centenary Conference, Leicester University, 1980.*

Middlemarch has achieved a unique status as both paradigm and paragon in discussion of the novel as a literary form. If a teacher or critic wishes to cite a representative example of the nineteenth-century English novel at its best, the chances are that it will be *Middlemarch*. Indeed it is scarcely an exaggeration to say that, for many critics, *Middlemarch* is the *only* truly representative, truly great Victorian novel—all other candidates, including the rest of George Eliot's fiction, being either too idiosyncratic or too flawed. Barbara Hardy was surely right when she said in her introduction to *Middlemarch: critical approaches to the novel* (1967) that 'if a poll were held for the greatest English novel there would probably be more votes for *Middlemarch* than for any other work';[1] while one of her contributors, Hilda Hulme, quoted a judgement that 'every novel would be *Middlemarch* if it could'.[2]

That symposium edited by Barbara Hardy probably registered the highwater mark of *Middlemarch*'s modern reputation. More recently criticism has begun to express a more reserved admiration for George Eliot's masterpiece, echoing and amplifying Henry James's suave judgement on reviewing *Middlemarch*: 'It sets a limit, we think, to the development of the old-fashioned English novel.'[3] George Eliot's realism is now regarded not as a kind of timeless truthfulness to human experience (as implied by the

* This paper was originally presented at the George Eliot Centenary Conference held at Leicester University, 4–6 July 1980. Some six months later, Dr Colin MacCabe, of whose work it is in part a critique, became the centre of a widely publicized controversy at the University of Cambridge. I record this sequence of events to make clear that my essay should in no way be interpreted as an oblique comment on the Cambridge 'affair', or a taking of sides in relation to it. My disagreement with Professor MacCabe (as he now is) on points of literary theory and literary history does not diminish the respect I have for his work or the stimulus I have obtained from it.

tribute, every novel would be *Middlemarch* if it could), but as an historically conditioned, ideologically motivated construction of 'the real'. J. Hillis Miller, for instance, while acknowledging that *Middlemarch* is 'perhaps the masterwork of Victorian realism',[4] is concerned to expose the rhetorical devices by which George Eliot achieves her 'totalizing' effect, and to reveal, beneath her apparently serene mastery of her fictional world, a gnawing epistemological doubt. A still more radical critique of George Eliot's realism, especially as displayed in *Middlemarch*, is to be found in a recent book by Colin MacCabe, *James Joyce and the Revolution of the Word* (1979), which I propose to use as my real starting point for this essay.

Colin MacCabe's book is an important and valuable study of Joyce, but gets some of its impetus from what seems to me a tendentious account of the nineteenth-century novel (the so-called 'classic realist text'), which is in its own way as misleading as the naive assumption that realistic fiction simply reflects a pre-existing reality more or less truthfully, and which should perhaps be challenged before it becomes a new orthodoxy.

Colin MacCabe is a British disciple (and an exceptionally lucid and articulate one) of that school of Parisian criticism to which I would give the general name of post-structuralism: in which the purely formal, semiological analysis of literary texts and genres, with which structuralist criticism was originally concerned, has been polemicized by the infusion of Roland Barthes's literary historicism, Jacques Lacan's reading of Freud, Louis Althusser's reading of Marx, and Jacques Derrida's deconstruction of the metaphysical basis of Western philosophy.[5] In this school of thought, the purely methodological separation made by Saussure between the signifier and the signified in the sign is given ontological status and importance. There is never a perfect fit between language and the world. It is impossible absolutely to say what we mean or mean what we say, since the subject who completes an utterance is no longer exactly the same as the subject who originated it, and the language used by the subject has its own materiality capable of signifiying beyond the subject's intention or control. The subject (what George Eliot would have called the individual man or woman) is not a concrete, substantial identity situated outside language, but is produced and continually modified by the entry into language. It is the ideas of language as a kind of 'material' and of consciousness and social relations as a kind of 'production' which perhaps enable proponents of this school of thought to reconcile their rather bleakly anti-humanist semiology with their commitment to revolutionary politics. Certainly they seem closer in spirit to Nietzsche than to Marx, and at times to come perilously near a kind of epistemological abyss of infinitely recessive interpretations of interpretations, rendering all human intellectual effort essentially futile. The underlying message seems to be that, however bleak and frightening this view of man and consciousness may be, it is true; and to deny it can only have the ill effects of all repression—whether in society, the psyche, or literature.

Colin MacCabe claims that Joyce's importance resides in the fact that he puts his readers to school in precisely this way, though his critics have misunderstood the lesson and obstinately persisted in trying to explain (or 'recuperate') his works, making them conform to a notion of stable 'meaning' such as it was precisely his intention to undermine. In his mature work, Joyce was concerned 'not with representing experience through language, but with experiencing language through a destruction of representation'.[6] To throw into relief Joyce's liberation of language, and destruction of representation, Colin MacCabe contrasts his fiction with 'the classic realist text', as represented by *Middlemarch*, 'which purports to represent experience through language'.

The 'classic realist text' is a term that derives from the criticism of Roland Barthes, especially *S/Z* (1970), and MacCabe is certainly indebted to Barthes in some ways. But his definition of the classic realist text is simpler, and I think less subtle, than Barthes'. According to MacCabe, a novel is a tissue of discourses— the discourses of the characters, as rendered in their speech, and the discourse of the narrator; and it is characteristic of the classic realist text that in it the narrative discourse acts as a 'metalanguage',[7] controlling, interpreting, and judging the other discourses, and thus putting the reader in a position of dominance over the characters and their stories. Joyce, in contrast, refuses to privilege one discourse over another in his writing, or to privilege the reader's position *vis-à-vis* the text. Even in his early work, such as the stories of *Dubliners*, superficially consistent with the techniques of classic realism, the narrator's discourse proves ambiguous and enigmatic on close examination; while in, for instance, the Cyclops episode of *Ulysses*, a characteristic specimen of his mature work, the conflicting discourses of the anonymous patron of Barney Kiernan's pub who narrates the main action, the Citizen, Bloom, and all the other characters in the bar, are interrupted not by the metalanguage of a reliable authorial narrator but by passages of parodic inflation and hyperbole (sanctioned purely aesthetically by the 'gigantism' theme of the episode)—a counter-text, MacCabe calls it, which 'far from setting up a position of judgement for the reader, merely proliferates the languages available'.[8] Thus the reader of *Ulysses* is never allowed to sink into the comfortable assurance of an interpretation guaranteed by the narrator, but must himself produce the meaning of the text by opening himself fully to the play of its diverse and contradictory discourses.

One symptom of Joyce's rejection of the conventions of reading and representation employed in the classic realist text, which MacCabe seizes on with understandable enthusiasm, is Joyce's refusal, from his earliest days as a writer, to employ what he called 'perverted commas' in rendering direct speech—using an introductory dash instead. It is the typographical marking off of direct speech from narrative by quotation marks that enforces the authority of the narrator's metalanguage, in MacCabe's view. 'The narrative prose is the meta-language that can state all the truths in the object-language(s) (the marks held in inverted commas) and can also explain the relation of the object-language to the world.'[9]

MacCabe uses George Eliot as a foil to show up certain features of Joyce's work, and an element of exaggeration and caricature is always apt to creep into such manoeuvres. Let us acknowledge that there is a real difference between the art of George Eliot and the art of James Joyce which MacCabe helps to define. Let us note also that MacCabe himself admits that classic realism is never absolute, and that within George Eliot's novels 'there are always images which counter the flat and univocal process which is the showing forth of the real'.[10] Nevertheless it seems to me that the distortion of George Eliot's practice implied by MacCabe's model of the classic realist text is sufficiently great to be worth contesting, and that this might be a way of extending our understanding of classic realism generally, and of George Eliot's art in particular.

What MacCabe calls a metalanguage (a term borrowed from linguistics and philosophy) will be better known to students of George Eliot as the convention of the omniscient and intrusive narrator, which has a venerable history as a subject of contention in criticism of her work. In the period of her relative eclipse, in the 1920s, 30s and 40s, when the Jamesian aesthetic of 'showing' rather than 'telling' was dominant in novel criticism, this feature of her work counted heavily against her. In the 1950s and 1960s several critics such as Wayne Booth, W. J. Harvey, and Barbara Hardy instituted a successful defence of the convention and George Eliot's exploitation of it, thus complementing on the aesthetic plane the reinstatement of George Eliot as a great novelist which F. R. Leavis had achieved on the ethical plane.

As Gérard Genette has observed, in his excellent study *Narrative Discourse*, the James-Lubbock distinction between 'showing' and 'telling', and the corresponding pair of terms, 'scene' and 'summary', derive from the distinction drawn between mimesis and diegesis in the third book of Plato's *Republic*; and MacCabe's discussion of the matter seems particularly close to Plato's (though it reverses Plato's preferences) because of the importance he gives to the marking off of speech from narration in the classic realist text. Plato illustrates the distinction between mimesis and diegesis by reference to the opening scene of the *Iliad* in which Chryses appeals to the Achaeans to let him ransom his daughter.

You know that as far as the lines

> *He prayed the Achaeans all,*
> *But chiefly the two rulers of the people,*
> *Both sons of Atreus*

the poet himself speaks, he never tries to turn our thoughts from himself or to suggest that anyone else is speaking; but after this he speaks as if he was himself Chryses, and tries his best to make us think that the priest, an old man, is speaking and not Homer.[11]

Mimesis, then, is narrating by imitating another's speech. Diegesis is narrating in one's own voice. To make his distinction clearer, Plato, through his mouthpiece Socrates, rewrites the scene from Homer in unbroken diegesis, in which Chryses' actual words are summarized in indirect form, *oratio obliqua*, and assimilated to the linguistic register of the narrator, Homer himself. A typology of literary modes (later to evolve into a typology of literary genres)[12] thus emerges: pure diegesis, as exemplified by dithyramb (a kind of hymn), in which the poet speaks exclusively in his own voice; pure mimesis, as exemplified by tragedy and comedy, in which the poet speaks exclusively in imitated voices; and the mixed form of the epic, which combines both modes. Needless to say, Plato greatly distrusted the most mimetic kind of writing, since it is ethically undiscriminating; and he will admit into the Republic only the most austere kind of writing—the purely diegetic, or that which combines diegesis with a little mimesis, but of good personages only.

Plato's discussion is more relevant to the comparison of George Eliot and James Joyce than might at first appear. Realism as a literary quality, or effect, of verisimilitude, is something we think of as very close to, if not quite synonymous with, the classical notion of mimesis or imitation, and we often describe the novel casually as a 'mimetic' literary form. In fact, of course, only drama is a strictly mimetic form, in which only words are imitated *in* words, and what is non-verbal—spectacle, gesture, etc.—is imitated non-verbally. Anything that is not dialogue in a novel, if only *he said* and *she said*, is diegesis, the report of a narrator, 'the poet himself' however impersonal. The only way of getting round this rule is to put the narrating entirely into the hands (or mouths) of a character or characters, as in the pseudo-auto-biographical novel or the epistolary novel: then the narrative becomes mimetic of diegesis. But as Genette concludes, 'the truth is that mimesis in words can only be mimesis of words. Other than that, all we have and can have is degrees of diegeses.'[13]

There is no *necessary* connection between mimesis and realism: some novels that consist largely of dialogue (Ronald Firbank, Henry Green, Ivy Compton-Burnett) are highly artificial; and some of the most realistic (i.e. convincing, lifelike, compelling) passages in *Middlemarch* are diegetic (for example the account of Lydgate's unpremeditated declaration to Rosamund in Chapter 31). But it is true that mimesis is inherently better adapted to realistic effect than diegesis, simply because it uses words to imitate words. The classic realist novel of the nineteenth century maintained a fairly even balance between mimesis and diegesis, showing and telling, scene and summary, and it did so at the expense of some degree of realistic illusion, in the interests of ethical control of the story and the reader's response.

The eighteenth-century novel began with the discovery of new mimetic possibilities in prose fiction—the pseudo-confessions of Defoe, the pseudo-correspondences of Richardson. But these achievements, remarkable as they were, tended to confirm Plato's fears about the morally debilitating effects of skilful mimesis of imperfect personages without diegetic guidance from the author. However highminded the intentions of Defoe (which is doubtful) or of Richardson (which is not), there is no way in which the reader can be prevented from delighting in and even identifying with the vitality, energy and resourcefulness of Moll Flanders or Lovelace, even in their wicked actions. Fielding, his mind trained in a classical school, restored the diegetic element in his 'comic-epic poem in prose'—though paradoxically in the interests of a more liberal morality than Richardson's or Defoe's. And it was Fielding's narrative method (though not his morality) which provided the model for the nineteenth-century novelists from Scott to George Eliot. In the classic Victorian novel, not only is there a great deal of narrative in proportion to speech, summary in proportion to scene, but the writers exploit the diegetic possibilities of the mixed form to speak very much 'in their own voice'—not merely reporting events, but delivering judgements, opinions, and evaluations about the story and about life in general. Even when characters act as narrators, (e.g. in *Jane Eyre*, *Great Expectations*) they behave more like novelists, shaping and improving their own stories, than do the naive memoir-writers of Defoe, or the pressured correspondents of Richardson.

With the advent of the modern novel, the pendulum swings back towards mimesis, in more subtle and sophisticated forms. Flaubert begins the process: in *Madame Bovary* the narrator is omnipresent, but it is impossible to discover what he thinks about the story he is telling. In James, the narrator is either a created character of doubtful reliability (e.g. the governess in *The Turn of the Screw*) or an authorial narrator who deliberately restricts himself to the limited perspective of a character (such as Lambert Strether in *The Ambassadors*) entangled in circumstances he does not fully understand. In Joyce, the author is progressively 'refined out of existence, indifferent, paring his fingernails'. The impersonal, but reliable and tonally consistent narrator of the early episodes of *Ulysses*, who tells us, for instance, that 'Stately, plump Buck Mulligan came from the stairhead, bearing a bowl of lather on which a mirror and a razor lay crossed,' or that 'Mr Leopold Bloom ate with relish the inner organs of beasts and fowls,' gradually disappears under a welter of different discourses, parodies and pastiches of journalese, officialese, obsolete literary styles, pub talk, women's magazine language, scientific description, and is finally displaced by the supreme example of mimesis in English narrative literature, the interior monologue of Molly Bloom.

I think there is some advantage to be gained from substituting the Platonic distinction between mimesis and diegesis for Mac-Cabe's distinction between language and metalanguage. Instead of seeing a total break of continuity between the classic realist text and the modern text, we see rather a swing of the pendulum from one end of a continuum of possibilities to the other, a pendulum that has been swinging throughout literary history. Mimesis and diegesis, like metaphor and metonymy, are fundamental, and, on a certain level, all-inclusive categories of representation, and a typology of texts can be established by assessing the dominance of one over the other. We are also better placed to show how MacCabe misrepresents the art of George Eliot. Two main points have to be made: (1) the distinction between mimesis and diegesis in George Eliot is by no means as clear-cut as MacCabe implies; and (2) the diegetic element is much more problematic than he allows.

When Plato refers to the epic as a mixed form, he means that it combines, or alternates between, mimesis and diegesis, the voice of the poet and the voices of the characters he imitates in dialogue. But the classic realist novel 'mixes' the two discourses in a more fundamental sense: it fuses them together, often indistinguishably and inextricably, through the device of free indirect speech by means of which the narrator, without absenting himself entirely from the text, communicates the narrative to us coloured by the thoughts and feelings of a character. The reference to this character in the third person pronoun, and the use of the past tense, or 'epic preterite', still imply the existence of the author as the source of the narrative; but by deleting the tags which affirm that existence, such as *he said*, *she wondered*, *she thought to herself*, etc., and by using the kind of diction appropriate to the character rather than to the authorial narrator, the latter can allow the sensibility of the character to dominate the discourse, and correspondingly subdue his own voice, his own opinions and evaluations. It was Jane Austen who first perfected the use of free indirect speech in English fiction, and thus showed succeeding novelists, including George Eliot, how the novel might combine Fielding's firm diegetic control with Richardson's subtle mimesis of character. The device is an extremely flexible one, which allows the narrator to move very freely and fluently between the poles of mimesis and diegesis within a single paragraph, or even a single sentence; and its effect is always to make the reader's task of interpretation more active and problematic. If we are looking for a single formal feature which characterizes the realist novel of the nineteenth century, it is surely not the domination of the characters' discourses by the narrator's discourse (something in fact more characteristic of earlier narrative literature) but the extensive use of free indirect speech, which obscures and complicates the distinction between the two types of discourse.

The work of the Russian literary theorists Mikhail Bakhtin and Valentin Volosinov, which goes back to the nineteen-twenties, but has only recently been translated into English, is very relevant here. They (or he—for they may be one and the same person) have suggested that it is precisely the dissolution of the boundaries between reported speech and reporting context (i.e., the author's speech) that characterizes the novel as discourse and distinguishes it from earlier types of narrative prose and from lyric verse. Bakhtin characterized novel discourse as 'polyphonic' or 'polyglottal', and maintained that, 'One of the essential peculiarities of prose fiction is the possibility it allows of using different types of discourse, with their distinct expressiveness intact, on the plane of a single work, without reduction to a single common denominator.'[14] Different types of discourse can be represented in fiction, of course, as the direct speech of characters, without serious disturbance to the authority of the narrator, as in the novels of Fielding or Scott. But once these discourses enter into the narrative discourse itself, in various forms of reported speech, or thought, the interpretative control of the author's voice is inevitably weakened to some degree, and the reader's work increased.

Derek Oldfield, in an essay entitled 'The Character of Dorothea', contributed to that symposium on *Middlemarch* edited by Barbara Hardy to which I have already referred, pointed out how George Eliot's narrative method is complicated by this alternation of narrator's and characters' voices, compelling to the reader to, in his words, 'zig-zag' his way through the discourse, rather than following a straight, well-marked path.[15] One of the examples he gives describes Dorothea's naive ideas about marriage at the beginning of the story. I shall cite the same passage, hoping to add a few points to his excellent commentary:

> She was open, ardent, and not in the least self-admiring; indeed, it was pretty to see how her imagination adorned her sister Celia with attractions altogether superior to her own, and if any gentleman appeared to come to the Grange from some other motive than that of seeing Mr Brooke, she concluded that he must be in love with Celia: Sir James Chettam, for example, whom she constantly considered from Celia's point of view, inwardly debating whether it would be good for Celia to accept him. That he should be regarded as a suitor to herself would have seemed to her a ridiculous irrelevance. Dorothea, with all her eagerness to know the truths of life, retained very childlike ideas about marriage.[16]

So far, this is diegetic: the narrator describes Dorothea's character authoritatively, in words that Dorothea could not use about herself without contradiction. (She cannot say or think about herself that she is not self-admiring, for that would be to admire herself. Nor can she acknowledge that her ideas about marriage are childlike without ceasing to hold them.) It is the justification of the diegetic method that it can give us such information, lucidly, concisely, and judiciously. In the rest of the passage, however, the narrator's discourse becomes permeated with Dorothea's discourse, but without wholly succumbing to it.

> She felt sure that she would have accepted the judicious Hooker, if she had been born in time to save him from that wretched mistake he made in matrimony: or John Milton when his blindness had come on; or any of the other great men whose odd habits it would have been glorious piety to endure; but an amiable handsome baronet, who said 'Exactly' to her

remarks even when she expressed uncertainty—how could he affect her as a lover? The really delightful marriage must be that where your husband was a sort of father, and could teach you even Hebrew, if you wished it.[17]

As Oldfield observes, the tag, 'she felt' is an ambiguous signal to the reader, since it can introduce either objective report or subjective reflection. Such colloquial phrases in the sequel as 'that wretched mistake' and 'when his blindness had come on', seem to be the words in which Dorothea herself would have articulated these ideas, though the equally colloquial 'odd habits' does not. Why does it not? Because, in unexpected collocation with 'great men' it seems too literary an irony for Dorothea, and so we ascribe it to the narrator. But that is not to imply that Dorothea is incapable of irony. '[W]ho said "Exactly" to her remarks even when she expressed uncertainty'—do we not infer that Sir James' illogicality has been noted by Dorothea herself in just that crisp, dismissive way? Then what about the immediately succeeding phrase, '—how could he affect her as a lover?' This is a really interesting challenge to analysis. If the immediately preceding phrase is attributed to Dorothea, as I suggest, then it would be natural to ascribe this one to her also; and the immediately following sentence is certainly Dorothea's own thought, communicated in free indirect speech: 'The really delightful marriage must be that where your husband was a sort of father, and could teach you even Hebrew, if you wished it.' But a problem of contradiction arises if we attribute the rhetorical question to Dorothea. For if Dorothea can formulate the question, 'How can Sir James affect me as a lover?' her alleged unconsciousness of her own attractions to visiting gentlemen is compromised. Is the question, then, put by the narrator, appealing directly to the reader, over Dorothea's head, to acknowledge the plausibility of her behaviour, meaning: 'You do see, gentle reader, why it never crossed Dorothea's mind that Sir James Chettham was a possible match for her.' There is such an implication, but the reason given—that Sir James says 'Exactly' when Dorothea expresses uncertainty—seems too trivial for the narrator to draw the conclusion, 'How could he affect her as a lover?' We can perhaps naturalize the utterance by interpreting it as Dorothea's likely response to a hypothetical question—'Do you think you could fall in love with Sir James Chettham?' But the fact is that mimesis and diegesis are fused together inextricably here, and for a good purpose. For there is a sense in which Dorothea knows what the narrator knows—namely, that Sir James is sexually attracted to her—but is repressing the thought, on account of her determination to marry an intellectual father-figure. When Celia finally compels Dorothea to face the fact that not only Sir James, but even the servants, assume that he is courting Dorothea, the narrator tells us that she was 'not less angry because details asleep in her memory were now awakened to confirm the unwelcome revelation'. One of those details was surely that very habit of Sir James's of saying 'Exactly' when she expressed uncertainty—a sign, surely, of his admiration, deference, and anxiety to please.

I am not claiming a Flaubertian *impassibilité* for the narrator of *Middlemarch*. The first part of the passage under discussion establishes very clearly the ethical terms in which Dorothea is to be judged: selflessness on the one hand, self-deception on the other. But as the writing proceeds to flesh out this diegetic assessment more mimetically, the reader is progressively more taxed to negotiate the nuances of irony and to resolve the ambiguities of deixis. Exactly how far Dorothea misconceives the nature of the great intellectual figures of the past; whether she is right or wrong in her assessment of Sir James Chettham's intelligence; whether she emerges from the whole passage with more credit than discredit, are questions which the reader must finally decide for himself. I think it will be granted that there are many other such passages in *Middlemarch*.

It is not, however, only because mimesis often contaminates diegesis in this way that MacCabe's account of the narrator's voice in George Eliot's fiction seems inaccurate.

The metalanguage within such a text refuses to acknowledge its own status as writing. The text outside the area of inverted commas claims to be the product of no articulation, it claims to be unwritten. This unwritten text can then attempt to staunch the haemorrhage of interpretations threatened by the material of language. Whereas other discourses within the text are considered as materials which are open to reinterpretation, the narrative discourse functions simply as a window on reality. This relationship between discourses can be taken as the defining feature of the classic realist text.[18]

The assertion that the narrator's discourse claims to be 'un-written' may be puzzling unless one traces it back to Derrida's argument that Western culture has always privileged the spoken word over the written, because the spoken word appears to guarantee the 'metaphysics of presence' on which our philoso-phical tradition is predicated. Speech implies the presence of a speaker, and by inference of an authentic, autonomous self who is the arbiter of his own meanings and able to pass them intact to another. But Derrida argues that this is a fallacy and an illusion. It is the absence of the addresser from the message which allows the materiality of language to generate its own semantic pos-sibilities among which the addressee may romp at will. Writing, in which such absence is obvious, is thus a more reliable model of how language works than speech; and writing which claims truthfulness by trying to disguise itself as speech, as the discourse of a man speaking to men, is in bad faith, or at least deluded.

Now it is true that the narrator's discourse in George Eliot's fiction is modelled on the I–thou speech situation, and certain that she would have endorsed Wordsworth's description of the writer as a man speaking to men. But in obvious ways, whether consciously or unconsciously, she reminds us that her narration is in fact written. This is particularly true of the more osten-tatiously diegetic passages, when she suspends the story to deliver herself of opinions, generalizations, judgements. To call these passages transparent windows on reality, as MacCabe does, seems quite inappropriate. They are in fact often quite obscure, or at least very complicated, and have to be scrutinized several times before we can confidently construe their meaning—a process that is peculiar to reading, and cannot be applied to the spoken word. Consider, for example, this comment on Mr Fare-brother, shortly after Lydgate has voted against him in the selec-tion of the hospital chaplaincy.

But Mr Farebrother met him with the same friendliness as before. The character of the publican and sinner is not always practically incompatible with that of the modern Pharisee, for the majority of us scarcely see more distinctly the faultiness of our own conduct than the faultiness of our own arguments, or the dullness of our own jokes. But the Vicar of St Botolph's had certainly escaped the slightest tincture of the Pharisee, and by dint of admitting to himself that he was too much as other men were, he had become remarkably unlike them in this—that he could excuse others for thinking slightly of him, and could judge impartially of their conduct even when it told against him.[19]

I would defy anyone to take in the exact sense of this passage through the ear alone. There are too many distinctions being juggled, and too many swerves and loops in the movement of the argument: first, we encounter the idea (stated in a double negative, and thus made more difficult to assimilate) that the modern publican and sinner may be combined with the modern Pharisee in the same person, unlike their Biblical prototypes. Is Mr Farebrother, who has just been mentioned, such a person, we may wonder, as we begin to negotiate this passage? This would be inconsistent with the previous presentation of his character, but we have to wait for some time to be reassured that this is *not* what the narrator means. Before we come to that point, we have to wrestle with another distinction—between faults of manners (arguments and jokes) and faults of morals (conduct)—a distinction which doesn't correspond exactly to the one between publicans and sinners and Pharisees. The exculpation of Farebrother is highly paradoxical: by admitting that he is too much like other men, he becomes remarkably unlike them: which is to say, that by admitting he is a publican and a sinner, he avoids being a Pharisee as well. So why has the narrator introduced the concept of Pharisee at all? It seems to be floating free, and we puzzle our way through the paragraph, waiting to see to whom it applies. We may be disconcerted to realize that it is applied, explicitly, only to 'the majority of us' ourselves. Perhaps it is also applied implicitly to Lydgate, whose conduct over the election, as he himself is well aware, was not entirely disinterested. On reflection we may decide that the negative comparison between Farebrother and Pharisee is justified by the fact that the Pharisees were a Jewish religious sect and that Phariseeism is an occupational failing of men of religion, but this explanation scarcely leaps off the page.

Mr Farebrother seems to emerge from these complex comparisons with credit. But only a few lines later, after a speech from Mr Farebrother in direct (i.e. mimetic) form—

'The world has been too strong for *me*, I know,' he said one day to Lydgate. 'But then I am not a mighty man—I shall never be a man of renown. The choice of Hercules is a pretty fable; but Prodicus makes it easy work for the hero, as if the first resolves were enough. Another story says that he came to hold the distaff, and at last wore the Nessus shirt. I suppose one good resolve might keep a man right if everybody else's resolve helped him.'[20]

—we encounter this diegetic comment:

The Vicar's talk was not always inspiriting: he had escaped being a Pharisee, but he had not escaped that low estimate of possibilities which we rather hastily arrive at as an inference from our own failure.[21]

This seems to check any inclination on the reader's part to over-estimate Mr Farebrother's moral stature; and if, in reading the preceding diegetic passage, we mentally defend ourselves against the accusation of Phariseeism by identifying ourselves with Farebrother's candid admission of his faults, we now find ourselves implicated with him in another kind of failing—complacency about one's faults. But if we make *another* adjustment, and take this as a cue to condemn Farebrother, we may be surprised and disconcerted once more, to find ourselves identified with Lydgate—for the passage immediately continues, and ends (as does the whole chapter) with this sentence: 'Lydgate felt that there was a pitiable lack of will in Mr Farebrother.' Since Lydgate has just been portrayed as subordinating his own will to expediency in the matter of the chaplaincy election, he is hardly in a position to throw stones at this particular moral glasshouse, and the sequel will show even greater 'infirmity of will' on his part in the matter of Rosamund.[22] To sum up, the authorial commentary, so far from telling the reader what to think, or putting him in a position of dominance in relation to the discourse of the characters, constantly forces him to think for himself, and constantly implicates him in the moral judgements being formulated.

I like to call this kind of literary effect, the 'Fish effect', because the American critic Stanley Fish has made the study of it so much his own in a series of books and articles published over the last fifteen years—primarily on seventeenth-century poetry and prose, but more lately with a wider range of reference.[23] Basically, his argument is that as we read, lineally, word by word, word group by word group, we form hypotheses and expectations about the meaning that is going to be delivered at the end of the sentence, or paragraph, or text; but, as Fish shows by skilful analyses of particular passages—action-replays of reading in slow motion—very often our expectations are disconfirmed, a different and perhaps entirely opposite meaning from that which we expected is formulated, yet without entirely abolishing the mistakenly projected meaning. In his early work Fish suggested that this effect was contrived by writers who had didactic, usually religious, designs upon their readers, using it to defamiliarize familiar truths; thus Milton reminds us that we are fallen creatures not merely by the fable of *Paradise Lost* but by constantly tripping us up with his syntax. More recently, Fish has argued that the effect is inherent in all discourse, but especially literary discourse, because the meaning of an utterance is determined entirely by its context and the interpretative assumptions that are brought to it—which, in the case of literary utterances, are never simple or fixed. I think both arguments are valid, and both apply to George Eliot's diegetic style, although such deviousness might, superficially, seem incompatible with her chosen stance as narrator: the privileged historian of the moral lives of characters who, it suits her purpose to pretend, are real people in real situations. The opening paragraph of Chapter 15 is *à propos*:

A great historian, as he insisted on calling himself, who had the happiness to be dead a hundred and twenty years ago, and so to take his place among the colossi whose huge legs our living pettiness is observed to walk under, glories in his copious remarks and digressions as the least imitable part of his work, and especially in those initial chapters to the successive books of his history, where he seems to bring his arm-chair to the proscenium and chat with us in all the lusty ease of his fine English. But Fielding lived when the days were longer (for time, like money, is measured by our needs). when summer afternoons were spacious, and the clock ticked slowly in the winter evenings. We belated historians must not linger after his example; and if we did so, it is probable that our chat would be thin and eager, as if delivered from a camp-stool in a parrot-house. I at least have so much to do in unravelling certain human lots, and seeing how they were woven and interwoven, that all the light I can command must be concentrated on this particular web, and not dispersed over that tempting range of relevancies called the universe.[24]

Colin MacCabe's comment on this paragraph is that 'Although at first sight, George Eliot would appear to be questioning her form, the force of the passage is to leave us convinced that we have finally abandoned form to be treated to the simple unravelling of the real.'[25] But this seems a very stubborn refusal to credit George Eliot with ironic selfconsciousness. It is patently obvious by Chapter 15 that the narrator of *Middlemarch is* ranging over the tempting range of relevancies called the universe, especially through her famous scientific analogies. And by comparing her own writing to Fielding's, she is implicitly placing it in a tradition of literary fiction, even if this admission is neatly disguised by invoking Fielding's description of himself as a historian. The Fish effect is immediately apparent in the opening of this passage: 'A great historian, as he insisted on calling himself. . . .' We don't know, yet, of course, who this historian is, and it is quite a time before we discover his identity, and that he is not a historian at all, but a novelist. '[A]s he insisted on calling himself . . .' might give us a clue that he wasn't a proper historian, but it might equally well be construed as meaning he was a proper historian who insisted on calling himself great. '[W]ho had the happiness to be dead a hundred and twenty years ago . . .' 'Dead' is surely a surprising word in the context. 'Who had the happiness to be alive' would be the more predictable formula, expressing that nostalgia for the good old days which George Eliot so often invokes in her fiction, though in fact seldom quite straight-forwardly. The paradox is resolved when we read, 'and so to take his place among the colossi whose huge legs our living pettiness is observed to walk under. . . .' Fielding was lucky to have died a hundred and twenty years ago, then, in the sense that he thus became a literary classic—though if he is dead it is hard to see how this brings him any happiness, and the reverence accorded to a classic seems somewhat undercut by the allusion to Shakespeare's Cassius. The narrator, at any rate, takes no responsibility for the analogy. 'Whose huge legs our living pettiness is observed to walk under. . . .' Observed by whom? By the makers of such extravagant analogies? '[G]lories in his copious remarks and digressions as the least imitable part of his work.' Was Fielding right in thinking them inimitable, or has George Eliot improved upon them? Of course, she disowns any attempt to compete with him, but then the whole passage is a digression disowning the intention to digress.

Several critics have recently pointed out the presence of paradox and contradiction in George Eliot's superficially smooth, unproblematic narrative style. J. Hillis Miller, for instance, in his article 'Optic and Semiotic in *Middlemarch*', identifies three groups of totalizing metaphors or families of metaphors, and comments, 'Each group of metaphors is related to the others, fulfilling them, but at the same time contradicting them, cancelling them out, or undermining their validity.'[26] Thus, for instance, the recurring image of the lives of the characters as a flowing web, an unrolling fabric, objectively there, to which the narrator brings a truthtelling light, is contaminated by other images of the subjectivity of interpretation, the inevitable distortions of perspective. The famous analogy of the candle-flame which confers pattern on the random scratches of the pier-glass, as Miller points out (and Leslie Stephen pointed out before him) applies as well to the narrator's perspective as to that of any character's. Stephen Marcus, in an interesting, if quirky article entitled, 'Human Nature, Social Orders and Nineteenth-Century Systems of Explanation: starting in with George Eliot' interprets her fondness for setting her novels back in the historical past (a feature of the classic Victorian novel in general) as a defence mechanism designed to control themes that she was both fascinated by and yet feared: sexual passion, class conflict and epistemological scepticism. He notes in her treatment of the past, as early as 'Amos Barton', the first piece of fiction she wrote, the Fish effect, moments when the irony of the narrator's discourse, with which the reader has been feeling a comfortable complicity, suddenly rebounds upon him:

> It is the reader himself who now suddenly discovers that he is being gently but firmly prodded in the ribs, although it is not altogether clear why he should all at once find himself on the wrong end of the stick. . . . The effect, however, is momentarily to loosen the reader's grip on the sequence of statements through which he has just worked his way and to cause him to look back, if only for a fraction of an instant, to see if he can ascertain the logical and syntactical course which led him to this uncertainly dislocated and suspended position.[27]

Very recently, Graham Martin, responding directly to Colin MacCabe's book, has argued that 'we learn as much about

The Mill on the Floss by looking at discontinuities between the authorial metalanguage and the narrated fiction, as by remarking on their fusion'.[28] All these critics tend to regard the fractures they discern in the smooth surface of George Eliot's narrative method as signs or symptoms of the tremendous stresses and strains she experienced in trying to deal truthfully and yet positively with an increasingly alienated and alienating social reality. But it is not necessary to see them as aesthetic flaws. On the contrary, it is precisely because the narrator's discourse is never entirely unambiguous, predictable, and in total interpretative control of the other discourses in *Middlemarch* that the novel survives, to be read and re-read, without ever being finally closed or exhausted. And this, paradoxically, follows inevitably from the post-Saussurian theories about language and discourse to which Colin MacCabe, and other critics of the same persuasion, subscribe. If it is true that language is a system of differences with no positive terms, that the subject is inevitably split in discourse between the 'I' who speaks and the 'I' who is spoken of, that the relationship between words and things is not natural but cultural, not given but produced, then George Eliot could not write fiction that was a 'transparent window on reality' even if she wanted to. The question, therefore, is whether in trying—or pretending—to do so, she was betrayed into false consciousness and bad art. It has been my purpose to suggest that she was well aware of the indeterminacy that lurks in all efforts at human communication, and frequently reminded her readers of this fact in the very act of apparently denying it through the use of an intrusive 'omniscient' authorial voice.

Notes

[Books cited were published in London unless otherwise indicated.]

1. Barbara Hardy, (ed.), *Middlemarch: critical Approaches to the novel* (1967) p. 3.

2. *Ibid.*, pp. 94–5.

3. Henry James, *The House of Fiction*, ed. Leon Edel (1962) p. 267.

4. J. Hillis Miller, 'Optic and Semiotic in *Middlemarch*', in *The Worlds of Victorian Fiction*, ed. Jerome Buckley, (1975) p. 127.

5. This catalogue of exotic names may be baffling and irritating to the uninitiated, but limitations of space preclude a detailed explanation of the ideas and theories involved. In fact, it is not necessary to be acquainted with the intellectual history behind the post-structuralist position to understand the argument between myself and MacCabe. Readers seeking further light on these matters, however, might consult the following sources, listed in an order corresponding roughly to a progressive shift of focus from structuralism to post-structuralism: Robert Scholes, *Structuralism in Literature* (1974); Terence Hawkes, *Structuralism and Semiotics* (1977); Jonathan Culler, *Structuralist Poetics* (1974); *Structuralism and Since*, ed. John Sturrock; and Catherine Belsey, *Critical Practice* (1980). The last of these is closest to Colin MacCabe's position, the theoretical bases of which are also expounded in his own book.

6. Colin MacCabe, *James Joyce and the Revolution of the Word* (1975) p. 4.

7. 'Metalanguage: a language or system of symbols used to discuss another language or system', Collins *New English Dictionary*.

8. MacCabe, *op. cit.* p. 100.

9. *Ibid.* p. 14.

10. *Ibid.* p. 27.

11. *Great Dialogues of Plato*, translated W. H. Rouse (New York, 1956) p. 190.

12. Gérard Genette has traced this process from Plato and Aristotle to the present day in his monograph, *Introduction à l'architexte* (Paris 1979), arguing that in developing Plato's distinction between three modes of poetic utterance into a theory of three basic genres (lyric, drama, epic), later poeticians not only misrepresented the classical authors, but created a good deal of confusion in poetics. For a short account in English of this work, see James Kearns, 'Gérard Genette: a Different Genre', *The Literary Review* No. 33, Jan. 1981, pp. 21–3.

13. Gérard Genette, *Narrative Discourse*, Translated by Jane E. Lewin, (Oxford, 1980) p. 164.

14. Mikhail Bakhtin, 'Discourse Typology in Prose' [an extract from *Problems in Dostoevsky's Poetics* (Leningrad, 1929)] in *Readings in Russian Poetics*, ed. Ladislav Matejka and Krystyna Pomorska, (Ann Arbor, 1978) p. 193. This anthology also contains an extract, entitled 'Reported Speech', from Volosinov's *Marxism and the Philosophy of Language* (Leningrad, 1930). For a survey of Bakhtin's work, and a discussion of the vexed question of his relationship to Volosinov, see Ann Shukman, 'Between Marxism and Formalism: the stylistics of Mikhail Bakhtin', *Comparative Criticism: a Yearbook*, ed. E. S. Shaffer, Vol. II, (Cambridge, 1980) pp. 221–34.

15. Barbara Hardy, (Ed.), *op. cit.*, pp. 67–9.

16. George Eliot, *Middlemarch* (Harmondsworth, 1965), p. 32.

17. *Ibid.*

18. MacCabe, *op. cit.*, p. 15.

19. *Middlemarch*, p. 217.

20. *Ibid.*, p. 217.

21. *Ibid.*, pp. 217–18.

22. Farebrother's allusions to the various versions of the Hercules myth are indeed full of proleptic irony in application to Lydgate, whose 'resolve' to make a contribution to medical science will be sacrificed to Rosamund's feminine and domestic desires (equivalent to 'holding the distaff'), and who will eventually wear the Nessus shirt of failure and disillusionment in his professional and emotional life.

23. See particularly *Surprised by Sin, The Reader in Paradise Lost* (1967); *Self-Consuming Artefacts: the Experience of Seventeenth-Century Literature* (Berkeley & Los Angeles, 1972); and *Is There a Text in this Class? The Authority of Interpretative Communities* (1981).

24. *Middlemarch*, p. 170.

25. Colin MacCabe, *op. cit.*, p. 19.

26. J. Hillis Miller, Buckley, (Ed.) *op. cit.*, p. 128.

27. Steven Marcus, 'Human Nature, Social Orders, and Nineteenth-Century Systems of Explanation: Starting in with George Eliot', *Salmagundi*, XXVI (1975), p. 21.

28. Graham Martin, '*The Mill on the Floss* and the Unreliable Narrator,' Anne Smith, (Ed.), *George Eliot: Centenary Essays and an Unpublished Fragment* (1980), p. 38.

14 James W. Gargano

What Maisie Knew:
the Evolution of a 'Moral Sense'

From *Nineteenth Century Fiction*, University of California Press, 1961, pp. 33–46.

Henry James's *What Maisie Knew* presents from a complex point of view the initiation of a young girl into a world of vortical activities and emotions. The novel, moreover, as an example of James's celebrated 'dramatic' method, contains ambiguities resulting from the special techniques (not to speak of stylistic eccentricities) he developed from 1896 to 1901, the period of the *The Awkward Age* and *The Sacred Fount*. It is not surprising, therefore, to find critics in radical disagreement as to what Maisie learns from the disruptions, reunions, and chance encounters that nourish her consciousness. Does she, as Beach maintains,[1] learn nothing, or does she, as Dupee declares, 'know at last ... that she is in fact an instrument of badness among [her parents and step-parents] and a not unwilling one so long as she goes along with them in her desire for support and affection?'[2] Are we to adopt the ambiguous view of Pelham Edgar, who, after insisting that the novel traces the development of Maisie's moral sense, confesses that 'as we close the book we are in the same predicament as Mrs Wix, and ask ourselves what, after all, did Maisie really know'?[3] Or is Canby right in assuming that in *Maisie* James, as a rather headstrong virtuoso, was concerned with 'stage effects, not character and personality'?[4]

Of the most recent studies of the novel, those of Bewley and F. R. Leavis are discerning and occasionally analytical.[5] Unfortunately, the controversy between the writers turns on the question of *Maisie*'s kinship to *The Turn of the Screw*. Yet, when they

[1] Joseph Warren Beach, *The Method of Henry James*, Yale University Press, 1954, p. 239.

[2] F. W. Dupee, *Henry James*, Methuen, 1951, p. 192.

[3] Pelham Edgar, *Henry James: Man and Author*, Grant Richards, London, 1927, p. 127.

[4] Henry S. Canby, *Turn West, Turn East*, Biblo and Tanner, 1951, p. 216.

[5] Marius Bewley, *The Complex Fate*, Chatto and Windus, 1952, pp. 96–144. This book contains two 'interpolations' by F. R. Leavis.

specifically discuss *Maisie*, they are, characteristically, almost completely at odds: Bewley finds in Mrs Wix's desire to keep Maisie an 'erotic' interest in Sir Claude, while Leavis assails this view as the 'oddest of ... perversities'.[1] The disputants also differ as to why Maisie finally chooses to return to England with Mrs Wix, and more importantly they put forth conflicting opinions concerning the 'tone' of the novel. Both writers agree, however, that Maisie herself is untainted by the evil that festers around her. Not until 1956 was it suggested (perhaps on the basis of Bewley's attempt to relate the novel to *The Turn of the Screw*?) that Maisie herself is so vitiated by the evil of her 'protectors' that she seeks to resolve her dilemma by offering to become Sir Claude's mistress.[2] If it can be substantiated, this interpretation of Maisie's character would further contribute to the element of 'horror' Bewley discovers in *What Maisie Knew*.

In spite of the disparity of critical opinion concerning *Maisie*, the novel has not been examined with the care that it merits. Generally, it has been praised, patronized, and explained in a few discursive paragraphs or pages. In attempting to determine what Maisie knows at the end of the novel, I shall examine the book's internal logic of episode and authorial commentary in the hope of capturing its staged revelations. For, despite obscurities, *What Maisie Knew* does possess an order and a lucidity in the precisely articulated preparatory scenes that consummate in the superficially ambiguous final chapters. In this study my aim has not been to promote another doctrinaire thesis, but to show, with a measure of documentation that critics of *Maisie* have avoided, the sure and deliberate architectonics through which James reveals his theme.

James's preface to *Maisie* emphasizes three aspects of the novel that should help direct the reader to its meaning. First of all, by describing his youthful heroine as endowed with 'an expanding consciousness', he establishes the novel's concern with the theme of growth. Second, he insists that Maisie must 'for the satisfaction of the mind' be 'saved';[3] this comment, enforced by his allusions to the child's moral insights and by his

[1] Ibid., p. 128.
[2] Harris W. Wilson, 'What Did Maisie Know?' in *College English*, XVII, Feb. 1956, 279–81.
[3] *The Novels and Tales of Henry James*, New York edition, XI vi–vii, Macmillan and Co., 1907–9.

observations on the moral value of two scenes, declares James's intention to deal affirmatively with Maisie's development. Finally, James's reference to 'our own commentary [which] constantly attends and amplifies',[1] calls attention to the authority of his interpolations—some of them surprisingly explicit— which explore and occasionally fix the significance of Maisie's thoughts and actions. I do not mean to imply that James mechanically glosses the difficulties of the dramatic scenes in set passages of exegesis. Instead, the wealth of authorial explanation is in a sense made integral by the basic technique of the novel—a central intelligence not altogether capable (as Strether is finally capable in *The Ambassadors*) of assessing and conceptualizing the value of her experiences. James, then, in his own words compensates for Maisie's limitations by 'going so "behind" the facts of her spectacle as to exaggerate the activity of her relation to them' without violating the unique sense of the child's response to those facts.[2]

Unless his preface is deliberately misleading, James puts on record how in a general way he intended *Maisie* to be read. I believe that his hints can be taken as serious guides to the meaning of the novel. In confessing this, I admit impatience with the sophistical arrogance that denies a writer, especially one with James's critical acumen, any authority to explain his own creations.

That the heroine's consciousness expands to self-understanding and moral awareness is proved both by her increasingly sensitive response to the events in which she plays a part and by James's comments on her development. The first important scene which shows the direction of Maisie's initiation occurs early and announces with singular clarity the motif of moral growth. At the outset of the novel, Maisie is caught in the continuing hostilities between her divorced parents, with each of whom she spends, in turn, six months of the year. Condemned to carry insults from one parent to another, she achieves her first 'expansion' when she refuses to report their abusive messages and thus thwarts their plans to make her a 'centre of hatred'. Almost too pointedly, James interprets her feigned stupidity as a 'great date in her small still life: the complete vision, private but final, of the

[1] Ibid., p. x.
[2] Ibid., p. x.

strange office she filled. It was literally a moral revolution and accomplished in the depths of her nature.' Clearly then, Maisie acquires 'vision', undergoes a profound spiritual alteration, and, by frustrating her mother and father's perverted sport, functions as a force for good. This scene alone, it seems to me, undermines Beach's argument that Maisie learns nothing from her experiences. Since James is here speaking *in propria persona*, the reader must accept the passage as incontrovertible evidence that Maisie is launched under fair auspices.

A favorable start, however, does not insure a safe arrival at distant ports. As Maisie grows older she must confront, with pathetically little assistance, the enigma of her situation. Her mother's marriage to Sir Claude and her father's marriage to Miss Overmore (now known as Mrs Beale) require from her a subtle allocation of loyalty that taxes her youthful ingenuity. To add to the confusion, her step-parents are soon involved in a 'relationship' strongly condemned by Mrs Wix, Maisie's comical but sturdily moral governess. Moreover, her mother's second marriage is followed by a series of 'attachments' to Mr Perriam, Lord Eric, and the Captain, while her father's denigration of conventional codes culminates in his being the paid lover of the Countess. But Maisie, in addition to being exposed to the sordid intricacies of her guardians' amours, is often present at uninhibited adult discussions of them. Nevertheless, her innocence remains surprisingly unsmirched in the immediate proximity of pitch.

And yet, as James shows in *The Awkward Age*, a close cousin to *Maisie*, innocence is not necessarily defiled by knowledge. Aggie's antiseptic education is a ludicrously inept preparation for life in a world with little resemblance to Eden, while Nanda's exposure leads to knowledge, growth, and self-sufficiency. Maisie, like Nanda, is 'a sort of drain-pipe with everything flowing through', and like Nanda too she remains uncontaminated. Less squeamish than many of his readers and critics, James did not subscribe to the Duchess's formula for creating in Aggie the perfect child, a paragon who should be nurtured 'privately, carefully, and with what she was *not* to learn—till the proper time —looked after quite as much as the rest'.[1]

---

[1] *The Novels and Tales of Henry James*, New York Edition, ix 53.

That Maisie's exposure to infection does not lead to paralysis, stasis, or corruption is apparent if the novel's basically simple focus, by no means simply achieved by the artist, is recognized: no matter how devious the adult intrigues, the center of interest always remains fixed in the child's acquisitive sensibility. In his preface, James himself warns against taking the Faranges and their associates as his subjects, for they are lacking in inherent interest because they are 'figures of too short a radiation'; they can only be invested with meaning by 'the child's own import-ance, spreading and contagiously acting'.[1] Beach's quaint de-rogation of Maisie's role seems to me to limit the novel's radiation and to reduce it to sparkling but empty virtuosity: 'Maisie herself has really no story. She is hardly more than an observer eagerly following from her side-box the enthralling spectacle of the stage.'[2] Far from being shunted to a side-box, the girl is constantly on stage in the midst of actions too urgent to be dismissed as mere spectacle.

There are at least four scenes (in addition to the episode des-cribing her moral revolution) which dramatize Maisie's journey toward knowledge and maturity. The first scene occurs when Sir Claude, about to turn Maisie over to Mrs Beale, asks her if she dreads seeing her father. In this situation, in which she might easily have condemned her father, she colors with 'an odd un-expected shame at placing in an inferior light ... so very near a relative as Mr Farange'. As interpreter of her increasing sensi-tivity, James characterizes her emotion, as 'more mature than any she had yet known'. He further indicates that at this moment Sir Claude, who is capable of fine discrimination, 'caught his first glimpse of her sense of responsibility'.

In other words, the child does not assume the facile irrever-ence that her stepfather too casually expects. Instead, with an unusual exhibition of propriety and force of character, she com-pels Sir Claude to take her conduct seriously. Once again she resists the adult tendency to make her a counter in an irrespon-sible game of hate. Her self-conscious integrity attests that her moral revolution has not proved abortive. Indeed, it has the subsidiary effect of modifying the cynicism and obtuseness of her adult associates; like Morgan Moreen in 'The Pupil', she

[1] Op. cit., p. xiii.
[2] Beach, p. 239.

contributes significantly to the education and refinement of those who should be enlightening her.

Of course I am not suggesting that Maisie can translate her reactions into abstract concepts; after all, though almost inordinately impressionable and discerning, she often lacks the maturity to understand what, in fact, is happening to her. As she unconsciously stores up sensations and insights, she is naturally less concerned with what she learns than with the wonder of the phenomena she observes; moreover, as the Preface warns, the experiences 'that she understands darken off into others that she rather tormentedly misses'.[1] The imaginative collaborator whom James assumes as his reader must then, with the author's assistance, supply the normative terms that describe her progress. The reader will not be disturbed, however, when after what seems a startling stretch of intelligence and feeling, Maisie lapses into childish naïveté. To expect an arbitrarily consistent development of all her faculties is to treat her as if she were a geometrical proof and not a child. Her mistakes, which are many and sometimes amusing, make her in James's words 'the ironic centre', but they do not nullify her slowly expanding vision.

A second incident showing the deepening of Maisie's nature is that in which her unbelievably stupid father takes her to the splendid house of the Countess. Here the girl's quick perceptions detect behind her father's attentions a desire to give his projected abandonment of her the best of appearances. The scene is triumphantly Jamesean in its rich and ingratiating evocation of Maisie's diversity, complexity, and not incongruous innocence. The child's aesthetic sense is vividly awakened; the daughter experiences filial palpitations and responsibilities; the imperiled little identity maturely considers her own interests; and her groping moral nature—never given a harsh prominence—slowly builds up to a vision of the ugly implications of what she has been exposed to. The gradual progression of the scene toward éclaircissement subtly illuminates James's moral intention, for though Maisie is child enough to feel enjoyment in the presence of the Countess's expensive possessions, she 'all in a moment'—her knowledge invariably comes in flashes—admits her father's degradation in allying himself with someone whom 'neither her mother, nor Mrs Beale, nor Mrs Wix, nor Sir Claude, nor the

[1] Op. cit., p. x.

Captain nor even Mr Perriam and Lord Eric could possibly have liked'. It might not be too extravagant to say that Maisie enters the house a child and leaves it precociously wise, for her initial pleasure in discovering herself in the enchanted world of the Arabian Nights is dissipated by the recognition of 'something in the Countess that falsified everything'. That she betrays, at the end of the scene, a juvenile delight in the money lavished on her by the Countess does not detract from James's moral purport; on the contrary, it is evidence that his moral sense does not interfere with the aesthetic rigor which demands that he be true to the child's nature.

Certainly a child who undergoes a moral revolution, learns responsibility, and rejects a revolting father is making rather wholesome progress. James never intimates that she is crushed or arrested by her experiences or that she is acquiring the calculated immorality to attempt to become her stepfather's mistress. In scene after scene, Maisie's accumulated insight is brought into play, but never more tenderly than when, with the Captain in Kensington Park, she desperately urges her companion to be loyal to her mother. With the 'small demonic foresight' James attributes to her in the preface, she envisions her mother's potential disaster.

> 'Good-bye.' Maisie kept his hand long enough to add: 'I like you too.' And then supremely: 'You do love her?'
> 'My dear child—!' The captain wanted words.
> 'Then don't do it only for just a little.'
> 'A little?'
> 'Like all the others.'
> 'All the others?'—he stood staring.
> She pulled away her hand. 'Do it always!'

Although a rigid moralist may condemn her encouragement of an illicit affair, she 'supremely' reveals a deep passion for loyalty and an understanding of the moral consequences of promiscuity. Her sense of responsibility, whose birth Sir Claude witnessed, has by now confronted those bitter realities not easily resolved by resort to simple moral fiat. Maisie's allegiance is obviously not to a restrictive code; unlike other James characters, notably Winterbourne, Mrs Newsome, and Mrs Pocock, she is emancipated from—or has never made—the narrow commitment that prevents humane action. Perhaps to act with responsible freedom is necessarily to transgress. Certainly, however, Maisie's earnest, even embarrassing approval of the Captain's love can seem immoral only to those who subscribe to the unbending dogmas of Woollett.

The scene with the Captain, in spite of its immediate impact—James saw in it, on rereading, an 'effect of associated magic'—is in a sense completed by the perfectly wrought episode dealing with Maisie's last meeting with her mother at Folkestone. The child, with almost motherly solicitude, tried to 'adopt her ladyship's practical interests and show her ladyship how perfectly she understood them'. Unfortunately, the battered but still arrogant parent is outraged at having the Captain—now 'the biggest cad in London'—recommended to her. Maisie matches her mother's angry explosion, but even anger is accompanied by a terrible prevision of tragedy.

> in the midst of her surge of passion—of which in fact it was a part—there rose in her a fear, a pain, a vision ominous, precocious, of what it might mean for her mother's fate to have forfeited such loyalty as that. There was literally an instant in which Maisie fully saw—saw madness and desolation, saw ruin and darkness, and death.

Such a dark vision—perhaps the key word in the novel is 'vision'—proves that the child has traveled a surprisingly straight course from the moment she decided not to feed her parents' mutual hatred. Without Mrs Wix's moral sense—which, though by no means contemptible, assesses human action by doctrinal requirements—Maisie wrests from the urgency of each of her predicaments a moral vision or a moral imperative.

Despite its inclusiveness, nevertheless, Maisie's vision is not complete until she has focused a true image of Sir Claude. For all her maturity, she would like to find in him not only a father-substitute, but the Prince Charming who, through the largess of treats, outings, and affection, instills romance into her life; their activities release her from the constricting classroom into the glamorous world of parks, restaurants, and foreign travel. His constant avowals of love and loyalty and his easygoing acceptance of her precocity, charm her into a state of devotion. Yet, James compels her to learn, a lesson terrible to a child, that her fairy-tale hero is incapable of ideal behavior in the real world. Her childhood dies with the death of her delusion. Maisie's most impressive act—the real measure of what she knows—is her precipitation of the situation which divests Sir Claude of his specious attractions and exposes his obsessively compromising nature.

Maisie does not, however, suddenly begin to judge Sir Claude at the end of the novel. From the beginning of their association, she occasionally observes in him a shiftiness with which she (like Mrs Wix) attempts to compromise. For example, when he asks if she might help him hide Mrs Beale from Mrs Wix's vigilance, she is described as gaining a 'first glimpse of something in him that she wouldn't have expected'. At another point, fear of leaving Mrs Wix drives her to tears, but she 'couldn't have told you if she had been crying at the image of their separation or at that of Sir Claude's untruth'. Still, she delusively believes that Sir Claude has been saved when, submitting to Mrs Wix's moral pressure, he flees with her to Boulogne. When the governess joins them, Sir Claude seems momentarily to have 'embraced his fine chance' and risen to ideal action. But Sir Claude proves himself a most unheroic hero when, accepting the first pretext, he announces his decision to return to England. In the ensuing debate with Mrs Wix, he confesses his fear of Mrs Beale and ultimately counters righteous arguments with a princely manner whose 'excess of light' draws 'depraved concession' from Mrs Wix. Though Maisie fails to support her governess's high-flying morality she astutely notices with 'slight oppression ... that [Sir Claude] has unmistakeably once more dodged'.

Sir Claude's defection is the prelude to a series of events that round out Maisie's education: Mrs Wix's desperate attempt to infuse a moral sense into her charge, Mrs Beale's dramatic appearance in Boulogne, and Sir Claude's return, as a 'different' man, into a situation likely to prove explosive. James's technical daring keeps the action moving, with imaginative brilliance and poise, through surprises, ironies, and charged, elliptical dialogue. Apart from its thematic function, the cluster of scenes displays a mastery of dramatic nuance, spectacle, and timing rarely equalled in James's work. Finally, however, the scenes mass the important characters in Boulogne and prepare for the showdown leading to Maisie's disenchantment with her hero.

Since the three events have a cumulative value, it is necessary to indicate their importance. In Mrs Wix's intense campaign to indoctrinate Maisie, the child performs like a dull student indeed. Her egregious 'stupidity' has persuaded many critics that, even after all her opportunities for 'accumulations', she knows next to nothing. These critics forget, however, that Maisie confronts Mrs Wix's query as to whether she 'really and truly' has any moral sense with clever dissimulation:

> Maisie was aware that her answer, though it brought her down to heels, was vague even to imbecility, and this was the first time she had appeared to practice with Mrs Wix an intellectual inaptitude to meet her—the infirmity to which she had owed so much success with papa and mamma. The appearance did her injustice.

In addition to her feigned ignorance, Maisie gives the appearance of childishness because she has no ready-made Sunday-school code to mouth with impressive facility. Almost pragmatically but most sensitively, she picks her way through the disorder and complexity of a world that Mrs Wix interprets in simple Biblical terms. Yet though the pupil does not, like her tutor, know the answers in the back of the book, she is not without values. Indeed, her life with depraved parents has ironically served to teach her 'one of the sacred lessons of home', that 'there were things papa called mamma and mamma called papa a low sneak for doing and for not doing'. In a sense Maisie is a more searching practical moralist than the literal-minded instructor whose formidable moral stance continually awes her. Moreover, through all of her disingenuous sallies, Maisie is motivated by the ideal of loyalty to Sir Claude—an ideal that Mrs Wix cannot sustain.

Mrs Beale's appearance in Boulogne demonstrates that Mrs Wix's moral sense can be rather easily trifled with. When Maisie's stepmother breathlessly courts the governess's support, Mrs Wix is so taken in by the extravagant display of kindness that she practically agrees to accept the woman she had earlier reviled. No wonder Maisie 'became on the spot quite as interested in Mrs Wix's moral sense as Mrs Wix could possibly be in hers'. Yet, strangely, in spite of James's persistently ironical view of Mrs Wix, most critics continue to accept her as the moral norm of the novel, forgetting that she is often actuated by materialistic considerations. Though it would be foolish to deny

Mrs Wix a measure of comic grandeur—her heroic speeches are always slightly preposterous—she is too high-pitched, narrow, and unsophisticated to embody James's sense of moral vision. On the whole, she has an old-fashioned, grandmotherly rectitude, but she is no vessel of wisdom. Her light is bright enough for the nursery, but it is no radiance. Her own complaint (perhaps her most touching utterance) that Maisie's affairs have led her into moral quicksands is a gauge of her limitations: 'I ask myself where I am; and ... say to myself that I'm too far, too far, from where I started.' I cannot agree with Bewley's contention that Mrs Wix is the only adult in the novel 'capable of being educated into fineness',[1] for 'fineness', with its suggestion of sensitive discrimination, is just what Mrs Wix will never achieve. Though she can, at times, burst into grotesque displays of moral energy, she rather resembles Mrs Micawber—as Mrs Beale cruelly points out—in her decision to 'never, never, never desert Miss Farange'. To the end she remains, in spite of her nagging and doctrinaire morality, 'peculiarly and soothingly safe; safer than anyone in the world'. It is indeed most characteristic of her that even after Maisie's sacrifice of Sir Claude she still wonders what the child really knows.

Mrs Beale's descent upon Maisie and Mrs Wix is for her the climactic event in a long struggle for security and power. The onetime governess, whom both Maisie and Sir Claude confess they fear, has designedly achieved status through her marriage to Maisie's father. Then, having quickly calculated that with Farange she is on a sinking ship, she attaches herself to the susceptible Sir Claude. The acute Maisie, reacting with childlike ambivalence, recognizes her stepmother's combination of beauty and strength: 'it took [Mrs Beale] but a short time to give her little friend an impression of positive power—an impression that seemed to begin like a long bright day. This was a perception on Maisie's part that neither mamma, nor Sir Claude, nor Mrs Wix ... had exactly kindled'. This 'power' is, in the Boulogne scenes, hurled with tremendous force against Mrs Wix's longstanding moral 'prejudice' concerning Mrs Beale's sinister influence on Sir Claude. Almost completely ignoring Maisie, who is only a pawn in her game, she wrings important concessions from her former enemy, but her masterful diplomatic *coup* gives

[1] Bewley, p. 101.

Maisie a vivid sense of a cold-blooded, intriguing nature: she lost 'herself in the meanings that, dimly as yet and disconnectedly, but with a vividness that fed apprehension, she could begin to read into her stepmother's independent move'. It is precisely the maneuver which subverts Mrs Wix's opposition that begins to enlighten Maisie and to prepare her to reject her stepmother.

Sir Claude's return to Boulogne after the grand entrance of Mrs Beale affords a picture of the indecisive man awaiting the moment of decision. Unlike the energetic and even dazzling Mrs Beale, he dreads the consequences that his sexual passions and moral shiftlessness have logically created. He torments himself with the necessity of accepting Mrs Beale (as he had earlier accepted Maisie's mother) as a terrible fate. Obviously, he is morally and psychologically capsized in a world where even hesitant action leads to commitment. His single free and seemingly responsible deed, his escape with Maisie to Boulogne, was a noisy and scared retreat, and not the 'miracle' she had supposed. For all Mrs Wix's rhetorical excesses, she accurately characterizes him as a soul lost by his slavery to passion. Even with his doom upon him, he continues to dodge, protesting to Maisie that since his return to France he has not seen his mistress. It is the beginning of Maisie's disenchantment that 'there settled on her, in the light of his beautiful smiling eyes, the faintest purest coldest conviction that he wasn't telling the truth'. When desperately he asks Maisie to sacrifice Mrs Wix, the child, with an ineluctable vision of his equivocal character, forces her life to its crisis by proposing escape from both Mrs Beale and Mrs Wix. Sir Claude's refusal to act enables Maisie to see the half-heartedness of his conversion and the inveteracy of his evasive, devious behavior.

Unmistakably, Maisie's proposal to Sir Claude and his reaction to it have all the ingredients of a climactic scene. Nevertheless, it must be granted that James presents the scene in a maddeningly elusive manner. In attempting to realize every emotional nuance of the charged situation, he resorts—to use favorite words of his—to audacious 'jumps' and 'leaps' that make less for precise accounting of motive than for dramatic tension. Emotional intensity is achieved by short questions, exclamations and broken sentences; the insistence on Maisie's 'whiteness' and 'fright' and on Sir Claude's 'whiteness' and 'fright', and the recurrence of words like 'temptation' and 'weakness' give an impression of agitated rather than minutely discriminated feelings. In short, the passage is affective and connotative; it is a tense dramatization and not a clarification. In a sense it is incomplete, and needs the illumination later shed on it by Sir Claude.

I do not believe that the 'obscurity' of the scene in terms of meaning (not as drama) is intended to disguise a naked appeal by Maisie to Sir Claude's sexual passion. Rather, the incident is the consummation of the novel's design in that the child rises above Sir Claude (and thus loses her hero) and above Mrs Wix, who before her final heroics shows that she too can compromise. Maisie's fear of herself, which can be misread as a fear of her rising sexual feelings, stems from her need to create an exigency which will prove or expose Sir Claude. Such a crisis will complete her vision, for her stepfather's reaction to it will, for all time, clear the troubled moral atmosphere. In asking no less than heroism from him she becomes herself heroic. And like other innocent heroines of James, she is doomed to ask too much. No wonder James says that she experienced 'something still deeper than a moral sense'.

My reading of this difficult and crucial passage is supported by Sir Claude's answer to Mrs Wix's accusation that he had destroyed the child's moral sense. In a spirit of revolt against the narrowness and tyranny of her views, he refuses to be 'treated as a little boy' (for Mrs Wix has a sort of moral arrogance) and finely declares:

'I've not killed anything,' he said; 'on the contrary I think I've produced life. I don't know what to call it—I haven't even known how decently to deal with it, to approach it; but whatever it is, it's the most beautiful thing I've ever met—its exquisite, it's sacred.'

I maintain that Sir Claude cannot be referring to an intended seduction. No amount of ingenuity concerning James's 'obliquity' or 'ambiguity' can evade the apparent significance of this speech.

The sum of Maisie's knowledge is not like the answer to a problem in addition, for in the Jamesean sense she knows 'everything'. But to be less oracular, Maisie reaches maturity when, by requiring her idol to satisfy her most strenuous spiritual demands, she refuses to accept life as a compromise. She has learned that Sir Claude's self-deceptive hopes to 'square' people —to work out with them convenient arrangements involving no moral decision—never actualize. Before taking her stand at the end of the novel, she had been abandoned by a father whose mistress 'falsified everything' and by a mother whose promiscuity may end in 'ruin and darkness and death'. When on the high ground of principle she provokes the situation which betrays Sir Claude's temporizing nature, Maisie surrenders her last childish fantasy. That her expanding consciousness has brought her a ripeness, a kind of perfection, is shown by Sir Claude's final panegyric:

> [Sir Claude speaks] with a relish as intense now as if some lovely work of art or of nature had suddenly been set down among them. He was rapidly recovering himself on this basis of fine appreciation. 'She made her condition—with such a sense of what it should be! She made the only right one.'

Ironically, the deflated hero, the man who prefers to be lost with Mrs Beale rather than 'saved' with Mrs Wix and Maisie, is the most sensitive appreciator of his stepdaughter. (Mrs Wix only dimly perceives what she has gained.) Yet, though he can fully evaluate his loss, the logic of events has stripped him of all illusions about his own character. Even when he pronounces Maisie to be free and laughingly proclaims her too good for himself and Mrs Beale, he accepts his own inescapable indecision as the queer law of his life. In the end, I am sure, this constantly frightened playboy is more afraid of Maisie's simple but intense heroism (as Vanderbank is of Nanda's in *The Awkward Age*) than he is of Mrs Beale's sexual power. When Maisie looks back from the steamer and fails to see him on the 'balcony', she must know that he knows his doom.

15 P. N. Furbank

Tess of the d'Urbervilles

From the *Introduction* to the New Wessex Edition, Macmillan (1974)

In the August of 1856 Thomas Hardy witnessed the hanging of Martha Brown of Birdsmoorgate, a tranter's wife who had killed her husband out of jealousy. It was the last public execution in Dorchester, drawing a crowd of three to four thousand, and it remained one of the most enduring memories of his life. In 1925, nearly seventy years later, he applied to his friend Lady Hester Pinney for details of the case, and in his letter of thanks for her information we catch sight, rather comically, of the cheerfully ghoulish and sado-masochistic side of his nature:

> My sincere thanks for the details you have been so indefatigable as to obtain about that unhappy woman Martha Brown, whom I am ashamed to say I saw hanged, my only excuse being that I was but a youth, and had to be in the town at the time for other reasons . . . I remember what a fine figure she showed against the sky as she hung in the misty rain, and how the tight black silk gown set off her shape as she wheeled half-round and back.
>
> I hope you have not felt the cold much: we have somewhat . . .[1]

T. S. Eliot, in a much-abused essay,[2] saw this as the essential Hardy and disliked him in consequence:

> He seems to me to have written as nearly for the sake of 'self-expression' as a man well can, and the self which he had to express does not strike me as a particularly wholesome or edifying matter of communication. . . . In consequence of his self-absorption, he makes a great deal of landscape; for landscape is a passive creature, which lends itself to an author's mood. Landscape is fitted, too, for the purposes of an author who is interested not at all in men's minds, but only in their emotions, and perhaps only in men as vehicles for emotion.

[1] See *Thomas Hardy and the Birdsmoorgate Murder 1856*, Monographs on the Life, Times and Works of Thomas Hardy, ed. J. Stevens Cox (Beaminster, 1966).

[2] In *After Strange Gods* (1934).

Of all accounts of Hardy it is Eliot's which most sticks in my mind. It won't quite do; it is altogether too hostile; but, so it seems to me, it points to the kind of author that Hardy was. It will perhaps catch a little of my meaning if I say that the artist he most reminds me of is Gustav Mahler. He was a late nineteenth-century emotionalist, like Mahler and Strauss, and he stands towards the humanistic, didactic, 'teaching' tradition in fiction—the school of George Eliot and Dickens—somewhat in the relation that they did to the Beethovian tradition in music. I must add at once that there was another aspect in which he was more akin to the George Eliot and Dickens school; I mean his humour, that very sane and clear-eyed humour which serves as a check to his more extreme assaults on our feelings; and this Eliot fails to allow for. Nevertheless, there is a respect in which we need some such epithet as *fin-de-siècle* for Hardy; and likewise the epithet 'Aesthetic'. 'Aestheticism' is a word which arouses prejudice; but consider, for instance, this extraordinary sentence from *A Laodicean*:

> A lavender haze hung in the air, the trees were as still as those of a submarine forest; while the sun, in colour like a brass plaque, had a hairy outline in the livid sky.

You would say, meeting it out of context, that it was the work of a Symbolist poet. Of course, every stroke in it is taken straight from nature, and there lies half its value; yet the strenuous, super-fine, rather rarefied sensibility registering these impressions is surely nearer to Mallarmé's than to George Eliot's? It lies in the high-aesthetic line; and the same is true of that whole, scenic, decorative and tableau-making art of his. He is concerned with life as a spectacle, a spectacle engaging our deepest feelings and appealing to our imagination but not capable of providing lessons. Thus it should not surprise us that Hardy should say, in *fin-de-siècle* accents, that: 'The "simply natural" is interesting no longer. The much decried, mad, late-Turner rendering is now necessary to create my interest.'[1] It can only confuse us to think of him as in the humanistic and moralistic tradition of George Eliot and Dickens.

For, after all, the basic enterprise of George Eliot and Dickens is to teach us how to live. They are provoking us all the time,

[1] F. E. Hardy, *The Life of Thomas Hardy 1840–1928* (1962), p. 185.

through the flux and reflux of sympathy, to pass moral judgements, which are meant to add up to some more comprehensive one. And somewhere, unstated, within their novels, lies the assumption that life in society can be lived successfully, and that moral judgement is the guide to this. It is an excellent tradition; but we are mistaken if we think Hardy belongs to it. He was not, in this sense, a teacher. He did not believe that life in society *could* be lived successfully. In his view—as he never tired of repeating—there was something fundamentally awry in the scheme of things; he even came to think of human emotion itself as a cruel flaw and mistake in creation. Thus, the attempt to find some consistent moral attitude in his novels is largely wasted.

Think, for instance, of two major creations of Hardy's: Clym Yeobright and Angel Clare. Both, at a certain point in their stories, achieve self-realization and find the way of life that suits them. For Clym it turns out to be neither money-making nor philanthropy but to become one of the children of Egdon, a furze-cutter, 'a brown spot in the midst of an expanse of olive-green gorse, and nothing more'. For Angel it is, as he discovers at Talbothays farm, to 'throw off the splints and bandages' of decorum and outer-directed living and 'to view life from its inner side'. Both these moments of self-discovery are wonderfully and convincingly rendered by Hardy. But, brought up on Forster and Lawrence, we tend to assume that self-realization must be good and have good consequences—if not, so the theory goes, then the self-realization must be false. This is not Hardy's vision. These self-realizations of Clym and Angel's are true ones; but for Hardy it does not follow at all that they must contribute to the general good. Indeed, they do not. Through the 'crass casualty' of circumstances, they turn out quite disastrously for Eustacia and for Tess, and we are not asked to make moral sense of this, but simply to witness the fact. I find this vision of Hardy's impressive, but it is not that of a moralist.

One cannot help thinking of Hardy himself in connection with Clym and Angel, the returned and the apprentice 'native', for in them, evidently, he is meditating upon aspects of his own return to 'Wessex'. When writing *Far from the Madding Crowd*, the first of his true 'Wessex' novels, he felt, almost as strongly as Clym himself, the urge to merge into the landscape.

So Hardy went on writing *Far from the Madding Crowd*—some-times indoors, sometimes out—when he would occasionally find himself without a scrap of paper at the very moment that he felt volumes. In such circumstances, he would use large dead leaves, white chips left by the woodcutters, or pieces of stone or slate that came to hand. He used to say that when he carried a pocket-book his mind was as barren as the Sahara.[1]

It was a moment of extreme joy for him, this finding of his true line as an artist, this discovery that every detail of his native scene 'spoke' to him, evoked inexhaustible knowledge in himself and told of a measureless, anonymous past, a past in which all par-ticular tragedies were reduced in scale, as if seen through the wrong end of a telescope. This was his own great moment of self-realization. Nevertheless, it entailed losses. Such a retreat from the city, where thought was active and social progress a hope, could look, in another light, like a return to the tomb.

For one thing, it means giving up a part of his vocation. At the outset of his literary career he had pictured himself as a 'modern' novelist, one who had seen deeply into modern experience and could interpret it and make moral and intellectual sense of it. He never renounced this vocation; nor was it absurd; but it was not one he was able to realize. He was not born to be a Dostoevsky or Ibsen or Lawrence, a writer who could handle the issues of the modern consciousness in realistic art. One has only to think of *The Hand of Ethelberta* and *A Laodicean* to see how, in them, he bungled a rich and promising theme: the theme of the social energy of the *parvenu* versus the spent forces of ancient families, with its converse, the ache of modernism versus the life-acceptance of the older aristocracy. Why he bungled it was, I should im-agine, because it was too personal. As we know, he hinted con-tinually about the 'swart thing', the modern dilemma, which had ruined his personal happiness; and why he only hints may have been not so much that the thing, no doubt sexual, was unavow-able as that he could never fully comprehend it. He seized first on another explanation, searching deeper and deeper into the nature of things, till at last, half-seriously, he threw the blame on the universe itself. Whatever the cause, he was unable to handle this intractable material directly, and he did not find himself as a novelist till he discovered a way of treating it by parable—the

[1] *Life of Hardy*, p. 96.

parable of an imaginary 'Wessex'. He called his philosophy only 'a confused heap of impressions'. A juster name would have been 'partial visions', and these partial visions, he found, were best presented by suggestion and analogy—by all those poetic analogies offered by the pastoral scene. It was a profound discovery and was his making as a novelist. However, it carried with it ironies too, and one of these he conveys in his poem 'On an Invitation to the United States':

> My ardours for emprize nigh lost
> Since Life has bared its bones to me,
> I shrink to seek a modern coast
> Whose riper times have yet to be;
> Where the new regions claim them free
> From that long drip of human tears
> Which people old in tragedy
> Have left upon the centuried years.

> For, wonning in these ancient lands,
> Enchased and lettered as a tomb,
> And scored with prints of perished hands,
> And chronicled with dates of doom,
> Though my own Being bears no bloom
> I trace the lives such scenes enshrine,
> Give past exemplars present room,
> And their experience count as mine.

The poem pictures England as a tomb and his own fictional creation as a compensation for personal frustration. And it is these feelings, I suggest, that lie at the roots of what I have called his 'aestheticism'.

But, indeed, the poem is altogether suggestive. For the ruling idea of Hardy in his 'Wessex' novels is, you might say, that of 'reading' a scene or a landscape—tracing out with a finger its 'chasing' and 'lettering' till a whole history is deciphered. He is obsessed with physical evidence and with evoking the numberless lives of the past from the rubbings and abradings they leave on objects. One can go further and say that he thought of stories as *telling themselves* and of humans as—through such traces—imprinting their own portrait, as in early experiments in photography. He is fascinated by shadows, or the 'shadows' represented by stains, blots and abradings. They represent, for him, an analogy to stories; and much of his strength as a writer lies in his Stoical refusal—as in his poem 'The Shadow on the Stone'—to delude himself into thinking them more than shadows. There is a most beautiful passage in *Tess of the d'Urbervilles* describing Tess and her companions returning from the fair at Chaseborough:

> Then these children of the open air, whom even excess of alcohol could scarce injure permanently, betook themselves to the field-path; and as they went there moved onward with them, around the shadow of each one's head, a circle of opalized light, formed by the moon's rays upon the glistering sheet of dew. Each pedestrian could see no halo but his or her own, which never deserted the head-shadow, whatever its vulgar unsteadiness might be; but adhered to it, and persistently beautified it . . . [pp. 101–2]

Here, to the idea of shadows, is added that of the halo, that self-projected, self-deceiving radiance which, we are to think, is all there is to human happiness.

Not only are we reminded of photography, we are reminded of the cinema. As many critics have pointed out, Hardy is extraordinarily cinematic (suggesting that, in some mysterious way, the cinema was called into being by nineteenth-century fiction). First he gives you a close-up of a hand, holding dice, then, with widening focus, moves up the arms, to the gambler's head, and to the scene behind his head. And, as in the cinema, one is first presented with an object and then has to decipher its meaning.

> Then, far beyond the ploughing-teams, a black speck was seen. It had come from the corner of a fence, where there was a gap, and its tendency was up the incline, towards the swede-cutters. From the proportions of a mere point it advanced to the shape of a ninepin, and was soon perceived to be a man in black, arriving from the direction of Flintcomb-Ash. [p. 361]

Physical objects, as it were, take the initiative. They enforce their own will on the observer; so that, seeing the smoke from a cottage chimney, one's thoughts are drawn down the chimney to the hearth and those sitting round the hearth. And to these proto-cinematic devices are added ones taken from painting—considerations of perspective and lighting; *how* you see things, how one solid object masks another or how an object may be lit from more than one source.

> Each girl sat down on her three-legged stool, her face sideways, her right cheek resting against the cow; and looked musingly along the animal's flank at Tess as she approached. The male

milkers, with hat-brims turned down, resting flat on their foreheads and gazing on the ground did not observe her. [p. 144]

As they crept along, stooping low to discern the plant, a soft yellow gleam was reflected from the buttercups into their shaded faces giving them an elfish, moonlit aspect, though the sun was pouring upon their backs in all the strength of noon. [p. 179]

These literal matters of perspective and lighting, intensely interesting to Hardy, link with his notions about viewpoint and perspective in the moral and authorial sense. Narration, for him, tends to be a matter of someone 'reading appearances'.[1] He likes to abnegate responsibility for the witnessing and interpreting of events and to shuffle it off on to the shoulders of his characters, converting them into eavesdroppers and *voyeurs*. Michael Millgate, in *Thomas Hardy: his career as a novelist* (1971), says:

> It is almost as though Hardy shrank from the responsibilities of omniscience, from the necessity of moral judgements and firm intellectual commitments, and found a certain security in adopting—usually quite inconsistently and on a scene-to-scene basis—the limited but essentially human perspectives available to particular characters.

It is a shrewd remark. But this trait of Hardy's has, I think, a wider bearing still, and connects with what I have said about his not being a 'teacher'.

The *how* is always an overriding interest of Hardy's. He is fascinated by contrivance: how exactly Angel contrives to carry the dairymaids over the flooded road, or how the weary Fanny Robin ingeniously contrives to employ a dog as a crutch; how Clym as a boy makes pigments out of flower-pollen, and the gamblers in *The Return of the Native* use glow-worms as lamps. In a rural existence, the suggestion is, everything has to be made out of the material at hand. Not only is this true in practical matters, it is equally true in moral ones. Eustacia has to construct a romantic lover out of the poor material of Wildeve, who is all that there is available; and Tess, rebuffed by church and society, improvises her own baptismal ceremony for her dying

[1] In the MS. of *Far from the Madding Crowd* (ch. 3) he included five drawings of the hoofmarks followed by Oak and Coggan in their pursuit of Bathsheba's horse.

baby. Out of the given materials, however unpromising, these unprivileged humans make up complete lives, complete self-expression. And there is the further rider that—as with Tess's sacrament or Jude's scholarship—the home-made article may be more genuine than its orthodox counterpart.

This brings me back to Hardy and the 'aesthetic' tradition. There was a time when critics would actually tell us that Hardy wrote 'like a countryman', meaning something rather hobnailed. It was a strange notion, considering the subtlety, venturesomeness and 'mad, late-Turner' effects of his artistic achievement. But it is true that, in his very personal and original conception of fiction— that 'reading of appearances' I have spoken of—he was drawing on an analogy from country skills. It is suggested by the very first lines of his first 'country' novel, *Under the Greenwood Tree*. 'To dwellers in a wood almost every species of tree has its voice as well as its feature.' It was a constantly returning theme for him:

> The countryman who is obliged to judge the time of day from changes in external nature, sees a thousand successive tints and traits in the landscape which are never discerned by him who knows the regular chime of the clock, because they are never in request.

His model, for himself as a novelist, was the countryman. He read histories and tragedies out of the Wessex scene, and out of the pages of county histories, with the same expertness with which Gabriel Oak and Giles Winterborne, from the visible scene, read the time of day and the approaching weather. He also had another *persona* as writer, that of the local antiquarian, a man professionally committed to minute descriptive accuracy. These disguises and analogies were a support to him; they gave him his convention as a prose-stylist. And what this convention reminds me of is something more familiar to us in another art, that of the decorative designer. Hardy saw the immense potentialities for literature, potentialities of feeling, in the convention by which, on a pot or a bas-relief, the limb of a satyr may be both a limb and the completion of a decorative pattern, or his neck be also the 'neck' of a jug. It is the best analogy I can find for those endless devices by which Hardy implicates his characters in landscape, so that they become part of it, or—to use his words in *Tess*—'an integral part of the scene'. This, surely, is the heart of Hardy's 'Wessex' style.

Tess is the culminating triumph of this extraordinary landscape art. She is implicated in landscape, seen as a part of it, and has her path in life dictated by landscape. She is the milkmaid in Hardy's poem of that name:

> The maid breathes words—to vent,
> It seems, her sense of Nature's scenery,
> Of whose life, sentiment,
> And essence, very part itself is she.

Much of our feeling for Tess derives from her helplessness, the economic helplessness of the dispossessed rural poor. Her actual journeyings by foot are, in a sense, her destiny; and thus Hardy's painstaking accuracy in tracing them—the accuracy of a surveyor or topographer—becomes a powerful engine of feeling. By 'landscape' one also means rural pursuits; and in Clare's courting of Tess amid the milking and skimming Hardy is once more using the method of *Far from the Madding Crowd* and *The Woodlanders* —in which, you might say, the character of Gabriel Oak and of Giles Winterborne is indistinguishable from what they do.

Nevertheless, the 'Wessex' cycle of novels really concludes with *The Woodlanders*, and *Tess* as a whole is a very different novel from its predecessors. For one thing, it is an allegory, or intermittently a whole series of allegories. The successive landscapes of Tess's life are plainly meant as Bunyanesque. They are also, obscurely, one feels, an allegory of Hardy's own sexual development; the comedy of Marian's finding 'queer-shaped flints'— petrified sexual emblems—in the fields of Flintcomb-Ash, and shrieking with laughter at them, has a note of confessional irony. And then , at another time, Tess, enslaved to the threshing machine, typifies traditional agriculture in its defeat. Angel, too, at moments, is truly an angel, harp and all, and Alec, plying his pitchfork among the flames, a devil. Allegory crowds upon allegory, till Tess, ending her Pilgrim's Progress upon the altar at Stonehenge, ritually suffers both for the secular cruelty of men and for the cruelty of their religion.

Here is one difference. Another is that, with his public position now assured, Hardy returns to his old commitment as a 'modern' novelist and embattled social critic. *Tess* is a sustained religious and social polemic, a turning-on-their-head of the pretensions of nineteenth-century Christianity—Tess representing true purity and true Pauline Christianity against its pharisaic Victorian travesty (as later Jude will represent 'true' scholarship as against the spurious Christminster version). He was better equipped now for such a novel, and in a portion of *Tess*, the Talbothays part, he masters it. In that account of Angel at Talbothays, where Angel feels himself coming into touch with 'the great passionate pulse of existence' and viewing Life from its 'inner side', it is extraordinary how completely, in fictional terms, Hardy has realized that 'vitalist' strain in philosophy which runs through Nietzsche and Bergson to Lawrence. Here truly are ideas in action, and what a 'modern' novelist is appointed to achieve. Angel with his conversion to 'life', and Tess, so much the 'life' that he is seeking yet so little perceived in her reality, or in any way understood by him: here is a large modern theme handled as finely and comprehensively, in concrete human terms, as it could have been by Ibsen. Hardy emerges here as the 'teacher', the committed artist-prophet, that it lay within his power to be.

But the same cannot quite be said of *Tess* as a whole. All that intricate knot of thoughts about ancient lineage with which he credits Angel—his disapproving of aristocracy socially and politically but relishing it imaginatively—is a knot that is never quite untied here, any more than it is in *A Laodicean*. Hardy presents it, convincingly enough, as a perversion, a weakness infecting Angel's will, one which prepares his fatal backsliding into conventionalism. He shows, very powerfully, how destructive these intellectual fancies are, and how they lead Angel to deny the living reality under his nose. (It is Angel who, though he thinks he has found in Tess a new and unspoilt piece of Nature, unconsciously strives, at every point, to bury her in the 'tomb' of the past—a theme marvellously rendered in the sleep-walking scene.) Nevertheless, dramatically speaking, Hardy fumbles and loses interest in these shifting motives and vacillations of Angel's; he fumbles Angel altogether at certain moments and seems to wash his hands of him. Thus, to revert to an earlier theme, we cannot, and must not try to, make sense of Angel as a whole. The fatal conjunction of Angel and Tess, so full of point and meaningful irony in the Talbothays part, becomes in the end just another meaningless 'crass casualty'. The novel, like his other novels, remains a series of partial visions, its unity being only the unity of a spectacle.

Eliot's 'He seems to me to have written as nearly for the sake of "self-expression" as a man well can' fits *Tess* especially. Hardy, one feels, expressed his heart more completely in this novel than in any other. He was, no doubt, Angel himself, as he was Sue Bridehead. In the clash of Angel and Tess he was dramatizing the life-denying and life-affirming elements in his own temperament. Tess, so vivid to us, so particularized as a presence, is at the same time the most generalized of all characters in his novels. She represents, among so many other things, the natural instinct of delight and truth of feeling, as against perversion—the perversions of bourgeois society, and equally the perversions of the 'modern' consciousness. Hardy had a strangely possessive attitude towards her; he liked to refer to her as 'my' Tess and has a way, in the novel, of talking of her as if she had been a real person. Plainly, too, Angel's tergiversations were, or had been, Hardy's own: was he a 'new' man, full of *parvenu* energy, or was he the effete survivor of a decrepit stock? One of the main clues to the novel is certainly that diary-entry for 30 September 1888.

> The decline and fall of the Hardys much in evidence hereabout. An instance: Becky S.'s mother's sister married one of the Hardys of this branch, who was considered to have demeaned himself by the marriage. 'All Woolcombe and Froom Quintin belonged to them at one time', Beck used to say proudly. She might have added Up-Sydling and Toller Welme. This particular couple had an enormous lot of children. I remember when young seeing the man—tall and thin—walking behind a horse and common spring trap, and my mother pointing him out to me and saying he represented what was once the leading branch of the family. So we go down, down, down.

As for Tess, she embodies the stoical virtues he sought for himself; and equally she was all that he found desirable physically—the framework for this erotic vision, given his temperament, having to be a hanging. She is an ideal; and idealized heroes and heroines, the ruin of novels in the realistic tradition, are possible for Hardy, whose 'Wessex' is only a parable.

But, then, Tess is so very many things, and Eliot's phrase about men as 'vehicles' is apt, though in no derogatory sense. Think how, in a curious passage in Chapter 13, Hardy explores through Tess the vices of the 'pathetic fallacy'.

> At times her whimsical fancy would intensify natural processes around her till they seemed a part of her own story.

Rather they became a part of it; for the world is only a psychological phenomenon, and what they seemed they were. The midnight airs and gusts, moaning amongst the tightly-wrapped buds, and bark of winter twigs, were formulae of bitter reproach. A wet day was the expression of irremediable grief at her weakness in the mind of some vague ethical being whom she could not class definitely as the God of her childhood, and could not comprehend as any other. [p.120]

Tess is in a morbid state at this moment; but, significantly, in this novel, which so shakes its fist at the universe, there is a general tendency to anthropomorphize physical objects, not normally characteristic of Hardy and more reminiscent of Dickens:

The fire in the grate looked impish—demoniacally funny, as if it did not care in the least about her strait. The fender grinned idly, as if it too did not care. [p. 270]

And now as he looked into the candle its flame dumbly expressed to him that it was made to shine on sensible people, and that it abhorred lighting the face of a dupe and a failure. [p. 309]

Tess is so many things that we may forget what she is not—I mean, a rounded character in the nineteenth-century novelist's sense. She is so vivid to us, we know so exactly what she looks like and what her voice sounds like, that we credit her with more coherence as a character than she possesses. I am thinking, for instance, of her articulacy, her Sixth Standard National School English: it is a trait that never fully sinks into our mind, and Hardy, in his opportunistic way, remembers or forgets it as it suits him.

But, then, it would have hindered his purposes for Tess to be a fully rounded character; for such characters belong to the realistic novel, and Hardy is writing in another *genre*. It is a genre in which he is almost as free as an Elizabethan dramatist to move from one mode to another. In *The Return of the Native* he gives us a close paraphrase of a scene from Webster's *The White Devil*, and it seems quite natural to us. In *Tess* we slip, just as naturally, into the mode of Shakespearian poetic comedy. I have in mind that wonderful scene in which Tess 'undulates' to Angel's harp and is wrought up to tell him her fearful imaginings:

'The trees have inquisitive eyes, haven't they?—that is, seem as if they had. And the river says,—"Why do ye trouble me with your looks?" And you seem to see numbers of tomorrows just all in a line, the first of them the biggest and clearest, the others getting smaller and smaller as they stand farther away; but they all seem very fierce and cruel and as if they said, "I'm coming! Beware of me! Beware of me!" . . . But *you*, sir, can raise up dreams with your music and drive all such horrid fancies away!' [p. 163]

That free inventiveness of Hardy's, his power of moving from mode to mode and turning everything to expressiveness, is even more commanding in *Tess* than in any of his earlier novels and makes me regard it, imperfect as it is, as his masterpiece.

16 Henry Nash Smith

the *Introduction to Huckleberry Finn*

From the Riverside Press Edition (1958), pp. v–xxix.

Most of the fifty thousand people who bought *Adventures of Huckleberry Finn* upon its publication in 1885 probably welcomed the book simply as another amusing specimen of the work of the post-Civil War literary comedians like Orpheus C. Kerr and Josh Billings and Bill Nye with whom Mark Twain was habitually associated in the public mind. On the other hand, readers who prided themselves on being refined considered these humorists rather vulgar. When the Concord Library Committee characterized *Huckleberry Finn* as 'the veriest trash', the denunciation was widely echoed in the press.[1] There was some basis for each of these views. The book does come out of the far from squeamish tradition of native American humour, and some things in it, such as the effort to make comedy out of Joanna Wilks's harelip, represent undeniable lapses in taste. But in our day critical opinion has vindicated the judgment of the few perceptive readers like William Dean Howells and Joel Chandler Harris who saw that whatever traits Mark Twain's novel might share, for better or for worse, with the buffoonery of the popular humorists, it was a literary masterpiece.[2]

A book so clearly great, yet with such evident defects, poses a difficult critical problem. There is little profit in making a mere checklist of faults and beauties. We must try to see the book integrally. How well has Mark Twain succeeded in organizing his material into a coherent and unified whole? And what does this whole mean? Let us begin by recalling the main outlines of the plot. Huck Finn, the thirteen- or fourteen-year-old son of the town drunkard of St Petersburg, Missouri, a boy accustomed to sleep in an empty sugar hogshead and to eat the

---

[1] Arthur L. Vogelback, 'The Publication and Reception of *Huckleberry Finn* in America', *American Literature*, XI, 260–72, November, 1939.

[2] Recent discussion of *Huckleberry Finn* is listed by Harry H. Clark in *Eight American Authors: A Review of Research and Criticism*, ed. Floyd Stovall, New York, 1956, pp. 347–55.

food chance brings within his reach, decides to run away. He needs to escape from the efforts of certain good women to 'sivilize' him and from the sadistic beatings of his Pap. On uninhabited Jackson's Island in the Mississippi he encounters the runaway slave, Jim. They join forces and are lucky enough to find a lumber-raft brought down by the spring flood. The ostensible narrative pattern of the story is provided by the journey of Huck and Jim some eleven hundred miles, as the River flows, from St Petersburg to the 'one-horse' plantation of Silas Phelps near Pikesville, Arkansas.

In a broad sense, the form of the narrative is thus picaresque. Like Gil Blas, the *picaro* or rascally hero of a celebrated story by Le Sage that Mark Twain had in mind as a possible model for a sequel to *Tom Sawyer*,[1] Huck and Jim are involved in a series of adventures more or less self-contained, and at the end of each they move on until they become involved in a fresh adventure. They are fugitives from the law, living by their wits, and Huck has an easy way with watermelons and chickens, as well as a marked propensity for lying. Yet the story is not basically picaresque. The difference becomes clear if we compare Huck with the Duke and the King, who are perfect examples of the literary *picaro*, but who are of course not the central characters. Huck does not have the *picaro*'s callousness; on the contrary, he is easily touched by the sufferings of others. And unlike the unscrupulous Gil Blas, he is 'engaged'— he is helping Jim escape from slavery.

The implied denunciation of slavery in *Huckleberry Finn* is more damaging than the frontal attack delivered by *Uncle Tom's Cabin* because Jim is so much more convincing as a character than is Mrs Stowe's Uncle Tom, who is almost an allegorical figure—a Black Christ. Yet if we read *Huckleberry Finn* simply as the story of Huck's and Jim's quest for freedom we run into difficulties. For in the last section (Chapters XXXIII–XLIII) Mark Twain seems to be burlesquing his own plot. Huck's efforts to help Jim escape, involving real danger and anguished inner conflict with the boy's conscience, give way to the elaborate foolishness of Tom Sawyer's schemes for conducting an Evasion according to rules he has deduced from *The Count of Monte*

---

[1] Mark Twain to William Dean Howells, Hartford, July 5, 1875, in *Mark Twain's Letters*, ed. Albert B. Paine, 2 vols., New York, 1917, I, 258,

268 Henry Nash Smith

Cristo and other melodramatic works of fiction. Jim is reduced to the status of a 'darkey' in a minstrel show; the reader is evidently expected to laugh at his discomforts from the rats and spiders Tom introduces as stage properties. And at the last moment it is revealed that Jim was freed two months before through the highly implausible deathbed repentance of his owner, Miss Watson. We feel as badly sold as did the audience for the Duke's and the King's presentation of *The Royal Nonesuch*.

The puzzling change of attitude toward Jim results from the presence of Tom Sawyer, whose conventional imagination cannot embrace the full recognition of Jim's humanity. He conceives the Evasion (which he knows to be unnecessary) as a means of achieving fame for himself and Jim through the artistic perfection of the scheme. When Tom re-enters the story at the beginning of Chapter XXXIII, he causes an abrupt change in the perspective from which Jim is viewed. The runaway slave imprisoned in the cabin on the Phelps plantation has little in common with the Jim of the great middle section of the story. After the final escape, when Jim emerges from his hiding place and gives up his chance of freedom because he will not desert the wounded Tom, it is as if he has been underground. The reader is gratified that in the end Mark Twain consummates Jim's dignity by giving him an opportunity to make a heroic sacrifice of himself comparable to Huck's decision to go to hell for the sake of his friend. But this return to the earlier perspective on Jim cannot fully redeem the long chapters in which Tom Sawyer has been allowed to play pranks on him.

Indeed, Jim's quest for freedom receives such cavalier treatment in the Phelps plantation sequence that one is forced to ask whether it is the true imaginative centre of the story. If we examine the place which the theme of Jim's escape occupies in the book as a whole, we discover that it is by no means always central to the action. The first seven chapters, where the author has to manage the transition from the state of affairs at the end of *Tom Sawyer* to the quite different atmosphere of the sequel, offered no occasion for dealing with the new problem. Not until Huck makes his Robinson-Crusoe-like discovery of Jim's campfire in Chapter VIII does the reader know that Jim has run away. We then have eight chapters during which the two friends make their way southward on the raft, with pauses for such episodes as the exploration of the 'House of Death' and the wrecked steamboat *Walter Scott*. But at the end of Chapter XVI Mark Twain faced a crisis in the management of his plot, for at this point he must have discovered that the original plan of his narrative would no longer serve his purposes.

Early in Chapter XVI Huck and Jim are approaching the mouth of the Ohio at Cairo, Illinois. Jim is understandably excited. He has conceived the idea that 'he'd be a free man the minute he seen it [Cairo], but if he missed it he'd be in the slave country again and no more show for freedom'. Jim's notion that he would be free as soon as he entered the mouth of the Ohio was oversimplified, but that river was certainly his pathway to freedom.[1] It made no sense for Huck and Jim to move a single mile farther past the mouth of the Ohio than they were forced to. If Mark Twain took Jim down the Mississippi he committed himself to a narrative plan that was very unlikely to lead Jim to freedom. His only alternatives would be to leave Jim in slavery (which, however faithful to historical probability, would have created a sombre ending quite out of keeping with the comic tone of the book), or to free him by some such *deus ex machina* device as the supposed deathbed repentance of Miss Watson.

Why then did Mark Twain not cause Huck and Jim to make

[1] It is not clear how thoroughly Clemens had understood the legal status of runaway slaves in Illinois when he was a boy, or what he remembered about this complex subject when he wrote *Huckleberry Finn*. But everyone in Hannibal must have been generally familiar with the state of affairs just across the River. In the 1840s Cairo, in southern Illinois, was rather less safe for a runaway slave than would have been the Illinois shore just opposite Hannibal. To be sure, the farther the fugitive travelled in any direction the harder it was for agents sent out by his owner to overtake him. But in the 1840s a system of 'indentured labour' hardly distinguishable from slavery was in full legal force in Illinois, and the laws of the state directed county officials to arrest any Negro who could not show freedom papers signed by his former master. Generally speaking, pro-slavery sentiment and the eagerness of sheriffs to capture runaway slaves increased as one moved southward in the state (Norman D. Harris, *History of Negro Slavery in Illinois and of the Slavery Agitation in That State*, Chicago, 1906, esp. pp. 22–3, 53, 109–10). Jim seems to have been familiar with the status of Negroes in Illinois, for in calmer moments he and Huck had wisely planned to go far up the Ohio River by steamboat, perhaps as far as the state of Ohio, where they might have established contact with the Underground Railway. With this sort of help they would have had a good chance to reach Canada, in the manner of Eliza and George Harris in *Uncle Tom's Cabin*. Only in Canada would Jim be immune from arrest and delivery back to his mistress.

their way up the Ohio? To ask this question is to answer it: he did not know the Ohio. But he had known the lower Mississippi intimately for four years as cub and pilot. As Huck and Jim float past Cairo, Mark Twain's desire to write a story drawing upon his memories of the lower Mississippi comes into conflict with the idea of telling the story of Jim's escape from slavery. When he wrote Chapter XVI he apparently did not see any escape from the dilemma. 'By-and-by', says Huck, 'we talked about what we better do, and found there warn't no way but just to go along down with the raft till we got a chance to buy a canoe to go back in.'

This plan represents a dead end for the original plan of escape. The destruction of the raft at the end of Chapter XVI registers the author's recognition of the fact. As Walter Blair has demonstrated recently in a brilliant study of the composition of the novel,[1] Mark Twain broke off his manuscript in 1876 near the end of Chapter XVI and laid it aside for at least two years. He took it up again—probably during the winter of 1879–80—and added the two chapters (XVII and XVIII) dealing with the Grangerford feud. Huck and Jim are separated during this sequence, and no travel farther south is involved. Thus there was no need to solve here the larger problem of how Huck and Jim could be plausibly represented as floating on down the river. Near the end of Chapter XVIII Mark Twain again laid his manuscript aside, and did not return to it for some months—apparently not before the summer of 1880, when the evidence suggests that he wrote Chapters XIX, XX, and XXI.

He was now able to carry the narrative beyond the end of the feud sequence because he had at last thought of a plan which, without sacrificing plausibility, would allow Huck and Jim to float down the River indefinitely. This plan called for the resurrection of the raft (a note of Mark Twain's written in 1879 or 1880 shows that he had not meant to use the raft again when he related how it was destroyed by the steamboat)[2] and the introduction of the Duke and the King. When these immortal rascals

---

[1] 'When was *Huckleberry Finn* Written?', *American Literature*, XXX, 1–25, March, 1958. I wish to acknowledge Mr Blair's kindness in offering me expert advice on other matters connected with *Huckleberry Finn*.

[2] Quoted by Bernard De Voto in *Mark Twain at Work*, Cambridge, Mass., 1942, p. 67.

come aboard, each fleeing a mob of outraged townspeople, they dominate the raft by virtue of their superior cunning and their sheer physical superiority to Huck, who is rightly afraid of violence from them. The raft, carried downstream by the current, is the ideal mode of transportation for the Duke and the King because they are constantly in need of a means of escape from one imbroglio and of approach to another. It is an additional advantage for them that Huck and Jim can be made into servants. And in the end, Jim can always be turned in for some kind of reward.

Bringing the Duke and the King into the story was a master stroke. Not only are they themselves comic and satiric creations of the highest order, but their mode of life makes plausible a narrative pattern which allows Mark Twain to deal with any desired aspect of life on the River or along the shore. From the beginning of Chapter XIX to the disappearance of the two rogues appropriately 'astraddle of a rail' and 'all over tar and feathers', at the end of Chapter XXXIII, the narrative consists of a series of episodes dominated by the Duke and the King. In between, the raft floats ever southward.

But the journey which begins in Chapter XIX is quite different from the journey described in Chapters XII–XVI, for it has nothing to do with Jim's escape and therefore no purpose in the sense that the journey from St Petersburg to Cairo had a purpose. Once Mark Twain had worked out in his mind a plausible device for taking Huck and Jim downstream, he seems to have forgotten about the original plan of escape up the Ohio. Even before the Duke and the King enter the story, when Huck and Jim set out on the raft from the Grangerford plantation, the earlier plan has sunk from sight. Huck now says that as soon as the raft had got out to the middle of the River, 'we . . . judged that we was free and safe once more. . . . We said there warn't no home like a raft, after all. Other places do seem so cramped up and smothery, but a raft don't. You feel mighty free and easy and comfortable on a raft.' When Huck goes ashore in Chapter XIX to look for berries, just before he meets the Duke and the King, he mentions finding a canoe without giving any indication that this is precisely what he and Jim need to make their way upstream. It should be emphasized that these incidents occur before Mark Twain has actually brought into play his device of subjecting Huck and Jim to the coercion of the Duke and the King. Thereafter, although theoretically Huck and Jim might be expected to seize the first opportunity of escaping from their captors in order to head back upstream, we are not surprised that they fail to do so. When they momentarily elude the Duke and the King after the Wilks episode (at the end of Chapter XXIX). Huck says: '. . . away we went, a sliding down the river, and it *did* seem so good to be free again and all by ourselves on the big river and nobody to bother us'.

In these moments of spontaneous reflection Huck has simply forgotten Jim's assertion that below Cairo 'he'd be in the slave country again and no more show for freedom'. What has happened is that Mark Twain has abandoned his original narrative plan and has substituted for it a different structural principle. During the journey from the Grangerford plantation to Pikesville, the action is not dictated by the reasonable if risky plan for Jim's escape but by the powerful image of Huck and Jim's 'a sliding down the river', 'free and easy' on the raft.[1] This image now embodies the only meaning which freedom and safety have in the narrative. It becomes the positive value replacing the original goal of actual freedom for Jim. The new goal is a subjective state, having its empirical basis in the solitude of the friends in their 'home' on 'the big river' but consisting in a mode of experience rather than an outward condition. There is some suggestion, to be sure, of a pastoral sanction for the state of mind attained by Huck and Jim when they are alone on the raft. The physical setting, the River, sometimes becomes vaguely but powerfully benign, as in the ecstatic opening of Chapter XIX. But the journey considered as movement from one determinate place to another has lost its meaning. It literally leads nowhere. The Phelps plantation where it ends, from the standpoint of

---

[1] The pattern is repeated at the beginning of the Phelps plantation sequence when Tom asks Huck what his proposal for rescuing Jim is. Huck says they should simply take Jim out of the cabin at night and 'shove off down the river on the raft, with Jim, hiding daytimes and running nights, the way me and Jim did before'. But he welcomes Tom's more splendid and complicated plan for the rescue, recognizing with unconscious irony that it 'would make Jim just as free a man as mine would, and maybe get us all killed besides' (Chapter XXXIV). Again, in the last chapter Tom says he had intended, after the Evasion, 'for us to run [Jim] down the river, on the raft, and have adventures plumb to the mouth of the river, and then tell him about his being free'.

geography eleven hundred miles downstream from St Petersburg, is from the standpoint of Mark Twain's imagination very near the starting-point of Huck's and Jim's journey. It is his fictional rendering of the farm of his uncle John Quarles, thirty miles inland from Hannibal, where he spent summers as a child.

The new structural principle which supplants the original linear movement toward freedom is bipolar. It is a contrast between the raft—connoting freedom, security, happiness, and harmony with physical nature—and the society of the towns along the shore, connoting vulgarity and malice and fraud and greed and violence. The raft, when those invaders from the shore, the Duke and King, can be got out of the way or even just put to sleep, is always the same. The towns are very much alike also; Pokeville, Bricksville, and Peter Wilks's home town all embody Mark Twain's memories of Hannibal. Huck is drawn ashore repeatedly, and repeatedly returns to the raft, but this apparent movement is merely an oscillation between two modes of experience, and the successive episodes are restatements, with variations, of the same theme: the raft versus the town, the River versus the Shore. Yet this thematic plan is not so different as it might seem at first glance from the original narrative plan of linear movement toward a geographical goal. The book has a basic unity of theme despite Mark Twain's pronounced shift in overt structure. For not only does the River connote freedom; the Shore connotes slavery, bondage in a more general sense than the actual servitude of Jim. Huck and Jim share a common quest, not merely because Huck is helping Jim, but because Huck too is fleeing from slavery. On occasion it is implied that the contrast between freedom and slavery is even more general, that Jim's and Huck's predicament is that of every man, and their quest a universal human undertaking.

In the six or seven years between the time when Mark Twain wrote the opening chapters and the time when he wrote the last half of his book, he had become aware of a meaning in Huck's and Jim's situation that transcended (while still including) his original concern with Jim's escape from slavery. Slavery in the actual pre-Civil War South had come to seem to him only an extreme example of the constraints imposed by that society on all its members, white as well as black. And the historical South itself, remembered with such unexampled vividness from Mark

Twain's boyhood, had tended to become a metaphor for the human condition. This generalizing of the concrete situation is strikingly evident in Colonel Sherburn's speech to the mob, which comes significantly at the beginning of the final continuous spurt of composition in the summer of 1883. Sherburn's speech, as Mr Blair has pointed out, is very close in ideas to a passage Mark Twain had written in his own person earlier in the same year for inclusion in *Life on the Mississippi*. The passage was omitted from that book, but Mark Twain did not abandon his opinion that the 'civilization' of the United States (the reference here, as in Sherburn's speech, is not limited to the South) amply deserved Mrs Trollope's criticisms, 'being slavery, rowdyism, "chivalrous" assassinations, sham godliness, and several other devilishnesses. . . .' 'She was holily hated for her "prejudices",' Mark Twain continued; 'but they seem to have been simply the prejudices of a humane spirit against inhumanities; of an honest nature against humbug; of a clean breeding against grossness; of a right heart against unright speech and deed.'[1]

One is reminded of Eric Auerbach's remark that Rousseau by contrasting the natural condition of man with existing social reality made this reality a problem for the writer and thus provided the intellectual basis for literary realism[2]. We can see in Mark Twain's description of the river towns a coming-into-being of realism as a fictional mode, even though the novel as a whole is not realistic but symbolic in structure. Lionel Trilling has advanced a similar generalization, recalling Wordsworth's boys 'upon whom the shades of the prison house are inevitably to fall', and noting the constant recurrence of the image of a prison in fiction of the past century and a half. The image, he thinks, implies a new recognition of society as coercion—by the family, by the professions, by the code of respectability with its ideas of faith and duty, by the very language men speak. 'The modern self,' he concludes, 'like Little Dorrit, was born in a prison. It assumed its nature and fate the moment it perceived, named, and denounced its oppressor.' In contrast with the image of society as a prison, of course, Huck's and Jim's way of life on the raft is an embodiment of what Mr Trilling calls 'the modern

---

[1] *Life on the Mississippi*, New York, 1944 (Heritage Press edition), p. 392.
[2] *Mimesis, The Representation of Reality in Western Literature*, trans. Willard R. Trask, Princeton, 1953, p. 467.

imagination of autonomy and delight, of surprise and elevation, of selves conceived in opposition to the general culture'.[1]

The middle section of *Huckleberry Finn*, with its superb series of little towns along the River, is rich in passages illustrating the thematic opposition between the bondage imposed by society and the freedom (at least the potential freedom) of the raft. Let us glance at the most elaborate of the interludes on shore, the sequence laid in the nameless Tennessee town where Peter Wilks the tanner has just died and the King and the Duke are trying to make away with his considerable property. In the early part of this episode Huck is a passive observer feeling almost equal distaste for the 'scamps' who are bent on gulling the townspeople and for their victims—'a lot of prejudiced chuckle-heads' eager to be deceived and exploited. The arrival of the adventurers in the guise of the long-awaited Wilks brothers from England produces a sensation that is described with the broad strokes of caricature. 'The news,' Huck says (at the beginning of Chapter XXV), 'was all over town in two minutes . . . '; people came 'tearing down on the run'; by the time the newcomers reach the Wilks house, 'the street in front of it was packed'. Through Huck's unconscious exaggerations, Mark Twain passes judgment on the villagers. He condemns two traits: their greed for sensation, a kind of tropism that focuses all their attention on any event that breaks the monotony of everyday life; and their sentimentality, their tendency to luxuriate in emotion for its own sake. Both these traits bespeak a lack of freedom, and both are outgrowths of a mob spirit. The townspeople are shown in deliberately grotesque postures (putting on their coats as they run toward the Wilks house), and are compared to soldiers obeying the commands of a drill master. A condensed metaphor even likens them to animals in a herd (they are 'trotting along with the gang').

The evil in the culture of the village results from the deference paid by the people to a false set of values, a collection of approved and prescribed attitudes which derive from an outworn Calvinism and from the eighteenth-century cult of feeling. The King is able to impose himself on the people by pretending to be a clergyman and addressing them in a burlesque of pulpit

[1] *The Opposing Self, Nine Essays in Criticism*, New York, 1955, Preface, pp. x–xiv.

rhetoric. He 'works himself up and slobbers out a speech, all full of tears and flapdoodle' about the 'sore trial' (that is, the death of his supposed brother) which is however 'sweetened and sanctified to us by this dear sympathy and these holy tears'. Then he 'blubbers out a pious goody-goody Amen, and turns himself loose and goes to crying fit to bust'.

Although Huck does not analyse the situation in abstract terms, his narrative suggests to the reader that the King's hearers are helpless because they do not react to situations spontaneously but according to stereotyped patterns of feeling and behaviour. The town's culture does not express the true feelings of the people, and since they are not aware of what their true feelings are they lie at the mercy of an impostor who can manipulate the dead symbols to which they are bound by habit and by the desire for status. In a telling metaphor, Huck remarks that the ostentatious grief of the King and the Duke 'worked the crowd'—like a strong physic.

The only scepticism and common sense in the town are represented by Dr Robinson and the lawyer Levi Bell, the nearest approach to intellectuals among the populace, and 'a big rough husky' named Hines from up the River who happened to see the King's party board the steamboat only a few miles above the village and thus knows for certain that they are lying about their supposed arrival straight from England. For a time the sceptics seem to be free of the conditioning that binds everyone else in the community. Lawyer Bell proposes settling the question of identity by comparing specimens of handwriting, and when this plan is frustrated suggests digging up Peter Wilks's corpse in order to examine the tattoo mark. Yet even these men are in the end controlled by the same tropisms that control the crowd. Hines, who is holding Huck by the wrist, loses his head when the bag of gold is discovered in Wilks's coffin; he 'let out a whoop, like everybody else', says Huck, 'and dropped my wrist and give a big surge to bust his way in and get a look. . . .' Robinson and Bell apparently make the same mistake: the King and the Duke also escape when 'the excited fools . . . let go all holts and made that rush to get a look. . . .'

The implication of this passage is that Huck is not subject to the social pressures holding the townspeople in bondage. But the situation is not so simple as this. With respect to the great issue of the overt action, Jim's escape from slavery, Huck is divided against himself. His inner freedom is menaced by attitudes imposed upon him by society. The culture of the Shore had invaded his personality by implanting in him a conscience which is the internalized mores of the community. When Huck faces a crisis of decision about his loyalty to Jim, his conscience significantly addresses him in the language of the official culture a tawdry and faded effort at a high style that is the rhetorical equivalent of the ornaments of the Grangerford parlour. The following sentence, for example (in Chapter XXXI), has a complexity of structure which is foreign to Huck's own mode of speech, as are the cant theological phrases: 'And at last, when it hit me all of a sudden that here was the plain hand of Providence slapping me in the face and letting me know my wickedness was being watched all the time from up there in heaven, whilst I was stealing a poor old woman's nigger that hadn't ever done me no harm, and now was showing me there's One that's always on the lookout, and ain't agoing to allow no such miserable doings to go only just so fur and no further, I most dropped in my tracks I was so scared.' Parallel clauses are built up to a monitory climax in a pattern Huck must have heard used by preachers and politicians: 'It was because my heart warn't right; it was because I warn't square; it was because I was playing double. I was letting *on* to give up sin, but away inside of me I was holding on to the biggest one of all. I was trying to make my mouth *say* I would do the right thing and the clean thing, and go and write to that nigger's owner and tell where he was; but deep down in me I knowed it was a lie—and He knowed it. You can't pray a lie—I found that out.'

In passages such as these, the polar opposition between the River and the Shore, between freedom and bondage, is restated as a division within Huck's own mind. The intuitive self, the spontaneous impulse from the deepest levels of the personality, is placed in opposition to the acquired conscience, the overlayer of prejudice and false valuation imposed upon all members of society in the name of religion, morality, law, and culture. Huck's triumph over his conscience is his most nearly heroic moment, falling short of grandeur only because his youth and ignorance prevent him from undertaking a decisive action.

What is the source of the power by which the true self triumphs over the false conscience? It is conveyed indirectly a few lines later, in a passage which is the emotional and thematic climax of the book, and one of its supremely beautiful moments. This is the voice of freedom, spontaneity, autonomy of the individual; of brotherhood, of the River as opposed to the Shore. Huck actually writes a letter to Miss Watson giving Jim away; but then he 'laid the paper down and set there thinking . . . And went on thinking. And got to thinking over our trip down the river; and I see Jim before me, all the time, in the day, and in the night-time, sometimes moonlight, sometimes storms, and we a floating along, talking, and singing, and laughing.' There is more of this, but the quotation will suggest the extraordinary intensity of emotion together with the convincing representation in words of the free flow of reminiscence and emotion, devoid of the artifices of official rhetoric, undisciplined by syntax (although cunningly controlled in rhythm), and overwhelmingly concrete: a torrent of emotionally charged images.

The Huck who could not harden himself against Jim is the 'real' or 'true' Huck, the boy who has, as Mark Twain said when he described the book ten years later, a 'sound'.[1] The depraved conscience is unreal; it is an intrusion from without, just as the Duke and the King on the raft are invaders from the shore, and its threat is overcome. The narrator of the story, looking back over his experiences, knows that he has been victorious in his struggle with his conscience. The remembered struggle merely lends richness and depth to his character. Basically this character is natural man, pure and spontaneously good. But we must remember the pattern of values Mark Twain has established for his story: the contrast between the River and the Shore. Huck's goodness has to be defined in opposition to the standards of propriety and respectability that prevail in organized society. He is the Bad Boy—he is dirty and ungrammatical, he steals chickens and watermelons, he is an accomplished liar, he runs away and lives a vagabond existence with an escaped slave. In the moral system of the novel, these traits of the Bad Boy simply establish his innocence

[1] Notebook #28a [I], TS, p. 35 (1895), Mark Twain Papers, University of California Library, Berkeley. The entry refers to *Huckleberry Finn* as 'a book of mine where a sound heart & a deformed conscience come into collision & conscience suffers defeat'.

and purity. It is a scheme having something in common with the heart-of-gold formula popularized by Bret Harte but more profound because much more serious, more deeply felt by the author.

Yet this disreputable vagabond with a good heart beneath his rags, although a fully realized character, is after all a character, not an actual person. He is conceived by Mark Twain deliberately for a specific technical purpose. He establishes a point of view, a perspective from which the events of the story can be observed and described. And since the author identifies himself with Huck by using the first person, Huck is evidently a mask, a narrative persona. In this respect Huck derives from a series of narrative personae devised by Mark Twain experimentally for earlier books: the persona of the ignorant tourist (innocent mainly because of his ignorance) in *The Innocents Abroad*; that of the tenderfoot undergoing initiation in *Roughing It*; that of the inspired idiot in *A Tramp Abroad* who professes to have come to Europe to study painting and the German language, to make pedestrian tours (which always lead him to the first vehicle he can catch), to climb the Alps (by means of a telescope). Yet earlier literary ancestors of Huck are Simon Wheeler, who tells the story of 'The Celebrated Jumping Frog of Calaveras County', and other characters in Mark Twain's sketches who represent his apprentice efforts to reproduce in written prose the effect of the deadpan manner cultivated by oral storytellers in the American backwoods tradition.

Late in his career Mark Twain composed the ars poetica of the oral humorous tale, which he pronounced a native American genre entirely distinct from the comic story of the English or the witty story of the French. 'The humorous story is told gravely,' he asserted; 'the teller does his best to conceal the fact that he even dimly suspects that there is anything funny about it. . . .' Mark Twain mentions as masters of the technique Artemus Ward (the mentor and guide he met in Nevada) and James Whitcomb Riley. He describes how in telling a certain story Riley assumed 'the character of a dull-witted old farmer' and 'perfectly simulated' the farmer's 'simplicity and innocence and sincerity and unconsciousness. . . .'[1] Artemus Ward had

[1] 'How to Tell a Story', in *The Writings of Mark Twain*, Definitive Edition, 37 vols., New York, 1922–5, XXIV, 263–70, esp. 266–7.

used a similar technique, well indicated by the title which he always announced for his humorous 'lectures' without regard to their wildly irrelevant and rambling content: 'The Babes in the the Wood'. The art which Mark Twain praised in Artemus Ward and Riley was, of course, the art he brought to perfection in his own platform appearances. A perceptive newspaper reporter once characterized it as the pose of 'Innocence victimized by the world, flesh, and devil'.[1]

Huck Finn is the literary culmination of this deadpan manner. Through Mark Twain's use of Huck as narrator he is able to wear the mask of innocence—not only in the sense of unspotted goodness, but also in the sense of ignorance, inexperience, and a simple-mindedness not in the least impaired by Huck's evident native shrewdness. Because the narrator of the story is represented as being less sophisticated than the author and the reader, the reader is made to perceive virtually every incident on two levels: that of Huck, and that of the author. The contrast between the two levels of perception creates an almost unbroken irony. Sometimes the effect is rather simple comedy, as when Huck says that after he and Jim found a wooden leg in the deserted house floating down the river, they 'hunted all around' for the other one. A more complex passage—in which comedy blends with a kind of naïve lyricism—is Huck's description of the circus (introduced rather incongruously into Chapter XXII). Huck himself never realizes that the antics of the acrobat disguised as a drunken tramp have been carefully rehearsed with the ringmaster. Indeed, when he proves unable to grasp the point of Buck Grangerford's prehistoric riddle about where Moses was when the light went out, we are forced to recognize that the comedy of the book, while it is conveyed to us in Huck's words, is lost on Huck himself. The narrative persona is a character without a sense of humour.

In its simplest form, this device reinforces comic effects by contrast (as Mark Twain noted in his description of Artemus Ward's and Riley's technique of oral story-telling). But in Mark Twain's hands it proves to have capabilities quite beyond the range of the earlier humorists. For example, Huck's imperviousness to comedy deepens into a predominantly melancholy

---

[1] Washington *Post*, November 25, 1884.

cast of temperament. Wise beyond his years in the mischances of life, he has the imagination of disaster. The thumbnail autobiographies he invents, usually as a means of getting himself out of a tight place, but often carried beyond the demands of utility for sheer love of the art, are uniformly sombre. When he plans his escape from Pap (Chapter VII), he does so by imagining his own death and planting clues that convince everyone in St Petersburg, including Tom Sawyer, that he has actually been murdered.[1] In the crisis of Chapter XVI, when Huck overcomes the temptation to betray Jim, his heightened emotion leads him to produce on the spur of the moment a harrowing tale to the effect that his father and mother and sister are suffering from smallpox on a raft adrift in mid-river, and he is unable to tow the raft ashore by himself. The slave-hunters he encounters are so touched by the story that they give him forty dollars in gold and careful instructions about how to seek help—farther downstream. Huck tells the Grangerfords 'how pap and me and all the family was living on a little farm down at the bottom of Arkansaw, and my sister Mary Ann run off and got married and never was heard of no more, and Bill went to hunt them and he warn't heard of no more, and Tom and Mort died, and then there warn't nobody but just me and pap left, and he was just trimmed down to nothing, on account of his troubles; so when he died I took what there was left, because the farm didn't belong to us, and started up the river, deck passage, and fell overboard. . . . ' (Chapter XVII).

These yarns—and others like them, for Huck uses the device often—are improvisations on the themes of his own life. Although comic because they are fabrications, making the hearers into dupes, they reinforce the narrative by adding a kind of resonance to it; they make Huck's experience seem of a piece with many other lives of farmer-folk along the river. As projections of Huck's unconscious, they reveal the gloomy substratum of his personality. His memory is stored with images of violence and calamity, bereavement, sickness, separation of families, and

[1] Mr Franklin Rogers, in 'The Role of Literary Burlesque in the Development of Mark Twain's Structural Patterns, 1855–1885' (unpublished dissertation, University of California, Berkeley, 1958), suggests that at one time Mark Twain had in mind a plot for the novel involving Jim's being brought to trial for the supposed murder of Huck.

especially of boys left alone in the world by the death of parents.

Yet another use to which Mark Twain perceived the deadpan mask of the oral story-teller could be put is satire. In one sense the manoeuvre was familiar: Goldsmith's Chinese Citizen of the World and Voltaire's Ingénu from the wilds of North America are only two among dozens of deliberately naïve observers who had described Europe from an external point of view during the eighteenth century. Huck's description of the Grangerford-Shepherdson feud, which has few comic touches, is close to the traditional technique. But no one had used the device for such a brilliant blending of comedy and satire as Mark Twain achieves in Huck's celebrated description of the Grangerford parlour (Chapter XVII). This passage gains much of its effect from the fact that Huck sincerely admires the taste of the Grangerfords and is genuinely humble in his statement that *The Pilgrim's Progress* is 'about a man that left his family it didn't say why.' He even tries to 'sweat out a verse or two' in memory of Emmeline Grangerford because her diligence as an elegist entitles her to an elegy of her own.

It is remarkable how consistently Mark Twain maintains Huck's point of view. When the book was published in 1885, Henry James had hardly begun to be aware of the technical effects to be achieved by excluding the author from the novel, and Howells, for all his critical sophistication concerning other men's work and his admiration for both Mark Twain and James, never did perceive that management of point-of-view was the central technical development in modern fiction. If we accept (as we must) the arbitrary convention that Huck as narrator is able to recall the exact words he has heard other characters utter, we can find only the most trifling departures from plausibility in *Huckleberry Finn*, with the one significant exception of Sherburn's speech to the mob in Chapter XXII which has been mentioned earlier. Here the mask drops, the narrative persona is forgotten, if only for a moment, and the illusion is for that moment dispelled.

Elsewhere, however, it is Huck, not Mark Twain, who speaks. The point is worth making because of its bearing on the much-discussed declaration of Huck which ends the novel: '. . . I reckon I got to light out for the Territory ahead of the rest, because Aunt Sally she's going to adopt me and sivilize me, and I can't stand it. I been there before.' This is a deliberate echo of the opening pages of the story, where Huck has told the reader: 'The Widow Douglas, she took me for her son, and allowed she would sivilize me; but it was rough living in the house all the time, considering how dismal regular and decent the widow was in all her ways; and so when I couldn't stand it no longer, I lit out. I got into my old rags, and my sugar-hogshead again, and was free and satisfied. But Tom Sawyer, he hunted me up and said he was going to start a band of robbers, and I might join if I would go back to the widow and be respectable. So I went back.' Huck is merely summarizing here the last pages of *Tom Sawyer*, and as far as plot is concerned the opening chapters of the sequel are a continuation of the earlier book. When Huck's Pap forces him to leave the Widow Douglas's house for the cabin across the River, Huck quickly resumes his old ways and for two months is quite content. 'I didn't want to go back no more,' he says. 'It was pretty good times up in the woods there, take it all around.' This escape is purely negative in meaning: he is glad not to have Miss Watson 'pecking' at him. It is true that he is presently forced to escape from a more serious menace, his Pap's dunken brutality; and when he joins forces with Jim his flight takes on a still deeper meaning. But when the Evasion from the Phelps plantation under Tom Sawyer's leadership restores the mood of the opening chapters, Huck's desire to escape is stripped of the meaning it had acquired in the middle section of the book. We are brought back to the situation at the end of *Tom Sawyer*. Even the robber gang reappears, for Tom's imagination peoples the territory with robbers in his 'nonnamous letters' of warning. It is Tom, again, who conceives the plan to 'go for howling adventures amongst the Injuns, over in the Territory, for a couple of weeks or two'. When Huck says he means to set out ahead of the others, there is nothing in the text to indicate that his intention is more serious than Tom's.

This reading of Huck's last sentence contradicts a view that has been gaining in popularity among critics, a view which sees a portentous meaning in Huck's final escape on the theory that he has become disgusted with a society that tolerates slavery and is making a drastic, final gesture of alienation and rejection. Such a reading of the passage presupposes first, that the question of slavery as an actual institution in the Old South is central to the entire novel, and second, that Huck has matured in the course of the narrative so that his last decision has a depth not characteristic of his attitudes and actions at the beginning. Huck's maturity, according to this view, now enables him to perceive that slavery is evil.

But what is the evidence that Huck has arrived at such an insight? We can recognize that he made a thrilling step toward emotional maturity when he humbled himself to ask Jim's forgiveness for deceiving him, at the end of Chapter XV. But some if not all of this emotional growth has been sacrificed when Huck accepted Tom's leadership during the Evasion sequence, without any indication that he perceived the consequent degradation of Jim. And he is still living in Tom's fantasy-world of robber gangs and literary Indians at the end of the book. What he is trying to escape from is not a society corrupted by slavery, but the same petty harassments he had fled from at the end of *Tom Sawyer*.

The diminished Huck of the last chapters, then, is decidedly inferior to the character who had been capable of such a profound loyalty to his friend Jim in the middle section. But not even then had he been capable of arriving at the abstract proposition, 'Slavery is wrong.' The depth and strength of his character lie in integrity of emotion, not in intellectual acuteness. Indeed, Mark Twain's depiction of Huck's inner life suggests a contrast between thought and feeling that to some degree parallels the contrast between the Shore and the River. Huck's conscience, spokesman for the official culture, tries to beguile him with the abstractions of sin and property, the abstractions which underwrite institutions and thus provide society with the means of enslaving people in the towns. His loyalty to Jim enables him to evade these sophistries, but he does not have enough intellectual sophistication to deny them. He acts in defiance of a doctrine which he never ceases, on the intellectual level, to accept. Mark Twain makes this clear in his comment on *Huckleberry Finn* written ten years after it was published: ' . . . the whole community was agreed as to one thing—the awful sacredness of slave property'. This view, he added, was held not only by slave-owners, but by 'the paupers, the loafers the rag-tag & bobtail of the community, & in a passionate & uncompromising form. . . .' It was only natural that 'Huck & his father the worthless loafer should feel it' also; for 'the conscience—that unerring monitor—can be trained to approve any wild thing you *want* it to approve if you begin its education early & stick to it'[1] Huck's spontaneously good heart has dictated his actions, but his conscience has remained depraved, for it represents the community. And Huck is not able to think his way toward the perception that the community is mistaken.

Several topics touched upon earlier have led, by different routes, to the question of the language of *Huckleberry Finn*. Huck criticizes Peter Wilks's fellow-townsmen by means of derogatory metaphors embodied in his diction; the King is represented as perpetrating his fraud upon them by rhetoric; Huck's conscience tries to persuade him to betray Jim by the same means; vernacular speech is the principal device for maintaining the deadpan innocence of Huck as a narrative persona; the style of Emmeline Grangerford's verse burlesques nineteenth-century sentimental literature; Huck is prevented from seeing through the fallacies of the conventional attitude toward slavery because the lack of abstract terms in his vocabulary makes conceptual thought difficult for him. Beyond question, Mark Twain uses language in a variety of ways in this book to build up his meaning.

He himself calls attention to the language in his prefatory note, emphasizing the care with which he has discriminated seven dialects. 'The shadings have not been done in a haphazard fashion, or by guess-work,' he asserts; 'but pains-takingly, and with the trustworthy guidance and support of personal familiarity with these several forms of speech.' His claim to care in the representation of dialects is borne out by a comparison between the manuscript of about two thirds of the novel (now in the Buffalo Public Library) and the published text, which reveals thousands of changes in spelling and diction evidently made for the sake of accuracy of transcription. But even if we could prove that the dialects are accurately rendered (which we could do only by a difficult historical inquiry into the language actually spoken along the banks of the Mississippi

[1] Notebook #28a [I], TS, pp. 34–6.

in the 1840s), we should still have thrown very little light upon the novel as a work of art. What counts for literature is Mark Twain's success in establishing the illusion of accuracy, in making the reader accept a character's speech as lifelike. The discriminations that matter are those which differentiate characters from one another and confer individuality on them. Pap's diatribe against the 'govment' (Chapter VI), the Duke's effort to call back Hamlet's soliloquy from 'recollection's vaults' (Chapter XXI), old Mrs Hotchkiss's inspired monologue on the night of the Evasion (Chapter XLI)—the novel is filled with passages of this sort which give to each character his exactly appropriate idiom.

Just as effective as the individualizing of characters by their speech is Mark Twain's device of establishing a common diction and rhetoric for all characters the moment they try to claim for themselves a false pathos (as the Duke does when he announces the secret of his birth) or an undeserved moral authority (as the King does in the Wilks sequence). Different as the characters are in their natural selves, when they fall into pretence they all sound alike because they all begin to speak in a burlesque of the exalted rhetoric of the official culture. This 'high' language might be called the 'alas!' or the 'soul-butter' mode of speech. The Duke and the King are masters of it, and so was Emmeline Grangerford, if we are to judge from her verses and the titles she composed for her pictures. But almost any character can resort to this pompous language on occasion, even Huck's Pap (as when he takes the pledge at the end of Chapter V). When Tom Sawyer composes 'mournful inscriptions' for Jim to scribble on the wall ('Here a captive heart busted,' and so on, Chapter XXXVIII) 'his voice trembled, whilst he was reading them, and he most broke down.' And although Huck himself never reaches this level of self-deception, his conscience, as we have seen, commands no means of expression except soul-butter.

These uses of language represent an impressive accomplishment in the art of fiction. They are, however, expert management of well-established resources of the novelist rather than technical innovations. As long as Mark Twain uses Huck simply to report dialogue, whether his own or others', he is following a convention which was familiar to Mrs Stowe, or Cooper, or Scott, or for that matter Richardson: there was nothing new about having 'low' characters speak in dialect. Such a use of the vernacular implies no identification of the author with it; on the contrary, the contrast between the dialect within the quotation marks and the correct prose outside establishes a marked distance between author and character. But Mark Twain's use of Huck's vernacular speech as the narrative medium, outside quotation marks, is something new—a drastic, even a revolutionary shift in technique. For it means that the author has put on a mask, surrendering the right to express, except indirectly by means of irony, any ideas or emotions beyond Huck's range. He has made his story entirely dramatic in the sense that he has removed himself from the stage and has undertaken to say everything he has to say within the limits of a vocabulary not his own.

In *Huckleberry Finn*, as in Wordsworth's *Lyrical Ballads*, the language of literature gains a new life by being violently torn loose from its established moorings. For one thing, a new imagery becomes available. Speaking through Huck, Mark Twain can refer to 'the fish-belly white' of a man's face; he can call Henry VIII a 'bug'; he can say that after Pap had got drunk in the beautiful spare-room of the new judge's house, 'they had to take soundings before they could navigate it'. Furthermore, the systematic elimination of conventional associations removes the cake of custom from the visible universe and fosters a completely fresh treatment of landscape. A vision not distorted by inherited modes of perception, once fresh themselves but long since grown lifeless through over-use, can report sensory experience with supreme vividness. Taking as an example the description of the sunrise near the beginning of Chapter XIX, Leo Marx has skilfully demonstrated the change in Mark Twain's rendering of landscape in *Huckleberry Finn* as compared with his procedure in earlier books.[1] In *Tom Sawyer* and *Life on the Mississippi* he had not been able to free himself from a conventional vocabulary of landscape description, 'the literary counterpart of the painter's picturesque'. But when he 'looked at the river through Huck's eyes he was suddenly free of certain

[1] 'The Pilot and the Passenger: Landscape Conventions and the Style of *Huckleberry Finn*', *American Literature*, XXVIII, 129–46, May, 1956. I wish to thank Mr Marx for many suggestions about *Huckleberry Finn* in private correspondence.

arid notions of what a writer should write'. Huck's ignorance, his lack of exposure to formal culture, allows him to take the world as he finds it and report his sensations directly, 'without anxiously forcing meanings upon it'. The lyric intensity of the passage—a quality of which there is hardly a hint in the humorous tales from which Mark Twain's style is descended— is not an inevitable result of the use of the vernacular as a narrative medium, but is the outcome of a fortunate convergence of material (the author's boyhood memories of the River), theme (the River as a symbol of freedom), narrative technique (the choice of the vernacular persona as a means of telling the story), and language. Yet the language is the medium in which this convergence becomes possible: the point of view, as Mr Marx points out, has become a style.

We can justly apply to Mark Twain's achievement what Eric Auerbach says of Dante: '. . . this man used his language to discover the world anew.'[1] Yet it would be misleading to imply that Mark Twain's break with literary tradition was all clear gain. The official culture (which we perhaps too easily dismiss by calling it the Genteel Tradition) had indeed lost its power to nourish vigorous literature; an act of repudiation was necessary. But if Mark Twain rejected the affirmations proposed by the cultural tradition, what positive value was left to sustain his work as an artist? The answer proposed by *Huckleberry Finn* is: innate, natural human goodness, which would flower into brotherhood if it could only be protected against the taint of society. The vision of innocence and happiness on the raft was exhilarating, as the book itself shows, but the affirmation of natural goodness was unsatisfactory in the long run because it was contradicted by Mark Twain's own observation of human character. There was no refuge from society, even on the River. The experiment could never be tried, and even if it could have been one must doubt whether Huck and Jim can be taken as representative of humanity. If one part of Mark Twain's mind could conceive of the happiness and freedom of two comrades on the raft, another part, just as true to his over-all view of life, speaks through Colonel Sherburn's denunciation of the Bricks- ville mob—a denunciation which is extended to include 'the

[1] *Mimesis.* p. 183.

average all around', 'the average man', and verges upon the denunciation of 'the damned human race' that later became almost habitual for Mark Twain. (The persistence of the two contradictory attitudes is charmingly revealed in the Damned Human Race Luncheon Club which he founded in his lonely old age, with a membership limited to himself and three greatly loved friends.)

In *Huckleberry Finn* Colonel Sherburn asserts, for the author, that the average man is cruel and cowardly, perhaps cruel because cowardly—a helpless victim of mob spirit. In his next book Mark Twain would make one more effort to refute the charge, to establish at least the imaginative validity of the innocent vernacular character. He conceived a country-born blacksmith and horse-doctor who had come to town and become a master mechanic, able 'to make everything: guns, revolvers, cannon, boilers, engines, all sorts of labour-saving machinery'.[1] Hank Morgan, the Connecticut Yankee, is carefully labelled an ignoramus in matters of art and culture but is endowed with vigorous republican principles and all the power of modern technology. If no one could escape society altogether, could this grown-up Huck Finn hope to transform it so completely that decent creatures might live in it and be happy? A *Connecticut Yankee* was a genuine *roman expérimental*: the issue was in doubt and the author allowed his imagination to follow out what seemed the inevitable consequences of the given situation. The hero was defeated by prejudice and cowardice. His technology could give him limitless physical power but could not redeem a population debauched by social institutions. He came to despise the 'human muck' that he had hoped to educate into manhood,[2] and his Utopian experiment ended in the stench of twenty-five thousand corpses.

In the course of this novel the alienation from society that is hinted at in Colonel Sherburn's speech is established as the author's dominant attitude. The major direction of his thought thereafter takes him with increasing bitterness through 'The Man That Corrupted Hadleyburg' and *Pudd'nhead Wilson* to *The Mysterious Stranger*. In this fable Satan symbolically de-

[1] A *Connecticut Yankee in King Arthur's Court*, Definitive Edition, XIV, 5.

[2] A *Connecticut Yankee*, Definitive Edition, XIV, 430.

stroys the image of Hannibal which was Mark Twain's persistent metaphor for human society. The later books enable us to recognize that the contrast in *Huckleberry Finn* between the River and the Shore contains a latent anarchism and even nihilism. This perception should be kept in mind when we consider what the novel has meant to twentieth-century American writers. Although no one has yet undertaken to spell out the details of Mark Twain's influence on the literature of our day, the magnitude of that influence is obvious. Everyone has read Ernest Hemingway's flamboyant assertion that 'all modern American literature comes from one book by Mark Twain called *Huckleberry Finn*. . . .'[1] William Faulkner declared recently that Mark Twain was the father of Sherwood Anderson, who in turn was 'the father of my generation of American writers and the tradition of American writing which our successors will carry on'.[2] T. S. Eliot has maintained that in *Huckleberry Finn* Mark Twain 'reveals himself to be one of those writers, of whom there are not a great many in any literature, who have discovered a new way of writing, valid not only for themselves but for others. I should place him, in this respect, even with Dryden and Swift, as one of those rare writers who have brought their language up to date, and in so doing, "purified the dialect of the tribe".'[3]

Although Mark Twain's themes, especially his alienation from society, and the use of a deliberately naïve point of view have undoubtedly proved suggestive for later writers, Mr Eliot's emphasis on language seems historically justified. Malcolm Cowley attempted to specify what is implied here by suggesting that a 'Middle American' or Midwestern prose which Mark Twain took over from the early backwoods humorists and transmitted to the twentieth century has become the dominant language of American fiction. 'It was certainly Hemingway who made it popular,' continues Mr Cowley, 'but some of his contemporaries (including Fitzgerald and Dos Passos, but not Thomas Wolfe) seem to have approached it independently. It began to run riot among the novelists a little younger than

[1] *Green Hills of Africa*, New York, 1935, p. 22.
[2] In an interview with Jean Stein, *Paris Review*, XII, 46, Spring, 1956.
[3] *American Literature and the American Language*, Washington University Studies, New Series, Language and Literature, No. 23, St Louis, 1953, pp. 16–17.

Hemingway, like Steinbeck and Saroyan and Raymond Chandler'.[1] Mr Cowley places Gertrude Stein and Sherwood Anderson in this line of linguistic continuity, and the list of writers whom critics have seen as practitioners of a vernacular style derived from Mark Twain includes, among others, Sandburg Mencken, Thurber, Agee, and Salinger.

The historical facts are not fully established, but the main outlines of the phenomenon are clear enough in the work of such acknowledged disciples as Anderson and Hemingway. Different as they are from one another, both these writers illustrate the vividness and power of a prose patterned on the vernacular. But they also illustrate the consequences of the tendency toward primitivism that is implicit in *Huckleberry Finn*. The vernacular style greatly limited the power of Mark Twain and his successors to deal with abstract thought and thus has fostered anti-intellectualism. The repudiation of the Western European literary tradition, while in one sense a liberation for the writer, cuts him off from the accumulated experience of the past and commits him to the often wasteful enterprise of building from the ground up. Mark Twain's career, with its false starts and its lack of continuity, reveals the disadvantages as well as the advantages of the literary pioneer. Like the actual pioneer, he had to pay a high price for his conquest of new territory, and his debt was entailed upon his heirs.

Still—if the new territory was to be occupied, someone had to pay that price. Mark Twain took the risk, possibly without always understanding what dangers he ran, and the result is *Huckleberry Finn*: for all its imperfections, a great book, not only because it worked a revolution in American literary prose, but because of what it says—against stupid conformity and for the autonomy of the individual.

[1] 'The Middle American Style: D. Crockett to E. Hemingway', *New York Times Book Review*, July 15, 1945, p. 14.

17 Emile Zola

The Experimental Novel

First published 1893. From *The Naturalist Novel*, trans. Belle M. Sherman, Harvest House, Montreal, 1964, pp. 1–24.

In my literary essays I have often spoken of the application of the experimental method to the novel and to the drama. The return to nature, the naturalistic evolution which marks the century, drives little by little all the manifestation of human intelligence into the same scientific path. Only the idea of a literature governed by science is doubtless a surprise, until explained with precision and understood. It seems to me necessary, then, to say briefly and to the point what I understand by the experimental novel.

I really only need to adapt, for the experimental method has been established with strength and marvelous clearness by Claude Bernard in his 'Introduction à l'Étude de la Médecine Expérimentale'. This work, by a savant whose authority is unquestioned, will serve me as a solid foundation. I shall here find the whole question treated, and I shall restrict myself to irrefutable arguments and to giving the quotations which may seem necessary to me. This will then be but a compiling of texts, as I intend on all points to intrench myself behind Claude Bernard. It will often be but necessary for me to replace the word 'doctor' by the word 'novelist', to make my meaning clear and to give it the rigidity of a scientific truth.

What determined my choice, and made me choose 'L'Introduction' as my basis, was the fact that medicine, in the eyes of a great number of people, is still an art, as is the novel. Claude Bernard all his life was searching and battling to put medicine in a scientific path. In his struggle we see the first feeble attempts of a science to disengage itself little by little from empiricism,[1] and to gain a foothold in the realm of truth, by means of the experimental method. Claude Bernard demonstrates that this method, followed in the study of inanimate bodies in chemistry

[1] Zola uses empiricism in this essay in the sense of 'haphazard observation' in contrast with a scientific experiment undertaken to prove a certain truth. [Translator.]

and in physics, should be also used in the study of living bodies, in physiology and medicine. I am going to try and prove for my part that if the experimental method leads to the knowledge of physical life, it should also lead to the knowledge of the passionate and intellectual life. It is but a question of degree in the same path which runs from chemistry to physiology, then from physiology to anthropology and to sociology. The experimental novel is the goal.

To be more clear, I think it would be better to give a brief *résumé* of 'L'Introduction' before I commence. The applications which I shall make of the texts will be better understood if the plan of the work and the matters treated are explained.

Claude Bernard, after having declared that medicine enters the scientific path, with physiology as its foundation, and by means of the experimental method, first explains the differences which exist between the sciences of observation and the sciences of experiment. He concludes, finally, that experiment is but provoked observation. All experimental reasoning is based on doubt, for the experimentalist should have no preconceived idea, in the face of nature, and should always retain his liberty of thought. He simply accepts the phenomena which are produced, when they are proved.

In the second part he reaches his true subject and shows that the spontaneity of living bodies is not opposed to the employment of experiment. The difference is simply that an inanimate body possesses merely the ordinary, external environment, while the essence of the higher organism is set in an internal and perfected environment endowed with constant physico-chemical properties exactly like the external environment; hence there is an absolute determinism in the existing conditions of natural phenomena; for the living as for the inanimate bodies. He calls determinism the cause which determines the appearance of these phenomena. This nearest cause, as it is called, is nothing more than the physical and material condition of the existence or manifestation of the phenomena. The end of all experimental method, the boundary of all scientific research, is then identical for living and for inanimate bodies; it consists in finding the relations which unite a phenomenon of any kind to its nearest cause, or, in other words, in determining the conditions necessary for the manifestation of this phenomenon. Experimental science has no necessity to worry itself about the 'why' of things; it simply explains the 'how'.

After having explained the experimental considerations common to living beings and to inanimate, Claude Bernard passes to the experimental considerations which belong specially to living beings. The great and only difference is this, that there is presented to our consideration, in the organism of living beings, a harmonious group of phenomena. He then treats of practical experiments on living beings, of vivisection, of the preparatory anatomical conditions, of the choice of animals, of the use of calculation in the study of phenomena, and lastly of the physiologist's laboratory.

Finally, in the last part of 'L'Introduction', he gives some examples of physiological experimental investigations in support of the ideas which he has formulated. He then furnishes some examples of experimental criticism in physiology. In the end he indicates the philosophical obstacles which the experimental doctor encounters. He puts in the first rank the false application of physiology to medicine, the scientific ignorance as well as certain illusions of the medical mind. Further, he concludes by saying that empirical medicine and experimental medicine, not being incompatible, ought, on the contrary, to be inseparable one from the other. His last sentence is that experimental medicine adheres to no medical doctrine nor any philosophical system.

This is, very broadly, the skeleton of L'Introduction' stripped of its flesh. I hope that this rapid *exposé* will be sufficient to fill up the gaps which my manner of proceeding is bound to produce; for naturally, I shall cite from the work only such passages as are necessary to define and comment upon the experimental novel. I repeat that I use this treatise merely as a solid foundation on which to build, but a foundation very rich in arguments and proofs of all kinds. Experimental medicine, which but lisps as yet, can alone give us an exact idea of experimental literature, which, being still unhatched, is not even lisping.

I

The first question which presents itself is this: Is experiment possible in literature, in which up to the present time observation alone has been employed?

Claude Bernard discusses observation and experiment at great length. There exists, in the first place, a very clear line of demarcation, as follows: 'The name of "observer" is given to him who applies the simple or complex process of investigation in the study of phenomena which he does not vary, and which he gathers, consequently, as nature offers them to him; the name of "experimentalist" is given to him who employs the simple and complex process of investigation to vary or modify, for an end of some kind, the natural phenomena, and to make them appear under circumstances and conditions in which they are not presented by nature.' For instance, astronomy is a science of observation, because you cannot conceive of an astronomer acting upon the stars; while chemistry is an experimental science, as the chemist acts upon nature and modifies it. This, according to Claude Bernard, is the only true and important distinction which separates the observer from the experimentalist.

I cannot follow him in his discussion of the different definitions given up to the present time. As I have said before, he finishes by coming to the conclusion that experiment is but provoked observation. I repeat his words: 'In the experimental method the search after facts, that is to say, investigation, is always accompanied by a reason, so that ordinarily the experimentalist makes an experiment to confirm and verify the value of an experimental idea. In this case you can say that experiment is an observation instigated for the purpose of verification.'

To determine how much observation and experimenting there can be in the naturalistic novel, I only need to quote the following passages:

> The observer relates purely and simply the phenomena which he has under his eyes... He should be the photographer of phenomena, his observation should be an exact representation of nature... He listens to nature and he writes under its dictation. But once the fact is ascertained and the phenomenon observed, an idea or hypothesis comes into his mind, reason intervenes, and the experimentalist comes forward to interpret the phenomenon. The experimentalist is a man who, in pursuance of a more or less probable, but anticipated, explanation of observed phenomena, institutes an

experiment in such a way that, according to all probability, it will furnish a result which will serve to confirm the hypothesis or preconceived idea. The moment that the result of the experiment manifests itself, the experimentalist finds himself face to face with a true observation which he has called forth, and which he must ascertain, as all observation, without any preconceived idea. The experimentalist should then disappear, or rather transform himself instantly into the observer, and it is not until after he has ascertained the absolute results of the experiment, like that of an ordinary observation, that his mind comes back to reasoning, comparing, and judging whether the experimental hypothesis is verified or invalidated by these same results.

The mechanism is all there. It is a little complicated, it is true, and Claude Bernard is led on to say: 'When all this passes into the brain of a savant who has given himself up to the study of a science as complicated as medicine still is, then there is such an entanglement between the result of observation and what belongs to experiment that it will be impossible and, besides, useless to try to analyze, in their inextricable *mélange*, each of these terms.' In one word, it might be said that observation 'indicates' and that experiment 'teaches'.

Now, to return to the novel, we can easily see that the novelist is equally an observer and an experimentalist. The observer in him gives the facts as he has observed them, suggests the point of departure, displays the solid earth on which his characters are to tread and the phenomena to develop. Then the experimentalist appears and introduces an experiment, that is to say, sets his characters going in a certain story so as to show that the succession of facts will be such as the requirements of the determinism of the phenomena under examination call for. Here it is nearly always an experiment *'pour voir'*, as Claude Bernard calls it. The novelist starts out in search of a truth. I will take as an example the character of the Baron Hulot, in *Cousine Bette*, by Balzac. The general fact observed by Balzac is the ravages that the amorous temperament of a man makes in his home, in his family, and in society. As soon as he has chosen his subject he starts from known facts; then he makes his experiment, and exposes Hulot to a series of trials, placing him amid certain surroundings in order to exhibit how the complicated machinery of his passions works. It is then evident that there is not only observation there, but that there is also experiment; as Balzac does not remain satisfied with photographing the facts collected by him, but interferes in a direct way to place his character in certain conditions, and of these he remains the master. The problem is to know what such a passion, acting in such a surrounding and under such circumstances, would produce from the point of view of an individual and of society; and an experimental novel, *Cousine Bette*, for example, is simply the report of the experiment that the novelist conducts before the eyes of the public. In fact, the whole operation consists in taking facts in nature, then in studying the mechanism of these facts, acting upon them, by the modification of circumstances and surroundings, without deviating from the laws of nature. Finally, you possess knowledge of the man, scientific knowledge of him, in both his individual and social relations.

Doubtless we are still far from certainties in chemistry and even physiology. Nor do we know any more the reagents which decompose the passions, rendering them susceptible of analysis. Often, in this essay, I shall recall in similar fashion this fact, that the experimental novel is still younger than experimental medicine, and the latter is but just born. But I do not intend to exhibit the acquired results, I simply desire to clearly expose a method. If the experimental novelist is still groping in the most obscure and complex of all the sciences, this does not prevent this science from existing. It is undeniable that the naturalistic novel, such as we understand it to-day, is a real experiment that a novelist makes on man by the help of observation.

Besides, this opinion is not only mine, it is Claude Bernard's as well. He says in one place : 'In practical life men but make experiments on one another.' And again, in a more conclusive way, he expresses the whole theory of the experimental novel : 'When we reason on our own acts we have a certain guide, for we are conscious of what we think and how we feel. But if we wish to judge of the acts of another man, and know the motives which make him act, that is altogether a different thing. Without doubt we have before our eyes the movements of this man and his different acts, which are, we are sure, the modes of expression of his sensibility and his will. Further, we even admit that there is a necessary connection between the acts and their cause; but what is this cause? We do not feel it, we are not conscious of it, as we are when it acts in ourselves; we are therefore obliged to interpret it, and to guess at it, from the movements which we see and the words which we hear. We are obliged to check off this man's actions one by the other; we consider how he acted in such a circumstance and, in a word, we have recourse to the experimental method.' All that I have spoken of further back is summed up in this last phrase, which is written by a savant.

I shall still call your attention to another illustration of Claude Bernard, which struck me as very forcible: 'The experimentalist is the examining magistrate of nature.' We novelists are the examining magistrates of men and their passions.

But see what splendid clearness breaks forth when this conception of the application of the experimental method to the novel is adequately grasped and is carried out with all the scientific rigor which the matter permits to-day. A contemptible reproach which they heap upon us naturalistic writers is the desire to be solely photographers. We have in vain declared that we admit the necessity of an artist's possessing an individual temperament and a personal expression; they continue to reply to us with these imbecile arguments, about the impossibility of being strictly true, about the necessity of arranging facts to produce a work of art of any kind. Well, with the application of the experimental method to the novel that quarrel dies out. The idea of experiment carries with it the idea of modification. We start, indeed, from the true facts, which are our indestructible basis; but to show the mechanism of these facts it is necessary for us to produce and direct the phenomena; this is our share of invention, here is the genius in the book. Thus without having recourse to the questions of form and of style, which I shall examine later, I maintain even at this point that we must modify nature, without departing from nature, when we employ the experimental method in our novels. If we bear in mind this definition, that 'observation indicates and experiment teaches', we can even now claim for our books this great lesson of experiment.

The writer's office, far from being lessened, grows singularly from this point of view. An experiment, even the most simple, is always based on an idea, itself born of an observation. As Claude Bernard says: 'The experimental idea is not arbitrary, nor purely imaginary; it ought always to have a support in some observed reality, that is to say, in nature.' It is on this idea and on doubt that he bases all the method. 'The appearance of the experimental idea,' he says further on, 'is entirely spontaneous and its nature absolutely individual, depending upon the mind in which it originates; it is a particular sentiment, a *quid proprium*, which constitutes the originality, the invention, and the genius of each one.' Further, he makes doubt the great scientific lever. 'The doubter is the true savant; he doubts only himself and his interpretations; he believes in science; he even admits in the experimental sciences a criterion or a positive principle, the determinism of phenomena, which is absolute in living beings as in inanimate bodies.' Thus, instead of confining the novelist within narrow bounds, the experimental method gives full sway to his intelligence as a thinker, and to his genius as a creator. He must see, understand, and invent. Some observed fact makes the idea start up of trying an experiment, of writing a novel, in order to attain to a complete knowledge of the truth. Then when, after careful consideration, he has decided upon the plan of his experiment, he will judge the results at each step with the freedom of mind of a man who accepts only facts conformable to the determination of phenomena. He set out from doubt to reach positive knowledge; and he will not cease to doubt until the mechanism of the passion, taken to pieces and set up again by him, acts according to the fixed laws of nature. There is no greater, no more magnificent work for the human mind. We shall see, further on, the miseries of the scholastics, of the makers of systems, and those theorizing about the ideal, compared with the triumph of the experimentalists.

I sum up this first part by repeating that the naturalistic novelists observe and experiment, and that all their work is the off-spring of the doubt which seizes them in the presence of truths little known and phenomena unexplained, until an experimental idea rudely awakens their genius some day, and urges them to make an experiment, to analyze facts, and to master them.

II

Such, then, is the experimental method. But for a long time it has been held that this method cannot be applied to living beings.

This is the important point in the question that I am going to examine with Claude Bernard. The reasoning subsequently will be of the simplest; if the experimental method can be carried from chemistry and physics into physiology and medicine, it can be also carried from physiology into the naturalistic novel.

Cuvier—to cite the name of only one scientific man—claimed that experiment as applied to inanimate bodies could not be used with living beings; physiology, according to his way of thinking, should be purely a science of observation and of anatomical deduction. The vitalists even admit a vital force in unceasing battle with the physical and chemical forces neutralizing their action. Claude Bernard, on the contrary, denies all presence of a mysterious force, and affirms that experiment is applicable everywhere. 'I propose,' he says, 'to establish the fact that the science of the phenomena of life can have no other basis than the science of the phenomena of inanimate bodies, and that there are, in this connection, no differences between the principles of biological science and those of physics and chemistry. In fact, the end the experimental method proposes is the same everywhere; it consists in connecting by experiment, the natural phenomena to their conditions of existence or to their nearest causes.'

It seems to me useless to enter into the complicated explanations and reasonings of Claude Bernard. I have already said that he insists upon the existence of an interior condition in living beings. 'In experimenting on inanimate bodies,' he says, 'there is only one condition to be considered, that is, the exterior earthly condition; while among the higher living organisms there are at least two conditions to consider: the exterior condition or extra-organic, and the interior or inter-organic. The complexity due to the existence of an interior organic condition is the only reason for the great difficulties which we encounter in the experimental determination of living phenomena, and in the application of the means capable of modifying them.' And he starts out from this fact to establish the principle that there are fixed laws governing the physiological elements plunged into an interior condition, as there are fixed laws for governing the chemical elements which are steeped in an exterior condition. Hence, you can experiment on a living being as well as on an inanimate one; it is only a question of putting yourself in the desired conditions.

I insist upon this, because, I repeat once more, the important point of the question is there. Claude Bernard, in speaking of the vitalists, writes thus : 'They consider life as a mysterious and supernatural agent, which acts arbitrarily, free from all determinism, and they condemn as materialists all those who endeavor to trace vital phenomena to definite organic and physico-chemical conditions. These are false ideas, which it is not easy to root out once they have become domiciled in the mind; only the progress of science can dissipate them.' And he lays down this axiom: 'With living beings as well as inanimate, the conditions of the existence of each phenomenon are determined in an absolute manner.'

I restrain myself for fear of complicating the argument to too great an extent.

Thus you see the progress which science has made. In the last century a more exact application of the experimental method creates physics and chemistry, which then are freed from the irrational and supernatural. Men discover that there are fixed laws, thanks to analysis, and make themselves masters of phenomena. Then a new point is gained. Living beings, in which the vitalists still admitted a mysterious influence, are in their turn brought under and reduced to the general mechanism of matter. Science proves that the existing conditions of all phenomena are the same in living beings as in inanimate; and from that time on physiology assumes little by little the certainty of chemistry and medicine. But are we going to stop there? Evidently not. When it has been proved that the body of man is a machine, whose machinery can be taken apart and put together again at the will of the experimenter, then we can pass to the passionate and intellectual acts of man. Then we shall enter into the domain which up to the present has belonged to physiology and literature; it will be the decisive conquest by science of the hypotheses of philosophers and writers. We have experimental chemistry and medicine; we shall have experimental physiology, and later on an experimental novel. It is an inevitable evolution, the goal of which it is easy to see to-day. All things hang together; it is necessary to start from the determinism of inanimate bodies in order to arrive at the determinism of living beings; and since savants like Claude Bernard demonstrate now that fixed laws govern the human body, we can easily proclaim without fear of being mistaken, the hour in which the laws of thought and passion will be formulated in their turn. A like determinism will govern the stones of the roadway and the brain of man.

This opinion is to be found in 'L'Introduction'. I cannot repeat too often that I take all my arguments from Claude Bernard's work. After having explained that any completely special phenomena may be the result of the more and more complex combination and co-operation of the organized elements, he writes the following: 'I am persuaded that the obstacles which surround the experimental study of psychological phenomena are in great measure due to difficulties of this order; for notwithstanding the marvelous nature and the delicacy of their manifestations, it is impossible, so it seems to me, not to bring cerebral phenomena, like all the phenomena of living bodies, under the laws of a scientific determinism.' This is clear. Later, without doubt, science will find this determinism for all the cerebral and sensory manifestations of man.

Now, science enters into the domain of us novelists, who are to-day the analyzers of man, in his individual and social relations. We are continuing, by our observations and experiments, the work of the physiologist, who has continued that of the physicist and the chemist. We are making use, in a certain way, of scientific psychology to complete scientific physiology; and to finish the series we have only to bring into our studies of nature and man the decisive tool of the experimental method. In one word, we should operate on the characters, the passions, on the human and social data, in the same way that the chemist and the physicist operate on inanimate beings, and as the physiologist operates on living beings. Determinism dominates everything. It is scientific investigation, it is experimental reasoning, which combats one by one the hypotheses of the idealists, and which replaces purely imaginary novels by novels of observation and experiment.

I certainly do not intend at this point to formulate laws. In the actual condition of the science of man the obscurity and confusion are still too great to risk the slightest synthesis. All that can be said is that there is an absolute determinism for all human phenomena. From that on investigation is a duty. We have the method; we should go forward, even if a whole lifetime of effort ends but in the conquest of a small particle of the truth. Look at physiology: Claude Bernard made grand discoveries, and he died protesting that he knew nothing, or nearly nothing. In each page he confesses the difficulties of his task. 'In the phenomenal relations,' he says, 'such as nature offers them to us, there always reigns a complexity more or less great. In this respect the complexity of mineral phenomena is much less great than that of living phenomena; that is why the sciences restricted to inanimate bodies have been able to formulate themselves more quickly. In living beings the phenomena are of enormous complexity, and the greater mobility of living organisms renders them more difficult to grasp and to define.' What can be said, then, of the difficulties to be encountered by the experimental novel, which adds to physiology its studies upon the most delicate and complex organs, which deals with the highest manifestations of man as an individual and a social member? Evidently analysis becomes more complicated here. Therefore, if the physiologist is but drawing up his principles to-day, it is natural that the experimental novelist should be only taking his first steps: We foresee it as a sure consequence of the scientific evolution of the century; but it is impossible to base it on certain laws. Since Claude Bernard speaks of 'the restricted and precarious truths of biological science', we can freely admit that the truths of the science of man, from the standpoint of his intellectual and passionate mechanism, are more restricted and precarious still. We are lisping yet, we are the last comers, but that should be only one incentive the more to push us forward to more exact studies; now that we possess the tool, the experimental method, our goal is very plain—to know the determinism of phenomena and to make ourselves master of these phenomena.

Without daring, as I say, to formulate laws, I consider that the question of heredity has a great influence in the intellectual and passionate manifestations of man. I also attach considerable importance to the surroundings. I ought to touch upon Darwin's theories; but this is only a general study of the experimental method as applied to the novel, and I should lose myself were I to enter into details. I will only say a word on the subject of surroundings. We have just seen the great importance given by Claude Bernard to the study of those inter-organic conditions which must be taken into account if we wish to find the determinism of phenomena in living beings. Well, then! in the study of a family, of a group of living beings, I think that the social condition is of equal importance. Some day the physiologist will explain to us the mechanism of the thoughts and the passions; we shall know how the individual machinery of each man works; how he thinks, how he loves, how he goes from reason to passion and folly; but these phenomena, resulting as they do from the mechanism of the organs, acting under the influence of an interior condition, are not produced in isolation or in the bare void. Man is not alone; he lives in society, in a social condition; and consequently, for us novelists, this social condition unceasingly modifies the phenomena. Indeed our great study is just there, in the reciprocal effect of society on the individual and the individual on society. For the physiologist, the exterior and interior conditions are purely chemical and physical, and this aids him in finding the laws which govern them easily. We are not yet able to prove that the social condition is also physical and chemical. It is that certainly, or rather it is the variable product of a group of living beings, who themselves are absolutely submissive to the physical and chemical laws which govern alike living beings and inanimate. From this we shall see that we can act upon the social conditions, in acting upon the phenomena of which we have made ourselves master in man. And this is what constitutes the experimental novel: to possess a knowledge of the mechanism of the phenomena inherent in man, to show the machinery of his intellectual and sensory manifestations, under the influences of heredity and environment, such as physiology shall give them to us, and then finally to exhibit man living in social conditions produced by himself, which he modifies daily, and in the heart of which he himself experiences a continual transformation. Thus, then, we lean on physiology; we take man from the hands of the physiologist solely, in order to continue the solution of the problem, and to solve scientifically the question of how men behave when they are in society.

These general ideas will be sufficient to guide us to-day. Later on, when science is farther advanced, when the experimental novel has brought forth decisive results, some critic will explain more precisely what I have but indicated to-day.

Elsewhere Claude Bernard confesses how difficult it is to apply the experimental method to living beings. 'The living body,' he says, 'especially among the higher animals, never falls into chemical or physical indifference with the exterior conditions; it possesses an incessant movement, an organic evolution apparently spontaneous and constant; and notwithstanding the fact that this evolution has need of exterior circumstances to manifest itself, it is, however, independent in its course and movement.' And he concludes as I have: 'In short, it is only in the physical and chemical conditions of the interior that we shall find the principle that governs the exterior phenomena of life.' But whatever complexities may present themselves, and even when extraordinary phenomena are produced, the application of the experimental method is imperative. If the phenomena of life have a complexity and an apparent difference from those of inanimate bodies, they do not offer this difference, except by reason of determined or determinable conditions which belong to them. Therefore, even should the sciences dealing with life differ from the others in their application and in their special laws, they are not to be distinguished by their scientific method.

I must say one word as to the limits which Claude Bernard assigns to science. According to him we shall always be ignorant of the 'why' of things; we can only know the 'how'. It is this that he expresses in the following terms: 'The nature of our minds urges us to seek the essence or the "why" of things. In this we see further than the goal it has been given us to attain to; for experiment soon teaches us that we must not go beyond the "how"; that is to say, beyond the nearest cause or the condition of the existence of any phenomenon.' Further on he gives this example: 'If we can discover "why" opium and its alkaloids produce sleep, we shall know the mechanism of such slumber, and know "how" opium or its essence produces sleep; for slumber only takes place because the active substance is about to put itself in contact with certain organic elements which it modifies.' The practical conclusion of all this is the following: 'Science has precisely the privilege of teaching us what we are ignorant of, through its substitution of reason and experiment for sentiment, and by showing us clearly the limit of our actual knowledge. But, by a marvelous compensation, in proportion as science humbles our pride, it strengthens our power.' All these considerations are strictly applicable to the experimental novel. In order not to lose itself in philosophical speculations, in order to replace idealistic hypothesis by a slow conquest of the unknown, it must continue the search after the 'how' of things. This is its exact rôle, and it is from this that it must draw, as we are going to see, its reason for being and its moral.

I have reached this point: the experimental novel is a consequence of the scientific evolution of the century; it continues and completes physiology, which itself leans for support on chemistry and medicine; it substitutes for the study of the abstract and the metaphysical man the study of the natural man, governed by physical and chemical laws, and modified by the influences of his surroundings; it is in one word the literature of our scientific age, as the classical and romantic literature corresponded to a scholastic and theological age. Now I will pass to the great question of the application of all this, and of its justification.

III

The object of the experimental method in physiology and in medicine is to study phenomena in order to become their master. Claude Bernard in each page of 'L'Introduction' comes back to this idea. He declares: 'All natural philosophy is summed up in this: To know the laws which govern phenomena. The experimental problem reduces itself to this: To foresee and direct phenomena.' Farther on he gives an example: 'It will not satisfy the experimental doctor, though it may the merely empirical one, to know that quinine cures fever; the essential thing is to know what fever is, and to understand the mechanism by which quinine cures. All this is of the greatest importance to the experimental doctor; for as soon as he knows it positively, the fact that quinine cures fever will no longer be an isolated and empirical fact, but a scientific fact. This fact will be connected then with the conditions which bind it to other phenomena, and we shall be thus led to the knowledge of the laws of the organism, and to the possibility of regulating their manifestations.' A striking example can be quoted in the case of scabies. 'To-day the cause of this disease is known and determined experimentally; the whole subject has become scientific, and empiricism has disappeared. A cure is surely and without exception effected when you place yourself in the conditions known by experiment to produce this end.'

This, then, is the end, this is the purpose in physiology and in experimental medicine: to make one's self master of life in order to be able to direct it. Let us suppose that science advances and that the conquest of the unknown is finally completed; the scientific age which Claude Bernard saw in his dreams will then be realized. When that time comes the doctor will be the master of maladies; he will cure without fail; his influence upon the human body will conduce to the welfare and strength of the species. We shall enter upon a century in which man, grown more powerful, will make use of nature and will utilize its laws to produce upon the earth the greatest possible amount of justice and freedom. There is no nobler, higher, nor grander end. Here is our rôle as intelligent beings: to penetrate to the wherefore of things, to become superior to these things, and to reduce them to a condition of subservient machinery.

Well, this dream of the physiologist and the experimental doctor is also that of the novelist, who employs the experimental method in his study of man as a simple individual and as a social animal. Their object is ours; we also desire to master certain phenomena of an intellectual and personal order, to be able to direct them. We are, in a word, experimental moralists, showing by experiment in what way a passion acts in a certain social condition. The day in which we gain control of the mechanism of this passion we can treat it and reduce it, or at least make it as inoffensive as possible. And in this consists the practical utility and high morality of our naturalistic works, which experiment on man, and which dissect piece by piece this human machinery in order to set it going through the influence of the environment. When things have advanced further, when we are in possession of the different laws, it will only be necessary to work upon the individuals and the surroundings if we wish to find the best social condition. In this way we shall construct a practical sociology, and our work will be a help to political and economical sciences. I do not know, I repeat, of a more noble work, nor of a grander application. To be the master of good and evil, to regulate life, to regulate society, to solve in time all the problems of socialism, above all, to give justice a solid foundation by solving through experiment the questions of criminality—is not this being the most useful and the most moral workers in the human workshop?

Let us compare, for one instant, the work of the idealistic novelist to ours; and here this word idealistic refers to writers who cast aside observation and experiment, and base their works on the supernatural and the irrational, who admit, in a word, the power of mysterious forces outside of the determinism of the phenomena. Claude Bernard shall reply to this for me: 'What distinguishes experimental reasoning from scholastic is the fecundity of the one and the sterility of the other. It is precisely the scholastic, who believes he has absolute certitude, who attains to no results. This is easily understood, since by his belief in an absolute principle he puts himself outside of nature, in which everything is relative. It is, on the contrary, the experimenter, who is always in doubt, who does not think he possesses absolute certainty about anything, who succeeds in mastering the phenomena which surround him, and in increasing his power over nature.' By and by I shall return to this question of the ideal, which is in truth but the question of indeterminism. Claude Bernard says truly: 'The intellectual conquest of man consists in diminishing and driving back indeterminism, and so, gradually, by the aid of the experimental method, gaining ground for determinism.' We experimental novelists have the same task; our work is to go from the known to the unknown, to make ourselves masters of nature; while the idealistic novelists deliberately remain in the unknown, through all sorts of religious and philosophical prejudices, under the astounding pretense that the unknown is nobler and more beautiful than the known. If our work, often cruel, if our terrible pictures needed justification, I should find, indeed, with Claude Bernard this argument conclusive: 'You will never reach really fruitful and luminous generalizations on the phenomena of life until you have experimented yourself and stirred up in the hospital, the amphitheater, and the laboratory the fetid or palpitating sources of life. If it were necessary for me to give a comparison which would explain my sentiments on the science of life, I should say that it is a superb salon, flooded with light, which you can only reach by passing through a long and nauseating kitchen.'

I insist upon the word which I have employed, that of experimental novelists as applied to naturalistic novelists. One page of 'L'Introduction' struck me as being very forcible, that in which the author speaks of the vital 'circulus'. 'The muscular and nervous organs preserve the activity of the organs which make the blood; but the blood, in its turn, nourishes the organs which produce it. There is in this a social or organic solidarity, which keeps up a perpetual movement, until the derangement or cessation of the action of a necessary and vital element has broken the equilibrium or brought about some trouble or stoppage in the play of the animal machinery. The problem of the experimentalist doctor consists in finding the cause of any organic disarrangement, that is to say, in seizing the initial phenomenon. We shall see how a dislocation of the organism, or a disarrangement the most complex in appearance, can be traced to a simple initial cause, which calls forth immediately the most complex effects.' All that is necessary here is to change the words experimental doctor to experimental novelist, and this passage is exactly applicable to our naturalistic literature. The social circulus is identical with the vital circulus; in society, as in human beings, a solidarity exists which unites the different members and the different organisms in such a way that if one organ becomes rotten many others are tainted and a very complicated disease results. Hence, in our novels, when we experiment on a dangerous wound which poisons society, we proceed in the same way as the experimentalist doctor; we try to find the simple initial cause in order to reach the complex causes of which the action is the result. Go back once more to the example of Baron Hulot in *Cousine Bette*. See the final result, the dénouement of the novel : an entire family is destroyed, all sorts of secondary dramas are produced, under the action of Hulot's amorous temperament. It is there, in this temperament, that the initial cause is found. One member, Hulot, becomes rotten, and immediately all around him are tainted, the social circulus is interrupted, the health of that society is compromised. What emphasis Balzac lays on the character of Baron Hulot; with what scrupulous care he analyzes him! The experiment deals with him chiefly, because its object is to master the symptoms of this passion in order to govern it. Suppose that Hulot is cured, or at least restrained and rendered inoffensive, immediately the drama ceases to have any longer any *raison d'être*; the equilibrium, or more truly the health, of the social body is again established. Thus the naturalistic novelists are really experimental moralists.

And I reach thus the great reproach with which they think to crush the naturalistic novelists, by treating them as fatalists. How many times have they wished to prove to us that as soon as we did not accept free will, that as soon as man was no more to us than a living machine, acting under the influence of heredity and surroundings, we should fall into gross fatalism, we should debase humanity to the rank of a troop marching under the baton of destiny. It is necessary to define our terms: we are not fatalists, we are determinists, which is not at all the same thing. Claude Bernard explains the two terms very plainly: 'We have given the name of determinism to the nearest or determining cause of phenomena. We never act upon the essence of phenomena in nature, but only on their determinism, and by this very fact, that we act upon it, determinism differs from fatalism, upon which we could not act at all. Fatalism assumes that the appearance of any phenomenon is necessary apart from its conditions, while determinism is just the condition essential for the appearance of any phenomenon, and such appearance is never forced. Once the search for the determinism of phenomena is placed as a fundamental principle of the experimental method, there is no longer either materialism, or spiritualism, or inanimate matter, or living matter; there remain but phenomena of which it is necessary to determine the conditions, that is to say, the circumstances which play, by their proximity to these phenomena, the rôle of nearest cause.' This is decisive. All we do is to apply this method in our novels, and we are the determinists who experimentally try to determine the condition of the phenomena, without departing in our investigations from the laws of nature. As Claude Bernard very truly says, the moment that we can act, and that we do act, on the determining cause of phenomena—by modifying their surroundings, for example—we cease to be fatalists.

Here you have, then, the moral purpose of the experimental novelist clearly defined. I have often said that we do not have to draw a conclusion from our works; and this means that our works carry their conclusion with them. An experimentalist has no need to conclude, because, in truth, experiment concludes for him. A hundred times, if necessary, he will repeat the experiment before the public; he will explain it; but he need neither become indignant nor approve of it personally; such is the truth, such is the way phenomena work; it is for society to produce or not to produce these phenomena, according as the result is useful or dangerous. You cannot imagine, as I have said elsewhere, a savant being provoked with azote because azote is dangerous to life; he suppresses azote when it is harmful, and not otherwise. As our power is not the same as that of a savant, as we are experimentalists without being practitioners, we ought to content ourselves with searching out the determinism of social phenomena, and leaving to legislators and to men of affairs the care of controlling sooner or later these phenomena in such a way as to develop the good and reject the bad, from the point of view of their utility to man.

In our rôle as experimental moralists we show the mechanism of the useful and the useless, we disengage the determinism of the human and social phenomena so that, in their turn, the legislators can one day dominate and control these phenomena. In a word, we are working with the whole country toward that great object, the conquest of nature and the increase of man's power a hundredfold. Compare with ours the work of the idealistic writers, who rely upon the irrational and the supernatural, and whose every flight upward is followed by a deeper fall into metaphysical chaos. We are the ones who possess strength and morality.

IV

I have said before that I chose 'L'Introduction' because medicine is still looked upon by many as an art. Claude Bernard proves that it ought to be a science, and in his book we see the birth of a science, a very instructive spectacle in itself, and which shows us that the scientific domain is extending and conquering all the manifestations of human intelligence. Since medicine, which was an art, is becoming a science, why should not literature also become a science by means of the experimental method?

It must be remarked that all things hang together: If the territory of the experimental doctor is the body of man, as shown in the phenomena of his different organs both in their normal and pathological condition, our territory is equally the body of man, as shown by his sensory and cerebral phenomena, both in their normal and pathological condition. If we are not satisfied with the metaphysical man of the classical age we must, perforce, take into consideration the new ideas on nature and on life, with which our age has become imbued. We continue necessarily, I repeat, the work of the physiologist and the doctor, who have continued, in their turn, that of the physician and the chemist. Hence we enter into the domain of science. I will not touch on the question of sentiment and form, but will reserve that for another time.

Let us see first what Claude Bernard says about medicine: 'Certain doctors contend that medicine can only be conjectural, and they conclude that a doctor is an artist, who ought to make up for the indeterminism in particular cases by his genius and his personal tact. All sciences have necessarily commenced by being conjectural; there are still to-day in every science conjectural parts. Medicine is still nearly all conjecture. I do not deny that; but I only want to say that modern science should make an effort to come out of this provisionary state, which does not constitute a definite scientific condition—not any more for medicine than for the other sciences. The scientific condition will be longer in taking shape and more difficult to obtain in medicine by reason of the complexities of its phenomena; but the end of the medical savant is to reduce in his science, as in all the others, the indeterminate to the determinate.' The mechanism of the birth and the development of a science is here clearly defined. Men still look upon the doctor as an artist, because there is in medicine an enormous place still left to conjecture. Naturally, the novelist merits still more the name of artist, as he finds himself buried still deeper in the indeterminate. If Claude Bernard confesses that the complexity of its phenomena will prevent medicine, for a long time yet, from arriving at a scientific state, what shall we say of the experimental novel, in which the phenomena are much more complicated still? But this does not prevent the novel from entering upon the scientific pathway, obedient to the general evolution of the century.

Moreover, Claude Bernard himself has indicated the evolutions of the human mind. 'The human mind,' he says, 'at various periods of its progress has passed successively through feeling, reason, and experiment. First, feeling alone, dominating reason, created the truths of faith, that is to say, theology. Reason, or philosophy, becoming afterward the mistress, brought forth scholasticism. Finally, experiment, that is to say, the study of natural phenomena, taught man that the truths of the exterior world were to be found formulated, in the first place, neither in reason nor in feeling. These last are, indeed, our indispensable guides, but to obtain the truth it is necessary to descend into the objective reality of things, where they lie concealed under their phenomenal form. Thus it is that in the natural progress of things the experimental method appears, which sums up the whole, and which supports itself successfully on the three branches of this immovable tripod: feeling, reason, and experiment. In the search after truth by means of this method, feeling has always the initiative; it engenders the idea *a priori* or intuition; reason, or the reasoning power, immediately develops the idea and deduces its logical consequences. But if feeling must be guided by the light of reason, reason in its turn must be guided by experiment.'

I have given this passage entire, as it is of the greatest importance. It shows clearly the rôle that the personality of the novelist should play, apart from the style. Since feeling is the starting point of the experimental method, since reason subsequently intervenes to end in experiment, and to be controlled by it, the genius of the experimentalist dominates everything, and this is what has made the experimental method, so inert in other hands, such a powerful tool in the hands of Claude Bernard. I have said the word: method is but the tool; it is the workman, it is the idea, which he brings, which makes the *chef-d'oeuvre*. I have already noted these lines: 'It is a particular feeling a *quid proprium*, which constitutes the originality, the invention, or the genius of each one.' This, then, is the part taken by genius in the experimental novel. As Claude Bernard says again: 'The idea is the seed; the method is the soil which furnishes the conditions for developing and prospering it, and bringing forth its best fruits, according to nature.' Thus everything is reduced to a question of method. If you are content to remain in the *a priori* idea, and enjoy your own feelings without finding any basis for it in reason or any verification in experiment, you are a poet; you venture upon hypotheses which you cannot prove; you are struggling vainly in a painful indeterminism, and in a way that is often injurious. Listen to these lines of 'L'Introduction': 'Man is naturally a metaphysician and proud; he believes that the idealistic creations of his brain, which coincide with his feelings, represent the reality. Thus it follows that the experimental method is not innate and natural to man, for it is only after having wandered for a long time among theological and scholastical discussions that he ends by recognizing the sterility of his efforts in this path. Man then perceives that he cannot dictate laws to nature, because he does not possess in himself the knowledge and the criterion of exterior things; he realizes that in order to arrive at the truth he must, on the contrary, study the natural laws and submit his ideas, if not his reason, to experiment, that is to say, to the criterion of facts.' What becomes of the genius of the experimental novelist? The genius, the idea *a priori*, remains, only it is controlled by experiment. The experiment naturally cannot destroy his genius; on the contrary, it confirms it. To take the case of a poet, for example: To show he has genius is it necessary that his feeling, his idea, *a priori*, should be false? Evidently not, for the genius of a man will be so much the greater when experiment has proved the truth of his personal idea. Our age of lyricism, our romantic disease, was alone capable of measuring a man's genius by the quantity of nonsense and folly which he put in circulation. I conclude by saying that in our scientific century experiment must prove genius.

This is the drift of our quarrel with the idealistic writers. They always start out from an irrational source of some kind, such as a revelation, a tradition, or conventional authority. As Claude Bernard declares: 'We must admit nothing occult; there are but phenomena and the conditions of phenomena.' We naturalistic novelists submit each fact to the test of observation and experiment, while the idealistic writers admit mysterious elements which escape analysis, and therefore remain in the unknown, outside of the influence of the laws governing nature. This question of the ideal, from the scientific point of view, reduces itself to a question of indeterminate or determinate. All that we do not know, all that escapes us still, that is truly the ideal, and the aim of our human efforts is each day to reduce the ideal, to conquer truth from the unknown. We are all idealists, if we mean by this that we busy ourselves with the ideal. But I dub those idealists who take refuge in the unknown for the pleasure of being there, who have a taste but for the most risky hypotheses, who disdain to submit them to the test of experiment under the pretext that the truth is in themselves and not in the things. These writers, I repeat, accomplish a vain and harmful task, while the observer and the experimentalist are the only ones who work for the strength and happiness of man, making him more and more the master of nature. There is neither nobility, nor dignity, nor beauty, nor morality in not knowing, in lying, in pretending that you are greater according as you advance in error and confusion. The only great and moral works are those of truth.

What we alone must accept is what I will call the stimulus of the ideal. Certainly our science is very limited as yet, beside the enormous mass of things of which we are ignorant. This great unknown which surrounds us ought to inspire us with the desire to pierce it, to explain it by means of scientific methods. And this does not refer only to scientific men; all the manifestations of human intelligence are connected together, all our efforts have their birth in the need we feel of making ourselves masters of the truth. Claude Bernard explains this very clearly when he writes: 'The sciences each possess, if not a special method, at least special processes, and, moreover, they reciprocally serve as tools for one another. Mathematics serves as a tool to physics, to chemistry, and to biology in very different measure; physics and chemistry serve as powerful tools to physiology and medicine. In this mutual help which the sciences are to each other, you must distinguish clearly the savant who advances each science and he who makes use of it. The physician and the chemist are not mathematicians because they employ calculation; the physiologist is not a chemist or a physician because he uses chemical reactions or medical instruments, any more than the chemist and the physician are physiologists because they study the compositions or the properties of certain liquids and certain animal or vegetable tissues.' This is the reply which Claude Bernard can be said to make for us naturalists to the critics who taunt us with making pretensions to science. We are neither chemists nor physicians nor physiologists; we are simply novelists who depend upon the sciences for support. We certainly do not pretend to have made discoveries in physiology which we do not practice; only, being obliged to make a study of man, we feel we cannot deny the efficacy of the new physiological truths. And I will add that the novelists are certainly the workers who rely at once upon the greatest number of sciences, for they treat of them all and must know them all, as the novel has become a general inquiry on nature and on man. This is why we have been led to apply to our work the experimental method as soon as this method had become the most powerful tool of investigation. We sum up investigation, we throw ourselves anew into the conquest of the ideal, employing all forms of knowledge.

Let it be well understood that I am speaking of the 'how' of things and not of the 'why'. For an experimental savant, the ideal which he is endeavoring to reduce, the indeterminate, is always restricted to the 'how'. He leaves to philosophers the other ideal, that of the 'why', which he despairs of determining. I think that the experimental novelists equally ought not to occupy themselves with this unknown quality, unless they wish to lose themselves in the follies of the poets and the philosophers. It is surely an object large enough to try to know the entire mechanism of nature, without troubling one's self for the time being with the origin of the mechanism. If we some day succeed in knowing it, we shall doubtless owe our knowledge to method, and it is better then to begin at the beginning with the study of phenomena, instead of hoping that a sudden revelation will reveal to us the secret of the world. We are the workmen; we will leave to the metaphysicians this great unknown of the 'why' they have struggled with so vainly for centuries, in order to confine our efforts to that other unknown of the 'how', which is cleared away more and more every day by our investigation. The only idea which ought to exist for us, the naturalistic novelists, should be one which we can conquer.

Besides, in the slow conquest which we can make over this unknown which surrounds us, we humbly confess the ignorant condition in which we are. We are beginning to march forward, nothing more; and our only real strength lies in our method. Claude Bernard, after acknowledging that experimental medicine is in its infancy still, does not hesitate to give great credit to empirical medicine. 'In reality,' he says, 'empiricism, that is to say, observation or accidental experiment, has been the origin of all science. In the complex sciences dealing with man empiricism necessarily governs the practice much longer than in those of the more simple sciences.' And he is willing to admit that at the crisis of a disease, when the determinism or nearest cause of the pathological phenomena has not been found, the best thing to do is to act empirically; as, moreover, happens in the growth of knowledge, since empiricism invariably precedes the scientific condition of any branch of knowledge. Certainly if doctors must resort to empiricism in nearly every case, we have much greater reasons for using it, we novelists whose science is more complicated and less determined. I say once more, it is not a question of creating the science of man, as an individual and as a social being, out of the whole cloth; it is only a question of emerging little by little and with all the inevitable struggles from the obscurity in which we lie concerning our own natures, happy if, amid so many errors, we can determine one truth. We experiment, that is to say, for a long time still, we must use the false to reach the true.

Such is the feeling among strong men. Claude Bernard argues fiercely against those who persist in seeing only an artist in a doctor. He knows the habitual objection of those who pretend to look upon experimental medicine 'as a theoretical conception of which nothing for the moment justifies the practical reality, because no fact demonstrates the attainment in medicine of the scientific precision of the experimental sciences'. But he does not let this worry him; he shows that 'experimental medicine is but the natural outcome of practical medical investigation directed by a scientific mind'. And here is his conclusion: 'Without doubt it will be a long time before medicine becomes truly scientific; but that does not prevent us from conceiving the possibility of such a thing, and doing all that we can to help it by trying daily to introduce into medicine the method which is to lead us to it.'

All this, which I will not tire you by repeating, applies perfectly to the experimental novel. Put the word 'novel' in place of 'medicine', and the passage remains equally true.

I will address to the young literary generation which is growing up around me these grand and strongs words of Claude Bernard. I know none more manly. 'Medicine is destined to escape little by little from empiricism, and she will escape, as have all the other sciences, by the experimental method. This profound conviction sustains and controls my scientific life. I am deaf to the voices of those doctors who demand that the causes of scarlatina and measles shall be experimentally shown to them, and who think by that to draw forth an argument against the use of the experimental method in medicine. These discouraging objections and denials generally come from systematic or lazy minds, those who prefer to rest on their systems or to sleep in darkness instead of making an effort to become enlightened. The experimental direction which medicine is taking to-day is definitely defined. And it is no longer the ephemeral influence of a personal system of any kind; it is the result of the scientific evolution of medicine itself. My convictions in this respect are so strong that I endeavor to impress them clearly upon the minds of the young medical students who are following my course at the Collège de France. The students must be inspired before all else with the scientific spirit, and initiated into the ideas and the tendencies of modern science.'

Though I have frequently written the same words and given the same advice, I will repeat them here: 'The experimental method alone can bring the novel out of the atmosphere of lies and errors in which it is plunged. All my literary life has been controlled by this conviction. I am deaf to the voices of the critics who demand that I shall formulate the laws of heredity and the influence of surroundings in my characters; those who make these discouraging objections and denials but speak from slothfulness of mind, from an infatuation for tradition, from an attachment more or less conscious to philosophical and religious beliefs. The experimental direction which the novel is taking to-day is a definite one. And it is no longer the ephemeral influence of a personal system of any kind, it is the result of the scientific evolution, of the study of man himself. My convictions in this respect are so strong that I endeavor to impress them clearly upon the minds of the young writers who read my works; for I think it necessary, above all things else, to inspire them with the scientific spirit, and to initiate them into the ideas and the tendencies of modern science.' [...]

[...] The conclusion to which I wish to come is this: If I were to define the experimental novel I should not say, as Claude Bernard says, that a literary work lies entirely in the personal feeling, for the reason that in my opinion the personal feeling is but the first impulse. Later nature, being there, makes itself felt, or at least that part of nature of which science has given us the secret, and about which we have no longer any right to romance. The experimental novelist is therefore the one who accepts proven facts, who points out in man and in society the mechanism of the phenomena over which science is mistress, and who does not interpose his personal sentiments, except in the phenomena whose determination is not yet settled, and who tries to test, as much as he can, this personal sentiment, this idea *a priori*, by observation and experiment.

I cannot understand how our naturalistic literature can mean anything else. I have only spoken of the experimental novel, but I am fairly convinced that the same method, after having triumphed in history and in criticism, will triumph everywhere, on the stage and in poetry even. It is an inevitable evolution. Literature, in spite of all that can be said, does not depend merely upon the author; it is influenced by the nature it depicts and by the man whom it studies. Now if the savants change their ideas of nature, if they find the true mechanism of life, they force us to follow them, to precede them even, so as to play our rôle in the new hypotheses. The metaphysical man is dead; our whole territory is transformed by the advent of the physiological man. No doubt 'Achilles' Anger', 'Dido's Love', will last forever on account of their beauty: but to-day we feel the necessity of analyzing anger and love, of discovering exactly how such passions work in the human being. This view of the matter is a new one; we have become experimentalists instead of philosophers. In short, everything is summed up in this great fact: the experimental method in letters, as in the sciences, is in the way to explain the natural phenomena, both individual and social, of which the metaphysics, until now, has given only irrational and supernatural explanations.

18 F. R. Leavis

Anna Karenina:
Thought and Significance
in a Great Creative Work

From *Anna Karenina and Other Essays*, Chatto and Windus, 1963, pp. 9–31.

In addressing the Cambridge University Slavonic Society I felt acutely conscious of the fact that I know no Russian. I have been assured, however, by those familiar with Tolstoy's use of the language that it would be a mistake, as a critic, to feel altogether disqualified by a dependence upon Aylmer Maude, and I have permitted myself to accept the assurance. The real formidableness of my undertaking is constituted by the magnitude of *Anna Karenina*—the greatness and the largeness; the greatness that entails largeness. There is a necessary point made in the last phrase; or not necessary, you may prefer to say, since it hardly needs making. It is the range and variety of human experience going with the depth and vividness in the rendering that one would point to and start to comment on if, having ventured (as one might) that *Anna Karenina* was the greatest of novels, one were challenged to give one's grounds for expecting assent. The triad, 'range', 'depth', and 'vividness', however, doesn't satisfy one as an intimation of the nature of the greatness; one is left looking for a way of conveying another essential emphasis, and this way doesn't immediately present itself— doesn't present itself at all if what one is looking for is a word, or a phrase, or even two or three sentences. The emphasis regards the nature of the concern for significance that characterizes this art—an art so unlike that of Henry James. The cue for this comparative reference is given by what James himself (in a letter to Hugh Walpole of 1913) said about Tolstoy:

> Tolstoy and Dostoievsky are fluid pudding, though not tasteless, because the amount of their own minds and souls in solution in the broth gives it savour and flavour, thanks to the strong, rank quality of their genius and their experience. But there are all sorts of things to be said of them, and

in particular that we see how great a vice is their lack of composition and their defiance of economy and architecture.

It is 'him', of course, I'm concerned about; the 'them' and the 'their' are in any case unacceptable. The confident censure might seem astonishing, coming from so intelligent, and so intensely serious, a student of the novelist's art. When, writing in 1887, Arnold, having noted that there are 'many characters' in *Anna Karenina*, says 'too many, if we look in it for a work of art in which the action shall be vigorously one, and to that one action everything shall converge', and makes his intention plain by pronouncing that we are not to take Tolstoy's masterpiece as a work of art, but as a 'piece of life', we recognize the naïveté as inevitable in a critic of Arnold's education at that date (though *Little Dorrit*, *Great Expectations* and *Middlemarch* had appeared—as had also *Madame Bovary*, and the novels of Jane Austen). But James, who hadn't Public School Classics and Aristotle and Oxford behind him and didn't take it for an axiom that 'the crown of literature is poetry', is known for his concern to vindicate for the novelist's art its right to the fullest attention that sophisticated intelligence can devote to it. The explanation, of course, is what I pointed to in making the reference to James. The sense of the possibilities of the novel that informed his criticism was determined by his own creative preoccupations, and his conception of the art was personal and his own in a limiting way that (significantly for the criticism of his own achievement) he failed to realize: it is not without some implicit prompting from him that we are offered his collected Prefaces as 'the novelist's *vade-mecum*'. My concern in saying these obvious enough things is with the distinctive nature of Tolstoy's genius; I want to insist that the relation between art and life it exemplifies for us is the characteristic of the highest kind of creativity—a higher kind than James's. If Tolstoy gave no heed to any Jamesian canons it was not because he failed to give the most intelligent kind of attention to the demands of art. To confute James's critical censures and show what is the nature of the 'composition' that makes *Anna Karenina* superlatively a great work of art is to illustrate what D. H. Lawrence had in mind when he wrote:

The novel is a great discovery: far greater than Galileo's

telescope or somebody else's wireless. The novel is the highest form of human expression so far attained.

It is a large claim, but Lawrence made it with full intention; he was not talking loosely. He was prepared to say that by the 'highest form of human expression' he meant the highest form of thought, the thought in question necessarily being, for him, thought about the nature, the meaning, and the essential problems of human life. He didn't the less, of course, think of the novel, whenever it should answer to his account, as supremely art. Thought, to come at all near truth and adequacy, must engage the whole man, and relate in a valid way—such a way, that is, as precludes and defeats the distorting effects of abstraction and selection (both inevitable)—all the diverse elements of experience.

The organization of *Anna Karenina* expresses an intense devotion of this kind to the pursuit of truth, and Lawrence might have had the book in front of him when he wrote: 'The novel is the highest form of subtle inter-relatedness that man has discovered.' It was a significant lack of responsiveness to the given devotion that enabled James to find *Anna Karenina* lacking in 'composition' and defiant of economy and architecture. His ability to use the word 'architecture' betrays the difference between the idea of 'art' that informs his own work and that implicit in Tolstoy's. A limited and clearly conceived interest determined the 'composition' and economy of a Jamesian novel. A firm plan, expressing a definitive and masterful purpose and excluding all that doesn't seem necessary in relation to this, determines the perfection that James aims at. An addiction to 'art' in this sense entails a severe limitation in regard to significance—to the nature of the significance the artist's concern for which is the principle of organization that controls his creating. James's significances are those which, in relation to each given enterprise, he can bring, he feels, into the critical consciousness for thorough analysis, discuss with himself exhaustively, and provide for in relation to firmly grasped criteria.

The relation of art to life in Tolstoy is such as to preclude this kind of narrowly provident economy. It is an immensely fuller and profounder involvement *in* life on the part of the artist, whose concern for the significance in his art is the intense and focused expression of the questing after significance that characterizes him in his daily living. This, of course, amounts to saying that Tolstoy is a different kind of man from James—he is the kind of man the greatest kind of artist necessarily is. Tolstoy might very well have answered as Lawrence did when asked, not long before his death, what was the drive behind his creating: 'One writes out of one's moral sense; for the race, as it were.' 'Moral', of course, is an ambiguous word, but Lawrence was thinking of that manifestation of his own vitality of genius, the distinctive preoccupation with ultimate questions—those which concern the nature of one's deepest inner allegiances and determinations, the fundamental significances to be read in one's experience of life, the nature and conditions of 'fulfilment' (a word for what is to be sought that he finds more apt than 'happiness'). An artist of this kind will have strong didactic impulses. But it will be a certainly not less important characteristic of his to be, in the essential spirit of his art, intent on ensuring, with all its resources, that the didactic impulses shall not get out of hand.

'In a novel,' writes Lawrence, 'everything is relative to everything else, if that novel is art at all. There may be didactic bits, but they aren't the novel.... There you have the greatness of the novel itself. It won't let you tell didactic lies and put them over.' What Tolstoy has to guard against is the intensity of his need for an 'answer'. For the concern for significance that is the principle of life in *Anna Karenina* is a deep spontaneous *lived* question, or quest. The temptation in wait for Tolstoy is to relax the tension, which, in being that of his integrity, is the vital tension of his art, by reducing the 'question' into one that *can* be answered—or, rather, one to which a seemingly satisfying answer strongly solicits him; that is, to simplify the challenge life actually is for him and deny the complexity of his total knowledge and need.

While what makes itself felt as we read *Anna Karenina* is decidedly a positive or creative nisus, it affects us as an exploratory effort towards the definition of a norm. It necessarily, then, concerns itself everywhere—or is never long felt not to be concerning itself—with the relations between men and women: love in its varieties, marriage in its varieties, the meaning of marriage. The essential mode of the book carries with it the implication that there *could* be no simple statement of a real problem, or of any 'answer' worth having. It is the very antithesis of a didactic mode. The book says in effect, 'This is life'—which is a different thing from saying as Arnold does, 'It is not a work of art, but a piece of life.' The greatness of *Anna Karenina* lies in the degree to which, along with its depth, it justifies the clear suggestion it conveys of a representative comprehensiveness. The creative writer's way of arriving at and presenting general truths about life is that which Tolstoy exemplifies with such resource, such potency, and on such a scale, and there is none to replace or rival it. Only a work of art can say with validity and force, as *Anna Karenina* does, 'This is life.'

There is of course a character in the book particularly close to Tolstoy himself—Levin; and apart from biographical facts, we know this because Levin, we recognize, is the focus of what I have called the 'deep, spontaneous, lived question'. That, however, is not the same as saying that he *is* the author, the artist, directly present in the book; a point that can be enforced with the observation that Levin is *not* a great novelist. It is an essential difference. Taken together with the perceived intimacy of relation, it is important for the understanding of *Anna Karenina* as a great creative work, and it has its bearings (as I shall suggest) on the development of the author into the Count Leo Tolstoy who wrote *What then must we do?*, was tragically at odds with his wife, and died at Astapova railway station.

Levin, in fact, while being a great deal more besides, is the focal presence of the temptation (that essential element in the creative vitality). It is dramatized in him. Not that we think of him as a dramatized temptation—or tend to use the word at all (unless at the end of the book) in relation to him. The Constantine Levin whom we know with such intimacy is so much more than an earnest 'seeker', addicted to intense pertinacities of meditation on death, the meaning of life, and the behest (if only one could be sure what that was) of the living clear-sighted conscience. We have no difficulty in thinking of him as a Russian aristocrat, or believing that, different as he is from Vronsky and Oblonsky, he has had as such a normally 'immoral' past. It is as a matter of immediately acceptable fact that we see him finding Oblonsky, when he meets him at the club, a warmly *sympathetique* old friend, and joining happily in the epicure-choice of an expensive meal. He is a paternal but businesslike landlord, a modernizing farmer, a writer on agricultural economy, and a sportsman with the proper pride of a first-class shot. We almost inevitably credit him with Tolstoy's own very knowledgeable delight, which the account of the steeplechase conveys so powerfully, in the functional and vital beauty of thoroughbred horses. When in the book he first encounters Kitty it is on a winter's day at the Zoological Gardens, where he has a reputation he proceeds to justify of being the 'best skater'.

And here, of course, in this episode of the drama of his relations with Kitty, we come to what, in a brief post-Arnoldian account of *Anna Karenina* as a closely-organized whole, would figure as the essential main part that Levin plays in its significance—plays together with Kitty. Love, courtship, and marriage: it seems reasonable to say, harking back to the word 'norm' as I used it earlier, that Kitty and Levin have, for that crucial matter of the relations between men and women, a clear normative significance—that they represent, at any rate, the especially clear affirming presence of the normative spirit that informs the whole work. They certainly provide a foil to Anna and Vronsky.

When, however, we think of the way the book closes we may very well draw back from suggesting that a confident normative prescription has, in sum, been offered. The strong deep current of Levin's meditating on life, death, and the peasants moves, beyond question, towards consequences in regard to marriage that Kitty, if they should really threaten, couldn't do anything but fight. Nevertheless, the consequences lie outside *Anna Karenina*; and there is no sign that Tolstoy, the highly and subtly conscious artist, could have recognized the novel's significance as being anything but what the tragedy of Anna, implicitly commented on by the context in general and the Levin-Kitty theme in particular, conveys. Yet some inner prompting made him bring into the context, as the close of the whole organization, that quite other-than-clinching effect of Levin's later development.

It is a close in full keeping with the creative mode of the work; with the delicate wholeness of the 'sincerity' (the inverted commas a reminder that every great creative work compels us to reconsider the meaning of that word) with which Tolstoy pursues his aim of inducing life to propose and define the 'questions'—a process that is at the same time a conveying of such 'answers' as life may yield. There is in *Anna Karenina* no suggestion either of the controlled-experiment convention ·that the conditions of the theatre compelled upon Shakespeare for the treatment of his theme in *Measure for Measure* (where Angelo is the victim of a frankly contrived demonstration) or of the writing-up of findings and significances that forms the close of that play. Tolstoy, great creative power in the tradition of the novel that owes so much to Shakespeare, is great enough to vindicate, by showing it marvellously realized, the conception of the novel and of its supreme advantages I have adduced from Lawrence. That conception enforces the maxim: 'Art-speech is the only speech.' And by 'speech' Lawrence means the utterance of thought—thought of the anti-mathematical order.

It no doubt seemed to James as well as Arnold an instance of a characteristically large casualness in respect of form in *Anna Karenina* that the book, though committed to the two main actions (Arnold's phrase), each of which in Tolstoyan treatment entails a generous abundance—redundance, for James—of wide-ranging specificity, should open not with either, but with the trouble in the Oblonsky household. We, of course, see here the rightness and sure command of the great artist in terms of his own undertaking, and don't need explanations of the part played by the Oblonsky theme in relation to 'form' and significance. We aren't prompted to say that the 'normal' distinctively unideal and not happy married relations (though the marriage remains 'successful') between the goodnatured, life-loving, and irresistible Stephen Oblonsky and the wholly admirable Dolly provides a third main action. But the theme nevertheless continues, through the book, to keep us reminded of itself and of its relevance to the main action. And, unmistakably of the first importance for the significance we are to have seen, at the close, in Anna's fate, there are the married relations of Anna and Karenin, which are evoked with such pregnant economy and, for the evaluative response of our deepest moral sense, our innermost sense for what ultimately and essentially offends against life and what makes for it, such decisive power.

It will be an economy at this point, the title-theme being in question, the significance of which depends on the reader's full sense of the Tolstoyan ethos of art, to make a brief use of Arnold. And it will bring out by the way the force of Lawrence's contention that the discovery of the novel was a great advance for human thought. For Arnold was a man of distinguished intelligence, who didn't in general tend to slight the importance of literature, its place and function in life. And of the sequel to the episode of the steeplechase and of Anna's avowal to Karenin of her relations with Vronsky he writes,

> Hard at first, cruel, thinking only of himself, Karenin, who, as I have said, has a conscience, is touched by grace at the moment when Anna's trouble's reach their height. He returns to find her with a child just born to her and Vronsky, the lover in the house and Anna apparently dying. Karenin has words of kindness and forgiveness only. The noble and victorious effort transfigures him, and all that her husband gains in the eyes of Anna, her lover, Vronsky loses.

Having quoted from the painful scene at the bedside of the delirious Anna, Arnold goes on:

> She seems dying, and Vronsky rushes out and shoots himself. And so, in a common novel, the story would end. Anna would die, Vronsky would commit suicide, Karenin would survive, in possession of our admiration and sympathy. But the story does not always end so in life: neither does it end so in Count Tolstoy's novel.

But not only does it *not* end so; we find ourselves exclaiming: 'But that is *not* the story!' 'Karenin has words of kindness and forgiveness only. The noble and victorious effort transfigures him'—who would divine from that the disturbing subtlety of the actual presentment? The state of feeling actually produced in us is very different from that which Arnold suggests with his 'in possession of our admiration and sympathy'. The way we take the scene, its moral and human significance for us, is conditioned by all that goes before, and this has established what Karenin is, what Anna is, and what, inexorably, the relations between them must be. We know him as, in the pejorative Laurentian sense, a purely 'social' being, ego-bound, self-important, without any spontaneity of life in him and unable to be anything but offended and made uncomfortable by spontaneity of life in others. This is conveyed to us, not by statement, but in innumerable ways: mode of speech, for instance—so rendered by Tolstoy as to give us the tone and inflection. The same subtle power has suggested the effect, even before her 'awakening' by Vronsky, on Anna.

It is the effect conveyed with something like violence when, back at Petersburg after that first fatal encounter with Vronsky, she is persuading herself that nothing has happened, that her profound sense to the contrary was an illusion, and that she has towards her husband the proper feelings of a wife:

> He pressed her hand and again kissed it.
> 'After all, he is a good man: truthful and kind and remarkable in his own sphere,' said Anna to herself when she had returned to her room, as if defending him from someone who accused him and declared it was impossible to love him. 'But why do his ears stick out so? Or has he had his hair cut?'

In the scene of Anna's delirium (Part IV, chapter XVII) this inner conflict takes on, when Karenin comes into the bedroom, a nightmare intensity, the disturbing power of which as Tolstoy evokes the scene it would take a long quotation to suggest: 'With one hand she held him, while with the other she thrust him away'—what is summarized there is a prolonged dramatic immediacy that keeps us in acute discomfort through several pages. The reader, even at the moment when Karenin seems most noble and most commands sympathy and Anna's self-abasement is deepest, can hardly falter in his certainty that revulsion from Karenin is basic and invincible in Anna.

As for the 'noble and victorious effort that transfigures him', when (as Arnold puts it), 'he is touched with grace', the effect of the episode on us, even before we know that this is the way his admirer and consoler, the Countess Ivanovna will put it, is so embarrassingly painful because it is so much more complex than such an account suggests. Karenin's inability to bear the spectacle of acute distress and suffering (especially, we have been told, in a woman) doesn't impress us as an unequivocal escape from the ego: that disconcerting fact is what, added to Vronsky's repellent and horribly convincing humiliation, makes the scene so atrociously unpleasant. And it is in place to note again that the question, 'What is sincerity?', represents for us, as we inquire into the organization and significance of *Anna Karenina*, a sense we recurrently have of the nature of the creative energy in Tolstoy's art. As for the way the later relation between the Countess Lydia Ivanovna and Karenin reflects back on Karenin's 'noble and victorious effort', that is a clear instance of the kind of significant 'relatedness' (Lawrence's word) that Arnold ignores.

We are in no doubt about how we are to take the Countess's 'spirituality' or 'pietism', and it is plain beyond all question that she establishes and confirms Karenin in his 'religious' nobleness, the refuge he finds from self-contempt, by playing on his egotism, his conceit, and his self-deceiving animus. I must add at once that, if we are disposed to come at all easily to general conclusions about the nature, according to Tolstoy, of ostensible saintly goodness—of states of being 'touched with grace'—we had better consider Madame Stahl and Varenka and the episode of Kitty's temporary 'conversion'. The discrimination between the three is firmly and finely made—done in dramatic presentation. That Madame Stahl's spirituality is bogus, a compensation for the denial of more direct and ordinarily feminine self-satisfaction, becomes quite plain. Kitty's revulsion passes an unequivocal judgment on her own fit of dedicated Christian 'goodness': she recognizes that it wasn't sincere—that it falsified the reality of herself and was something to be ashamed of. 'I cannot live but by my own heart, but you', she says to Varenka, 'live by principle.'

But Varenka, Madame Stahl's companion and *protégée*, who herself has been disappointed in love, *is* really good. Yet—yet the whole affair of the proposal that didn't come off, Koznyshev's failure to decide ('Won't bite,' says the disappointed Kitty) and the relief felt by both of the mutually attracted pair as if they had escaped something, conveys a suggestion of critical reserves about both of them. What these amounted to we suspect that Tolstoy himself ('Never trust the artist, trust the tale') would not have been ready to say much about analytically. But we know well enough that we have an example of the characteristic significant organization of the book when, in the next chapter, the attitudes of Levin and his visiting half-brother, Koznyshev, towards the peasants are contrasted.

330 F. R. Leavis

Had Constantine been asked whether he liked the peasants he would not have known what to answer. He both liked and disliked them, just as he liked and disliked all human beings.

Of Koznyshev, the intellectual, on the other hand, we are told that 'his methodical mind had formed definite views on the life of the people', and it is made plain to us that he likes the peasants on 'principle' (to use Kitty's word).

Constantine considered his brother to be a man of great intellect, noble in the highest sense of the word, and gifted with the power of working for the general welfare. But the older he grew and the more intimately he came to know his brother, the oftener the thought occurred to him that the power of working for the general welfare—a power of which he felt entirely destitute—was not a virtue but rather a lack of something, not a lack of kindly honesty and noble desires and tastes, but a lack of the power of living, of what is called heart. . . .

—'Heart' was Kitty's word.

We can't help relating the whole exploration of 'sincerity' in religion that we find in *Anna Karenina* with Levin's own religious preoccupation—I am thinking in part of the way (there is an irony in it) in which the book leaves him identifying the idea of being 'good' with peasant-like Christian belief, inspired as he is by his intimate contacts with the peasants to feel, with that tense and pertinacious tentativeness of his, that he has almost grasped a saving certitude and prescription for his own use.

But to return to the main theme: whatever the old Leo (as Lawrence calls him) would have pronounced, the book confronts us with the impossibility, the sheer impossibility, of Anna's going on living with Karenin. How pregnant, and right (we feel), her diagnosis is when she says: 'If he had never heard people talk of love, he would never have wanted that word.' We too feel directly the revulsion she feels. The fact that we know the life-history that has made him like that doesn't make the revulsion less: *tout comprendre* is not *tout pardonner*—emotionally it can't be. Positive sympathy does indeed enter in for us, to render the full complexity of life in that marvellous way of Tolstoy's, when we suddenly have to realize that even in this repellently 'social' being the spontaneity can come to life, and something unquestionably real assert itself. There is the tenderness that takes him by surprise in his feelings towards the baby, Vronsky's child.

In that smile also Karenin thought he saw himself and his position ridiculed.

'Unfortunate child!' said the nurse, hushing the baby and continuing to walk up and down with it. Karenin sat down on a chair and with a look full of suffering and despondency watched the nurse as she paced the room. When the child was pacified and laid in her deep cot, and the nurse after smoothing the little pillow went away, Karenin rose, and stepping with difficulty on tiptoe approached the infant. For a moment he stood silent, regarding the child with the same despondent expression; but suddenly a smile, wrinkling the skin on his nose, came out on his face, and he quietly left the room.

He rang the bell in the dining-room and told the nurse to send for the doctor once more. He was vexed with his wife for not troubling about the charming baby....

But even if Anna had been aware of this development in Karenin, it could hardly have tended to make living with him seem less impossible. The stark fact of impossibility—that is immediate and final and inescapable for her. No one who had been fully exposed to Tolstoy's evocation of life, to the work of his creative genius, could question it. To say that, however, is not to take D. H. Lawrence's line: 'No one in the world is anything but delighted when Vronsky gets Anna Karenina.' 'O come!'—that gives my own reaction as I read the opening sentences of Lawrence's commentary on the book. What he is recognizing, of course, is the impossibility of Karenin for Anna, and that it is in her relations with Vronsky that she has come to life. But he ignores all the tormenting complexity—the same feelings that Anna, inevitably, can't escape, her sense of guilt, her perception of irreconcilable contradictions, Vronsky's sense that the son (Karenin's), so dear to Anna, is a nuisance. Lawrence asks 'what about the sin?', and answers: 'Why, when you look at it, all the tragedy comes from Vronsky's and Anna's fear of society.... They couldn't live in the pride of their sincere passion, and spit in Mother Grundy's eye. And that, that cowardice, was the real "sin". The novel makes it obvious, and knocks all old Leo's teeth out.'

It is astonishing that so marvellously perceptive a critic as Lawrence could simplify in that way, with so distorting an effect. What the novel makes obvious is that, though they might live for a little in the 'pride of their passion', they couldn't settle down to live *on* it; it makes it plain that to live on it was in the nature of things impossible: to reduce the adverse conditions that defeated them to cowardice is to refuse to take what, with all the force of specificity and subtle truth to life, the novel actually gives. Anna, we are made to see, can't but feel (we are considering here an instance of the profound exploration of moral feeling enacted in the book) that, though Karenin is insufferable, she has done wrong. The dreadful contradiction is focused for her in Seryozha, her son. It is given in the dream of hers in which he has two fathers. Further, what would be involved in getting her husband's necessary collaboration in the obtaining of a divorce is something that, for shame (nothing to do with Mrs Grundy), she can't face. She shrinks from analysing the dreadful *impasse* that torments her, but we are made to share her state, and we know the meaning of the curious withdrawal and the knit look between the eyes with which she meets Vronsky's attempts to start a discussion of the necessary steps towards the divorce that will put everything on a decent footing ('We can't remain like this'). She doesn't want to think about it; at the upper level she can half believe she hopes, but underneath she knows that there is no issue. He, not understanding, and, moreover, impatient, underneath, of the part played in her essential life by Seryozha, inevitably senses in her an indocile force of perverse and dangerous will. This phase of paralysis they suffer, this being held up in a perversity of cross currents and undertows, is wonderfully done in the novel—done (it had to be in order to convey its significance) as something long drawn out.

Lawrence, in a letter of an appropriate date in his own life, writes that Frieda 'had carefully studied *Anna Karenina* in a sort of "How to be happy though livanted spirit" '. Whatever he may be implying as to the lesson that Frieda might have learnt, he is referring, of course, to Anna's finally going off undivorced with Vronsky, and to the absence of any cheering example of happiness so won. We don't, I have suggested with some confidence, accept Lawrence's account, implicitly given in the later-written passage on *Anna Karenina* I have quoted, of the reasons for the Russian Livanters having been decidedly, and in the end disastrously, *less* successful than he and Frieda. We can use the challenged comparison as a way of bringing out the significance of Anna's and Vronsky's case as Tolstoy's art evokes it.

Anna was not an amoral German aristocrat—that seems to me an obvious opening comment. Frieda didn't give up *her* children without some suffering (*Look! We have Come Through*), but she got over that, and attained a floating indolence of well-being as, placidly undomesticated, she accompanied Lawrence about the world (we always see *him* doing the chores). There are delicacies in the way of offering to push further our divinations from such evidence concerning Frieda as we have, but we can see that what Tolstoy makes present to us in Anna is certainly something finer. Frieda's vitality and charm, in fact, have close affinities (she being as decidedly feminine as he is masculine) with those of Stephen Oblonsky—Stiva, Anna's brother, who 'can't believe that anything is wrong when it gives him so much enjoyment'. But the vitality that makes Anna's beauty irresistible manifests itself in a distinction of spirit that it is her brother's charm to be without. She has a delicate inner pride, a quick proud sense of responsibility towards life, that puts the easy accommodations of amoral 'realism' out of the question for her.

As for Vronsky, he is altogether unlike Lawrence. There is nothing of the artist in him. We are prompted to make the point in this way by the very fact that, in Italy, he tries to persuade himself, with some success for a while, that he *is* one. If we ask why he, the aristocratic ex-Guardsman (to *be* a Guardsman being his vocation) should have cultivated that illusion, we find ourselves inquiring into the whole problem that Lawrence, with his too simple diagnosis, dismisses. Why aren't Vronsky and Anna happy in Italy? Why don't they settle down to their sense of a solved problem? They have no money troubles, and plenty of friends, and, if happiness eludes them, the explanation is *not* Mrs Grundy or Society, at any rate in the simple way Lawrence suggests. All this part of the significance of *Anna Karenina* Lawrence ignores; he refuses (for I think it *is*, at bottom, that) to see the nature of the tragedy. And this is a serious charge, for the book gives the compelling constatation of a truth about human life. The spontaneity and depth of Vronsky's and Anna's passion for one another may be admirable, but passion—love—can't itself, though going with estimable qualities in both parties, make a permanent relation. Vronsky, having given up his career and his ambition for love, *has* his love, but is very soon felt to give out (and it is marvellous how the great novelist's art conveys this) a vibration of restlessness and dissatisfaction.

Lawrence *was* an artist—superlatively one. The conditions of his life with Frieda were the reverse of uncongenial to that extraordinary, inexhaustible, and endlessly inquiring intelligence of his. It ensured that he should never feel disorientated, vaguely lost, hanging in the wind. And yet—the point can't be made briefly with the proper delicacy—it is impossible (I think) not to feel that his work reveals a loss, a certain disablement, entailed by those conditions: the life of nomadic, childless, improvised, and essentially impermanent domesticities. Could he have written *Lady Chatterley's Lover*, written it as a vehicle of that didactic earnestness, if he hadn't lost his sense of what normal human life was like? The pamphlet, *Apropos of Lady Chatterley's Lover*, with which he followed the book up, implicitly admits the criticism—makes it; for the emphasis that, writing in ostensible vindication of the notorious novel, he now (with some inconsequence, one would think) lays on marriage and the family—and the whole manifesto is immensely impressive (it's a classic, I think)—can't but be taken by the reader as coming from a profound *corrective* impulse in Lawrence.

Vronsky's discovery of *his* vocation as an artist expresses merely his need of what, now he has left the army, he hasn't—a purpose, a sense of function, a place in life, a meaning. What he takes for the artist's vocation is what Lawrence in his tales deals with so well, the vocation of 'being an artist', and the pages of *Anna Karenina* that expose the bogusness of that should have appealed to the author of *St Mawr* and *Lady Chatterley's Lover*. Vronsky is too much of a man to find the lasting satisfaction in it that Lawrence's gentlemen-pseudo-artists find, and the way in which the reality drops out of it for Vronsky is done with the insight and astringent power of a novelist who is himself a real and great artist. There are the contacts with Mikhaylov, the *un*gentlemanly and unurbane genius, whose discomfort—his embarrassment when expected to take Vronsky's vocation and its products seriously—comes painfully home to us but brings no enlightenment to Vronsky, though the experience has its effect.

Vronsky can derive satisfaction from the reassuring flatteries and complacencies of his friends, but the impulse to work at his own portrait of Anna lapses after he has seen Mikhaylov's. The vocation of 'being an artist' lapses with it.

We then see Vronsky and Anna back in Russia. Vronsky is trying to find a place and meaning in life as a landowner and public-spirited local magnate. But the new vocation—its factitiousness is conveyed to us by means that brief quotation can't really suggest—is still not one that can give Vronsky what he lost when he left the army and the familiar milieu, the friends and comrades with whom he had lived in his old career.

And this is the point at which to say that *Anna Karenina*, exploring the nature of the moral sense and of sincerity, explores also, with an intimately associated subtlety, the relation between the individual *qua* locus of moral responsibility and his social context. It's all very well for Lawrence to talk of thumbing one's nose at society—that is what he says Vronsky should have done. *Anna Karenina* compels us to recognize how much less simple things are than Lawrence suggests. The book, in its preoccupation with the way—the ways—in which the individual moral sense is socially conditioned, leaves us for upshot nothing like a simple conclusion. We have in the treatment of this theme too the tentative, questing spirit. There is a good deal in the book that we can unhesitatingly take for ironic commentary on the way in which moral feeling tends to be 'social' in the pejorative sense; that is, to express not any individual's moral perception and judgment, but a social climate—to be a product of a kind of flank-rubbing. But on the other hand there is no encouragement given to think of real moral judgment (and I have in mind Tolstoy's normative concern) as that of the isolated individual. It is necessarily individual, yes; but not merely individual. That, however, is no simple conclusion—which is what *Anna Karenina*, in its range and subtlety, makes so poignantly clear to us. A study of human nature is a study of social human nature, and the psychologist, sociologist, and social historian aren't in it compared with the great novelists. Tolstoy's perception is infinitely fine and penetrating, and is inseparable from his sense of relatedness (Lawrence's term). You recall how Levin's, Vronsky's, Anna's, Oblonsky's sense of things—their sense that things are right or not right, in resonance or not with their moral

336 F. R. Leavis

feeling—changes with the shift from the familiar to the unfamiliar milieu: Moscow to Petersburg, town to country, one
social world to another.

Levin feels sure of his judgment and his criteria only when he
is at home on his estate, engaged in the duties and responsibilities and interests that are his real life. Vronsky, intense and
serious as we know his passion for Anna to be, lapses naturally
into the tone and ethic in which he has been brought up and
that fit the society to which he belongs, when talking with his
cousin, the Princess Betsy, at the Opera.

> 'And how you used to laugh at others!' continued the Prin-
> cess Betsy, who took particular pleasure at following the
> progress of this passion. 'What has become of it all? You are
> caught, my dear fellow.'
>
> 'I wish for nothing better than to be caught,' replied Vron-
> sky with his calm good-natured smile. 'To tell the truth, if I
> complain at all, it is only of not being caught enough. I am
> beginning to lose hope.'
>
> 'What hope can you have?' said Betsy, offended on her
> friend's behalf: *'entendons nous!'* But in her eyes little sparks
> twinkled which said she understood very well, and just as he
> did, what hope he might have.
>
> 'None whatever,' said Vronsky, laughing and showing his
> close-set teeth. 'Excuse me!' he added, taking from her hand
> the opera-glasses, and he set to work to scan across her bare
> shoulder the row of boxes opposite. 'I am afraid I am becom-
> ing ridiculous.'
>
> He knew very well that he ran no risk of appearing ridiculous
> either in Betsy's eyes or in the eyes of Society people generally.
> He knew very well that in their eyes the rôle of the disappoin-
> ted lover of a maiden or any single woman might be ridicu-
> lous; but that the rôle of a man who was pursuing a married
> woman, and who made it the purpose of his life at all costs
> to draw her into adultery, was one which had in it something
> beautiful and dignified, and could never be ridiculous; so it
> was with a proud glad smile lurking under his moustache that
> he put down the opera-glasses and looked at his cousin.

Anna, after the fatal meeting with Vronsky in Moscow (where
she had gone on her mission of reconciliation to the Oblonsky's),
returns to Petersburg:

> The feeling of causeless shame she had felt during the

journey, and her agitation, had quite vanished. In her accustomed condition of life she again felt firm and blameless.

She thought with wonder of her state the day before. 'What
had happened? Nothing! Vronsky said some silly things, to
which it will be easy to put a stop, and I said what was
necessary. It is unnecessary and impossible to speak of it to
my husband.' She remembered how she had once told her husband about one of his subordinates who had very nearly made
her a declaration, and how Karenin had answered that every
woman living in society was liable to such things, but that
he had full confidence in her tact and would never disgrace
himself and her by being jealous. 'So there is no need to tell
him! Besides, thank Heaven, there is nothing to tell!' she
said to herself.

Anyone who has read the book can, in twenty minutes, find a
dozen further examples, larger and smaller, of great diversity.
Not that any suggestion emerges tending to qualify personal
responsibility. A normative search after the social conditions the
individual needs for happiness, or fulfilment, and for the individual responsive moral sense that serves it—that is the preoccupation. Vronsky, in the country-gentleman phase, for all the
impressive outward show, has found neither the vocation nor
the social context that can restore his sense of purpose in life or
of rightness. Anna knows this, and even if she weren't tormented by yearning for her son, it would make an established happiness with Vronsky impossible. Her response is to be jealous,
and her jealousy has the inevitable effect on him: it makes him
feel cramped and tethered. The terrible logic or dialectic moves,
like an accelerating mechanism, to the catastrophe.

'Vengeance is mine; I will repay'—we remember Tolstoy's
epigraph. And there is Karenin's own orthodox formulation,
'Our lives are bound together not by men but by God', which
closes in terms that come to have meaning for Anna: 'that kind
of crime brings its punishment.' All the book is a feeling out, and
a feeling inwards, for an adequate sense of the nature of life and
its implicit laws, to break which entails the penalty. And to say
this is not to pass any naïve moralistic judgment on Anna—any
simple moral judgment such as was made either by Lawrence
('sincere passion') or by the old Leo.

The significance is brought out by the contrasting Levin case-
history. Does Tolstoy, or the 'tale', offer this as presenting the

'norm'? Not quite that; the case-history—the case—is not so clear or conclusive. *Anna Karenina* is a work of art, and Levin (who, of course, compels our full respect) is in it the self-distrusting, ever-exploring 'seeker'. He is after happiness—as is also (we may add here, by way of noting the characteristic play of contrast) Oblonsky—which prompts us to substitute the word 'fulfilment' when thinking of Levin. For Levin marriage is a matter of love, and love of marriage. Involved in his problems of farming, religion and relations with the peasants, he knows that (as Agatha Mikhaylovna tells him) he needs a wife, but we are in no doubt that it is love—the kind into which one falls —that in due course unites him and Kitty.

We are left with *him* as the book closes. And if, as we share his sense of what are the great problems, we seem very close to the author, we note also that Levin is content for the time being with some inconsistencies (he feels them to be) and a certain tentativeness. His sense of problems to be solved focuses on the one hand (in terms of social responsibility) on the peasants, and on the other on his own need of religious belief. Or can we say that the peasants have become, at the close of the book, something like a comprehensive focus? He is still troubled by the problem of the right relations with them. But there is now a very much strengthened tendency to associate the solution of that problem in an ominous way with the solution of what, for Levin, must surely be a very different problem—that of the good life. An ominous way—there is a clear intimation that, as Levin broods, he finds himself identifying them: the problems seem merging into one. The solution is to live with the peasants, to be a peasant among peasants. His problem of 'belief' (associated with his intense inner response to the fact of death[1]—we don't forget the grim evocation of the dying Nicholas, his brother) he sees as to be solved by his achieving the naïve 'belief' of the peasants. And this, in a curiously simple way, he identifies with being 'good'.

My summary has, as of course any summary of theme and significance in *Anna Karenina* must have, an effect of grossness from which one shrinks. The actual creative presentment is

---

[1] 'If you once realize that tomorrow, if not today, you will die and nothing will be left of you, everything becomes insignificant.' See the whole context, Part IV, chapter VII.

infinitely subtle, and comes as the upshot of an immense deal of immediately relevant drama and suggestion in the foregoing mass of the book. For example, I will point to chapters XI and XII in Part III, which give us Levin's visit, while still a bachelor, to his sister's village in order to look after farming interests of hers that need attention. He suspects that the peasants are cheating her over the hay harvest, and it turns out that his suspicions are well founded. Nevertheless, that matter settled, the deceits and grudges are forgotten, and he finds himself contemplating the peasants with warm idealizing sympathy as they cart the hay. The power of the episode depends upon a kind of sustained and typically Tolstoyan poetic life such as I had very much in mind when I spoke of what Tolstoy must lose in translation. This, with some cuts, is a passage of it :

Levin had often admired that kind of life, had often admired the folk who lived it; but that day, especially after what he had seen for the first time of the relations between Vanka Parmenich and his young wife, it struck him that it depended on himself to change his wearisome, idle and artificial life for that pure delightful life of common toil.

The old man who had been sitting beside him had long since gone home ... Levin ... still lay on the haycock, looking, listening and thinking. The peasants who were staying in the meadow kept awake almost all the short summer night. . . . The whole long day of toil had left upon them no trace of anything but merriment.

Just before dawn all became silent. The sounds of night—the ceaseless croaking of frogs, the snorting of horses through the morning mist over the meadow—could alone be heard. Awakening to reality, Levin rose from his haycock, and glancing up at the stars, realized that the night was nearly over.

Well, then, what shall I do? How shall I do it? he asked himself, trying to find expression for what he had been thinking and the feelings he had lived through in that short night. All his ideas and feelings separated themselves into three different lines of thought. The first was, how to renounce his old life and discard his quite useless education. This renunciation would afford him pleasure and was quite easy and simple. The second was concerned with his notion of the life he now wanted to lead. He was distinctly conscious of the simplicity, purity and rightness of that life, and convinced that in it he would find satisfaction, peace and dignity, the absence of which was so painful to him. But the third thought was the question of how to make the change from his present life to that other one ... Should he have a wife? ... 'but I'll clear it up later. One thing is certain: this night has decided my fate. All my former dreams of a family life were nonsense—not the right thing. Everything is much simpler and better than that...'

'How beautiful!' he thought, looking up at a strange mother-of-pearl-coloured shell formed of fleecy clouds, in the centre of the sky just above his head. 'How lovely everything is, this lovely night! And how did the shell get formed so quickly? A little while ago when I looked at the sky all was clear, but for two white strips. My views of life have changed in the same unnoticeable way.'

Leaving the meadow, he went down the high road towards the village.

He hears wheels and bells, and a coach comes by. In it, looking out as she wakes up, he sees Kitty. 'She recognized him, and joyful surprise lit up her face.'

This is before his marriage; it is in the period of disappointed love, and the last sentence makes the dawn for him, suddenly, that of a new hope. The hope proves no vain one, and in the close of the book, when the brooding on peasant-faith as a personal solution recurs, and so insistently, the dream he had dismissed as foolish has been achieved: Kitty is his wife, and they have a family. He doesn't say now that the dream was all nonsense. The assurance of an inner peace, a firm possession to be won of the saving truth, if only he can take the decision and put it into effect, has for context the incongruous preoccupations of family life, enlightened farming, his own developed interests as one of the intelligentsia, and the intellectual talk of his half-brother Koznyshev and Katavasov about Pan-Slavism. But the suggestion on which the novel ends is that the assurance, the half-grasped faith, is henceforward to be the central reality of Levin's life.

And the cogent force of the whole great work makes it plain that the answer he threatens to commit himself to with all the force of his will is a desperately simplifying one; that is, not an answer at all—unless a rejection of life is an answer. Levin's peasant solution gets no countenance from the preceding book;

quite the reverse. I will allow myself a final extract, from a passage (Part III, chapter XXX) that gives something like a summary, or paradigm, of the refutation conveyed by the novel as a whole. Agatha Mikhaylovna, Levin's old nurse, is the maternal ideal-peasant housekeeper of his bachelor establishment.

Having written for some time, Levin suddenly with particular vividness remembered Kitty, her refusal, and their last meeting. He rose and began to pace up and down the room.

'What is the use of fretting?' said Agatha Mikhaylovna. 'You should go to a watering-place now that you have got ready.'

'So I shall: I am going the day after tomorrow, Agatha Mikhaylovna, only I must finish my business.'

'Eh, what is your business? Have you not done enough for the peasants as it is! Why, they are saying, "Your master will get a reward from the Tsar for it!" And it is strange: why should you bother about the peasants?'

'I am not bothering about them: I am doing it for myself.'

Agatha Mikhaylovna knew all the details of Levin's farming plans.... But this time she quite misunderstood what he said.

'Of course one must think of one's soul before everything else,' she remarked with a sigh. 'There was Parfen Denisich, who was no scholar at all, but may God grant everyone to die as he did!' she said, referring to a servant who had died recently: 'He received Holy Communion and Extreme Unction.'

'I am not speaking about that,' he said. 'I mean that I am doing it for my own profit. My gains are bigger when the peasants work better.'

'But, whatever you do, an idler will always bungle. If he has a conscience he will work, if not, you can do nothing with him.'

'But you yourself say that Ivan looks after the cattle better now.'

'I only say,' answered Agatha Mikhaylovna, evidently not speaking at random, but with strict sequence of thought, 'you must marry, that is all!'

She herself may be said to represent peasant wisdom—anti-intellectual sanity, and profundity of intuitive insight and judgment. Her view of the peasants has incomparably more authority than Levin's. The disconcerting felicity of her 'you must marry, that is all' has for context something like a comprehensive insight into Levin's complexities of preoccupation—the passage makes that plain enough. 'Of course, one must think of one's soul before anything else.'—Of course, and Parfen's end was edifying; but when one says that, how much is said, peasant-life and reality being the question? She knows that any peasant would, with complete conviction, prescribe as she does—realizing with her what responsibilities, not to be shed, marriage would entail upon Levin. In so far as she glimpses Levin's religious-social ideas as they relate to the peasants, she knows that the peasants themselves would deride them. And it is impossible to believe that Tolstoy in writing this chapter had any sense of dissociation from *her* knowledge—that it wasn't for him at the same time his own. But Levin, married to the admirable Kitty, now the mother of his child, is shown once more cultivating a resolution that denies such knowledge—or defies it.

We may tell ourselves that he is merely a character in the book, and that the book makes its implicit comment on Levin. The significance of the book is what is conveyed by the whole, and the suggestion of the whole doesn't in the least encourage us to think of Levin as anything but ill-judging, ill-inspired, and in for disillusionment. With the advantage of hindsight, however, we can see that the breakdown of Tolstoy into the old Leo is here portended.

The later Tolstoy—a significant consistency, if you like—refused to see anything impressive in *Anna Karenina*. 'What difficulty is there,' he said, 'in writing how an officer fell in love with a married woman? There is no difficulty in it, and, above all, there is no good in it.' But we, most of us, have to recognize a higher authority in the art, the creative power, of *Anna Karenina* than in the wisdom of the sage and prophet. The later Tolstoy—the prophetic and tragic Tolstoy—insisted on a simple answer.

Anna Karenina one of the great European novels?—it is, surely, *the* European novel. The completeness with which Tolstoy, with his genius, was a Russian of his time made him an incomparably representative European, and made the book into which his whole experience, his most comprehensive 'relatedness', went what it is for us: the great novel of modern—of our

—civilization. The backwardness of Russia meant that the transcendent genius experienced to the full, taking their significances with personal intensity, the changes that have produced our modern world. In a country in which serfdom has been recently abolished, the characters of *Anna Karenina* travel as a matter of course by railway between the two capitals. The patriarchal landowner participates in a cosmopolitan culture, and, using French and English in intercourse with members of his own class, is intellectually nourished on the contemporary literature and thought of the West. Anna herself, having had at the outset of the book the shock of the fatal accident that marks her arrival at Moscow, ends her life under the iron wheels. The apparition of the little peasant with the sack who horrifies her, and is so oddly associated with the wheels and the rails, acts on our imagination as a pregnant symbol and a sinister augury (he is seen, too, later in a nightmare by Vronsky).[1] The disharmonies, contrasts, and contradictions are challenging in a way that makes the optimisms of Progress impossible for Tolstoy— as the inability of Levin, the earnest and public-spirited, to see duty in Zemstvo-attendance very characteristically intimates. *Anna Karenina*, in its human centrality, gives us modern man; Tolstoy's essential problems, moral and spiritual, are ours.

See Part IV, chapter III. And see also Part III, chapter IV.

Acknowledgements

The editor and publisher wish to thank the following for their permission to reproduce copyright material:

Edward Arnold Ltd for extract from *Aspects of the Novel*, 1927, by E. M. Forster; Northrop Frye and Princeton University Press for 'Specific Continuous Forms' in *Anatomy of Criticism* © 1957 by Princeton University Press, Princeton Paperback, 1971; the Estate of the late Mrs Frieda Lawrence and Laurence Pollinger Ltd for 'Why the Novel Matters' from *Phoenix*, 1936 and for 'Morality and the Novel' from *Phoenix*, 1936; Wayne C. Booth and University of Chicago Press for extract from *The Rhetoric of Fiction*, 1961; Georg Lukács and The Merlin Press for extract from *Writer and Critic*, 1970; Didier-Erudition for extract from *Les formes de la création romanesque à l'époque de Walter Scott et de Jane Austen*, 1977; Dorothy van Ghent and Holt, Rinehard and Winston Inc. for 'On Wuthering Heights' from *The English Novel: Form and Function*; Columbia University Press for excerpts from 'The Complete Poems of Emily Jane Brontë' included in *The English Novel: Form and Function* by van Ghent; G. Robert Stange and the National Council of Teachers of English for 'Expectations Well Lost: Dickens's Fable for His Time' from *College English*, Copyright © 1954; U. C. Knoelpflmacher and Princeton University Press for extract from *Religious Humanism and the Victorian Novel: George Eliot, Walter Pater, and Samuel Butler* © 1965 Princeton University Press, Princeton Paperback, 1970; David Lodge and The Open University for '*Middlemarch* and the Idea of the Classic Realist Text'; James W. Gargano and The Regents of the University of California Press for extract from Volume 16 Number 1 of *Nineteenth-Century Fiction*; Macmillan Publishers for the Introduction to the New Wessex Edition of *Tess of the D'Urbervilles*, 1974; Henry Nash Smith for the Introduction to The Riverside Press Edition of *Huckleberry Finn*, © 1958; F. R. Leavis and Chatto and Windus Ltd for 'Anna Karenina' from *Anna Karenina and Other Essays*.

Index[1]

[1]Major references are italicized.